A BRUTAL
FRIENDSHIP

ALSO BY SAÏD K. ABURISH

The Rise, Corruption and Coming Fall of the House of Saud

A BRUTAL FRIENDSHIP

★ ★ ★ ★ ★ ★ ★

The West and the Arab Elite

SAÏD K. ABURISH

St. Martin's Press 〽 New York

A THOMAS DUNNE BOOK.
An imprint of St. Martin's Press.

Library of Congress Cataloging-in-Publication Data

Aburish, Saïd K.
  A brutal friendship : the West and the Arab elite /
Saïd K. Aburish.
    p.   cm.
  "A Thomas Dunne book."
  Includes bibliographical references (p.   ) and index.
  ISBN 0-312-18543-X
    1. Arab countries—Politics and government.
  2. Arab countries—Foreign relations—United States.
  3. United States—Foreign relations—Arab countries.
  4. Legitimacy of governments—Arab countries.
  5. Consensus (Social science)—Arab countries.
  6. Elite (Social science)—Arab countries. I. Title.
DS63.18.A28   1998   98-3342
327.73017'4927—dc21   CIP

First published in Great Britain by Victor Gollancz,
an imprint of the Cassell Group

First U.S. Edition: August 1998

10 9 8 7 6 5 4 3 2 1

For Clare and for Edward –
Good times

Contents

Acknowledgements

I include no list of people who helped me write this book. Many who were interviewed over a period of three years and others who provided advice did so on condition of anonymity. Most of those who helped openly are mentioned in the text. I owe a huge debt of thanks to all of them. However, the opinions expressed in this book, like its shortcomings, are mine alone. In writing it I am addressing the question of why the Middle East is misreported and mishandled by Western and Arab powers, both of which selfishly perpetuate its problems. I feel it is my Arab and human duty to spotlight the unsoundness of their policies and to try to contribute towards the development of better ones.

PART ONE

Sponsored Illegitimacy

1 · A Cruel Harmony, a Brutal Friendship

There are no legitimate regimes in the Arab Middle East. The House of Saud, King Hussein of Jordan, Presidents Husni Mubarak of Egypt, Saddam Hussein of Iraq, Hafez Al Assad of Syria, Yasser Arafat of the Palestinian Authority and the remaining minor Arab heads of state run various types of dictatorships. They depend on phoney claims to legitimacy while representing small special interest groups – minorities whose members owe their allegiance to them rather than the state as the representative and guardian of the interests of the people. The result is religious, tribal, army-based or hybrid ruling cliques and leaders who have one thing in common: they are opposed to the desire of the majority of the Arab people to have or develop legitimate governments.

Yet the West deals with all these regimes as if they were legitimate. Even the ones which the West opposes are not rejected by reason of their lack of legitimacy. Questioning the lack of legitimacy of unfriendly regimes would inevitably extend such scrutiny to friendly ones. This is why Western attacks on Saddam's Iraq or Qaddafi's Libya avoid this issue and Bill Clinton and other Western leaders attribute all criminality to the persons of Saddam and Qaddafi rather than to the nature of their governments. Furthermore, the West seldom speaks of relations with Egypt, Jordan or Saudi Arabia but of the policies of President Mubarak, King Hussein and the House of Saud.

By overlooking the absence of legitimacy and affording dictatorships unqualified recognition, the West, directly and indirectly, supports the paramountcy of individual leaders, army groups, sects, clans and families who run the Middle East and determine its shape and direction. The existing division of the Arab Middle East into friendly and unfriendly governments and groups has little to do with their true nature. Historically, legitimate nationalist regimes were rejected when they were considered a threat to Western interests while friendly illegitimate ones were supported regardless. Perpetuating Western political hegemony and protecting economic interests from real or imagined threats take precedence over considerations of legitimacy.

In the states under discussion legitimacy is synonymous with acceptability: a legitimate government is no more than one which is acceptable to its people. In the Arab context, however, acceptability or legitimacy should not be confused with a democratic system of government such as exists in the West. Acceptability can result from having a popular leader. Nasser of Egypt, a dictator who expressed the aspirations of his people and the rest of the Arabs, had enough popular support to make him legitimate. Another way of attaining legitimacy is for a government to espouse a popular indigenous ideology, and this includes the use of religion in a way supported by the majority of the people. For example, when the PLO's policy of resistance to Israel reflected the wishes and will of the Palestinian people, the PLO was their legitimate representative.

A third way of attaining legitimacy is to have a state structure which expresses the ideal of the people and protects their rights. This, the creation of acceptable state institutions which have primacy over ruling groups, is a first step against dictatorial abuse of power, even when the structure is not fully democratic. Unhappily, except for brief flirtations with free elections in Syria and Jordan in the 1950s and 60s, there are no examples of creating institutions which both reflect the will of the people and protect their rights. Naturally, the bases for legitimacy overlap and hypothetically it is possible to have a country with a popular leader, an ideology which reflects the will of the people and an organized, benevolent state structure – a functioning democracy.

Democracy in a Western sense is the process which can confirm and support these bases of acceptability. Democracy may or may not come after one or more of them are attained, because there are no recent Arab democratic traditions, and state structures haven't been built. First the responsive leader, acceptable ideology or functioning structure, or any combination of these, and then democracy or something akin to it.

There is no better way to demonstrate the existing shortage of legitimacy and hence acceptability than to examine the governments (or rather the leadership, because they are dictatorships) of the countries I have already mentioned; how they justify their own existence to their people and others; and the needed claim to legitimacy all of them purport to have.

The Saudi state uses religious ideology, the teachings of the Wahhabi sub-sect of Sunni Islam, to claim the right to rule. The Wahhabis of Saudi Arabia are a mere 20 per cent of the population of the country and are favoured in a way which allows them to control all aspects of public and private life in the Kingdom. But the teachings of Wahhabism are rejected by the rest of the people (the Saudis are the only people in the world named after their royal family). Furthermore, there are now clear signs of serious divisions within this sub-sect. Among others, the Committee for the Defence of the Legitimate Rights of the Saudi people (CDLR), is anti-House of Saud, but is made up of Wahhabis and accuses the ruling family of perverting Wahhabism and giving it a bad name. Because CDLR and other Wahhabi opposition groups are popular, the House of Saud is reduced to reliance on a fragment of this sub-sect, a very small part of the total population of Saudi Arabia. What remains is a religious-ideological claim supported by the House of Saud and their lackeys. In fact, the House of Saud's claim to legitimacy is so thin and questionable that most Western leaders avoid discussing it and settle for supportive statements about the friendly nature of Saudi Arabia's government and leadership.

King Hussein of Jordan heads an artificial state created by the British in 1922. His claim to legitimacy rests on two phoney foundations. The Hashemites, the family of King Hussein, are descendants of the Prophet Muhammad and, according to them, this lineage entitles them to occupy the office of the traditional caliphate. So Hussein's is a personal religious claim. To most of the people of Jordan and the Middle East, perpetuating the caliphate is an out-of-date and unpopular idea. Even in 1924, King Hussein's great-grandfather, Hussein I, lost the throne of the Hijaz after he had declared himself caliphate. He failed to use this lineage to generate Muslim support for his claim at a time of greater belief in the holiness of his family. In 1951, King Abdallah, King Hussein's grandfather, was gunned down by an assassin who objected to his closeness to Israel, and there were no repercussions. Yet later, in 1958, King Hussein's cousin, Faisal, was overthrown and killed in Iraq. The army officers who carried out the coup and applied the sword to Hashemite necks were popular, and the holiness of the Iraqi royal family failed to save them. Even if Hashemite holiness was acceptable, King Hussein's behaviour, his marriage to a foreigner, the fact that he has not observed the Koran's strict injunction against alcoholic drinks and his friendliness to Israel, vitiate his claim to religious legitimacy among those inclined to accept it.

King Hussein's second claim to legitimacy, his supposed popularity among his country's Bedouins, despite the idea's appeal to Western romantics, is equally flawed. Today there are fewer Bedouins than when Jordan was created and their loyalty, as shown by the support many of them gave the PLO in the 1960s and 70s, is suspect. But, while their loyalty is not questioned, even in the 1940s and 50s they were a minority whose importance was inflated by Glubb Pasha and other Orientalist-agents. They have become much more of a minority since non-Bedouin Palestinians moved to Jordan in 1948 and now account for more than 60 per cent of its population. So, neither descent from the Prophet nor dependence on Bedouins, nor the attempt to combine both, is a valid source of legitimacy in the eyes of Jordan's people. The West accepts King Hussein's claims while knowing better.

Amazingly, the Lebanese government resembles that of Saudi Arabia. In Lebanon, a Maronite minority elevated to special status by the French colonial administration after the First World War still runs the country and reduces its non-Maronite citizens to second-class status. Non-Maronites cannot hold high office, including that of president, just as non-Wahhabis are denied the right to belong to the important Saudi Council of Ulemas, the religious body which decides the laws of the country. And, as in Wahhabi Saudi Arabia, the Maronites place their co-religionists in government jobs and afford them special treatment in the field of commerce. This is unacceptable to 80 per cent of the people of Lebanon (the Maronites represent approximately 20 per cent of the total population). Lebanon is run by a minority non-monarchical religious sect which imposes its will and ways on the non-Maronite majority of the country. This is the primary reason for the civil war which racked that country for fifteen years and produced casualties in the hundreds of thousands. The West is still committed to a Maronite-controlled Lebanon.

Egypt is saddled with an uninspiring leader, Husni Mubarak, whose claim to legitimacy, a pretence that he runs a democracy, is phonier than most. In reality Mubarak depends on the army, security forces and Western political and economic support to remain in power. His three sources of support are unacceptable to his people. In fact, so lacking is he in popularity that he often refuses to appoint a vice-president and successor to himself lest the occupant of the post become a magnet for his people's disaffection. Unlike under Nasser, the political party Mubarak uses to justify and underpin his phoney democratic rule, the National Party, has no street following. Meanwhile Mubarak's party achieves results at elections that no one believes; according to him, 96 per cent of the Egyptians elected him president. This tactic has backfired and the ensuing dissent has forced Mubarak into relying on harsh dictatorial methods. His recent attempts to stifle mounting press criticism of his ways have led to the enactment of totally undemocratic press laws. The increasing opposition to his government by Islamic groups has produced a level of state violence against them unprecedented even in the Middle East. To the horror of most Egyptians, Islamists are detained without trial, tortured, tried by military courts and executed in large numbers. Despite Mubarak's total reliance on force, the West supports him unconditionally.

In terms of its lack of legitimacy, the Iraqi government of Saddam Hussein is no different from all the governments that have ruled that country since its creation in 1922. All have depended on an officer class made up of the country's Sunni minority, who represent between 20 and 25 per cent of the population. They have consistently ignored the wishes of the Shia majority and the country's Kurds. Over the years Saddam has tried to assume the role of a popular leader and build a state structure capable of creating legitimacy for his regime. He has failed in both aims. He remains unpopular among the Shias and Kurds and his elaborate state structure, though impressive and not without credits, is mainly aimed at oppressing his people rather than expressing their will. Saddam's continued dependence for survival on a Sunni-officered army translates into an abusive, cruel, minority government. The West, though opposed to the person of Saddam, has continued to ignore the unsoundness of his Sunni state, the continuation of the one the British created in the 1920s. Advocating a legitimate Iraqi state might mean the emergence of a religiously militant Shia state which could act as a model for others and, to the West, might lead to consequent instability throughout the Middle East. The West prefers an unsound Sunni state, even with Saddam as leader, to the other prospects.

Since the late 1960s Syria has been run by a minority Alawi regime to which President Assad belongs. The Alawis are a mere 15 per cent of the population of Syria and, like Saddam, Assad has tried to create a personality cult. Furthermore, he has tried to claim legitimacy through building a state structure based on the teachings of the pan-Arab Ba'ath Party. Because religious affiliation is stronger than allegiance to the state, Assad's efforts have failed and he depends for the continuance of his regime on an army commanded by Alawi officers. In this case too, the West's occasional opposition to Assad has nothing to do with the lack of legitimacy of his regime. It has to do with his friendly or unfriendly policies.

Until the peace accords with Israel and the emergence of the Palestinian Authority of Yasser Arafat, the Palestine Liberation Movement (PLO) was the legitimate representative of Palestinian aspirations. For years Arafat's personal popularity lent additional legitimacy. However, in opting for a questionable peace without consulting his people or taking their misgivings into consideration, Arafat forfeited the blanket support his organization had hitherto commanded. Moreover, his penchant for undignified histrionics, his dictatorial inclinations, the corruption of many of his aides and his police's treatment of fellow Palestinians and denial of freedom to the press have undermined his standing with his people and cancelled the legitimacy of the Palestinian Authority. The West opposed Arafat when he was legitimate and it supports him now when he follows a Western line unacceptable to most of his people. Arafat's present situation is as exact as a mathematical formula: the more dictatorial he becomes in order to carry out the deficient and unpopular Western-sponsored peace plan, the less acceptable he becomes to his people.

The claims of the Arab states and leaders to personal, ideological or structural legitimacy, different as they are, do not meet the minimum level of acceptability by their people. And in all the countries discussed, maintaining good relations with the West – along with other historical reasons – stands in the way of attaining legitimacy. Meanwhile, the West goes beyond simply accepting illegitimate governments and actively opposes the forces which support legitimacy. The West backs the House of Saud, although its claim to legitimacy is unsatisfactory and has become even less so. The West is committed to a Maronite Lebanon, despite the self-destructiveness this engenders. King Hussein's pretence to a non-existent holiness and his reliance on a small Bedouin constituency are used by the West to grant him support which guarantees his survival and consequent adherence to disastrously unpopular policies – for example, amity with Israel and the corruption of his court. Mubarak's unpopularity, and allegations of corruption and open dishonesty in his regime, find the West with little to say about the violence of his government against his people and less to offer in terms of making him pursue a different course of action.

Iraq is a prime example of Western lack of interest in legitimate regimes or in using political openings, such as Saddam's current vulnerability, to institute legitimate ones. Instead of supporting Iraqis calling for a system which grants equal rights to the Shias and Kurds, the West, despite occasional pretences to the contrary, is looking for another Saddam who would use the army to perpetuate a pro-West Sunni primacy. And the West's opposition to Assad of Syria is in proportion to his acceptance or rejection of Western plans to impose its policies on the Arab Middle East and has nothing to do with legitimacy.

To the West, the leaderships of Saudi Arabia, Jordan, Lebanon, Egypt, Iraq, Syria and the Palestinian Authority offer stability. In this context, stability means governments which behave in a predictable manner and ones whose systems preclude the emergence of forces that are opposed to the West or wish to deal with it on an equal basis. Stability means dictator-ships and an ensuing coercion of the people which eliminates the chances of attaining legitimacy and democracy. Moves to legitimize these regimes and make them acceptable to their people would create an 'instability' that would threaten the status quo, the 'devil you know', the forces which underpin Western political hegemony over the Middle East and perpetuate its economic control of the area. The West views governments responsive to the will of the people as ones which might want to charge more for oil, control its refining and distribution and develop a petrochemical industry or, because of the absence of secular forces, ones with Islamic inclinations – or both. (In the 1950s and 60s the West helped overthrow freely elected – but to them uncooperative – governments in Syria and Jordan.)

So, in Western eyes, stability is what endows the present dictatorial regimes with respectability, while instability means having legitimate governments which are assumed to oppose the West and promote radicalism, violence and terrorism. Even when the people calling for change advocate peaceful change, and many Muslim groups do, the notion of violence and terrorism adheres to them. And, as we will see, the images created by this blanket definition of stability and instability turn the official Western attitude into a policy acceptable to Western people who become as imperialist as their governments.

Western acceptance of stable dictatorial regimes in the Arab Middle East has to do with considerations which go beyond their treatment of their people (which embraces frequent imprisonment, torture, killing and kidnapping). It includes the regimes' behaviour towards Arab, Islamic and other issues. There is a convergence of interests. Arab leaders suppress their people to stay in power and use their control of their countries to provide a stability which serves Western political and economic interests within the countries concerned and beyond. The West, even when uneasy about the behaviour of its stable partners and friends towards their people, accepts an implicit bargain and recognizes the need to be dictatorial. (The West supported Saddam until he threatened the West's oil interests, and the threat to oppose Assad is the result of his studied refusal to accept Western hegemony.)

If the demise of the USSR has eliminated the need for an alliance between the Arab regimes and the West to confront communism, then the overriding 'international' issues in today's Arab Middle East are the control of oil and the Arab-Israeli problem. The West supports regimes which guarantee the flow of oil at a low price and ones which are committed to bringing an end to the Arab-Israeli situation in accordance with a Western formula. And while the West regards the present regimes' relationship to their people as subsidiary to these considerations – to keep Western backing, to intercept any possible understanding between the

West and the Arab people on these issues (a reformist Islamic regime which would continue the present oil policy of Saudi Arabia or Palestinians who would accept a sensible peace agreement) – the present regimes are always willing to give the West more than their people are willing to offer. This is why oil is sold to the West at even cheaper prices than is warranted, regardless of the effect on the Saudi people, and why Arafat concedes more to the West and Israel than is acceptable to the local leadership of Gaza and the West Bank. This eliminates any chance of interest by the West in popular movements and widens the gap between the regimes and those who advocate sensible dialogue and the people. The Middle East governments settle for depending on a narrower popular base, political opposition groups are undermined and the people become more unhappy and militant. The West follows obvious short-term interests and becomes more supportive of the accommodating regimes. The people become anti-West.

This is why former British Prime Minister Harold Macmillan spoke of being 'forced to support reactionary regimes'.[1] And this is what happened recently when Arafat signed the Oslo peace accord which gave the Israelis more than what Palestinian delegates, unlike him negotiating in the open in Washington, came close to attaining. He pre-empted an agreement by delegates who were a genuine expression of the Palestinian people by giving more (see Chapter 5). It is a vicious cycle which perpetuates itself. This is what has existed, in different forms and for different reasons and through different pro-West control groups, since the First World War. And this situation justifies focusing on the historical background that created what we have today.

Except for some sheikhdoms along the Gulf, Western colonialism did not come to the Middle East until during and shortly after the First World War. The West's declared and immediate aim was to eject Ottoman Turkey, Germany's war ally, from the region which it had controlled under the banner of an Islamic caliphate for over four centuries. Instead of attempting to conquer the Arab Middle East militarily, and because their armies were fully engaged on the Western Front, the West chose to undermine Turkey's hold on the territory comprising today's Syria, Iraq, Lebanon, Palestine, Jordan and much of Saudi Arabia by sponsoring uprisings by the indigenous Arab population. In addition, bringing an end to Turkey's rule of fellow Muslims required an ideological counter-weight to the undoubted pull of Islam, and this meant supporting the then new idea of Arab nationalism and relying on local Arab leaders with tribal or religious followings to promote this movement to fight Turkey.

The plans as to how to sponsor indigenous uprisings were, in the main, improvised by the British officers of the Arab Bureau in Cairo. The British backing for the idea of Arab nationalism represented a policy, but the alliances with traditional leaders such as Hussein I of the Hijaz and Ibn Saud of central Arabia had no master plan behind them; it was the convenient expression of this policy.

Judged by the contradictory agreements and unenforceable promises they made to Arabs and their chiefs and the ones made to the Zionists and shared with France, the whole British approach – and Britain was the country that mattered – was aimed at realizing short-term benefits without paying attention to their long-term consequences. There was no coordination between the Arab Bureau in Cairo, the body which controlled day-to-day regional developments, and higher authorities in London. There was an inclination by field operatives to promise too much and deceive; an absence of qualified people to oversee field operations; and an attachment to, and acceptance of, Bedouin culture and importance which perverted what the Arab Middle East needed and its people wanted.

Even the 1917 Balfour Declaration was contradictory and contained the seeds of its own destruction: it promised a national home to the Jews without prejudicing the rights of the Arab people of Palestine. Indeed, the declaration was so shady that there was an attempt to keep its contents secret. Of course there were the British promises to Hussein I which supported his claim to the caliphate and primary Arab leadership (Lawrence, McMahon and others including a letter which used eighty-two words to describe his title). But Hussein I was being promoted while Captain William Shakespeare of the British India Office and later Sir Percy Cox and others were making contrary promises to his arch-rival, Ibn Saud. The British pretended to support Arab unity, the creation of an Arab state comprising all the countries mentioned except Egypt, while secretly signing the 1916 Sykes-Picot Agreement with France to create small states and share in their control (the contents of this agreement were kept secret until 1921, when a copy fell into the hands of the Bolsheviks) and while the Orientalist-agent Gertrude Bell claimed that there was no Arab nation.[2] Sir Arthur Hirtzel of the India Office took matters further and made clear that Britain's aim was to divide the Arabs rather than to unify them.[3] Even Lawrence of Arabia, commonly accepted as the champion of the Arab cause, described the Arabs as a 'limited, narrow-minded people'.[4]

This confusing, unattractive picture of double-dealing aside, there were fundamental considerations which determined the whole approach of Britain and France to the area. Above all, the central governments of both countries didn't like the Arabs or respect their leaders, and using them to defeat Turkey was no more than a tactical move. The view that both governments took of the Arabs was the result of historical prejudices and they saw them as a backward Muslim people, the possessors of an inferior culture, manners and behaviour.[5] This traditional opinion of the Arabs was coupled with the British desire to safeguard the routes to India – the wish to control the holy cities of Mecca and Medina and use them as a lever in handling the Muslims within its empire – and the Christian belief of some members of the British government in the creation of a Jewish state in Palestine. In turn, the French, using tenuous connections to the Maronites of Lebanon which went back centuries, were committed to promoting the divisive interests of their wards. And even then, for both countries but more so for Britain, there was the lure of oil, for this was being produced in Iran and beginning to be discovered in Iraq.

The basic attitudes and interests of the governments of Britain and France eventually either transcended or supported the whims of their field officers and their schemes. But the contradictions between what these officers were told and what mattered to Britain and France escaped the Arabs, who were in a deplorable state of 'social, political and moral decay'.[6] It was this state of decay which encouraged the West to pursue its post-First World War plans for indirect control of the weakened region. Colonialism was dying, direct rule of the region would have been expensive, and the French and British armies were occupied elsewhere; controlling the Arab Middle East through a neo-colonialism based on the use of willing native collaborators became the order of the day.

This neo-colonialism meant dividing the simple and naive people of the Arab Middle East into two groups: one that ruled and one that was ruled. The first group was made up of sherifs (descendants of Muhammad), traditional tribal sheikhs, religious leaders and the subsidiary groups of merchants, anti-Turkish intellectuals and some Arab officers who had served in the Turkish army. Although some members of these groups were genuinely misled and quarrelled with the Western powers later, initially all of them were the willing servants of the British and French. Real Arab aspirations either didn't matter or were satisfied through false promises, and this meant ignoring the ruled.

Because of the importance accorded their religious lineage and the fact that they joined forces with the British early and started the anti-Ottoman rebellion in 1916, the Hashemites were identified, more than any other family or group, with the post-First World War arrival of the colonial powers. Descendants of the Prophet, they had been the loyal servants of Ottoman Turkey and for centuries appointed by it as governors of the Hijaz and the holy cities of Mecca and Medina. Their alliance with Britain was concluded after lengthy negotiations with the Arab Bureau in Cairo, the British office in charge of developing the needed Arab support against Turkey.

The Arab Revolt, as the Hashemite uprising against Turkey came to be known, was not a mass movement and had very little to do with the Arab people.[7] It was 'an Anglo-Hashemite conspiracy'[8] which depended on Bedouin mercenaries, British money and a number of Arab officers in the Turkish army who had defected to Britain. The city people of the Hijaz, the relatively educated majority of the people in the territory where the rebellion started, had very little to do with it. Only some Syrian and other intellectuals accepted the Hashemites, because they saw in them the means to gain Western support for Arab independence, and this support was short-lived.

Judged realistically, the Arab Revolt was a reflection of personal and family ambitions. To concentrate on the image of the romantic Bedouin mercenary fighting for 'independence' promoted by Lawrence of Arabia and others, and on the ephemeral support of other groups, is to ignore the misgivings of the majority who preferred the Muslim Empire of Ottoman Turkey to the infidel West.

To the east of the Hijaz, in central Arabia, a similar event was taking place. The British administration of India, the India Office, gave support to another traditional leader after years of hesitation. The contacts with Ibn Saud (Abdel Aziz Abdel Rahman Al Saud), the leader of the Wahhabi puritan and warlike sub-sect, in reality a religious order, started in answer to his various pleas to become a servant of Britain.[9] But he was rebuffed until Britain decided that war with Turkey was inevitable and began to use him against pro-Turkish chiefs of central and eastern Arabia.

Ibn Saud, like Hussein I of the Hijaz, enhanced his religious claim by using British money to buy Bedouin loyalty. However, largely because of local circumstances, there were no former Arab officers of the Turkish army in his territory and he identified more closely with the Bedouins while relying on direct British help in the form of money, arms and occasionally officers.

The third group sponsored by the British to rise against Turkey originally appeared in a supporting capacity. This was the already mentioned Arab officer class of the Turkish army, who played a central role in the Arab Revolt, helped create Iraq and later ran it as a pro-British government. Here, once again, was a group who had little connection with the

people; in this case the officers had defected because they were resentful
of the Turkish monopoly of high ranks in the Ottoman army. The most
prominent personalities of this group, the Iraqis Nuri Saïd, Ja'afar Al
Askari, Jamil Madfai' and Ali Jawdat Ayoubi, were Kurds and the Egyptian
Aziz Al Masri was a Circasian, and none of them had a claim to popular
leadership. Even if we include the Arab members of this group – prominent
among whom were the brothers Taha and Yassin Al Hashemi – except
for the highly educated Askari what we have is a clique for hire who saw
a better future in cooperating with Britain than in remaining with Turkey.
They had little interest in the ruled. In fact, they represented the first
attempt by a colonial power to create a new class of army officers beholden
to it, the precursor of CIA-sponsored officer groups which took over Arab
countries in the 1950s and 60s.

The remaining pro-British groupings mattered less. The Bedouins followed whoever controlled the purse-strings to the extent of switching
allegiance between Hussein I and Ibn Saud. In some instances, for example
Sheikh Mubarak in Kuwait and Auda Abu Tayi, the Jordanian Sheikh
who assisted Lawrence, the British used money to deal with Bedouin
chiefs directly. In addition, merchants, mainly non-Arabs in Syria, Lebanon
and Egypt, favoured the West because they saw a better future for themselves than under a disintegrating Muslim Turkey. Lastly, there were the
small group of intellectuals in Syria and Lebanon who were resentful
of Turkish dictatorial methods and accepted the West's promises at face
value.

France, Britain's junior partner in plans to control the Middle East,
addressed the question of the smaller territory allocated to it by the secret
Sykes-Picot Agreement: Syria and Lebanon. Its concern with maintaining
a Middle East position through the use of local people found it supporting
the Maronite Lebanese in creating a country twice the size of the Mount
Lebanon of history, the basis of the Lebanese claim to a state separate
from Syria, the mother country which considered Lebanon an integral
part of its territory. In addition, there were other French attempts to
fragment Syria further, which led to the short-lived creation of Alawi and
Druze states from its territory. In fact, the French conquest of Syria was
followed by the recruitment of thousands of members of these minority
religious sects and others to serve in the French Troupes Spéciales, the
forces the French used to subdue the majority of the people after their
1920 conquest. Use of religious minority groups in Syria was similar to
the British use of Ibn Saud. And, to repeat, the use of the Maronites and
Ibn Saud to claim and create new territories and turn them into subservient
states based on religion is strikingly similar.[10]

The small groups which supported the British and French during the First World War became even smaller after the defeat of Ottoman Turkey exposed Western designs, schemes and cynicism. In fact, the period following the war, from 1918 until 1925, saw the first confrontation between the Arabs and the West this century and reveals a West so determined to have its own way that even Hussein I, its first and most important ally during the war, turned against it.

The British and French, however muddled and improvised their wartime plans were, proceeded to develop a cohesive policy whose aim was to divide the Arab Middle East into small weak states.[11] Because most of the Arab people opposed this, the Arab patriarchy and the special interest groups who continued to support them were no more than collaborators who had a similar interest in dividing the region along new, self-serving political and economic lines. Except for Egypt, the boundaries of every state which emerged after the war were drawn by European powers. Indeed every Arab state of the time was run by what Desmond Stewart calls a 'client dynasty'[12] or under the direct control of the West. But geographically, religiously, politically, economically, socially and despite Western persistence in trying to secure religious and tribal sanction through sponsored chiefs, what resulted suffered from faulty design. And despite the absence of cohesive groups capable of political action in opposition to Western designs in most territories, a response to the new creations became inevitable. The responses were feeble, different from one place to another and so disjointed as to represent no threat. Even so, they served ample notice that there existed an Arab people who desired something different and that it was early enough for the West to change direction or to couple its support for client dynasties, sects and groups with safeguards against unacceptable future developments, the inevitable abuse of the common people by what they had created. In fact, the West's refusal at this point to consider any moves to correct its obvious mistakes, or accommodate the wishes of the people and future developments, provides ample proof that its neo-colonialist designs were the result not of a lack of cohesion among the Arabs but of a desire to control the Arabs and keep them down.

The first problem to confront the West after the First World War was what to do about its leading former client, Hussein I. Adamant that British promises made to him during the war included support for the Arab position in Palestine and his kingship of all Arabs in a united country, and angry over the contrary, perfidious promises Britain had secretly made in support of the Zionists, Hussein I retreated into deep melancholia and a state of non-cooperation. With no Turkey to fight, and because his holiness had been deliberately exaggerated and was no longer of use, Hussein I had outlived his purpose. The response of the British to his challenge was swift: they withdrew their support and switched it to the more accommodating Ibn Saud.[13] Their preference for the leader of the Wahhabi minority was part of their plan to divide the Arabs and prompted their refusal to stop his invasion and occupation of Hussein's territory of Hijaz – something that they had done in the past.[14] Hussein's fate was sealed and he abdicated in favour of his son Ali, who, lacking support, lost the Hijaz to the British-sponsored Ibn Saud in 1925.

Meanwhile, in 1920, Hussein's more pro-British and accommodating son, Faisal, had assumed the throne of Syria, in this case in response to the call to become its king by the country's educated and relatively sophisticated bourgeoisie, unlike others a class capable of running an independent country. But Syria had been given to the French by the Sykes-Picot Agreement.

The French, viewing Faisal's accession to Syria's throne as an act of usurpation, in 1920 brought an end to it in four months. Initially they issued an ultimatum to Faisal to accept their primacy. Surprisingly, perhaps because of awareness of what was happening to his father, Faisal, but not the Syrians, accepted the French demand. Claiming the acceptance of their ultimatum had come too late, the French army marched into Syria, dethroned Faisal and declared the country a mandate territory in accordance with the rules of the League of Nations.

Another of Hussein's sons (and Faisal's brother), Abdallah, the one member of his family who believed in British primacy to the point of never questioning it, put together an army and marched from the Hijaz towards Syria to eject the French. However, relying on his inherent weakness for obeying them, the British intercepted his march and offered him a new country, the Emirate of Jordan, as compensation. In reality, the British knew Abdallah was incapable of regaining Syria for the Hashemites and their action had another motive behind it. A Jordan with a pro-British emir would be friendly to the Jews, and Abdallah could be used to check the increasingly popular anti-Zionism of the time.[15] Jordan was nothing more than the Bedouin part of Palestine east of the River Jordan, its people the least advanced Palestinians and its purpose to thwart the wishes of the more educated majority (the use of Jordan's King Hussein against the Palestinians smacks of this to this day).

Then, in 1921, in a cynical stroke of the pen, the British decided that Faisal, though not as pliant as his brother or as divisive as Ibn Saud, had learned his lesson and become 'manageable' enough to be used. They decided to make him King of Iraq, a state stitched up from the former

Turkish *vilayets* (provinces ruled by a governor) of Baghdad, Basra and Mosul. The majority Shias of the country were opposed to the imposition of a Sunni king and in 1920 the first inkling of Britain's plans led them to start a serious rebellion which cost the British four thousand casualties and £20 million. But it was no use; the British determination to award the 'reformed' members of the Hashemite family with thrones – perhaps as a compensation for losing out on Arab unity – saw them deport the local contender to the country's throne, Sayyid Taleb Al Naqib, to Ceylon. They followed this with a rigged referendum which favoured Faisal (rigging is alive and well in those countries in the Middle East which purport to hold elections).

Almost simultaneously, in 1921, the British engineered the election to the post of Mufti of Palestine of Haj Amin Husseini, another descendant of the Prophet who lacked the basic qualifications of office (see Chapter 5). The British plans to give Palestine to the Jews, the infamous Balfour Declaration of 1917, had been revealed by the Bolsheviks a short time before and the consequent disturbances in Palestine required an establishment religious figure to accommodate British designs.

North of Palestine, in 1920, the French sanctioned the creation of a greater Lebanon than was historically justified and put the Maronites in control against the wishes of the country's Muslim population and Syria, the country from which most of the Lebanese territory was taken. And, of course, the French continued with their threat to create states for the Alawi and Druze sects and reduce Syria further.

By 1925 the Arab Middle East which emerged was not only a Western design, it didn't even subscribe to many of the original neo-colonialist pretences. Ibn Saud controlled most of the Arabian Peninsula and ran it in accordance with friendship treaties with Britain which ceded the conduct of his country's foreign relations to his mentors. Abdallah's new state, Jordan, the ultimate expression of artificiality, was dependent on British subsidies and was run by British officers as much as it was run by him. Iraq was under Faisal and the cabal of former Turkish army officers who were elevated to prominence during the Arab Revolt – an alien Sunni group with little sensitivity to the needs of the country's majority Shias.

In fact, the British suppression of the Iraqi Shias went as far as using their own leaders against them; the British resurrected old land-ownership laws and gave Shia tribal leaders huge tracts of land to bribe them to keep their people quiet. Palestine, the historical seat of Pilate, was wrenched by conflict between Arabs and Jews, and the British insistence on fulfilling the promise made in the Balfour and other pro-Jewish declarations led them to use the Mufti to keep Arab protest under control. The French were consolidating the Maronite minority control of Lebanon by granting them commercial and legal rights denied to the non-Maronite people of the country. Kuwait, originally part of the Iraqi *vilayet* of Basra, was bound to Britain by an illegal agreement signed in 1896; after the First World War the British reconfirmed this agreement to keep Kuwait separate from Iraq. Egypt, a historical nation state, had been reduced to the status of a British protectorate free from its historical ties to Turkey in 1914, after a combination of Western-sponsored overspending and palace corruption had bankrupted it. What emerged was another British-controlled country reduced in status, a surrogate state with an originally Albanian royal family, who owned huge tracts of land and had little connection with the Egyptian people, in charge. (This explains Lord Curzon's statement that the 'British didn't govern Egypt, we only govern the governors of Egypt'.[16])

It was Syria which provided the difference. In Syria the landowning class was nationalist and, along with educated circles, produced a leadership which unceasingly put pressure on the French to grant them independence and successfully forced France to cancel the plans for more minority states in addition to Lebanon. And the Syrians not only never gave up their claim to Lebanon itself, but made recovering it part of their national policy. The most successful popular resistance to Western designs and hegemony emerged in Syria in the 1920s and 30s.

What the West created after the First World War involved cynicism, instability, inefficiency and corruption. The cynicism showed early and clearly; instead of being liberators, the military commanders of Britain and France, Generals Allenby and Gouraud, were seen as Christian conquerors by their governments and people.[17] This was followed by reneging on the various promises which had been made. Instability was built-in, the new countries' claims to statehood, which should have provided them with enduring stability, were arbitrary and unacceptable to their people (for example, no attention was paid to demography in creating Iraq, and the Palestinians continued to call themselves southern Syrians until the early 1930s). And corruption and inefficiency were approved of when Western-sponsored leaders, not the most competent people available, received foreign subsidies and pocketed them. These were the trademarks of the new regimes. Only Western support for the rulers or ruling classes mattered. Except for a brief period after the French left Syria in the mid-1940s, not a single country among the new creations has ever had a leadership which was pro-West and acceptable to its people at the same time. As early as the 1930s, Syria, Saudi Arabia, Palestine, Egypt and Iraq produced serious popular protests and uprisings against the Western-backed leaderships of their countries.

In many countries, particularly Saudi Arabia and Jordan, the leadership, with British blessing, compounded its lack of acceptability by an archaic dependence on the Bedouins, the people the Koran described as 'hardened in their impurity and hypocrisy'. It was a case of impure leadership expanding its impurity by depending on an impure minority to produce an impure, out-of-date system of government. In Iraq former Turkish army officers friendly to the British ran the country, claimed much of the public land as their own and became a new exclusive and abusive governing class. In Palestine British dependence on a religious figure, the Mufti, refusal to deal with the people and reliance on a small number of establishment families produced an inability to solve the Palestinian problem in a satisfactory way. In Lebanon things got worse and the original religious division assumed a socio-economic character which threatened to perpetuate itself and the divisions it contained. The only country in the Arab Middle East not created by the imperialist designs which followed the First World War was Egypt, then the most advanced of them all. But even in Egypt, the British depended on the alien monarchy, the abusive landowning pashas and the Greek and Jewish merchants of the country, and the ensuing protest by the intellectual class rendered the country unstable. This completed the picture: after the First World War the West gave birth to governmental illegitimacy, right across the Arab Middle East.

This dismal picture, the unacceptable fabrications the West created or adopted following the First World War, is still with us to this day. The perpetual convergence of interest between obsolete monarchies (Saudi Arabia, Kuwait and Jordan), minority religious sects (the Maronites), special interest groups (Saddam Hussein and Arafat and the Palestinian establishment) and army-based rule (Mubarak of Egypt and Assad of Syria) and the West remains intact.

Today there is greater dependence by the West and the illegitimate regimes on the military, but this is a natural development, a product of the times which represents nothing more than an advanced version of the original use of the Bedouins. Even in the 1920s, in Iraq, one of the only relatively advanced countries among the new creations, the use of the army came naturally. Egypt, another advanced and a fairly developed country, was occupied by British forces, who were then replaced by the Egyptian army as the power behind the state. And in others, particularly Saudi Arabia and Jordan, today's armies are an extension of the Bedouins who supported the original regimes, and to this day their loyalty is bought with ready cash. In the rest of the region, even armies with no Bedouin background have been accepted as a new oppressive class. Today's military cliques are no different from the original élite in their policies toward their people and the West. New control groups have either been added to the old ones or have replaced them, among them being the one which put the Iraqi Ba'ath Party and Saddam Hussein in power (see Chapter 4).

In the West, this period also saw a change which did not affect the determination to maintain hegemony over the Arab Middle East – the replacement of the original predominant neo-colonialist country, Britain, by the United States. There was American ideology immediately after the First World War, when the country had no direct interest in the Middle East. But it had disappeared and was replaced by self-interest later. The Americans moved into the Middle East after the Second World War, dispensed with the tired and bankrupt French in no time and reduced the British to a junior partner. Britain's original wish to safeguard the strategic routes to India was replaced after the Second World War by the Americans' determination to control the region against communist expansion. On other regional problems, Palestine in particular, the American commitment to keeping the area divided and weak to support Zionist designs differed from the original British designs only in its openness and crudeness of method. And later, after the creation of Israel, the country was allowed to deputize for America in a manner which allowed it to provide support for the Jordanian monarchy and the Maronites of Lebanon.

The one determining factor, the importance of which has grown in terms of the West's control of the Middle East, is oil. The discovery of Arab oil in vast quantities and consequent American dependence on it for economic survival made control of oil the cornerstone of America's Middle East policy. Until the need for oil, the Cold War and the desire to manipulate the outcome of the Arab-Israeli conflict forced it into the open as the dominant power in the Middle East, republican non-colonial America was acceptable to the Arabs. Even in the late 1930s the Arabs believed in America's neutrality on the problem of Palestine, as confirmed by the findings of the King-Crane Commission. Moreover, the Arabs admired Woodrow Wilson's proclamations calling for the granting of independence to various national groups and making the world safe for democracy, and saw both as the antithesis of the policies of the traditional colonial powers. But America discarded its ideology, followed oil interests, turned a blind commitment to anti-communism into a wish to involve all people in this issue and manifested a desire to please Zionism and win elections at home at the expense of the Arabs. America has, during the past four decades, followed its replacement of the old, tired colonial powers by adopting policies similar to theirs. In the process America became colonialist and made the Middle East unsafe for democracy.

This book is a collection of case studies of the deterrence of democracy and the promotion of governmental illegitimacy in the Arab Middle East by France, Britain, the United States and, in a subsidiary role, Israel. It is not an exhaustive history of this subject in terms of covering all that has happened, but it examines major representative examples of how and through whom this has been achieved. The result has been the cruel enslavement of the Arab people and the fire on the way: the Islamic-West confrontation in the making.

Contrary to accepted opinion in the Middle East, the conspiracy behind what has happened is mainly implicit. While there have been situations which required the two allied sides, the West and the Arab élite, to consult, cooperate, plot coups and develop joint plans to meet the common enemy, the Arab people, more often than not both sides arrived at similar conclusions relatively independently. This is why we have had the occasional aberration, albeit temporary, of a misreading by one side of the other's commitment and intentions. (King Hussein's support for Saddam Hussein during the Gulf crisis could be seen in this light.)

The terms 'establishment', 'élite' and 'patriarchy' as used throughout this book, though obviously not the same, are interchangeable and embrace the aristocracy, monarchical and otherwise, but are not limited to those. They have a broad meaning covering army officers who elevated themselves, mainly with outside help, to a privileged ruling class (the Sunni army officership in Iraq), special moneyed groups who hijacked a whole political movement (the pro-West money-men behind Yasser Arafat) and small nations endowed with sudden riches which enable them to be élitist and to exercise regional influence and power (Kuwait). In essence, the groups under discussion are best described by the Arab expression '*elly bihel we burbut*', 'those who loosen and bind', the groups in a position to decide the fate of the countries covered by this study.

The West-Arab establishment hegemony and control of power has not gone unopposed. The challenges to it which followed the First World War were weak and lacked cohesion, but the challenge of Nasser's Arab Nationalism in the 1950s and 60s was a substantial one which gathered hitherto diverse elements in one populist movement and came close to achieving success: an independent Middle East. With Nasser's disappearance, the West, as usual, assumed that the forces which rallied behind him had disappeared. Superficially they have, and Nasser's failure brought an end to secular resistance to the traditional and new establishments and Western hegemony. But, as we will see, the abusive nature of the harmony between the West and the Arab establishment, the brutal friendship which binds them together, inevitably leads to either the re-emergence of these forces in a different guise or new forces which follow similar policies. With secularism discredited, initially by Nasser's and other failures to deliver on the promises of their movements, and more recently by the destruction of secular Iraq during the Gulf War, people have turned to religion to express grievances which are nearly a century old. The result is the predominance of Islamic fundamentalism.

To appreciate the destructive nature of the West-Arab establishment informal alliances – mainly called friendship – one has to examine major, known problems which have racked the Middle East during the past four decades. The West used friendly Arab regimes to undermine Arab efforts against Israel in 1948; in particular King Abdallah of Jordan followed an openly traitorous anti-Arab policy in collusion with Britain and Israel (see Chapter 7). Britain and France tried to reduce Nasser to size in 1955 and 56 – on occasion tried to eliminate him – because he objected to their economic abuse of Egypt through control of the Suez Canal. In 1967, because Nasser placed regional consideration ahead of the West's preoccupation with communism, the United States, assured by Nasser that he was not about to start a war, looked the other way while Israel attacked him. In 1970 the West supported Jordan's suppression of the Palestinians in a bloody civil war because Jordan followed a more accommodating policy, one closer to that of the United States, *vis-à-vis* Israel. The Kurdish rebellions of 1948, 56, 67 and 75, like the present one, have had little to do with Kurdish aspirations and more to do with Iraq's unwillingness to follow a pro-West line. The Lebanese civil war had Maronite sectarian dominance as its primary reason. The 1962–7 war in the Yemen continued because the West, though it showed signs of vacillation, was afraid that democracy in the Yemen might undermine friendly Saudi Arabia's absolute feudal monarchy. One justifiable way of seeing the intifada is to view it as a grassroots movement of the disenfranchised against a situation dictated by powers committed to denying the Palestinian people their rights. And the first Gulf War, between Iran and Iraq, lasted nine years because the West and its Arab allies used it to weaken both sides and divert them from challenging their alliance. The second Gulf War, a direct, greater challenge to the West's Middle East position than anything before it, completed the picture. With the popular forces opposed to Western hegemony on the decline since 1967, the West was able to opt for direct interference without major popular opposition, while counting on the support of its Arab establishment friends who paid the West back for its support.

What connects these situations to the West-Arab establishment alliance is clear: the survival of Western policy through tributary regimes, allies/friends. However, there are situations which are more difficult to follow, and others which remain secret. The West has used economic sanctions against unfriendly regimes and groups to undermine them and replace them with friendly ones (Iraq and Libya now). Selectively, anti-West regimes are accused of being dictators unacceptable to the modern world, or new world order (Iraq and Libya). The security forces of friendly countries, the secret police they use against their citizens, are trained by the West (Saudi Arabia, Kuwait et al.). Surrogate forces are sponsored to fight unfriendly regimes and groups (the Kurds against Iraq and the Maronites against the Palestinians). Even some moderate groups which oppose the pro-West dictatorial regimes are dubbed a 'threat to peace' (the Muslim Brotherhood in Egypt and the Islamic Saudi opposition in London). In other words, the process of Western opposition to everything except client-states led by brutal-friendly leaders, beyond being policy, has become a tradition which can express itself in many different ways.

All attempts to undermine the West-Arab establishment alliance, be they peaceful, confrontational, popular, governmental or any combination of these, have failed. Their failure has led the opponents of the alliance to adopt new ideologies which have not been tainted by failure; most are Islamic and some incorporate extremist positions. The extremists are an expression of the escalating confrontation between the Arab establishment and the Arab people. The level of abuse and state violence in the Middle East is greater than ever before, and most responses to it, though understandable, are equally reprehensible. In Egypt political opponents are executed after trials by courts the legitimacy of which has been challenged by international human rights organizations. The House of Saud kidnaps, imprisons and tortures dissidents. Bahrain denies its majority Shias equal rights and the Western-supported regime kills them when they demonstrate. The largest building in Amman belongs to the internal security apparatus, whose function is obvious. Yasser Arafat's police, a new entrant in the ugliness stakes, controls the press and tortures and eliminates opponents. Iraq's present government is rightly condemned for eliminating people but the West wants to install a similar regime in power, without the demonized Saddam in charge. Kuwait, unable to control or support them, denies hundreds of thousands of its Bidoon people citizenship. And conditions in Syria are best described through the recent amnesty of five thousand political prisoners, people we hadn't heard anything about until their release.

The preceding, in view of Western connivance in some crimes and silence about the rest, supports my contention that the West and its clients are still in the business of suppressing and eliminating all opposition. Meanwhile, because the cynicism, inefficiency, corruption and resulting structural instability which plagued the area after the First World War are worse than ever before, and because the Arab people are now too educated and advanced to tolerate this unhappy state, the opposition to what exists is growing. One has only to think of the bombing of the World Trade Center, the reports of attacks on tourists in Egypt, the two explosions which destroyed buildings housing American troops and their dependants in supposedly stable Saudi Arabia, open dissent and riots in Jordan and Bahrain, the identity crisis racking Kuwait and the increasingly dictatorial behaviour of Yasser Arafat, and it becomes clear that total reliance on police power to decide what exists cannot continue.

The opposition forces which first surfaced eighty years ago have lost battles and have often gone silent, but they have never disappeared. Because they are operating under an Islamic banner with wider appeal and have grown to the point of threatening Western and establishment interests in a more serious way than their mainly secular predecessors, both the West and the establishment are using the threat to their dominance to perpetuate it. To them, the Islamic movements are made of extremists with whom one cannot hold a dialogue; their suppression is therefore justified.

If we accept that serious trouble is on the way, then solutions to avert disaster – total or partial – are needed. The ever-changing nature and breadth of the Middle East's problems preclude making a list of tactical remedies to recommend to policy-makers, so I will limit myself to advocating a strategic change in the attitude of the West which would produce an atmosphere conducive to the emergence of specific solutions. What needs to exist between the Arabs and the West, what has always been needed, is a state of friendly tension, a pervasive, inclusive atmosphere which recognizes the interdependence of the two sides while accepting the existence of differences in their interests and opinion and the need to overcome these obstacles in a friendly fashion. In other words, neither side should take the other for granted, or follow policies aimed at taking the other for granted. This would automatically end the system of indirect control, eliminate the need for illegitimate deputy sherifs who accept being taken for granted and involve the Arab people. Unlike the pro-West rulers, the people don't need protection to survive and want to deal with the West as equals and not as 'petitioning schoolboys'.[18]

PART TWO

*The Counterfeit
Middle East*

2 · Images and Reality

To the noted British writer and Middle East expert David Gilmour the British are saddled with the Victorian notion that, 'Everything good about the Middle East comes from the desert and everything bad is from Levantine fleshpots.'[1] American news correspondent Christopher Harper offers a more topical refrain: 'The problem which the Arab world has in the United States is the image of Islam.'[2] The image of Islam which Harper has in mind is made of the hostage crisis in Iran and the bombings of the American Embassy and marine barracks in Lebanon, the World Trade Center in New York and the American army compound in Al Khobar, Saudi Arabia.

The statements of the two experts (Harper spent more than five years in the Middle East as correspondent for *Newsweek* and ABC) are not contradictory; they are complementary. Gilmour's statement expresses an embedded historical attitude which is more British than American while Harper's opinion is a more contemporary one which concerns how the media and the people in America see things. Beneath the surface the statements are true of both countries. The few Americans, mainly missionaries and educators, who knew the Middle East earlier this century were not as romantically inclined as the British colonialists who served there, but they did have an attachment to Bedouin life and the generous, kind and colourful Arab of the desert. And the ordinary Briton accepts the prevailing image of Islam and the Arabs described by Harper. The difference between the two countries has nothing to do with the Arabs or their overall image, but with the difference between British and American thinking: the fact that one defers to history more than the other.

The picture Western governments and people have of the Arabs, based as it is on a romantic past and an unhappy present, is the greatest obstacle to a better understanding between the Arab Middle East and the West. Nobody tries to demonstrate the fallacy of depending on a past which is no more, or to explain that celebrating desert people, Bedouins, and setting them above educated city folk was always a serious mistake and produced unhappy results. Nor is anybody willing, or able, to explain the unhappy

state of affairs which exists now as a result of a huge historical misunderstanding: the Western support of unpopular leaders which persists to this
day. There are no attempts to solve the real problems which produce the
bomber. The few academics who have addressed these problems – Edward
Said's and Noam Chomsky's efforts are worthy of note – talk to a special,
highly educated audience of government officials, academics, specialists
and experts and sadly their preaching does not reach the average American
or Briton.

We see the Middle East through indelible good and bad images which
exaggerate, reduce, supersede, overlook, twist or replace simple facts. The
final product is the brainchild of the West and its Arab friends and is
moulded to serve their common purpose which invariably precludes their
taking into consideration the feelings and interests of the Arab people.
The average Arab, neglected and ignored, is not the Bedouin noble savage,
the backward Arab whose interests and demands do not clash with those
of the West. He is the educated or semi-educated city dweller who has
social and political grievances which are unacceptable to the West's clients
and indirectly to the West. The bomber is not a Bedouin or a supporter
of a Bedouin state or a Western-sponsored dictatorship; he is the unacceptable 'other Arab', the original unromantic figure who opposes Western
hegemony.

'We deal with everyone except the common man,' is a statement attributed to the former Chairman of the US Senate Foreign Relations Committee, William Fulbright.[3] Ignoring or subordinating the interests of the
Arab people and relying on small groups of traditional or new dictators
to accommodate Western political and economic interests, even if successful for long periods, produces an untrue picture and a consequent inability
to cope with the real and continuing problems of the Middle East. These
cannot be solved when the West manufactures consent, deliberately confuses the consent of the few with the consent and interests of the Arab
people. Nor can they be solved by focusing on individual events, however
unacceptable, without dealing with the grievances behind them. The
West's small circle of clients–cum–friends adopt one of two stances: they
claim that everybody accepts their ways and opposition doesn't exist, or
they misidentify their opponents and label them fanatics and demons. So,
bombings are the work of people who don't exist or people who are
intrinsically evil. We never penetrate these descriptions to know the people
who carry out the atrocious acts to express their non-existence or supposed
inherent criminality.

The dependence of the West on 'clients', 'deputy sherifs', minority
religious or ethnic groups, backward sheikhs, despots, military cliques,

unpopular monarchs, a moneyed class of people, intellectuals with a Western bent or an aristocracy, or combinations of these, continues. And this despite the many empirical examples which, throughout this century, have demonstrated the utter unsoundness of creating images intended to elevate unpopular and unworthy Western clients and their countries to the status of acceptable, stable and organized entities; in short, of substituting images for reality. Before 1958 and the bloody but popular overthrow of the Iraqi monarchy, we created an image of stability for Iraq and benevolence for its ruling family only to discover that Iraq was not stable and the royal family was neither benevolent nor popular. Something similar happened in Iran, where the West and its deputy sherif, the so-called modern Shah, opted for Westernization, were dismissive of the wishes of the people and convinced themselves that what they were doing was working. Khomeini proved the contrary in 1979; the West could do nothing to keep the Shah on the throne. After the Camp David Accord of 1978 we deluded ourselves by thinking that Sadat and his policies were popular until he was gunned down by Islamic elements in his own army in 1982.

The self-delusion continues. We judge Middle East leaders by what is acceptable to the West and not by what their people, the arbiters of their fate, want. For example, as a result of the image they have in the West, whatever King Hussein does is good and whatever Saddam Hussein does is bad. Events in which either man is involved are subordinated to the larger image that the West holds on to. Little publicity has been given until recently to the involvement of some members of King Hussein's family in the arms trade, his friends' drug running, how Hussein calls in favours to ensure favourable election results, the torture of detainees in Jordanian prisons and the overall corruption of Hussein's administration. His performance at the funeral of the murdered Israeli Prime Minister Yitzhak Rabin, sobbing in public and calling Rabin 'a friend and a brother', was utterly unacceptable to his own people, who thought it unIslamic (a Jew cannot be called a brother) and shameful, but the West saw it completely differently. How Hussein behaves towards them and their beliefs and feelings is of greater concern to the Jordanian people than the fact that he attended Harrow and Sandhurst and that he has a pretty American wife, which are what the West highlights when judging him.

Saddam is the other side of the coin; in his case the bad image is so pervasive that we are denied the right to judge him correctly. It is because of this bad image that some people believe that Saddam organized the bombing of the World Trade Center, though there is no evidence to support this allegation. And Saddam came to mind and was mentioned after the Oklahoma bombing, the bombing in October 1995 of a building full of military advisers in Riyadh and the June 1996 bombing in Al Khobar. Again, there is no evidence to support these allegations. In the West, nothing has been written about Saddam's eradication of illiteracy and health care programmes – the first one of the most successful efforts of its type in history and the second a broader one than exists in the rest of the Arab world. Nor is anything said about his championing of women's rights and how, on occasion, the Kurds fared better under him than in Iran and Turkey. To his people, even his evil acquisition of unconventional weapons is seen as an attempt to master modern technology (he did send a rocket into outer space). While the evil nature of the man is undisputed, the exaggerations, omissions and outright lies preclude judging him sensibly and responding correctly to his evil ways. So, good King Hussein is always good and bad Saddam is always bad.

In the West, mechanisms are in place – and, when necessary, created – to control, form and doctor the image of Arab leaders and countries to suit their usefulness to Western needs. Facts are subordinated to images, and what filters through to the knowledgeable and the average person alike is aimed at inducing them to concur with what has already been decided. The barriers that are set up thwart any possibility of a situation being judged by the facts which created it. True in normal circumstances, this is more so when a person or a country becomes 'a story'. In fact, the bigger the story the more the likelihood of distortion, and this is why Saddam is immediately connected to stories for which he is not responsible.

Taking Saudi Arabia as an example of a country which is facing serious political, economic and social problems and which has recently received wide press coverage, we find that most of the news which has reached the West has the same natural conclusion: the West is better off with the House of Saud than without them. The image becomes a story-line and persists despite frequent reports of human rights violations (Middle East Watch, Amnesty International and Article 19); a home-made economic crisis (*Business Week International, Wall Street Journal, Sunday Telegraph, Washington Post* and many others); or an abusive, absolute monarchy which refuses to share power with its citizenry (*Foreign Affairs* and *New Statesman* et al.). Even the recent bombings of buildings housing American military advisers and personnel and their dependants and the prospect of an Islamic fundamentalist takeover of the Kingdom, with a consequent increase in the price or interception of the flow of oil, are not enough to change the picture of how Saudi news is treated. In this case the image is not altered by available evidence, even by people, reporters and diplomats, who know or present this evidence themselves. Instead, the evidence is used, perverted, to reconfirm the policies which led to the failure and created the story. Instead of saying that the bombings are evidence that the policies of the House of Saud have been a failure, what the press and others say is that the bombings confirm that the good House of Saud needs and deserves our support more than ever before. What caused the problem is totally ignored.

Of course, the opposite is also true. An austerity programme initiated by Qaddafi is never seen as an attempt to control his country's budget at a time when oil prices are low. It is seen as a sign of the bankruptcy of his policies, another reason why bad Qaddafi should go. Similar austerity programmes in Saudi Arabia are the work of wise men who are trying to solve an economic problem sensibly and they are applauded.

The processes through which the efforts of the West and its friends, clients and Arab deputy sherifs, merge are there for everybody to see, but we are dealing with elaborate, institutionalized efforts which overshadow and overwhelm contrary voices. Writers who take a view different from established images are ostracized. For example, Noam Chomsky's books are no longer reviewed by the mainstream press in America. Others are accused of having lost their balance: Edward Said is suffering this fate because he objected to the US-sponsored peace agreement between the PLO and Israel. Alexander Cockburn's anti-Israeli views couldn't be left at that: he has been vilified and accused of being a writer for hire. I myself have been slandered, accused of being an agent of the Mossad, for writing a book about the House of Saud which didn't subscribe to the image, the accepted norm. Other writers and journalists who do know what is happening see what institutional image-making can produce and avoid taking the plunge; the price of calling things by their right name is too high.

Of necessity, the image-creating processes start with governments. What Clinton, Christopher, Major, Hurd, Rifkind, Chirac and their spokespersons, officials and heads of departments say represents the official policies of their governments. Even when their statements are crude (Reagan: Qaddafi is a mad dog) or not newsworthy (Clinton: President Mubarak is our friend and Saudi Arabia is vital to the interests of the West), they still represent an official, implicitly or explicitly acceptable term of reference regarding a Middle East leader or a country. Occasionally there are more subtle statements aimed at helping friends and discrediting their enemies. Responding to questions in the House of Commons in April 1995 about the activities of dissident Arab groups in London, the then Foreign Secretary, Douglas Hurd, making it clear he was speaking about the Saudi opposition, stated that Her Majesty's Government had no intention of allowing London to become a centre for terrorist activity. Hurd was talking about the anti-House of Saud efforts of the Committee for the Defence of the Legitimate Rights (of the Saudi people), the CDLR. This is a strange comment to make about an Islamic group with a solid record of advocating the use of peaceful means to change a rotten regime; not only does it put the CDLR in a bad light, it indirectly elevates the House of Saud to fighters against terrorism.

According to the 1994 *Human Watch World Report*, President Clinton has made several critical statements about the human rights records of Libya, Iraq and Iran, but not a word about the equally dismal records of Egypt, Saudi Arabia and Jordan. Clinton's selective morality is infectious; most Western officials follow his lead. Not a single Western leader has spoken of the human rights problems in these countries. 'Friendly' countries in the Middle East are omitted from the list of countries which abuse their citizens, even when, as in the case of Saudi Arabia, they eliminate some of them.[4] This is why the citizens of those countries lose hope, turn against their governments and their Western supporters and resort to violence.

The second source of the image we have of the Arab Middle East is the press. With very few and mainly minor exceptions, newspapers, magazines and radio and television reporting is subject to unwritten constraints which are transmitted, albeit implicitly, from the management of these establishments to their reporters. The *Washington Post* is solidly pro-Israeli and sends a particular signal to its reporters. A *Financial Times* correspondent has to think twice before endangering the sale of his newspaper's syndicated services, and the BBC is normally too sedate to delve into the personal misbehaviour of members of the House of Saud, even when the spendthrift ways of King Fahd and his relations are ruining his country. Essentially, except for ideological commitment, there is nothing to gain from supporting anti-establishment behaviour or groups. Sometimes this goes further and produces amusing situations. In 1982 NBC correspondent Steve Mallory came close to losing his job for using the term 'Israeli war machine'. To NBC, the 1982 Israeli invasion of Lebanon that Mallory was reporting was not carried out by a war machine, but by an Israeli Defence Force which, in accordance with NBC's definition of self-defence, was already 150 miles inside Lebanese territory.

Accepting the images created by governments forces an imperceptible but real redefinition of what constitutes news. The present minority government of Bahrain, unacceptable to the island's Shia majority, is friendly to the West. This has resulted in little coverage of the riots which have racked the island for the past two years (beginning in March 1995).

The new press laws in Egypt, to Article 19's Saïd Es Soulami a confirmation that 'Egypt is taking steps backwards',[5] have not featured in the Western press because Egypt is a 'friend'. A statement by Wahhabi cleric Ahmad bin Jibreen, a man appointed to his post by King Fahd, contained the words 'the Shias are heretics and idolaters who should be eliminated', condoning the elimination of 15 per cent of his country's population. Nothing was made of this either, nothing near what we hear when unfriendly Iran abuses Baha'is, who are less than 1 per cent of the population of Iran. The Western press followed an official line which accepted the prospect of the extermination of a significant part of the population of a friendly country.

Neglecting news stories is followed by outright attempts to overlook the obvious. In January 1984, *Time* correspondent Bill Stewart described Saudi Arabia as being blessed with 'an astute leadership', a near repeat of the United States' official line, when the whole world was beginning to judge King Fahd's rule as nothing short of a disaster. More recently, in September 1995, Jon Snow's interview of Yasser Arafat on BBC TV's highly rated *Newsnight* programme found him reluctant to question Arafat's word. To me, Snow allowed Arafat to play cute, and he accepted some answers at face value even when they didn't deserve it. For example, Arafat's ridiculous analogy between his idea of sharing Jerusalem with Israel and the sharing of Rome by Italy and the Vatican should have produced the obvious retort that he is comparing willing partners with unwilling ones.

In August 1995 the world press reported Husni Mubarak's reaction to the attempt on his life while he was in Addis Ababa attending an African summit conference. The Egyptian President identified the Sudan as being behind the attempt on his life before any culprits were caught or interrogated, let alone made a confession. His statement was taken at face value, with no questions touching on prior knowledge or a direct line to the powers which control life and death. Again in September 1995, Saddam Hussein's son-in-law, to the Iraqi people a murderer and a leading participant in some of the ugliest acts of Saddam's regime, was glamorized when he defected to Jordan. Very little was said about his past; by going to Jordan he became, for the West, our thug, a totally different person from the man the press vilified a few months before.

Perhaps the most persuasive example of accepting statements from friendly sources regarding important events has to do with the Mosque Rebellion in Mecca in 1979, the attempt by Muslim zealots to capture the Holy Mosque and spread the word from there. Because Saudi Arabia is a closed country, most of the Western press relied on official statements.

In this case those statements changed direction every day of the two-week siege of the rebels. Saudi Arabia accused them of being in the pay of the USSR, then Libya, then Yemen and after that they became followers of Sadat (the Saudis were quarrelling with him at that time) and – of course – Zionist agents. I find it amazing that only the *Wall Street Journal* took exception to these contradictory statements while the rest of the Western press accepted them as gospel.

In fact, but for a brave few, and most of them still compromise to survive to write the occasional good story, many reporters go further than accepting the dictum 'my country's and organization's interests first'; they make the situation worse through sheer ignorance. Most of the correspondents covering the Arab Middle East speak no Arabic, know very little about the history of the region and are disposed to reporting stories within the framework created by their governments. To most of them, Qaddafi is indeed a mad dog, and Saddam, whom many of them praised until he invaded Kuwait, is the source of all evil. As a result, working within their governments' rules as to who and what is good or bad, something which suits the policies of their management, foreign correspondents resort to innocent simplifications which often result in outright perversion. In May 1993 a *Sunday Times* report about Saudi Arabia described Islamic fundamentalism as a new sect, a bad one but a sect nevertheless. A year before, the *Spectator* magazine, writing about the plight of the Kurds in northern Iraq, referred to Irbil as Iraq's second largest city when in fact it rates sixth. In 1994, the *Washington Post* claimed that most of the people of Saudi Arabia belong to the Wahhabi sect, when they are only 20 per cent of the population. Because the House of Saud are Wahhabis, that story indirectly inflated their constituency. A mere two weeks after the November 1995 anti-American bombing in Riyadh which killed six people and wounded over sixty others, the London *Independent*, ignoring dozens of signs to the contrary and with no justification, stated, 'there is little sign of opposition in Saudi Arabia itself'.

Mistakes favourable to the House of Saud are not surprising. After all, the Saudi royals, despite the Lockheed and Yamama 2 pay-off scandals, a television film about how they beheaded one of their females, *Death of A Princess*, and dozens of small and large examples of financial and moral corruption, human rights violations and other crimes, are still 'our friends'. Reporters know King Fahd to be lazy, corrupt, ignorant and a drunk, but little is written about these things and he is still the West's man. This and a deep-rooted belief that there is nothing new in an Arab being lazy and ignorant cancels the story.

But it goes further than that. In hiring native experts, reporters and correspondents, the Western press invariably recruits members of minorities, just as the colonial powers, to control the majority of the people, used minorities in the armed forces and the police, among them the Troupe Spéciale in Syria and Assyrian Levies in Iraq. For example, the *New York Times* correspondent Yussuf Ibrahim is a Copt; Adel Darwish of the *Independent* is half Copt and half Jewish; Hezir Temourian of *The Times* is a Kurd; Noura Bustani of the *Washington Post* is a Maronite; and Lamis Andoni of the *Christian Science Monitor* is a Christian Palestinian, as is the well-known freelance journalist Daoud Khuttab. I am far from suggesting that any of these people got his or her job simply on the basis of religion, and in fact most are talented journalists indeed. However, the predominance of news correspondents from minority groups reflects a lack of acceptance by the Western media of Sunni or Shia reporters, adherents of the two major sects of Islam. This has to be true, for there are many qualified Sunni and Shia reporters whom Western media organizations wouldn't think of employing.

Think-tanks and universities, though mainly not in the business of affecting public opinion and directly creating images of the Arab Middle East, contribute to this process through providing governments, the press, corporations and concerned people with information and analyses which fit this picture. Because they too depend on Western and Middle Eastern official sources, their record is one of dismal failure. Most of the speakers at the oldest think-tank in the world, the Royal United Services Institute (RUSI) represent an official or pro-West partisan point of view. People who hold independent points of view – even experts in specific fields, myself included – have been pressured out of RUSI or not invited to specific functions where their opinions might conflict with the accepted norm. Some think-tanks accept grants from interested parties (Saudi Arabia) and adopt accommodating attitudes towards their sponsors and their policies. Very few think-tanks pay attention even to the most moderate of opposition groups. A think-tank is a proper venue for anyone wishing to make a presentation about the eradication of illiteracy in the Middle East, but that subject is never broached because it would show Saddam in a good light. Instead, General Prince Khalid bin Sultan of Saudi Arabia, the commander of the Arab forces during the Gulf War, makes a presentation about his country without anyone thinking of asking him how he acquired his huge fortune. Crown Prince Hassan of Jordan gives a presentation which celebrates the good relations between his country and Israel – and nobody thinks of asking how the Jordanian people feel about this. Members of the Dayan Center at Tel Aviv University give a self-serving day-long presentation about Islamic fundamentalism throughout the

Middle East without being questioned about the well-known and accepted fact that Israel has often supported Islamic groups, first against Nasser's Arab nationalism and more recently to undermine the PLO.

The American writer Steve Emerson has disclosed that dozens of American universities (among them Duke, Georgetown and Southern California), former diplomats (Talcot Sealey, Andrew Kilgore et al.) and think-tanks (the Aspen Institute) receive money from Saudi Arabia.[6] While it is true that the former diplomats render services and often valuable ones, the Saudi connection does nothing to enhance their ability to proffer unencumbered opinion.

It is illogical that a Middle East or Near East department of a university which receives money from the Saudis would – openly and willingly – do anything to undermine this connection. Very often the money is received 'without any strings attached', as in the case of funding a chair at Magdalen College, Oxford (the Khalid bin Abdel Aziz Chair in International Relations) and a recent £1 million donation, also by Saudi Arabia, to create a chair at the University of London's School of Oriental and African Studies. In fact, the strings are there, are implicit in the act itself, or else we have to believe, against all empirical judgement, that the House of Saud has become a sponsor of learning and the arts. How could an occupier of either seat speak freely about conditions in the Middle East when the country which sponsors him exercises complete control over its press, bribes the press of other Arab countries to doctor its reporting and overlook some issues while emphasizing others and 'bribes', mainly indirectly, most of the Western press into friendly silence?

By contrast with think-tanks and academe, Middle East governments contribute directly to the processes of image manipulation. Their efforts are enhanced by the use of Western writers for hire and corporations which have concessions or do business in their countries. Though government propaganda is unsurprising, it still receives more attention and greater funding than in other parts of the world, and it is uglier. The Saudis spend hundreds of millions of dollars establishing and buying newspapers, magazines, wire services and television stations (*Al Hayyat*, United Press International and Middle East Broadcasting, radio stations in America and France etc.). In a libellous statement which no one challenged, a 1993 story in the Saudi-owned *Al Hayyat* accused all those objecting to Saudi hegemony over the Arab press in London of being 'frustrated CIA and Mossad agents'. In 1991 all Arabic newspapers sponsored by the anti-Saddam Arab states printed a story about how Iraqi soldiers in Kuwait killed babies in incubators. The way the story was carried by the world's press is an example of how local press is used to influence the rest of the world. In fact, the whole story was no more than a fabrication by the Kuwaiti government-in-exile and its supporters.[7]

There is no end to the efforts of the established Arab regimes to promote their images and contribute to a joint picture that they and their Western supporters can live with. The Saudis and Kuwaitis have on occasion hired the biggest public relations firm in the world, Hill and Knowlton. Qatar, with a population of four hundred thousand, has huge press offices in London, Paris and Washington. What the Qataris are trying to promote is anyone's guess. Until the Gulf War, when Iraq was still acceptable, the Iraqis had twenty-four people in their London press office, usually headed by a Saddam loyalist from their home town of Tikrit. The others are not far behind; Jordan's London press office is too big and independent to be housed with the embassy. Throughout the world the press officers of the various Arab countries compete with the military attachés to be ranked second to the ambassador, and in some cases they come ahead of him.

But the most serious manifestation of the extent of their efforts to maintain a certain image is their hiring of established Western writers. This, and the mainly secret assistance that friendly countries receive from corporations such as Mobil, ARAMCO and others, is an activity at which Middle Eastern governments excel. There are six established journalists in London who receive regular salaries from Saudi Arabia, some while they are full-time employees of national newspapers. Many members of think-tanks in the United States do the same. Publications specializing in the Middle East receive Saudi, Kuwaiti and Qatari money and refrain from writing anything critical about their sponsors or reviewing books which contain the mildest criticism of them. Many American and British journalists receive favours, free airline tickets, visas denied to impartial reporters, and so on, and some accept Christmas presents of cases of expensive champagne. And although the interests of corporations are obvious, the distortions created by journalists 'friendly' to Saudi Arabia are more serious. The British writers in the pay of Arab governments go beyond image creation; they write misleading articles, review books in a way which pleases their paymasters, spread rumours and influence newspaper, magazine and book publishers.

In a way, independent Western writers who accept their government's maxims and believe in one or both of the elements which determine our attitude towards the Middle East – the celebration of the noble savage and a commitment to the devil we know – are a more dangerous group. Because they are not mercenaries and their opinions are not vitiated by that association, it is their belief, to which they are totally entitled, in engineered images which becomes a problem.

John Marlowe, an established writer and a leading authority on Palestine under the British, allowed an embedded image in his mind to distort the truth when he wrongly attributed the assassination of Lebanese Prime Minister Riad Solh to extremist Palestinian elements.[8] Thomas Friedman's book *Beirut to Jerusalem* won the Pulitzer Prize, but it contains some serious mistakes which render some of its conclusions questionable. Friedman states that 85 per cent of the Israeli settlers in the occupied territories live thirty minutes from Tel Aviv.[9] This is nonsense. Ma'ale Adumim, a settlement housing well over 10 per cent of the settlers, is considerably further away, as are the settlements east of it, most of the ones in Gaza and so on. Former President Jimmy Carter is a decent man who makes a serious mistake when he 'accuses' King Fahd of Saudi Arabia of 'aiding women's rights'.[10] Gerald de Gaury, an old-fashioned pro-Bedouin monarchies writer, describes Iraqi president Abdel Karim Kassem, the man who overthrew the Iraqi monarchy in 1958, as deranged.[11] While I have no problem supporting Kurdish aspirations, I must take exception to John Bulloch's and Harvey Morris's statement that 150 Kurds held up a whole Iraqi army division, an unsupported glorification of the Kurds at a time when the pro-Kurd sentiments became fashionable simply because they were fighting bad Saddam.[12] Alan Hart is so adoring of Yasser Arafat that he claims his biographical subject stopped a convoy of twelve Israeli armoured cars in 1948.[13] This is an Arafat story; the Israelis didn't have that number of plated armoured cars in 1948. Then there is Paul Johnson's assertion in his book *Modern Times* that the Iraqi invasion of Kuwait 'came as a surprise'.[14] The list of such misunderstandings is endless.

To describe every instance of image creation – including the efforts to muffle or discredit holders of contrary opinions – and how it came about would take a very long book indeed. But it is worth remembering that images may be created by some participants in the image-creating process without help from others who are working to the same purpose. Governments can do it alone, and they certainly give implicit direction to the press and others, but the image they want created is more widely accepted when think-tanks and the press repeat, amplify and expand the official message. Think-tanks alone can influence the press, and governments can often prevail on think-tanks and so on down the line to create an atmosphere which allows an enterprising writer for hire to stop the publication of a book that is critical of Hussein or the House of Saud. This is why, despite their records, most books about them have been friendly: the atmosphere forbids publishing books critical of these friends. Even when a publisher is inclined to issue such a book, there is no market for it, because conditioned Western readers don't want to read hostile things about 'friends'.

The examples which follow are representative of how the efforts of Western governments, the Western press, modern Orientalists or pretenders to this dubious honour, former diplomats, think-tanks and academic centres and the governments of the Middle East and their hired writers and corporate supporters contribute to the creation of accepted and rejected images in situations of vital concern to the West and the Arab world. If we accept the axiom that the Middle East is heading towards disaster, and even news organizations which support traditional rulers and regimes indirectly admit this, then the people and organizations who create images contrary to fact are guilty of a major crime: they produce images which rule out finding acceptable solutions to problems which concern both the Arabs and the West.

The combined efforts of Western governments, groups and organizations and their client regimes produce five major categories of images. There are people (and in this context, because we are dealing with dictatorships, countries' images always follow those of leaders and not the other way round) who are permanent 'friends'. They are the good kings, presidents or leaders who have consistently followed policies acceptable to and approved of by the West. King Hussein of Jordan, despite his brief deviation during the Gulf War, is a permanent friend. Sadat belonged and Mubarak belongs to this category, as do King Fahd of Saudi Arabia and members of his family and the sheikhs and emirs of the Gulf. Permanent friends are the people who – regardless of merit – escape Western critical judgement. The real King Hussein is exposed elsewhere in this book, but in the West little is known about Sadat's drinking and vanity[15] and less about the Mubarak regime's corruption. King Fahd's disastrous personal and public record, losing $6 million in one night of gambling, and the decline of the per capita income of the average Saudi in 1994 to a third of what it was in 1982, are wrapped in more white sheets than there are in the whole of Saudi Arabia.

The late Nuri Saïd, until his murder by his own people in July 1958 Prime Minister of Iraq fourteen times and its virtual ruler for thirty years, and arguably the most unpopular twentieth-century political leader in both his own country and the whole Arab world, was the greatest example of a permanent friend. The man's end and what followed it are the clearest example of the short-sightedness of elevating unfit leaders acceptable to the West to the status of statesmen, and then depending on them. His career is detailed in Chapter 3.

The second group comprises people who are the opposite: permanent enemies. George Habbash, the leader of the socialist Popular Front for the Liberation of Palestine, is one such enemy. Habbash's violent activities are known and I find them unacceptable and reprehensible, but he is a popular leader with a clean record and a strong appeal to educated Palestinians. He deserves a more methodical analysis than he gets. Colonel Muammar Qaddafi of Libya is another permanent enemy. Unpredictable and on occasion plain dangerous and idiotic, he has a bad image that overshadows his championing of women's rights and some of his popular housing, land reclamation and distribution schemes. Once again, my aim isn't to absolve bad people, but to accord them fair judgement in order to understand them, their popularity and the problems they create and represent.

Third on the list are the 'revolvers', the leaders who have no permanent image and who are treated as friends or enemies depending on the subject under consideration and the state of relations between them and the West. King Faisal of Saudi Arabia (1962–75) was of this ilk. He was a friend when he stood up to Nasser and sponsored anti-communist and anti-Arab nationalist Islamic groups and schemes, but he became a temporary enemy when he participated in the 1973 oil embargo. Because he depended on the West for protection and support, he revolved within that orbit and can be considered 'a pro-West revolver'. Nowadays, President Hafez Al Assad of Syria is the occupier of this unique middle ground. He has gone from being 'a supporter of terrorism', to the man who brought peace to Lebanon and a wise participant in Operation Desert Storm (the Gulf War). Recently we have seen signs that his refusal to sign a peace agreement with Israel will once again reduce him to unacceptability in Western circles. Assad, because he does not trust the West and rejects its hegemony while occasionally accepting the need to work within it, is an anti-West revolver. Interestingly Faisal's and Assad's brutal records on human rights are ignored or resurrected in accordance with their behaviour on issues which affect the West directly. Yet, to their people, any judgement of either man which does not take into account his record on human rights is an unsound one. It neglects their concerns, which are different from the criteria by which the West judges them.

The fourth group consists of those who begin as friends and turn into enemies when their policies clash with those of their former admirers or sponsors, or on occasion with those who helped them attain power. The earliest example of the 'renegades', King Hussein I of the Hijaz, though never acceptable to his people,[16] was a friend when he joined Britain and declared a jihad against Ottoman Turkey during the First World War. He became an enemy after he insisted that Britain live up to its promises to grant the Arabs independence. Nasser assumed power in Egypt with the knowledge and support of the CIA. He became an enemy as a result of buying arms from the communist bloc, nationalizing the Suez Canal and taking the Arabs' feelings into consideration. All this happened even though he first tried to obtain arms from the West, was forced into nationalizing the Suez Canal and was known to be anti-communist (see Chapter 3). Even Saddam Hussein, our friend at the time of the 1963 anti-socialist coup in Iraq and during his war against Khomeini, belongs to this category (this story is detailed in Chapter 4).

The last group is composed of those who begin as enemies and become friends, 'the converts'. Yasser Arafat, originally mislabelled terrorist, is the best example of this group. As Chairman of the Palestine Liberation Organization (PLO) in the 1960s, 70s and 80s, despite a pro-establishment bent and an essentially pro-West one, he and the organization he represented were unacceptable to Western governments because they were 'terrorists'. Now Arafat and the PLO are friends because he has signed a peace agreement with Israel which accords with Western plans more than it does with his own people's wishes. The fact that his previous mildly revolutionary stance was more popular with his people is irrelevant. Former Chairman of the US Senate Foreign Relations Committee Claybourn Pell speaks of Arafat as, 'The only man who can deliver peace.' How the Palestinian people feel about the agreement is ignored.[17]

There is no better way to demonstrate how the image-creation process works than to examine two major problems confronting the West in the Arab Middle East: Iraq and Islamic fundamentalism. Iraq, diminished as it is by the Gulf War and still the subject of an embargo which has reduced its people to starvation, is one of two enemy Arab states in existence. Libya is not part of the geographic Middle East covered by this study; Syria and Yemen occupy an uneasy middle ground; and Saudi Arabia, Egypt, Jordan, Kuwait, Oman, the Palestinian Authority, the United Arab Emirates and the rest are satellite states where the traditional client relationship with the West governs their leaders' behaviour towards their people, regional and Arab issues and their overall foreign policies.

The other enemy is Islamic fundamentalism. In this case, the West is unwilling to tolerate movements which endanger its client regimes because undermining or toppling these threatens the West's special relationship with such countries and its hegemony over the Arab Middle East. There is nothing new in this: the West's opposition to Islamic fundamentalism is no different from its 1950s and 60s opposition to Nasser's Arab nationalism or from any movement, regional or local, which has threatened its reliance on known, friendly entities. Two things differentiate the present confrontation between the West and Islam from others. The first is that it contains the greater danger of being an all-inclusive cultural one. The second is the inability of the West's client regimes to oppose the Islamic movements wholeheartedly; because they are Muslims who can't reject Islam, they are forced to redefine what the Islamic movements stand for and saddle them with the notions of militancy, regression and unreason.

Iraq was one of twelve states created by the Western powers after the First World War. Except for Lebanon, it is more of a fabrication than the rest because it lacks a unified national identity. Made up of Sunnis, Shias, Kurds, Turkomans, Assyrians and smaller groups, and seriously divided along socio-economic lines, it has no cohesion and suffers the stresses of having to reconcile the diverse interests and inclinations of the groups which make it. In 1921 the British installed King Faisal on the throne of the country they designed in the hope that his credentials as a descendant of the Prophet and a leader of the Arab Rebellion against the Turks might bring a semblance of unity. It didn't work and Faisal himself spoke of his sadness because 'there isn't an Iraqi people in Iraq'.[18] In the absence of an Iraqi people, it was the military who always held the country together. From its creation until now, Iraq's regimes have been kept in place by the only organized group capable of maintaining the structure of a state: the army.

In dealing with Iraq we are dealing with a dictatorship. Under the monarchy it was a pro-West dictatorship, perhaps the classic example of Western cooperation with traditional regimes. Since the overthrow of the monarchy in 1958 there has been a leftist dictatorship, a pro-Nasser Arab nationalist dictatorship and, beginning in 1968, a Ba'ath Party dictatorship, originally through a shared leadership and since 1979 one run by Saddam Hussein, the man whose brutality exceeded that of all other dictators who preceded him but who, through longevity and design, is a much more serious challenge to analysts of Iraq, its make-up and its relations with the rest of the world.

There is little need to examine Saddam Hussein's current image in detail. He is the man who started a nine-year war against Iran, used chemical weapons against the Kurds of his country, developed biological weapons capable of killing most of the people of the Middle East, threatened, then invaded, Kuwait and started the Gulf War, and came very close to making an atomic bomb. Meanwhile, within his country, Saddam executed people at random, imprisoned and tortured thousands of others, placed all power in the hands of his family and relations and allowed them to steal, rape and murder scores of innocents.

Saddam the embodiment of evil is known to us. But we discovered him only after he invaded Kuwait and paved the way for the Gulf War. His record between 1968 and 1990 was not exposed to us until he became an enemy in a way which precluded reintegrating him as a client or even as a tolerable nuisance. In fact, there is ample solid evidence that for at least sixteen years we helped Saddam and nurtured him. Though he was never a client in the mould of the traditional monarchies or the military dictatorships that the West installs, he was a willing tool in the hands of the West. It is when he stopped being a pliant friend, when the harmony between Saddam's interests and the West ceased to exist that he was demonized and we were enlightened as to what our erstwhile partner was all about.

Although a great deal has been written about the cynicism of the West in dealing with Saddam, there is vital and dramatic material which has escaped the attention of other writers. This material concerns the West's relations with its previous ally in the areas of armament, his use of chemical weapons and the background to the invasion of Kuwait.

There are three phases to Saddam's complicated relations with the West. The first phase is from 1968 until the 1979 war with Iran. This is when the West wanted to keep Saddam from falling irretrievably under the influence of the USSR and did everything possible to loosen its hold on Iraq, something the Soviet Union exercised through trying to be his major if not sole arms supplier. During this period the West gave Saddam a green light to buy arms in the West – *and there were no limits or restrictions.*

In the mid-1970s, through work with Arab Resources Management (ARM) of Beirut, I was involved in Iraqi negotiations to acquire British-made fighter and bomber aircraft, French-made helicopters and military electronic gear and the original design for a chemical warfare plant. Neither British Aerospace nor Westland Helicopters, Dassault or the supplier of the chemical plant design, Pfaulder Corporation of Rochester, New York, had anything to hide.[19] They all acted with the full knowledge and blessing of their governments.

This period of Western support and encouragement for Saddam's acquisition of arms, including unconventional weapons, was followed by the period of the Iran-Iraq War. Ostensibly neutral and pretending to embargo the sale of lethal weapons to both combatants, the West continued to supply Saddam with armaments. The exact number of Western corporations which operated within the policies of their governments and supplied Saddam with lethal and other weapons is disputed, but the figure was definitely over four hundred.

The reason for this was simple: Saddam was seen as a lesser evil and threat than Khomeini of Iran. Because the efforts to supply Saddam with military hardware, directly or through friendly countries such as Egypt, Jordan and Saudi Arabia, continued for the nine years of the Iran-Iraq War, combining this period with the one before, when we wanted to keep him from embracing the USSR, produces sixteen to eighteen years of connivance in arming Saddam and supplying him with Western technology. This answers the vital questions of how Saddam acquired so much military hardware and technology without our hearing much about it.

The continuing demonization of Saddam has to do with the fact that he is no longer a client, that, like Hussein I of the Hijaz, he has outlived his usefulness. Moreover, the West's efforts to present him as the ultimate evil man have been so successful that there is no way of altering this image. Meanwhile, Iraq's inability to sell oil on the international market serves another purpose: it is helpful to the West's client states of Kuwait, Saudi Arabia and the rest. Finally, the recent defection of Saddam's son-in-law to Jordan confirmed the absence of ideology in the Western battle against Saddam. Initially, Western governments and the Western press glamorized the defector Hussein Kamel Hassan, a Saddam protégé who is as evil as his creator. After he was fully debriefed and no longer of any use, his background was dredged up, used against him and he was dropped. Yet later, when he returned to Baghdad and was executed by his father-in-law, he became a victim of a criminal regime. What the West is after in Iraq is a new client, a brutal dictator who would replace Saddam and once again follow its lead.

Lack of knowledge makes it more difficult for the average person in the West to oppose an idea or an ideology than to oppose a person. Despite this, and despite the social constraint against criticizing religions, presently people in the West are predominantly anti-Muslim. According to Zakki Badawi, the head of London's Islamic College, 'The last acceptable racism is anti-Muslim.' What concerns us is not the historical picture which has already been covered by other writers, but today's image of Islam, the extension of the historical term of reference, the picture of one billion Muslims as a militant, backward people who threaten Western interests and the West. Relying on the press for guidance, following what it says is easier, and it reflects, embellishes and expands official policies. What we should address is exemplified by topics such as 'Islamic Rage', 'The Islamic Threat', 'Islam's Battlecry', 'Islamic Masses', 'Ragheads', 'Square Beards' and 'The Sword of Islam'.

The existing popular image of Islam is inclusive. In thinking of Islam, Western people include Saddam and Qaddafi, with all their faults secular leaders who themselves are threatened by militant Islamic movements.

And it goes further and includes even friends of the West: because they are oil-rich, the governments of Saudi Arabia, Kuwait and the rest. But however disliked the latter group are for subscribing to a religion which has a pervasively bad image, what matters more is the fact that they are 'friends'. Muslim 'friends' are acceptable because they escape criticism from official circles, the press, academe and think-tanks.

The image of Islam in the twentieth century has undergone three different phases and transformations. Immediately after the First World War there was the subdued Islam inherited from Ottoman Turkey and conquered by Field Marshal Allenby, the French General Gouraud and others.[20] This was when the West used a pliant Islam to impose leaders who believed in Western supremacy, the heyday of the hegemony of the traditional patriarchy over the masses. King Hussein I of the Hijaz allied himself to the West to create a pro-West caliphate. Ibn Saud of Saudi Arabia, leader of the Wahhabi puritan sect, signed treaties of subservience which guaranteed him British support to conquer the Arabian Peninsula. The Grand Mufti of Jerusalem, another claimant to descent from the Prophet, was appointed to his post by the British. All political leadership of the time depended on Islam for legitimacy and all political leaders were pro-British. Islam was the tool to legitimize the rule, tyranny and corruption of Arab leaders. To the West, Islam was acceptable; it could be and was used.[21]

The second phase occurred when the old order of Muslim leaders acceptable to the West came under threat, the period of Nasser's Arab nationalism, which started in the 1950s and continued until his death in 1970. This is when the traditional leadership which purported to represent the Arabs and Islam was confronted by Nasser's secular movement and the West supported a more activist Islam to resist the Nasser challenge to its interests, often in conjunction with traditional leaders but occasionally without them. Even the United States, new to the Middle East and ostensibly more committed to reform and secularism than the colonial powers, changed direction in the mid-1950s and began supporting Islamic movements.[22]

The third phase began after the Arab defeat in the 1967 War and flourished after Nasser's death, when Arab nationalism lost its momentum as the outlet for the frustration of the masses. The Islamic movements which replaced Arab nationalism at this point were the same ones which had been sponsored by the West. However, the political problems of Palestine and Lebanon and Western sponsorship of unpopular leaders and their absolute and abusive ways, forced the Muslim movements to change direction and to respond to the wishes of their followers, some after the

Iranian revolution of 1979 and others beginning in the mid-1980s. The once pro-West Islam was making its own claim, and this is the same Islam and Islamic image which we confront today.

Reducing these historical stages to simple formulas we have the period when Islam and Arab rulers were one, a second when Islam was used against anti-Western rulers and the present phase of an Islamic threat to pro-West rulers, Western interests and the West. Nowadays, Saudi Arabia, Egypt, Jordan, the Palestinian administration of Yasser Arafat, all allied to the West and following a pro-West line, are threatened by indigenous Islamic movements and others with regional reach. And Syria, Iraq and Libya, although not client countries in the mould of the first group, are experiencing an Islamic threat to their stability which finds the West conniving to support their governments because losing them to Islam is worse than keeping them under their present rulers and might provoke a regional chain reaction which could prove difficult to control or contain.

But what is behind this confrontation between Islam and the West? Is it a matter of misinterpreting the Islamic teachings? What perception do both sides have of each other and how did it come about? Is the situation controllable or is it too late?

The primary reason behind the confrontation between the West and Islam is the assumption by Islamic movements of the role of defenders of people's rights. Because the West and its clients have succeeded in destroying all the secular movements in the Arab Middle East without making any attempt to solve the real problems of the region, Islam has emerged as the only force opposed to the Western-Arab establishment hegemony. The lamentable results of this hegemony over the Arab Middle East for most of this century are there for all to see. There is no democracy anywhere, not even a semblance of it; the gap between the haves and have-nots has widened; corruption has spread; the state has failed to act as a magnet for people's loyalties and the West continues to depend on traditional leaders or invent new ones who perpetuate this unhappy state of affairs. Because all relationships with the West have resulted in failures and matters are becoming worse, and because other recourses for solving regional problems – adopting socialism and forging alliances with enemies of the West, communism – have been tried and have also failed, religion comes to the fore as an alternative. It combines the provision of an identity with a cushion against disappointment.

The Islam represented by Hussein I, Ibn Saud, the Mufti and others produced allegiance to rulers in a manner which allowed them to govern in accordance with an Islamic divine right of kings. The pro-West anti-Ottoman Arab Revolt that Hussein I declared during the First World War was no more than the work of a family which wanted to supplant Ottoman Turkey as leader of the Muslim and Arab worlds. Ibn Saud's Wahhabi hordes, in particular the Ikhwan warriors, were as fanatical and determined to impose uncompromising Islamic ways as any movement in existence today. The Mufti rose to paramountcy by manipulating Islamic organizations such as the Supreme Islamic Council, and his British-sponsored control of these organizations provided him with legitimacy and placed him in an unassailable position *vis-à-vis* his people.

The West did not love or accept Islam then. It condoned the rulers' use of Islam because they were 'friends' who were beholden to it and who aided its colonial policies. Unlike its parent in the Hijaz, the Syrian government which resulted from the 1917 Arab Revolt had Arab intellectuals and thinkers as its backbone. It was rejected out of hand when France invaded Syria and reduced it to a mandate territory. Hussein I himself, regardless of his Islamic credentials, was abandoned when he questioned Britain and demanded fulfilment of promises to grant the Arabs independence and support their unity. Ibn Saud received British financial and other support and his Islamic credentials were highlighted because he followed a totally pro-British policy. First he was allowed to subdue the relatively more advanced Al Rashids, the claimants to the rule of central Arabia. Later he was given a green light to conquer the Hijaz. In Palestine, the British looked the other way while the Mufti, appointed to office through their connivance (see Chapter 5), used his leadership of the Supreme Muslim Council to keep in check populist and popular movements advocating a stronger line against British plans to divide Palestine.

So the West's first twentieth-century contact with Islam was a cynical one. Operating from within the accepted Western perception that Islam is a backward enemy which was subdued when Ottoman Turkey was conquered, the West proceeded to use it to legitimize client-rulers. Because Islam was not actively opposed to Western plans, its bad image was an intellectual one which did not affect the attitude of Western governments and the media. In reality, Islam was used because the West thought it was bad, and certainly because it did not advocate independence and democracy in the way the intellectuals of Damascus and the founders of small secular political parties in the Hijaz and Palestine did.

The selective use of Islam during the period following the First World War continued well into the 1930s. King Faisal I of Iraq was imposed on that country by the British, who exploited his descent from the Prophet Muhammad. In the process of imposing Faisal the British discriminated against the country's Shia majority, who wanted nothing to do with him and started a rebellion. Support of Ibn Saud's rule, based as it was on religious and tribal foundations, overlooked his non-acceptance by his country's Shias and mainline Sunnis, who didn't belong to the Wahhabi sect. In Syria the French used the minority Alawi and Druze sects to suppress the educated majority of the country. In Lebanon a Christian minority was allowed to create a client state against the interests of Muslim Syria and Lebanon's Muslim majority.

The initial period of selective use of Islam to legitimize traditional leaders was challenged in the late 1930s and the 1940s and the challenge blossomed in the 1950s. The Bakr Sidqi coup in Iraq in 1937, whatever its more immediate motives, diminished the power of the country's monarchy, which used Islam as the foundation of its claim to the throne. The 1940–1 pro-Nazi and anti-British government of Rashid Ali Keilani, which temporarily forced the Iraqi royal family to flee the country, confirmed the erosion of the monarchy's Islamic base. In Syria the nationalist movement forced France to forgo its plans to use religion to divide the country and create separate Druze and Alawi states. In Palestine the people forced a nationalist stance on the Mufti at the expense of his religious credentials. But it wasn't until the 1950s and the emergence of Nasser and other secular Arab nationalist movements that the West began using mass Islamic movements instead of traditional Islam to prop up the sagging fortunes of the traditional leaders.

In the 1950s and later, the West opposed the secular Arab nationalist movement for two reasons: it challenged its regional hegemony and threatened the survival of its client leaders and countries. Specifically, there was nothing to stop a secular movement from cooperating with the USSR; in fact, most of them were mildly socialist. Furthermore, most secular movements advocated various schemes of Arab unity, a union or a unified policy, which threatened and undermined the pro-West traditional regimes of Saudi Arabia, Jordan and other client states. The West saw it as a challenge that had to be met.

Because the appeal of Arab nationalism was ideological and regional, the West's opposition to it had to be similar. In the Fertile Crescent (Syria, Iraq, Jordan and Palestine) there were occasional Western moves to support the avowedly fascist Parti Populaire Syrien (PPS) as a counterweight to Nasser and Arab nationalism, but this party was limited to these countries, commanded a small following and had a Christian leadership. Islam was the obvious choice, and Islam was acceptable by the traditional regimes.

According to CIA agent Miles Copeland, the Americans began looking for a Muslim Billy Graham around 1955.[23] This was after Nasser tilted towards the USSR and the United States gave up trying to control him but, unlike Britain and France, saw the need for a mass movement rather than a colonial use of force or exclusive reliance on the traditional regimes. When finding or creating a Muslim Billy Graham proved elusive, the CIA began to cooperate with the Muslim Brotherhood, the Muslim mass organization founded in Egypt but with followers throughout the Arab Middle East.

The Muslim Brotherhood was created in 1928 by a teacher by the name of Hassan Al Banna. It was not opposed to monarchies or traditional regimes so long as they followed the tenets of Islam. Because it went back and forth in its opposition to King Farouk and the Egyptian government, its 'political transactions' were obscure.[24] However, it was solidly opposed to socialism and the Soviet Union, became opposed to Nasser when he followed both and was adopted by the CIA and the West in 1955.

This signalled the beginning of an alliance between the traditional regimes and mass Islamic movements against Nasser and other secular forces. Taking its lead from the CIA, Saudi Arabia funded the Muslim Brotherhood.[25] Jordan allowed it and allowed the movements to operate freely at a time when all other political movements were banned. Pro-American Syrian governments followed Jordan's lead. And the US went as far as providing the movements with operating bases in friendly Muslim countries such as Pakistan.

The struggle between Nasser and the Muslim Brotherhood and its offshoots and Western and traditional Arab regimes' supporters continued until the 1967 War. Western support for Islam was provided openly and accepted by the leadership of the Islamic movements without reservation.[26]

It was another short-sighted alliance of convenience which produced agreement between the Western governments, press and thinkers. There is nothing in the statements of Western leaders of the time which suggests misgivings about what the movements preached, then as now: the application of harsh Islamic punishment, the re-establishment of the caliphate and rigid rejection of Western ways and thinking. And, in examining several hundred pages of newspaper reports covering this period, I discovered nothing to suggest that the press did anything but follow the official position and concentrated on reporting how strong and anti-communist the Muslim Brotherhood and other Islamic groups were. Temporarily Islam had a good image.

The third phase in the development of Islamic movements occurred after the 1967 War. The defeat of Nasser was a defeat for the force he represented, secularism, and with Nasser diminished, the Islamic movements moved to assume the political leadership of the masses of Arab

Middle East. Their efforts were aided by King Faisal of Saudi Arabia, a traditional leader who lost no time in backing moves and movements opposed to secularism and supportive of Islam (see Chapter 3).

Faisal's efforts triumphed soon after Nasser's death in 1970. Nasser's successor, Sadat, unacceptable to most of the leaders and people of Egypt, needed popular support. His response was to release the leadership of the Muslim Brotherhood from Nasser's prisons and to use them to gain popular approval.[27] In fact, Sadat's efforts in this regard went further and he and Faisal joined forces and bribed the Islamic leadership of Al Azhar, Islam's oldest university, to support their Islamic inclinations.[28] Even new Islamic movements such as Al Dawa and I'tisam were supported by Sadat and Faisal.

However, the mass Islamic movements were intrinsically opposed to the ways and foreign policies of Sadat, Faisal and the rest of the traditional regimes; a split between them began to appear at this point. It is indeed an irony that Islam was behind the murder of both men. Faisal's killer was a nephew, but he carried out his act to avenge the execution of his Muslim zealot brother, who had been executed by Faisal for attacking a television station, to him an invention in violation of Islamic teachings. And Sadat was gunned down in October 1981 by members of Takfir wa Hijra, a militant offshoot of the Muslim Brotherhood. These weren't the only signs that Islamic groups were turning militant and against their former sponsors. In 1982 there was a full-fledged revolution in the Syrian city of Hamma which pitted the Muslim Brotherhood against the Syrian government and produced some twenty thousand casualties. The writer Patrick Seale alleges that the Hamma Muslim rebels used US-made equipment to fight the Syrian army.[29]

Hamma, the assassinations of Sadat and Faisal and less portentous acts didn't interrupt Western and Arab client regimes' support for the Islamic movements, and Saudi Arabia and Egypt allowed pro-Islamic use of their state propaganda apparatus. Furthermore, the US prevailed on both countries to increase their support of Islam to help the Afghanistan Mujahideen, who were battling with the Russian army, and to send volunteers to fight with them. And Israel, forever inclined to back divisive movements, surfaced as another supporter of Islam and began to fund the Muslim Brotherhood and the Palestinian Islamic movement Hamas.[30]

Briefly, it was a four-way alliance of the West, Israel, the traditional regimes and the Islamic movements. But suddenly, in the early 1980s, further signs appeared that the Islamic movements were beginning to act independently. To understand this, one has to remember that even when dealing with movements instead of governments, the West could not penetrate the surface and reach the people, and the followers of the Islamic movements were never consulted about cooperation with the West. The second thing to remember is that, particularly after the death of Faisal, there was no traditional leader strong enough to pre-empt these movements. In fact, the Islamic movements were growing because the existing leaders were weak and unacceptable. Moreover, even when supported by the West and the traditional regimes, the populist nature of the mass Islamic movements set them on a collision course with the élite and governments made up of the élite, the very same ones which initially backed them against Nasser, communism and Arab nationalism and later used them to combat the Soviet Union in Afghanistan and resist Soviet penetration of the Horn of Africa. Kept under check for a while by an alliance of convenience, the Islamic movements' commitment against foreign hegemony finally surfaced to face its main sponsor, the West.

The inevitable confrontation between the Islamic movements and the West and its clients was the result of the same old reason – the West's total commitment to client states – and some new ones. The regimes of Saudi Arabia, Jordan, Egypt, Kuwait and other countries beholden to the West were and are corrupt and undemocratic and followed foreign and oil policies unacceptable to their people. The West, though obviously willing to cooperate with Islamic groups against mass movements threatening its interests and to prevent the Soviet Union from penetrating the Middle East, was unwilling to accommodate their demands for reform and, in the absence of a Soviet threat, to accept that the time had come for these countries to adopt an independent foreign policy.

The absence of a communist or socialist threat which bound the Islamists and the West together, and the surfacing of the conflict inherent in their totally different positions, were given impetus by several new factors, or old ones re-formed. There is the problem of Palestine and the issue of the control of Jerusalem, Islam's third holiest city. Lebanese and Western support for a Christian bastion in the middle of a Muslim world is always an issue. Lack of Western interest in the fate of the Shias in Kuwait, Saudi Arabia and Bahrain, and the West's support for governments which suppress and abuse them, is a third issue. Western support for the secessionist Christian movement in the Sudan, seen as an anti-Muslim move, is yet a fourth. And this was capped by a massive Western-led coalition to invade a Muslim country, Iraq, in 1991. The Gulf War and its consequences were followed by the war in Bosnia. While Saddam is frowned on and considered Islamically unacceptable, the Gulf War against Iraq is seen as a major manifestation of an anti-Muslim Western attitude which sanctions devastating military action against a Muslim country while it absolves others guilty of similar crimes against Muslim Bosnia. The two issues complement each other.

Meanwhile, the West's traditional client leaders and states have decided that the mass Islamic movements are the enemy and have turned against them. In Jordan they are no longer the ally permitted to operate freely and have become a threat to the throne. This has led to illegal imprisonment of their leaders, closure of their publications and denial of the right to compete in free elections without government interference. In Egypt the situation is considerably worse and imprisonment of thousands of members of Islamic groups was followed by the setting up of military courts to try, sentence and execute them. Naturally they are denied the opportunity to run for office without interference and some are disqualified without reason. In Bahrain members of Islamic movements are practically denied all rights and most of the leaders are in prison. In Saudi Arabia harsher measures are the order of the day, the government continues to promote its version of Islam and people still disappear in the middle of the night. And Kuwait, the country which caused the Gulf War, persists in denying its considerable Shia minority, over 30 per cent of the population, the most basic rights.

It is because the established regimes have declared war against the same Islam they once used to assume power and later used to confront popular demands under a secular banner that we have a conflict between the Islamists and the West's clients. And the West, unable to devise long-term policies which take the modicum of popular demands into consideration, affords these regimes unconditional and uncritical support. This has translated into an anti-West policy by Islamic groups, a policy which identifies the West as the guarantor of the abusive regimes of these countries. The extension of this policy is the attacks on the West and its clients and interests throughout the world. These attacks are what people in the West know and resent, but what led up to them and continues to cause them is neglected.

Nowadays we hear about Hizbollah, Hamas, Hizb Al Tahrir, Islamic Liberation Group, the Committee for Islamic Change, Jama'at Al Dawa, Jama'at Al Jihad, the Army of Allah, the Army of Muhammad, the Islamic Front and many other Islamic groups whose very names conjure up a picture of militancy and violence. While this is often so, there is still little effort to solve the problems that forced these groups into extremist positions and to distinguish them from less militant ones which, unsurprisingly, command greater support among the people of their countries.

For the most part, the Islamic movement in Jordan is a moderate one which operates openly and rejects violent means. Recognizing them for what they really are is undermined by King Hussein's efforts to demonize them and present them as a threat to his regime and hence to the West. In Egypt the mainstream Muslim Brotherhood is also opposed to violence and has openly condemned the actions of militant Islamic groups, including some who were originally part of it. This has not stopped President Mubarak from unjustifiably dismissing their claims and imprisoning many of them, turning them into an enemy of his regime and the West. Instead of dealing with small groups which number in the hundreds, Mubarak has created an enemy with a following in the millions. The Islamic Committee for the Defence of the Legitimate Rights (of the Saudi people) is the largest Islamic group in Saudi Arabia. It advocates the use of peaceful means, is ready to conduct a dialogue with the West and accepts the need for cooperation regarding the supply of oil to the West. However, the Saudi regime has imprisoned and tortured some of its members, accuses it of advocating violent means and calls for its suppression. The main Islamic opposition to the Bahraini and Kuwaiti regimes is made up of moderate groups who are saddled with the same labels and receive the same treatment.

Any fair analysis of the history of Islamic movements in the Arab Middle East must take into consideration their whole history, including their previous alliances with the West and what turned them into a magnet for anti-West popular feeling in the Middle East. Their image, when we consider that the major groups are moderate, is undeserved. The use of this image to add to the bad historical perception of Islam is nothing short of stupid. The adjectives applied to Islamic groups now are the same ones which were used to describe Nasser. In reality it isn't Islam the West is battling, but the notion of populist, popular political movements which represent a threat to the West's clients and interests. The bad image the West creates for them isn't meant to explain them; it is meant to justify declaring war on them. The West's persistence in supporting unpopular regimes will guarantee the success of the Islamists. Dealing with their moderate wings, if it isn't already too late, is what the West should do. Amazingly, their image of the West does not preclude discourse.

PART THREE

Oil, Arms and Blood

3 · The Gift of God, a Gift from Satan

Control of countries' wealth shapes their governments. The royal families, army cliques and political cabals which run the countries of the Arab Middle East exercise undivided control over their economies. Because political and economic power are expressions of each other, this control frustrates the possibility of economic development contributing towards political development. Instead, it confirms the status of the traditional establishment and supports the claim of new ruling groups to primacy and membership of that establishment.

The relationship between the West and today's Arab dictatorships, be they traditional, new or hybrids, consolidates the dictatorships' control of their economies to the benefit of both sides. The West accepts this centralization of economic power because it makes the dictatorial regimes stable and less vulnerable to the pressure of anti-West popular forces, and the governments repay the West by using this power in predictable ways which serve Western political and economic interests.

An example of how this works is a friendly dictatorship dependent on Western help to survive which uses its total control of its economy to buy more Western arms than it needs (Kuwait). Another is a major oil producer which pays for Western political support by keeping the price of oil low (Saudi Arabia). And there is the case of the unfriendly but stable country which buys goods from the West and sells it its oil, even when it can do better trading with others, to maintain a balanced relationship between them to stop the West from turning against it and destabilizing it (until the Gulf War, Iraq).

Both sides accept the merger of political and economic interests. The question of whether US support for Saudi Arabia is the reason its government keeps the price of oil low or the opposite is an academic, self-cancelling one because we are dealing with a barter-like simultaneous exchange. Kuwait spreads its financial deposits among all its Western supporters in accordance with the importance of the political support it receives from them. Iraq's trade with the US flourished under Reagan and Bush because both presidents accepted Saddam Hussein, restored diplomatic relations with Iraq and provided the country with credits, most of which were used to buy American goods and arms from friendly countries. The ways in which regimes use their control of their country's wealth differ, but the common thread is the use of it to bribe the West in return for protection, support or acceptance.

This background provides the West with control or influence over the two commodities which shape today's Middle East: oil and arms. Through this the West is able to perpetuate its political influence and optimize the economic benefits to itself. If the oil policy or arms purchases of a country do not fall within the Western sphere of influence or control, then that country becomes an enemy and it is opposed (Nasser's purchase of Soviet arms in 1955), subjected to trade restrictions (Iraq in 1961, when it followed an independent oil policy) or attacked (Iraq's invasion of Kuwait in 1990 threatened to wrest control of the oil market from the West).

Saudi Arabia's economic policies are compatible with those of the West. The ruling Al Saud family consists of between seven and nine thousand male members who view the country named after them as a piece of family real estate. According to published reports, there are over fifty billionaire princes, the cost of the king's palaces is estimated at $17 billion and the budget of the royal family is between $6 and $7 billion. The effects of the abuse of the country's wealth on the ordinary citizen are huge. The squandering of the country's reserves and income and the decline in the price of oil reduced the per capita annual income in the country to $6000 in 1993 from $14,600 in 1982.[1] The royals have not been affected by this. The West guarantees the continuance of the House of Saud in return for the country supplying it with all the oil it needs at a low price and the purchase of huge quantities of American, British and French military hardware.

The horrific abuse of Saudi Arabia's wealth goes beyond the accumulation of wealth by individual members of the royal family. The economic suffering of the citizens is made worse by a commitment by the ruling family to use much of the country's income to guarantee their retention of power. To this day, the Saudi regime buys the loyalty of tribes, neighbouring Arab countries, Muslim countries and groups and the Western powers. Bedouin tribes provide the regime with internal support; Arab countries are bribed into friendly silence; Muslim countries and groups grant Saudi Arabia a measure of religious legitimacy and Saudi Arabia finances CIA operations from the Horn of Africa to Central America, as well as supplying the West with cheap oil and buys billions of dollars' worth of military hardware. These expenditures take priority over using the oil income to solve the country's water shortage or to build schools and hospitals. This is why so little has been done to improve the standard of living of the country's poor Shia community, the people at the bottom of the social scale. The short-term benefits to the West are obvious; the long-term ones keep the royal family in power. Meanwhile the divide between the rich and the poor, one of the worst in the whole world, grows wider by the day.

The costs of the Saudi monarchy's survival, mainly underwritten by pro-West policies, represent the ugliest expression of dynastic economic monopoly. But other countries do the same. The economic policies of Kuwait, despite a People's Assembly which has produced voices of dissent and attempts at financial control, are still subject to the whims of an insensitive royal family. With no tribes to bribe, the Kuwaiti royal family corrupts other indigenous centres of power. It provides financial backing to local newspapers and favours the trading establishments of some of the leading families with government contracts. Externally, Kuwait's behaviour resembles that of Saudi Arabia, though it stops short of sponsoring Western political schemes around the world. However, very much like Saudi Arabia, it follows an accommodating oil policy and buys arms it cannot use to equip an army incapable of defending it against outside aggression. As with Saudi Arabia, the West sells Kuwait arms, gets its oil at a low price and guarantees the continuance of the royal family.

Jordan, without an oil income but with a parliament which is constrained by King Hussein's dictatorial inclinations, follows in the footsteps of Saudi Arabia and Kuwait. The way the country's budget is allocated has more to do with the royal will and King Hussein's inherent wish to protect and perpetuate the monarchy than it does with economic sense. The country's army, the king's survival kit, is larger than it should be, consumes a disproportionate amount of the country's budget and is still predominantly Bedouin. The king goes beyond supporting the country's abusive internal security apparatus lavishly: it is such a vital component of his government that its directors become Prime Ministers (like Muddar Badran) or are elevated to royal political advisers (like Muhammad Rasul Al Keilani). Huge amounts of money the country can ill afford are spent on buying the loyalty of local journalists and retaining expensive international public relations firms and experts to promote the image of the king and his brother, Crown Prince Hassan, who has his own PR man in London.

In the case of economically poor Jordan the payback to the West is essentially political. The West exercises indirect control on the army through being its sole arms supplier, and the army maintains the friendly regime. The West, despite Jordan's poverty, connives in Hussein's use of precious funds to maintain the army and the security apparatus. Expenditure on the army and the security forces takes precedence over the need to build schools and hospitals or the development of small industries.

Egypt, poor and with meagre resources, maintains a standing army of over four hundred thousand soldiers, despite a fifteen-year-old peace agreement with Israel. The pro-West regime, totally dependent on the armed forces for survival, uses more than 9 per cent of the country's gross national product to maintain them. The security forces are an added drain on the economy and their budget is so high that the figures are not published.

The Egyptian armed forces produce the leaders, keep them in office, are used to exert Egyptian-Western influence on neighbouring countries and provide the managerial talent for the industries of the country. The economy of Egypt is controlled and run by the pro-West officer class, which uses the wealth of the country to maintain its power base. (Interestingly, the officers hated the Russians because the latter didn't bribe them.) Egypt has been reduced to a country occupied by its own armed forces. The West likes the policies of this regime to the extent of helping to equip and maintain the army and the security forces and, in the process, sanctions the misuse of the country's wealth.

Iraq is another example of an army organization using the wealth of the country to perpetuate its control of power. In the case of Iraq the officers have greater cohesion than in Egypt: they come from the same religious sect and social background. They are a clique which assumed a military identity and elevated one of its members to a dictator.

The exact amount of Iraqi national income spent on sustaining the clique of Sunni army officers who run Iraq, most of whom hail from Saddam Hussein's home town of Tikrit, is difficult to quantify, but it has been more than 15 per cent of the national budget for the past two decades. When Iraq was pumping oil, the army and one of the most elaborate security systems in existence came first. After that, Iraq did spend money on land reclamation, education and cultural endeavours. The West did not object to Saddam Hussein's maintenance of a million-man army which needed considerable Western military hardware until he used it against its interests, to invade Kuwait.

Syria is similar to Egypt and Iraq. As with Iraq, most army officers belong to a specific sect, in this case the Alawis, and they are a privileged class which uses between 15 and 20 per cent of the country's income to maintain a force of three hundred thousand. Naturally, there is the ever-present security organization, the French-inspired Deuxième Bureau, which employs tens of thousands of people and needs billions of dollars to maintain.

The officer class not only runs the country behind President Hafez Al Assad; its needs take precedence over all else. In fact, the military are the source for managerial talent; no aspect of life escapes their attention and they have replaced the old landowning and merchant classes as the ruling élite. The army's control of the country's wealth is total and it perpetuates itself without opposition.

The only time the West mentions the disastrous economic effects of maintaining a huge Syrian army is in connection with its possible use to oppose Western policies or when it buys its military hardware from non-Western countries. When the latter occurs Western leaders manifest a sense of selective morality and object to the amounts of money Syria spends on arms while failing to mention that many of their client states spend more on the same, both in absolute terms and as a percentage of national income.

Yasser Arafat's new administration differs substantially from the rest because it has no oil and no army. However, Arafat, as discussed earlier, is beholden to a new class of Palestinians who became wealthy in the oil-producing countries and to the governments of these countries. The rich Palestinians and the oil-producing countries support Arafat's pro-West policies. Arafat's consequent use of his police to suppress political opponents is an expression of the will of pro-West wealthy Palestinians and Arab governments who oppose the emergence of threatening forces. In other words, a special group and the countries on which they depend impose pro-West policies to maintain Arafat's new, dictatorial regime. Beyond manipulating Arafat's policies, the rich Palestinians hope to control the economy of his regime. The West is happy to have a financially powerful group deputize for it, just as the monarchies and army groups deputize for it in other countries.

Except for Arafat's indirect adherence to this policy, the ruling groups in the Middle East use income from oil and their armed forces (including the security forces) to stay in power. Because the West controls or influences the acquisition of arms which make the armed forces effective and because it manipulates the oil market through oil companies which decide where to buy, refine, distribute and use the income generated from oil, it relies on both tools to determine the policies of these countries. This is why the West, in cooperation with friendly regimes and against the wishes of unfriendly ones, seeks to perpetuate its monopoly of both businesses.

*   *   *

Oil has been a major factor in the West's attempts to control the Middle East since the late nineteenth century. It was first discovered in Iran and gained added importance when the British Navy switched from coal to oil and the Italians used it to fuel military aircraft. During the First World War control of Romanian and Baku oil was part of the combatants' strategy and in 1916 there was an oil shortage. By the end of the war, oil was a major factor in how the Middle East was divided.

The original post-First World War scramble for Middle East oil provided the model for what followed. It involved the sanctioning of monopolistic consortia and oil was a determinant in creating, dividing, controlling and supporting countries. The original concession for the oil of Mosul (now in northern Iraq), discovered in 1908, was awarded by the then government of Ottoman Turkey to a consortium of the Anatolia Railway Commission and Deutsche Bank. In 1912–13 there was fierce Anglo-German competition to participate in exploiting it and different temporary consortia were set up for this purpose.

The results of the Great War changed this picture and placed Britain ahead. It was because of oil that the British considered their paramountcy over Mesopotamia among their major war aims in the Middle East. In fact, their military advance towards Mosul in 1917 and their total insistence that it be separated from Turkey and incorporated into a new country, Iraq, had oil behind it.[2] Later, in 1919, the British interest in the Mosul oil led them to renegotiate the Sykes–Picot Agreement with France. Britain kept Mosul, originally part of the proposed Syria which France had been awarded, in return for giving France a completely free hand in Syria and Lebanon. This is why Britain looked the other way when the French removed Britain's protégé, King Faisal, from the Syrian throne.

By 1921 Turkey had been driven out of Mosul, Syria had been redefined and a new country, Iraq, was created under a pro-British king, Faisal I. These geopolitical moves confirming oil's importance were sanctioned by the San Remo Treaty of 1920 and followed by elaborate British, French and American scheming to share a new concession. The United States, afraid of being squeezed out by the colonial powers, advocated what it called an Open Door policy; as the name suggests, it used the idea of free trade to support its determination to participate in the future monopoly of oil.

The whole business of controlling Iraq's oil was so shady, conspiratorial and subject to backroom manipulations that an Armenian entrepreneur with wile and connections, Calouste Gulbenkian, ended up holding 5 per cent of the 1925 concession that replaced the old Turkish one. And Britain, to avoid trouble in the future and because the expected profits were so great, saw fit to include the French and the Americans, albeit as junior partners.

So the first phase of the scramble for the Middle East saw the West using oil to determine the shape of the Arab Middle East and its leadership. The awarding of the concession was an inter-West happening over which Arab leaderships were not consulted and in which they did not participate. Naturally the Arab people, the ruled, were not involved on any level.

In the lower Gulf oil was not discovered until later. But Britain had turned tribal chiefs into leaders of statelets and shackled Saudi Arabia with 1915 and 1927 treaties which reduced it to a dependency. But the increasing awareness by the governments and companies of the potential of Middle East oil led them to formalize plans for its future exploitation. The result was a corporate umbrella, the pooling of interest by the oil companies. The companies, with governments' blessings, assumed direct control of exploiting the oil resources of the region to their mutual benefit, without quarrelling over it. The governments absolved the companies from the restrictions of anti-trust and other laws which enjoined them from forming cartels in other parts of the world.

The initial agreement adopted by the companies, the Red Line Agreement, was hammered out between the British and French governments in 1928. It called for a blatant sharing of the oil wealth of the former Turkish territories, allocating percentages of future oil production in these territories to British, French and American companies. Iran and Kuwait, subject to separate treaties with Britain, were left outside this arrangement.

Having supervised the overriding but illegal Red Line Agreement, the governments were happy to surrender to the companies its tactical implementation, the actual carrying out of the exploitation without deferring to the interests of the countries: what amounted to a theft. The implementation scheme, the As-Is Agreement, was the work of the heads of oil companies who met at Achnacarry Castle in Scotland and agreed on production and pricing policies governing their control of Middle East oil. This agreement too was made in secret, was later described as 'not only the work of the oil companies'[3] and, because of its one-sidedness, wasn't exposed until 1952.

The first phase of the scramble for Arab oil led to the creation of, or the support for, kings and sheikhs who did not question the West's plans to exploit the oil and afforded it the necessary local sanction to control the main economic resource of the Arab Middle East. Although this phase lasted until the mid-1950s, there was no change during this thirty-year period in the monopolistic structure and the way it affected the Arab countries, people or the position of their leadership. Neither the overt transfer of the control of oil to the companies nor the emergence of the Americans as independent oil exploiters had any effect on the political scene. The small countries' income from oil continued to be used to strengthen the governments created by the West. It was a perfect full circle.

America's appearance as a major player on the Middle East oil scene came about by accident: the conspiring, government-backed adherents to the Red Line Agreement lacked sufficient interest to pay proper attention to Saudi Arabia. Prospecting for oil in Saudi Arabia had been carried out by the British Eastern and General Syndicate from 1923, before the Red Line and As-Is agreements came into being. Oil was not found. The founder of Saudi Arabia, Ibn Saud, used his British adviser, Harry St John Philby, to try to induce other British companies to pick up the concession. For many reasons, but mainly the abundance of supplies from Iran and Iraq, there were no takers. Meanwhile the 1929 depression affected the number of Muslims making the hajj so badly that it came near to reducing Ibn Saud to a pauper.[4] In 1933, a year after it had discovered oil in the island of Bahrain, a few miles off the eastern coast of Saudi Arabia, Standard Oil of California (SOCAL) bought the right to prospect for oil in Saudi Arabia for a mere $250,000.

So America's entry into the Middle East oil stakes involved something resembling a bribe which went into the pocket of a spendthrift king, Ibn Saud. Compared with how the British-made Faisal was elevated to King of Iraq and what little say he had regarding the oil concession that Britain obtained in his country, bribing Ibn Saud amounted to an acceptance of the principle of consulting host governments, the elevation to partner of an accommodating local chief. The co-signatories to the Red Line and As-Is agreements, still unconcerned with Saudi oil or the man who controlled it, did not object.

They were proven wrong when Saudi oil was discovered in 1938, almost simultaneously with its discovery in Kuwait. The vastness of the Saudi potential prompted SOCAL to invite Texaco, Mobil and Standard Oil of New Jersey to form a joint company to exploit its concession and form the Arabian-American Oil Company (ARAMCO). This huge American commitment to Saudi oil had the solid support of the Roosevelt administration, which, operating under the guidance of Interior Secretary Harold Ickes, had already seen the future American dependence on Middle East oil, set aside the anti-trust laws governing oil exploitation in America and encouraged the companies to cooperate. The existence of the all-American consortium meant the *de facto* death of the Red Line Agreement, and indeed America served official notice of non-subscription to it two years later. But this was an inter-company quarrel with little effect on the relationship with the producing countries.

The differences between the consortia who subscribed to the colonial agreements and the Americans reflected their national character. The British companies were assumptive, directly dependent on the political muscle of their government to maintain concessions, allocate production and post prices. Arab leaders created by the colonialists and dependent on them for their very existence never questioned the companies' policies – no one dared. On the other hand, the Americans, unaccustomed to colonial behaviour and the resulting economic exploitation, 'cooperated' with the local chief, Ibn Saud. He was totally dependent on what they paid him, and they knew that 'the concession is always in jeopardy unless his (personal) demands are met'.[5] The results were similar: the rulers were sustained in power by what the oil companies paid them.

The British and American exploitation of oil, which continued until the 1950s, produced increases in production, company profits and a voluntary rise – mainly out of embarrassment or because they thought it wiser to do so – in the level of royalties. But the relationship between the companies and the host governments didn't change. For the most part, the money went into the pockets of the ruling families, with small amounts devoted to public expenditure and savings. In the 1940s 99 and 82 per cent of the oil revenues went into the pockets of, respectively, the Bahraini and Kuwaiti royal families.[6] The cost of maintaining the garages of Ibn Saud in 1946 was $2 million, while expenditure on education during the same year amounted to $150,000.[7] The increase in royalties amounted to an increase in subsidizing friendly chiefs.

The higher royalties had little effect on public expenditure and the issue of what to do with financial reserves did not arise until later. Meanwhile, the political use of the oil income by leaders went beyond building palaces, buying fleets of cars when there were no roads and King Saud's daily need for thirty lambs and two hundred chickens to feed his staff, and assumed two new forms. The oil companies, with their governments and intelligence services behind them, began their direct participation in the moral degradation of leaders and in the creation of narrow constituencies to support them.

In Kuwait the Getty Oil Company provided some royals with blondes. King Saud's preference for little boys was not a barrier[8] and the CIA and oil companies provided them. The British-controlled Iraqi Petroleum Company built a palace for Iraq strongman Nuri Saïd. The activities of the oil companies extended to countries through which they built oil pipelines and in 1949 the Americans bribed Syrian President Husni Zaim to allow them to build the Trans-Arabian Pipeline (TAPLINE) through his country. The corrupting efforts didn't stop at rulers or people who held office: they extended to members of their families. Groups of Saudi princes were flown to the United States for tours which included outright pimping by ARAMCO. In Iraq, Nuri Saïd's mentally deficient son Sabah was given incentive by non-existent advisory jobs with IPC (Iraqi Petroleum Company). Many Kuwaiti royals also held phoney jobs.

Corruption of the leaders and their families was followed by moves to confirm the position of these families by creating support groups beneath them. The twin effort towards this showed in the business and education fields. What the Kuwaitis pioneered was followed by others and the businesses which emerged as a result of the oil wealth were placed in the hands of groups loyal to the monarchies and sheikhdoms. In Iraq the employees, contractors and suppliers to the oil company were hired, used and fired in accordance with their political loyalty to the throne. In Saudi Arabia the family of the chief financial adviser to the king, Abdallah Suleiman, set up a construction and trading company which came close to monopolizing contracts. Even the king's English adviser and suspect convert to Islam, St John Philby, was awarded the agency of the Ford Motor Company. This was followed by giving other agencies to the Zamil, Ghoseibi, Zahid, Hamad and Al Khadi families – all pro-House of Saud.[9] In all cases, even in awarding agencies, the oil companies had a say in who got what.

The other activity aimed at creating a support group, a loyalist class, was in the field of education. Whatever money was allocated to education by both the oil companies and the governments concentrated on a small group of loyalists, with the rest of the people coming way behind. Members of the Kuwaiti and Bahraini royal families were sent to Beirut and Cairo schools at the expense of the oil companies. IPC, because the imported Iraqi royal family was small in number, educated the sons of the tribal sheikhs and loyalist bourgeoisie. In 1952 the Saudi students attending the International College in Beirut comprised eight Sudeiris (kin to the royal family), the son of the Minister of Post and Telegraph, five sons of advisers to the king, four sons of tribal sheikhs and two sons of army generals.[10] Providing schooling for the offspring of important people was a form of indirect payment to their parents.

Not only were there very few deserving commoners among the Saudis sent to Beirut at this time; not a single one of the privileged made the honours list, most repeated their classes and, later, one of them took eleven years to obtain his bachelor's degree at a second-rate American college. It didn't stop there, and the corrupt oil culture with which they were imbued found them bribing teachers to get passing grades, frequenting whore-houses and being rude to servants and helpers.

Overall there was a distinct political character to the way the oil money was being used on every level. The perversion of the leadership was coupled with creating a loyalist class and perverting it. In both groups, the new merchants and their so-called educated children, there resulted a preference for Western ways, including wearing jeans, chewing gum, eating hamburgers and calling a glass by its English name. Amusingly, those who benefited in countries where the British controlled the oil industry scoffed at their counterparts in countries where the American oil companies prevailed. In building a new socio-economic structure to support the political structure fabricated by their governments, the companies again failed to reach the groups with whom they had a problem, the thinkers and the average people. This was particularly true of ARAMCO, which, because of the hugeness of its operations, operated like a state within a state with a bias towards House of Saud followers regardless of qualifications.

With exceptions, this is what existed until the 1950s. The oil companies and governments behind them operated through corrupt traditional leaders and a new class of loyalists moulded by them and there was very little economic logic to it all. To repeat, the increase in the royalties they paid the governments was a decision they made themselves, because of an embarrassment of riches or acting on the advice of their governments – for the same reason. For example, the American government's advice to ARAMCO to pay the Saudis more money was coupled with a decision to allow the participants in the ARAMCO consortium to write off these payments against taxes in America, a scheme which came to be known as the 'Golden Gimmick' (not a credit against tax, but a total write-off). Even before that, in 1941, the American government, in an extraordinary step, used Lend-Lease to pay Ibn Saud money to sustain him in power. Preserving leaders or regimes determined how the oil money paid to countries was used. And it is worth repeating that the companies were making considerably more profit than they paid the countries.[11]

The developments which were to challenge this came from a non-Arab country, Iran, and an Arab country which then had no oil of its own, Egypt. In 1951, in a move which had a direct bearing on the relations of the oil-producing countries with the companies and the governments behind them, Iranian Prime Minister Muhammad Mossadeq nationalized the Anglo-Iranian Oil Company. Four years later Gamal Abdel Nasser of Egypt began speaking of 'Arab oil' and a little while later of 'Arab oil for the Arabs'. The act of nationalizing a Western oil company amounted to reclaiming the inalienable right of a producing country to control a natural resource and Nasser's appeals were aimed at having the masses participate in the benefits of their countries' wealth.

The Iranian move, a threatening model which could have been copied by the rest of the oil producers, was opposed every step of the way. When possible, the companies bought oil from other countries and there were boycotts, embargoes, military threats and interference by British intelligence and the CIA. The battle lines were drawn, Mossadeq proved nationalization was possible and the solid opposition of the companies and governments to his move demonstrated their determination and capabilities. But it was Nasser's shrill attacks on the oil companies which gave impetus to a widespread popular wish to change things and paved the way for the second phase of the relationship, the creation of OPEC (Organization of Petroleum Exporting Countries).

The appeals of Nasser against the inequitable concession agreements produced reactions from the two parties they threatened, the governments of the oil-producing countries and the oil companies. Most leaders of the oil-producing countries, particularly those of Iraq, saw Nasser's challenge as a political one and responded to it negatively. To deflect his threat they and the companies agreed on a slight increase in royalties and coordinated their efforts against him in Western circles. Surprisingly, it was Saudi Arabia's King Saud who in 1954 made an unexpected move towards breaking the total monopoly of the oil companies by forming a tanker company, in partnership with the Greek shipping magnate Aristotle Onassis, to transport his country's oil. The companies of the ARAMCO consortium, unwilling to cede even the smallest part of their monopolies, called on the US government for help.

The US government openly assumed the mantle of protector of American companies' rights and moved to oppose Saud. Secretary of State John Foster Dulles maintained that ARAMCO had the right to transport Saudi oil. The US Ambassador to Saudi Arabia, George Wadsworth, bluntly told the king that America might stop extracting oil in his country. Threat followed threat. The American response revealed two elements: it was control of the oil rather than its availability which mattered to the US and the previous pretence that, unlike others, US companies were not imperialist came to an end. Still, the Americans succeeded in forcing Saud to cancel the agreement to form a tanker company and ARAMCO once again reigned supreme.

The Saudi challenge resurfaced in 1959, when the newly appointed Oil Minister and Nasser protégé, Abdallah Tariki, organized a meeting of the Arab Petroleum Congress in Cairo. The purpose of convening the conference, to review the Arabs' relationships with the oil companies, was enough of a challenge, but when Tariki discovered that his Venezuelan counterpart was there as an observer, business moved ahead of schedule. The two met in secret and agreed on the need to do something about the total control of the posted price of oil by the companies. What Tariki and Alfonso Pérez needed to convince other producers to join them to give substance to their challenge was a palpable demonstration of how the companies' control of prices was damaging the economies of the producing countries. In August 1960 the companies, oblivious to the winds of change swirling around them, gave Tariki and Pérez what they needed.

With Esso in the lead, and as disinclined to consult the producing countries as ever, the companies decided to reduce the posted price of oil by 7 to 9 per cent. Coming as it did after the Cairo conference, the decision amounted to a response by the companies to Tariki and Pérez and a direct defiance of the countries' rights to have a say in their pricing policy.

But instead of being cowed, Tariki and Pérez capitalized on the move. Iraq, with a new government which had, in 1958, overthrown the pro-West pro-oil companies monarchy, in September 1962 hosted a meeting to discuss cooperation among the producers. Pérez suggested the creation of an organization and gave it its name, and his proposal was adopted unanimously. Saudi Arabia, Venezuela, Iraq, Iran and Kuwait were founding members. Iraqi leader Abdel Karim Kassem hosted a huge dinner party for the delegates and egged them on. The OPEC cartel came into being to face the cartel of the oil companies (the 'Seven Sisters'). The only reason Tariki was able to join Pérez as a founding father was because the government behind him was weak and torn by a family feud between King Saud and Crown Prince Faisal. Neither of them was strong enough to intercept the Oil Minister's popular oil policies. As Tariki owed his allegiance to Nasser, indirectly the founding of OPEC was a political move by the most popular Arab leader this century.

The companies' response to the creation of OPEC confirmed that the precipitous price reduction was not an accident. They resorted to both old and new techniques to undermine the organization. Their first move was to punish Iraq for hosting the first OPEC meeting and cancelling their right to exploit some areas of the country where the companies had failed to extract oil. The companies hadn't drilled for oil there and they were happy determining the production levels of each country among themselves, but they still saw the Iraqi move as nationalization or a prelude to it and took steps to retaliate by buying less Iraqi oil. The CIA and MI6 moved to support the companies and punish Iraq, by increasing their aid to the rebellious Kurds in the north of the country. The open economic and political warfare against Iraq culminated in the CIA's support in 1963 for the Ba'ath Party, to which Saddam Hussein belonged, to overthrow the government of Abdel Karim Kassem and replace it by one friendlier towards the companies (see Chapter 4).

With the companies and the governments behind them operating as one, the CIA unleashed an across-the-board attack on OPEC. CIA agent Bill Eveland used *New York Times* Chief of Middle East correspondents Sam Pope Brewer to plant several new stories in that paper. The stories were dismissive of OPEC and predicted that it would fall victim to internal squabbling and be short-lived. The CIA went further and prevailed on Lebanese newspapers, notably *Al Hayyat*, to run stories resurrecting old feuds between the member countries in an attempt to foment trouble and stop them cooperating. According to Abdallah Tariki, the British and Americans used intelligence and diplomatic channels to approach individual countries, in particular Kuwait, to prise them loose by promising a greater share of the market at the expense of vulnerable populous ones such as Iraq and Saudi Arabia.[12]

The companies even resorted to smear tactics and blackmail. They pressured newspapers to use innuendo and to refer to Tariki as the Red Sheikh. They spread stories about Tariki's past life purporting to show that his activities had more to do with personal pique, for being treated like a black in America, than with sound economics. They went further and had him shadowed during his frequent visits to Beirut. They wanted to uncover aspects of personal misbehaviour that they could use to undermine him.

The companies' efforts failed. And Nasser's background exhortations created a popular atmosphere which stopped the Saudi royal family from trying to foil the activities of its oil minister. Tariki himself managed to unbalance the companies; he accused them of doctoring their figures and demanded that they submit their books for examination. The companies refused; the first round went to OPEC. Fuad Ottayem of the Middle East Economic Survey and the leading independent Arab oil expert told me, 'It [the creation of OPEC] is a popular move, like wanting independence.'

Nineteen sixty-two saw the end of the first phase of OPEC and the reassertion of the power of the traditional establishment. Faisal replaced Saud as King of Saudi Arabia and set the ball rolling by firing Tariki. With Tariki out of the way and the largest oil exporter back under the undivided control of the conservative, pro-West House of Saud, relations with ARAMCO improved and the oil companies confirmed this improvement by recognizing OPEC. But the recognition was an empty gesture:

the new Saudi Oil Minister, Ahmad Zaki Yamani, took his instructions from Faisal and didn't lead, and Faisal wanted to end the confrontation between the producing countries and the companies. The remaining producers followed the lead of the largest oil exporter and lacked the will and the production power to continue the initial independent policies of OPEC. Instead, using Saudi Arabia as a friend within the enemy camp, the companies moved to manipulate OPEC. The political alliance between Saudi Arabia and the United States, a *de facto*, convoluted one, was determining the direction of OPEC.

Saudi Arabia could have withdrawn from OPEC, but the organization's policies were too popular with the people and there was no way for Faisal and his front man Yamani to do that without causing turmoil or even to appear to withhold support from it. This is why they turned to reducing its concerns and effectiveness from the inside. The OPEC meetings from 1962 until the 1967 Arab-Israeli War dealt with royalties and production programming, in particular variations on the 50 per cent share of profits. Amazingly, Saudi Arabia, determined to stay on good terms with America and ARAMCO and consistently unwilling to lead, did not get what the others got until the early 1970s. The Saudi leaders' sacrifice of their own interests to please outsiders did not escape the Saudi people or the people of the conservative countries which followed the Saudi lead.

But it was the outcome of the 1967 War which undermined the Saudi policy. Arab passions were inflamed and expressed themselves openly and the Saudi government, afraid that it might be overthrown, reacted to the Arab defeat by imposing a selective embargo on countries which supported Israel: the US, Britain, Germany and others. But this was rescinded by Faisal through Yamani after one month and the Oil Minister, despite all evidence to the contrary, served notice that oil and politics do not mix.[13] Unable to maintain an embargo without Saudi Arabia, the other Arab countries followed suit. Yamani, the man Anthony Sampson described as 'he seems to be acting all the time', was having it his way. Instead of a nationalist oil minister, Saudi Arabia had a pro-West, wealth-seeking dandy at the top.

Because there were too many OPEC meetings which dealt with price increases and production quotas, outlining the behaviour of the Arab countries within its offshoot, the Organization of Arab Petroleum Exporting Countries (OAPEC), is more to the point. In 1968 and after, the Saudis advocated participation (holding a share of the concession) when the other Arab countries were calling for nationalization. Later the same year they accepted a 20 per cent share when Libya and Algeria were getting 51 per cent. The Saudis resisted price increases and attempts at closer coordination of production. It was what one-time Tariki collaborator Anton Sarkis called 'Playing Don Quixote to protect US interests, even if it means sacrificing their interests and the rest of OPEC's.'[14]

But, weakened by the 1967 defeat to the point of depending on Saudi Arabia and Faisal for economic aid, Nasser was forced to stop his propaganda attacks on Faisal and the oil companies. It was an opening that both sides used to retard the natural confrontation between the countries and the oil companies. OPEC followed the policies of the largest producer and Nasser's death in 1970 gave it additional breathing space until the October War of 1973.

The background to the 1973 embargo is worth examining. By 1973 Sadat, Nasser's successor, had reduced his links with the USSR to the extent of getting rid of its military advisers and was following a pro-Saudi, pro-American policy. Wrongly, he and the Saudis assumed that this would lead to American pressure on Israel to end the occupation of the Egyptian territory that it had taken in 1967. But the Americans, seeing no threat to their oil interests, did nothing and the Israelis showed no signs of planning to leave Sinai.

Faisal feared two things. He didn't want Egypt to revert to radical politics and attack his oil policy, and his own people were restive (there were several coup attempts) and favoured his use of the 'oil weapon' against Israel. Time and again he pleaded with America and made statements to the press in an effort to help Egypt. Early in 1973 he used ARAMCO president Frank Jungers to transmit a message that failure to accommodate Egypt threatened the flow of oil. When his attempts to get America to act failed, Faisal had no option but to support Sadat's decision to go to war, and to use the oil weapon.

What followed came close to strangling the West economically, but it was the result of a series of mishaps rather than a Saudi policy aimed at that end. The Saudi policy of Faisal had two purposes: to serve notice that American inactivity was endangering its friends and the twin goal of buying time against the rising anger of his people and other Arabs. It didn't represent a deviation in Faisal's pro-West, pro-oil companies policies: it represented his personal interpretation of conditions on the ground and doing the minimum to contain them before things got out of hand. The last thing Faisal had in mind was a total oil embargo.

The war started on 6 October 1973 and Faisal immediately offered Egypt $200 million in aid. Soon after, hoping to prevent America from helping Israel out of its initial military setback, Faisal and fellow Arab oil producers announced a 5 per cent reduction in their output. On 16 October the reduction was increased to 10 per cent and a promise was given of a further 5 per cent cut every month. The threat of additional cuts was just that, and not a foregone conclusion.

When America dismissed the cuts and threats of more and opted to supply Israel with $2.2 billion worth of arms, Sheikh Zayyed of Abu Dhabi responded to the Nixon administration's dare by announcing a total oil embargo. Suddenly the lovers' quarrel was out of control. Faisal, afraid of the reaction within his country and the Arab and Muslim worlds, had no choice but to follow Zayyed's lead.

Oil prices soared and shortages were the order of the day, but Saudi Arabia worked to lift the embargo as soon as practicable. The records of the meetings between Secretary of State Henry Kissinger and King Faisal during the following three months reveal an unmistakable Saudi desire for a face-saving formula to end the impasse. In the middle of this, in February 1974, America reaffirmed its commitment to the House of Saud by selling Saudi Arabia more planes, tanks and other arms than it had ever done.

On 19 March 1974 Faisal lifted the embargo without gaining anything for the Egyptians or the Palestinians: the ostensible reason for enforcing it. Still, because the embargo was a popular move, Faisal came out of it with his Arab and Muslim credentials enhanced.

The suffering of the Western consumer should be judged in terms of this strengthening of the position of a pro-West leader and of what might have happened had the Arabs followed Iraq in demanding a total severance of trade relations with the West. On balance, the West came out ahead: not only was oil in safe hands, but the embargo having produced no concrete results, the potential use of the oil weapon in the future was unlikely.

Market conditions, a situation favourable to the suppliers, helped maintain the price increases which resulted from the 1973 Arab oil embargo. Faisal attributed the improvement in economic conditions to his policy. Meanwhile Saudi Arabia, because of its immense oil potential, tried to pump oil to keep prices down, but the squeeze on supplies persisted and the Saudi policy fell foul of two unexpected contrary forces. The Shah of Iran, succumbing to megalomania, needed high prices to build a huge army and spread his hegemony over the Gulf. And there was the amazing reappearance of Abdallah Tariki and former Iraqi Oil Minister Adnan Pachachi as advisers to Libya and the consequent commitment of that country to a policy of high oil prices. OPEC was reduced to a debating forum between Saudi Arabia, pro-West, pro-low oil prices, and the advocates of price increases.

The period from the mid-1970s until 1984 saw the third phase of the

relationship between the Arab oil producers and the West. Inevitably
Saudi Arabia re-emerged as the leading oil power and because it followed
traditional oil policies which subordinated its interests, as well as those of
its people and the rest of the Arabs to its political relationship with the
West, then it is safe to call this the Saudi era. And the Saudi era was the
creation of the man who, acting as a loyal servant of the Saudi crown,
translated into an oil policy the Saudi royal family's wish to maintain a
special relationship with the West. It was the Yamani era and, despite his
claims, politics were behind it.

The record of OPEC meetings between 1974 and the Iranian revolution
of 1979 show a Yamani dismissive of the interests of fellow OPEC
members, a man who was totally oblivious to the sensibilities of the Saudi
people and other Arabs. Every single meeting produced a Yamani
instructed to call for lower prices than the rest. He operated from within
his country's position as a swing producer – that is, capable of producing
enough oil to flood the market and keep prices down but also willing to
curtail them to raise prices. Because he always advocated keeping them
down, Yamani was popular in the West and hated in Saudi Arabia. In a
way, low oil prices was the ticket for Yamani to join the Arab establishment.
Very much like Arab leaders, his concern was to become the darling of
the West.

While OPEC meeting after meeting found Yamani holding a line against
the rest of the OPEC and OAPEC members, market conditions still
favoured higher prices. There were times when the Saudi policy came
near to the perverse and the country sold oil at $14.75 a barrel when it
was fetching $35 on the open market, but even this didn't halt the overall
trend. And higher oil prices produced the sudden increase in the income
of the oil-producing countries and ushered in a new era.

What matters to us at this point is how the producing countries saw
the future, how they used their money and what lasting effects the accumulation of wealth had on the ruling families and the societies of the oil-
producing countries. A summary of this reveals what effect the Arab oil
boom had on relations between the ruling families and the West.

Most of the money was used foolishly. Anthony Sampson speaks of
some of the people of countries accumulating untold wealth still living in
shacks.[15] The Arab economist and historian Ramzi Zakki deals with a
broader problem and contends that 'there was no attempt at structural
change'.[16] The refrains of both authors about using the money wrongly
are especially true of countries with close connections with the West. The
people in power lined their pockets and the budgets of the Saudi, Kuwaiti,
United Arab Emirates and other royal families skimmed off high percent-

ages of their countries' incomes. The divide between the rich and the poor widened. There were expensive and unnecessary show projects like the building of an Olympic stadium in Saudi Arabia, a four-lane highway which led nowhere in Kuwait, international airports in Sharja where there was no international air traffic, and ministry buildings which had more offices than there were employees. Western companies, planners and advisers were behind all these schemes. Only in countries which followed policies independent from the West did we see an attempt at sensible utilization of oil income. For example, Libya and Iraq did reclaim more land than the rest and there was greater emphasis on education, improving health standards, social security coverage and other services.

But personal abuse of wealth and misallocation of money, though serious, are less telling than the more subtle abuse of it. Many billions of dollars of the colossal surpluses (at one point a total of $220 billion) that the Arabs were accumulating were predestined, and in a way which, despite newspaper and other reports about Arab ownership of too much of the West, was acceptable to Western governments.

First, the surplus from oil was linked to the world capital market controlled by US, British and French banks (the latter through consortia such as the Union de Banque Arabe-Française (UBAF), which the French created especially for this reason). Placing the surpluses in Western banks ensured the continued use of money to fuel Western economies, to act as the primary lenders in the world financial market, and meant that the depositor countries realized less benefit than is available through different routes. There was no attempt to use the surpluses to develop the Middle East and whatever money trickled through towards regional development was comparatively small.

Secondly, as has already been mentioned, some countries used their oil wealth to sponsor Western policies, to front for the West. Saudi Arabia sponsored anti-communist elements in Angola, the Horn of Africa, Central America and Afghanistan. Kuwait favoured pro-West Palestinian elements, the Afghani Mujahideen and anti-communist factions in Yemen. Sadat got help from both countries and the United Arab Emirates to pursue his pro-West policies. King Hussein received money for his personal use and more to continue his pro-West policies, which included undermining the Palestinians. All three countries used more money to bribe tribal chiefs throughout the Middle East than aiding educational programmes.

Thirdly, there was the attempt to recycle the oil wealth through buying arms. Saudi writer Tewfic Al Sheikh claims that Saudi Arabia bought a third of all US arms exports in 1981.[17] Kuwait changed its tanks every five years, practically before members of its armed forces learned how to use them. The United Arab Emirates, with a total native population of three hundred thousand people, bought forty French Mirage aircraft for its air force. These deals were followed by others, equally large and mainly useless.

The drain of personal abuse, depositing money in Western banks where it realized the least return, spending on political schemes in which the people of these countries had little interest and buying more Western arms than needed was coupled with prohibitive factors. The countries were discouraged from developing their petrochemical industries, moving into refining and distribution, investing in the industries of the West or any moves towards a more equitable distribution of wealth. (When Kuwait acquired 19 per cent of British Petroleum (BP), the British government forced them to sell most of it.)

In fact, the failure of the oil countries and their Western supporters to use the sudden and monumental gush of wealth to create legitimate regimes acceptable to the people was a mistake as huge as their original one to build regimes which depended exclusively on minorities. It isn't only the unbelievability of people living in shacks in the middle of untold wealth: the pro-West regimes acquiesced in some serious moves to perpetuate an unhealthy situation both within and outside these countries.

One major move was the creation in 1979 of the Gulf Cooperation Council (GCC). Comprising Saudi Arabia, Kuwait, the Emirates, Qatar, Bahrain and Oman, it amounted to a rich countries' club with a special relationship with the West which separated it from the rest of the Middle East. The two aims of the GCC were to protect these countries against outside threats and to guard against internal turmoil in any member country.

Protecting against an outside threat, despite the very special case of the Iraqi invasion of Kuwait, served the purpose of inducing the small countries with a total population of sixteen to eighteen million to use their oil wealth to buy more Western arms. Surprisingly, their arms purchases were not coordinated and were never integrated and there was nothing to the effort beyond the actual sales and the commissions which resulted from them. Another reason for creating this bloc within the larger Arab one was to persuade the governments to continue to invest their money in Western banks instead of channelling it towards the larger Arab development. The danger of having extremely rich small states within an area of larger poor ones, with the instability this might cause, was accepted by the governments of these countries and their Western backers.

Within these countries the creation of the GCC reinforced the feeling of separateness and the fear of revolutions. All regimes spent a considerable amount of money on buying security equipment and hiring Western security experts, naturally ones approved by the Western governments. With the rulers and their tribal and merchant followers enjoying the fruits of oil wealth, the rest of the people were subjected to what amounts to a reimposition of feudal tyranny.

Not a single country among the GCC members subscribes to the International Bill of Human Rights. There is no free press, freedom of speech, right of assembly or written laws, and foreign publications are censored. Arbitrary arrests take place in all of them, women are discriminated against and the citizenship of dissidents is revoked without a due process of law. Despite this, and because the formation of the GCC amounts to another divisive move, Bush, Thatcher, Major, Hurd, Christopher and leaders of the French government have spoken of this entity as 'a stabilizing factor in the region'. Even taking steps backwards, as when the dissolution of parliament by Kuwait and Bahrain led to the reimposition of absolute rule, went unopposed.

Nineteen seventy-nine produced serious signs of discontent with the combined political-economic controls of the Middle East regimes beholden to the West. The non-Arab Shah was overthrown by Khomeini and replaced by a militant Islamic regime opposed to the phoney Westernization of Iran. And in Saudi Arabia there was an abortive rebellion by Islamic extremists who, above all, wanted to end their country's dependence on the West. The Mosque Rebellion in Mecca failed and sixty-one rebels were executed publicly, but instead of leading to changes aimed at intercepting what caused the turmoil, these two developments were used by the House of Saud to justify strengthening the old political reliance on the West.

What emerged was tantamount to Saudi Arabia running OPEC while the US ran Saudi Arabia. To compensate for the temporary absence of Iranian oil, the Saudis increased their production from seven to ten million barrels a day and again sold it for less than the going market price. According to Pierre Terrezian, this cost the Saudis $23 billion.[18] Saudi production capacity kept other producers in line. Even later, Saudi Arabia went on overproducing to keep the price down and Yamani told NBC News in 1981, 'We engineered the surplus.'

From 1981 to 1983 the battle was rekindled between the Saudi advocates of low prices and the Iranian camp, who clamoured for the opposite. A war had broken out between Iran and Iraq, and Saudi Arabia, acting with the approval of the United States, supported Iraq and pumped more oil to finance the Iraqi war effort and keep the price down. In the background, the CIA, World Bank and OECD, among others, predicted further increases in the price of oil. The prospect of a price increase damaging to the economies of the West was taken so seriously that US energy tsar James Schlesinger and others threatened direct military intervention to maintain its flow at a reasonable price.[19]

The predicted oil shortage and price increase never came. Conservation measures, North Sea oil, the emergence of small producers and moves towards natural gas produced an oil glut which led to a price collapse in 1985. The price of oil plummeted to $9 per barrel and the US, concerned that this might put its high-cost domestic oil producers out of business, sent Vice-President George Bush to Saudi Arabia to plead with King Fahd to reduce production and raise prices. Fahd did what America wanted. This was the third phase of the political use of Middle East oil, a reverse shock which led the Saudis to protect Western oil, and in some ways that is what is with us today.

The glut and resulting decline in price was the work of Yamani, who had been fired by King Fahd in 1984. The reasons for Yamani's dismissal, in all likelihood a personality clash, will probably remain secret for ever, but more importantly his departure had no bearing on Saudi Arabia's oil policy. The country has continued to balance its level of production ever since to keep the price of oil at $16–$18 a barrel – lower in real terms than what it was in 1973.

Since the mid-1980s OPEC has ceased to matter. Whatever the Saudis say goes, except for occasional overproduction by other pro-West countries, which also leads to lower prices and helps Western interests. It was one of these occasions, a US-inspired decision by Kuwait to overproduce without needing to, which threatened another price collapse in 1990 and drove needy Iraq to either start or advance its plans to occupy its neighbour.[20]

The Gulf War brought into perspective all the elements of the economic conspiracy governing the production, price and use of oil. The feudal governments of the Gulf funded the whole war effort and increased production to replace that of Iraq. The defeat of Iraq saw Saudi Arabia pick up 90 per cent of its OPEC share.[21] The buyers' market which Yamani engineered in the mid-1980s prevails. Says an expert at the Oxford Energy Centre, 'The price can be increased, but the United States won't let them do it.' Funnily, it is Yamani's Centre for Global Energy Studies which administers the judgement on the policies he started: 'By mid-1996, unless oil producers cut back, the price of oil will collapse once again with serious consequences for the producers.'[22]

The famous oil boom – through the inevitable filtering of benefits to the average citizen – produced an educated class of people in the oil-rich countries, clamouring for change in the political and economic structure. On a long-term basis this is the major result of the boom. The dialogue between producers and consumers to develop lasting policies to govern this strategic commodity ended when things looked brighter for the West, in 1975. There is no substantial petrochemical industry to absorb the shock of low oil prices on the producers and whatever petrochemicals are produced by them are subject to high tariffs in the West in accordance with a determination to continue to control this industry. Conversely, the important creation of the oil boom, the educated Arabs, are determined to change the governments which squandered their oil wealth, made no structural changes to their economies, settled for minimum contributions to the development of the Middle East and continued to follow what the West dictated. They are on the edge of rebellion. Foolish in everything else, perhaps the oil producers also managed to sponsor their own coming downfall. The West-Establishment control of oil is not considerably different from what it was early this century. However, judged by the prospects, failure is on the way.

Heads of state aside, the most famous Arab of our times is arms dealer Adnan Khashoggi (pronounced 'Khashog-ji'). This is one way of judging the importance of the armaments business in the Middle East. Another way is to state that the Arab countries of the Middle East allocate over 8.6 per cent of their national incomes, more than in any other region of the world, to the purchase of military hardware.[23]

Spending tens of billions of dollars on buying arms, like the notoriety of arms dealers, is relatively new, but supplying or denying arms to control the political direction of the Middle East under specific ruling classes is not. It has been with us since the formative arrival of the West after the First World War and it promises to stay with us for the foreseeable future.

Except for Lebanon and brief interregnums in Syria, Egypt and Jordan, the Middle East has been run by various forms of dictatorship for most of this century. Dictators need armies, organized or otherwise, to stay in power, and armies need arms, which, because there are no local armament industries, they buy from outside. Dependence on arms from outside means being beholden to the supplier, for most of this century to a West determined to use this business to further its political plans. This is what prompted Saddam Hussein's lament that, 'No country which relies on importing weapons is completely independent.'[24]

There are three phases to the West's use of its virtual monopoly of arms supplies to determine the political direction of the Middle East. The first started with British sponsorship of the Arab Rebellion of 1915 and lasted until the early 1930s, the post-First World War period, when the West supplied arms to its protégés, to create or run countries, or both. The second period, which included the 1948 Arab-Israeli War, lasted until 1955, when Nasser broke the Western monopoly of this business by buying arms from Czechoslovakia, resulting in the emergence of the communist bloc as an arms supplier in competition with the West. The third period, which exists today, began after Nasser's death. This is when the West re-emerged as the primary arms supplier and used its position to maintain friendly regimes by equipping their armies and to destabilize and diminish unfriendly regimes by denying them arms while often providing them to their opponents. This period has seen the merger of Western governmental and corporate policies to sell huge quantities of arms to recapture much of the oil income of the area.

The key concept governing all three periods is the one that the West employs to justify its political actions: stability. Arms were used to confirm pro-West leaders in power and provide them with the means to control their territories and people. For example, the fabrication called Jordan would be unstable without an army to maintain it. For nearly thirty years this army was officered and equipped by the designers of Jordan, the British. Now, the US equips Jordan's native army for the same reason: to maintain pro-West King Hussein against the wishes of his people.

Providing regimes with military hardware to create stability was followed by the use of arms to further specific political aims, as when the West stopped supplying the Arab armies fighting in Palestine to assure a Jewish victory, or when the West wouldn't sell arms to Nasser, to keep him in check. Nowadays it is a case of supplying or refusing to supply arms depending on the policies of a government, political group or special situation. And, in addition to the need to recycle the oil income, there is the cynicism of corrupting leaders to make them more dependent on their source of commissions, the West.

Not only is King Hussein's army equipped to keep him in power, but Saddam was supplied with arms to fight Iran. In different circumstances, the Kurds were armed to unbalance Saddam. Meanwhile, the leaders of Saudi Arabia have become so accustomed to income from commissions that they wouldn't know how to live without them. Of course, their total dependence on this income is behind the payback: their willingness to follow internal and external policies which fit Western designs.

The first instances of using the supply of weapons to influence the shape of the Middle East occurred during and immediately after the First World War. The British supplied them to King Hussein I, to start the

Arab Rebellion against their Turkish enemies. Some time later, after the British decided that Hussein had outlived his usefulness, they stopped providing him with arms while they supplied the forces of his arch-enemy, Ibn Saud. In both cases British agents used money and weapons to talk both leaders into undertaking military campaigns which suited British political designs.[25]

As with the purely political aspect of what was happening early this century, both supplying and withholding arms were governed by short-term considerations rather than firm policy. Between 1904 and 1911 Captain William Shakespeare supplied the leader of Nejed, Ibn Saud, with money and arms to rise against the Turks and conquer Hasa (the eastern part of modern Saudi Arabia) and fight his rivals, the pro-Turkish Al Rashid family. The relationship with Ibn Saud was suspended when the British directed their attention to backing the more important Hashemite family in western Arabia and began to supply them with more money and arms than they had provided for Ibn Saud.[26] This is when the Hashemite chief, King Hussein I, used what Britian gave him to buy the loyalty of tribes which had followed Ibn Saud. This situation ended when the British switched their support back to Ibn Saud, who offered the Bedouins superior guns.

The use of arms helped turn Iraq and Jordan into countries. Having decided to make Faisal I, the third son of Hussein, King of Iraq, the British proceeded to create an Iraqi army and use former Arab officers of the Turkish army to run it. Because the people of Iraq, the Shias in particular, were against the alien monarchy, the British created an army which guaranteed that the country's unity was made up of the minority Sunnis. That is when British arms were used to subdue the mainly Shia rebellion of 1920 and when the tradition started of a Sunni army running a country against the will of its people. How similar to what we have under Saddam Hussein today!

If Iraq was made up of three Turkish *vilayets* (Baghdad, Basra and Mosul) with little popular commitment to Iraq as a nation state, Jordan was an even more untidy fabrication. After deciding to create it, to make a country out of a ghastly desert blank and set it up as a buffer state made up of the Bedouin part of Palestine east of the Jordan, the British made Abdallah, Hussein's second son, its Emir. The population was sparse and Bedouin, and the British hurried to turn them into an army which reported directly to them. The first commander of this army was Colonel F.G. Peake; the second was the legendary Glubb Pasha. With a mercenary Bedouin army paid and officered by them, the British proceeded to use Jordan to further the political aims which were behind its creation.

The initial stage of supplying arms to help pro-West chiefs rise against Turkey, and the subsidiary stage of doing the same thing to create armies to guarantee their survival as British-backed heads of state, were followed by a more serious manifestation of the use of arms to discredit leaders who refused to follow a British line. When Hussein I demanded that the British fulfil their wartime promises to make him leader of all the Arabs at a time when he was no longer needed, the British decided to cut him down to size, then opted to get rid of him.[27]

Ibn Saud, on the sidelines for most of the war, was resurrected after Hussein refused to accept the divisions of the Middle East created by the San Remo conference and to sign a treaty of subsidiarity to Britain in 1921.[28] The British denied arms and money to Hussein and gave them to his enemy, allowing Ibn Saud to use them to conquer Hussein's territory. The inexcusability of turning against an old ally was made more perfidious by the fact that they had restrained Ibn Saud's wish to expand in the past. It was Britain's supply to Ibn Saud of armoured personnel carriers which sealed Hussein's fate. Naturally Ibn Saud repaid the British for their support. After the 1915 treaty, a replica of what Hussein had turned down because it infringed on his independence, he signed in 1927 a second treaty with them two years after his defeat of Hussein. This treaty also ceded the conduct of his new country's foreign affairs to the British.

In 1929, the Ikhwan, the zealous Muslim fighters behind Ibn Saud's military victory and unification of the Arabian Peninsula, rebelled against his closeness with Britain. With his British adviser St John Philby at his side and his armoury replenished with a 'motorized battle fleet',[29] Ibn Saud fought them, defeated them and took no prisoners. The British triumph of arms was followed by an appeal by the few survivors to be allowed refuge in Iraq, but the British wouldn't have it. The Ikhwan leader Faisal Duwaish was handed over to Ibn Saud to die in prison in mysterious circumstances.

In Iraq in the early 1930s something similar but not as threatening took place. King Ghazi, who succeeded his father in 1933, was manifestly anti-British but, flamboyant and always in military uniform, he became very popular with his army. Unable to distance him from the organization which held the country together, the British sought to undermine his power base by inciting the Assyrians and Kurds to armed rebellion in northern Iraq. Both rebel sides were provided with British arms,[30] but to the surprise of the British the Iraqi army proved equal to the occasion and suppressed the rebellions mercilessly.

The Saudi use of British arms to eliminate local opponents and British supply of arms to rebels to undermine an unfriendly government were new examples of how the British intended to use their monopoly of military hardware. However, the Sunni army of Iraq, created as the backbone of the state, used its victory against the British-sponsored rebels to stake its own political claim. In 1936 Iraqi officers led by General Bakr Sidki staged a coup in support of Ghazi. The British-equipped army got out of control.

The British response to the coup was to stop the flow of arms, including spare parts. But the late 1930s saw the emergence of Italy and Germany as an alternative source of military hardware and both governments made offers to supply arms to Baghdad. In 1937, the same anti-British General Bakr Sidki, ignoring the fact that his country's treaty with Britain stipulated buying British arms, was assassinated in the northern city of Mosul while on his way to visit Italy and Germany to negotiate an arms deal. His assassin was never tried, but the pro-West Iraqi government which followed his death returned as a purchaser of British arms.

The man the British reinstated in power following Bakr Sidqi, Nuri Saïd, was an old general who likewise built a power base within the army. He bribed army officers into acquiescing with his policies by promising them modern equipment from Britain. Although this worked for a while, the army rebelled again and the culmination was the 1941 pro-Nazi coup which forced Nuri and pro-British members of the royal family out of the country. Among the aims of the new army officers who staged the coup was the wish to end the British monopoly on military hardware.

The British put down the rebellion in four months by landing troops in Basra and using Jordan's Arab Legion. This was proof that the Arab Legion, equipped, maintained and officered by the British, had little to do with the defence of Jordan, which wasn't threatened by outsiders. The well-equipped Bedouin army was nothing but a surrogate British force ready to implement British policy, something which was to show more clearly and disastrously during the 1948 Arab-Israeli War.

On the eve of the 1948 War, all the Arab armies which mattered, the Egyptians, Iraqis and Jordanians, were British-equipped. The Syrian army, which had come into being three years earlier, was lightly and poorly equipped and trained. The Saudi army was made up of Bedouin irregulars with no more than rifles to their name and in any case Ibn Saud didn't send it to fight in Palestine anyway. Britain, the arms supplier to the Arabs, was in a position to control the effectiveness of the Arab armies through choking off supplies of military hardware and ammunition. That is exactly what Britain did to implement its pro-Jewish plans. According to the noted Egyptian writer Muhammad Heikal, it went as far as 'Giving the Egyptian army *matériel* to enter the war, but not enough to win.'[31]

According to Gamal Abdel Nasser, the Egyptian forces, denied British arms because of an embargo, 'were dashed against solid fortifications unprotected by armour'.[32] The Iraqi and Jordanian armies suffered because 'all British deliveries including ammunition' had stopped[33]. The denial of arms, coupled with direct orders to the commander of the best fighting Arab force, Glubb Pasha, to refrain from entering territory allocated to the Jews by the United Nations,[34] helped determine the results of the 1948 War. The Egyptians went home defeated. The Iraqis, with a solidly pro-British government at the helm, withdrew soon after a cease-fire was declared. And the Jordanians, led by twenty-one British officers who took their orders from London, retained the part of Palestine left to the Arabs by the United Nations: the West Bank.

There was more to the Arab defeat than Britain's withholding of arms and ammunition, and that includes divisions among the leadership and lack of organization, but the British control of the Arab military lifeline mattered considerably. After the 1948 War finding a reliable source of arms became an issue for some Arab governments and all the Arab peoples. Obtaining them, particularly without strings attached and even at the expense of butter, became a magnet for the frustration of the masses. The West knew this and redoubled its efforts to use arms to influence developments in the Middle East.

The three *coups d'état* which took place in Syria between 1949 and 1951 were led by army cliques who sought popularity through pronouncing a desire to modernize the equipment of the Syrian army.[35] In Egypt the press declared war on the government for sending a poorly equipped army to Palestine. Iraqi officers, including the man who eventually overthrew the monarchy in 1958, General Abdel Karim Kassem, began plotting against the government, which accepted the British denial of arms. Only in Jordan was the picture different. There Glubb Pasha turned his well-equipped force into an inward-looking one and used it to subdue, with force, the Palestinians Jordan had acquired through Arab defeat (see Chapter 9).

If arms were initially used to design countries directly or through the collaborationist establishment and later to eliminate opponents and undermine unfriendly regimes, then their use in 1948 amounted to completing the last part of the design which was developed by the West after the First World War: the creation of the state of Israel. However, the perpetrators of this policy and their followers ignored the changes in the international arena and in Arab thinking. Some new governments in the Middle East, born as they were out of opposition to this policy, were determined to free themselves from total dependence on Western military hardware.

It was Nasser who first expressed this wish. In 1955, wanting to buy weapons for his army and ready to pay cash for them, he refused whatever strings the West wanted to attach to supplying him with what he needed. After the lengthy negotiations detailed earlier (see Chapter 2) and which found the West determined to use arms supplies to control or influence Egyptian policy, Nasser, with Russian blessing, struck a deal with a communist Czechoslovakia.

This was more than an arms deal: it was a challenge to Western control of the Middle East. There were threats to attack him, attempts to intercept the deal, offers of replacements and bribes and outright anger. It wasn't only Britain, France and the United States which saw the arms deal as a challenge to their position: the traditional pro-West regimes felt the same. After all, they controlled their countries through reliance on Western arms and the availability of weapons from another source meant that their opponents were able to satisfy the wishes of counterforces and threaten their control.

Syria, forever nationalist and adrift, followed the Egyptian lead in 1956 and 1957. After the 1958 coup which toppled the monarchy, Iraq did the same. The arms deals with the communist bloc signalled a new type of independence, and the armies of these countries became its protectors. The Russians, happy to undermine the Western strategic position in the Middle East, expanded their arms supply contracts and signed economic and friendship treaties. The resulting alliances weren't as binding or limiting as the ones the West required, and the Arab leaders who signed them were not unaware of Russia's selfish interests, but arms determined the picture of the new Middle East.

In the late 1950s and the 60s there was open competition between the communists and the West as to who could best equip their friends. Colonial France reacted to Nasser's support of the Algerian rebellion and peevishly armed Israel against him. Britain sold arms to Jordan and Saudi Arabia. Because of pro-Israeli sentiment in Congress, America was unable to supply sophisticated military hardware to the Arabs but it still encouraged Britain and France towards specific arms deals. Russia poured arms into friendly countries and sought to control them through monopolizing its supply. The Middle East became an arms bazaar.

The supply of armaments played a decisive role in every war, civil war, rebellion, uprising, coup or political conspiracy of the 1960s. It began with the civil war between monarchists and republicans in Yemen, which pitted Soviet arms supplied to Egypt against American arms sold to Saudi Arabia. It was the Saudis' fear that America might cut off their arms supplies that on two occasions moved them to seek a solution to the problem.

Among other interpretations, the 1967 Arab–Israeli War can be seen as a triumph of Western technology over its Russian equivalent and the traditional establishment publicized this fact to undermine Nasser and condemn his reliance on Russia. Between 1961 and 1963 the West armed rebel Kurds to rise against the government of Iraqi strongman Abdel Karim Kassem. In 1963, two days after his overthrow by a regime with friendly ties to the West, the United States provided the new Iraqi government with arms to fight the same Kurds they had armed.[36] Meanwhile the West was busy equipping the inward-looking armies of Saudi Arabia and the Gulf states, armies which these countries used as security forces to keep their people down.

This state of affairs continued until Nasser's death in 1970. With Nasser out of the picture, the traditional regimes were in the ascendant and one of Sadat's major acts in distancing himself from Russia was his ejection in 1972 of the Russian military mission to Egypt. This ended Russia's role as Egypt's chief arms supplier and cancelled its political influence on the country.

Sadat's move signalled a reversion to an exclusive dependence on the West by all the Arab governments except Iraq and Syria, which continued to use Russian military hardware. However, seen in their proper context, these two exceptions are easy to explain. Syria, consistently more militant on the subject of Palestine, which until 1917 was part of it, could find no way free from constraints to purchase Western arms with which to fight the Israelis. There were several occasions when Syria wanted to buy Western arms, particularly from France, but there were implicit or explicit strings attached and Syria found in Russia a less demanding supplier. The political considerations which kept Syria dependent on non-Western suppliers continue to this day.

Iraq is another story. The country's alliance with Russia was always an uneasy one. After a period of cooperation in the late 1960s and early 70s, the Ba'athist regime persecuted the local Communist Party while relying on Russian armaments.[37] This is one of the reasons, despite a friendship treaty between Russia and Iraq signed in 1972, why the Russians in the mid-1970s stopped supplying Iraq and Saddam Hussein with modern weapons. Saddam, feeling hemmed in, started buying arms from a welcoming West which had decided to reclaim Iraq as a Western sphere of influence.

In 1974 Saddam retained the all-Palestinian consulting firm of Arab Projects and Development to help with his civilian and military plans. Although involved in planning railways and land reclamation projects, APD was also asked to study the possibility of Iraq obtaining atomic weapons. They advised Saddam to concentrate on the cheaper and more easily made chemical and biological weapons while continuing to pursue his atomic dream. APD and Saddam took a vital first step in this direction when they managed to repatriate 4612 Arab scientists and engineers capable of mastering unconventional weapons from all over the world. One of the biggest brain steals in history, this afforded Saddam the ability to purchase 'unfinished' plants and assemble them himself.

This was followed by an approach to Russia to buy a plant to manufacture chemical weapons. Companies engaged in such business require government approval, and when the Russians turned him down, Saddam saw it as a betrayal and used his Palestinian advisers to get a chemical warfare plant from the West. His anger with Russia's attempt to keep him under control went further and he decided to buy Western-made military aircraft and helicopters from France and the United Kingdom.

Saddam's decision was timely. The West was looking for ways to prise him loose from Russia's political hold and was in a mood to accommodate him. Selling him arms was the perfect way to achieve Western political goals. After lengthy negotiations in 1974–6, the Iraqis bought French-built Mirage 1 aircraft and Gazelle and Lynx helicopters from the British company Westland.

Buying a plant to manufacture chemical weapons proved more difficult. Recognizing the plant for what it was, British, French and German multinationals turned the request down, not because their governments objected to it, but on moral grounds or because they couldn't meet the Iraqi delivery schedule. (For example, ICI and Babcock Wilcox refused to be involved.)

It was an American company, Pfaulder Corporation of Rochester, New York, which in 1975 supplied the Iraqis with a blueprint which enabled them to build their first chemical warfare plant.[38] With this in hand, Saddam used the repatriated scientists and engineers to buy the components for the plant piecemeal from different countries and assembled it himself. The site of Saddam's first chemical warfare plant was at Akhashat in north-western Iraq, and the cost was $38 million for the plant and $40 million for safety equipment.

The purchase of the Mirage F1s, Westland helicopters and chemical warfare plant was followed by other efforts to supply Saddam with military and intelligence hardware to maintain his independence from Russia. The most telling sale, one of greater political than commercial significance, was that of a complete mobile telephone system to be used by the Ba'ath Party faithful to protect the regime against any attempts to overthrow it. This sale, and mobile telephone systems were mainly in the military domain at the time, was made by the Karkar Corporation of San Francisco with the full knowledge and the requisite approval of the United States government.

By 1979 Saddam's arms purchases in the West had produced the desired results for himself and for his suppliers. Russia, afraid of losing him altogether, changed direction and replenished his armoury. And the West continued to try to drive a wedge between Iraq and Russia at a time when Saddam was waging a war against the Kurds, suppressing his country's Shia majority. In a way, Saddam managed to reverse the traditional situation: instead of suppliers dictating policy, the purchaser was determining the policy of the suppliers in return for political benefits.

But there were voices in the West beginning to question the soundness of this policy. The Carter administration in particular began showing signs of unease and some Iraqi requests, including one for helicopters, were turned down. But any change in policy was forestalled by an event which overwhelmed everything in its way. The Shah's overthrow by Khomeini and the subsequent Iranian threat to the security of Iraq led to the start of the Iran-Iraq War in 1979 and the decision to continue to supply Saddam.

Seeing Khomeini as a more serious threat to its position in the Middle East, the West decided that secular Iraq was the only country capable of stopping the march of his Islamic movement and opted to continue to back Saddam. According to Alan Friedman, author of *Spider's Web*, it included the supply to Iraq of satellite pictures of Iranian positions under the direction of the CIA's William Casey.[39] This was the second phase of accommodating Saddam. The two phases lasted until the end of the Iran-Iraq War in 1989 and throughout this period there was no official Western effort to deny Saddam the arms he needed or wanted. It even included an American offer to supply Iraq with Harpoon missiles with which to attack shipping and other targets in 1983, when the tide of battle was running against the Iraqis.

I myself was approached by a major American arms dealer who, after describing the French-made Exocet missile the Iraqis were using as 'an ancient weapon', advised me that the US would view with favour the supply of the more sophisticated and lethal Harpoon. At the time the Harpoon was the most advanced missile in America's arsenal and some US army units trained in its use still hadn't received it. The Iraqis' response was positive and I set off for Washington with an authorization to buy $230 million worth of Harpoons. However, by the time I arrived, the fortunes of war had turned in Iraq's favour – they had stopped the Iranian advance – and the United States had withdrawn its offer.

The two-decade green light, along with the presence in his country of competent scientists and engineers, gave Saddam time to conduct one of the biggest armaments-buying sprees in history and a chance to develop his own armaments industry. This explains much of what we hear about today: the existence in Iraq of one of the most extensive armaments programmes in the history of the Middle East and indeed the world.

During the war with Iran, Saddam set up buying offices throughout the West, such as Matrix Churchill and other corporations, whose aim was to acquire Western technology. The French, British and American governments did everything to guarantee an Iraqi victory. The French provision of arms was open and it went as far as providing the Iraqis with extended-range Super Etendard aircraft capable of hitting Iranian oil facilities in the lower Gulf. The British support was more complex, and the rules governing the proclaimed neutrality between the two combatants were bent every step of the way. For example, Plessey Electronics supplied Saddam with an electronic command centre while Prime Minister Thatcher was hiding behind the convenient constraint of not supplying either side with 'lethal weapons'. The United States stayed in the background unless there was a real threat that the Iranians might break through the Iraqi lines and defeat Saddam. As already mentioned, in 1983 I carried an American message to Saddam's government expressing an American willingness to supply Saddam with the ultra-modern Harpoon missile to stem the Iranian advance towards Basra and the southern part of Iraq.[40]

There were hundreds of small and big deals. The Western policies governing them always amounted to 'we'll find a way to do it'. There were two conspicuous methods. First, whenever the declared policies of the Western countries stood in the way of an arms deal, Western governments agreed to supply Saddam through the pro-West countries of Jordan and Egypt, which also agreed to act as a front for Iraq to please the West and Saddam and to oppose Khomeini. Using friendly third parties overcame all Congressional, parliamentary and press hurdles, even when it was obvious to military experts that Jordan and Egypt had no use for the weapons in question. The second way the West helped Saddam was through extending massive credits to him to buy all the arms he needed.

The Banco di Lavoro in America gave Saddam $4 billion worth of credits, ostensibly to buy food, which he rechannelled to buy arms; he bartered the American-supplied food for the same purpose. Britain's Export Credit Guarantee department kept increasing his credit and much of the money went to the direct purchase of arms. The French government guaranteed $6 billion worth of loans to French arms makers to sell Saddam whatever he wanted.

It was the weight and quality of Western arms and the West's financial support of Saddam which forced Iran to sue for peace, and Saddam emerged from the conflict with the trappings of victory. By the time the war with Iran ended Saddam had a standing, battle-tried army of over one million men, one of the best-equipped in the world. Moreover, he was well on his way to mastering unconventional weapons. His armaments purchasing offices, particularly the British company Matrix Churchill, had managed to buy more chemical plants, biological weapons plants and nuclear reactors and the mechanisms (triggers etc.) to convert them for the production of an atomic bomb.

The end of the war with Iran was the end of the extended honeymoon between the West and Saddam. With Iran humiliated and its danger reduced, the West, acting on what it knew about the Iraqi regime, cut off Saddam's armaments supplies and began demanding repayment of loans and exposing the evil nature of its client. The adopted child became a source of embarrassment, but the sudden change in attitude was difficult to sell to the Western public, which had followed its governments and accepted him as a friend. Saddam's response was to refuse to demobilize his army and, unable to provide the Iraqi people with the fruits of his victory against Iran, to threaten to use it. Israel was the natural enemy and making war on Israel would have made him extremely popular with the Arab masses, but whatever would have resulted wouldn't have solved his economic problems. Suddenly, Kuwait, forever the object of Iraqi claims and hate, gave him an excuse. By pumping more oil than it needed, it sent the price of this commodity down and endangered Saddam's position within his country. On 2 August 1990 Saddam hit back.

What followed is too well known to recount. Yet it is important to recall that the Iraqi claim to Kuwait is an historical one to which every single Iraqi regime has subscribed and that Kuwait had agreed to federate with Iraq as recently as 1962.[41] Moreover, there is evidence that, conniving with the CIA, Kuwait produced oil beyond its OPEC quota and financial needs.[42] This lowered oil prices, threatened Iraqi economic stability and Saddam's survival. Even after the Iraqi invasion of Kuwait the picture remained suspicious.

On 3 September 1990, a month after the Iraqi aggression commenced, *Newsweek* wrote that George Bush approved a CIA plan to overthrow Saddam, at a time when Bush was telling us that his sole aim was the ejection of Iraq from Kuwait. On 22 August 1990 the *New York Times* detailed how the US government was trying to block diplomatic solutions to the conflict. And on 5 March 1991 Michael Emery of the *Village Voice* showed that Iraq was willing to withdraw from Kuwait and that the US was in the business of avoiding a peaceful solution. But, despite their discoveries, both the *New York Times* and *Newsweek* supported war against

Saddam and very few people paid attention to what the *Village Voice* was saying. In the UK press, there were no dissenting voices. In fact, Britain's overall term of reference was totally colonial and many newspapers and pundits couldn't do better than recall that Iraq was a British creation, nothing more than a naughty child who had forgotten his upbringing and deserved to be punished.

What needs reiterating is the simple fact that it was Western arms and financial support which made Saddam. This was the most flagrant example of the policies of convenience which the West has followed since 1917. But, in essence, it is no different from the rest of them. Though the phrase has been touted by Western leaders for decades, there isn't a single case of arms supplies to Arab regimes subscribing to the notion of 'legitimate needs'. It has always been a case of arming people to follow certain policies or achieve certain aims in which legitimate needs didn't figure, and, as we will see from what followed, it was also a case of selling arms to continue to maintain regimes, corrupt them and make them more dependent on the West, as well as to make money. Iraq and its invasion of Kuwait was a case of the client going it alone without consideration of the supplier's reaction; in essence, it resembles the Israeli use of cluster bombs against innocent civilians despite restrictions included in the supply agreement by the United States.

Beyond opening the door for the West to use arms to convert to its own ways Middle East governments which had depended on Russia, the death of Nasser in 1970 had profound consequences on Arab governments already dependent on the West and, once again, on the West's ability to use arms to manipulate the outcome of local conflicts. Nasser had successfully propagandized against the oil-rich countries squandering their wealth in foolish ways and his absence freed the pro-West governments from this indirect constraint. And Nasser's absence coincided with the first oil shock, the 1973 massive increase in their income and the West's desire to sell them more arms to recycle their huge surpluses.

The 1970s were the age of the intermediary and the time when corporate greed and the attitude of the Western governments merged. The intermediary, fixer, commission agent, go-between, power broker, middleman is nothing more than a person who can help a foreign corporation obtain business through his or her connections with people in power. The person in power with whom the intermediary works is the 'skimmer' or 'intermedler', the person who decides what should be purchased, awards the contracts and obtains a hefty share of the intermediary's commission, sometimes a greater share than that of the intermediary. Because of their size and the commissions they generate, arms deals are ideal intermediary territory.

As stated before, the most famous intermediary of our time is the Saudi arms dealer Adnan Khashoggi. His importance is the result of the size of his business and his close connection with skimmer Prince Sultan bin Abdel Aziz, the Saudi Minister of Defence and second in line to the Saudi throne. In the 1970s Khashoggi represented the American Lockheed, Grumman, Northrop and Raytheon corporations, among others.

A typical Khashoggi-type deal would start with him convincing the Saudi royals of the need for military hardware made by a corporation which he represented or which was willing to work with him on a commission basis. This could start as an attempt to face a particular problem (to support the royalist Yemenis in mountainous terrain), replace obsolete military hardware (old tanks) or upgrade the equipment used by a branch of the armed forces (modern aircraft). Importantly, it could be an expression of a broader policy, an armaments programme aimed at equipping Saudi Arabia to face a real or imagined or even fabricated external threat in the Gulf.

After obtaining the consent of a purchaser, let's say Saudi Arabia, Khashoggi or another arms dealer would turn to organizing the commission payments with the company. Payments can be made in several direct or indirect ways. There are straight payments where the intermediary is described as an agent or a consultant and gets a small percentage of the value of the contract; payments are realized through awarding subcontracts to local Saudi companies which charge more than the business justifies and in which the agent or his mentor has an interest; and there is the bartering of oil for arms in a way which either overstates the value of the arms or understates the value of the oil to create a 'commission margin'. The combination of these three ways of realizing commissions produces huge sums of money. In the 1970s Khashoggi's straight commission from Northrop yielded $100 million and his commission from Lockheed topped that with $106 million.

The unknown in the Khashoggi-type formula is how much of this money goes to the skimmer. Although accusations have often been levelled at Khashoggi, he has always insisted that he makes no payments to higher-ups. But he has not denied the existence of royal patronage, nor has he distanced himself from allegations that he has maintained connections with highly placed US officials whose positions might help him with his business.[43] In fact, there is ample record of how connections with important people on the supplier side work. CIA Middle East Chief James Critchfield kept Khashoggi apprised of agency attitudes, CIA super-agent Kim Roosevelt set him up with Northrop Corporation and Nixon adviser Bebe Rebozzo acted as a go-between with the President.

The question here is why the United States didn't sell arms to Saudi Arabia without the intercession of a middle man. Armaments procurement orders which genuinely reflect the overused phrase 'legitimate needs of a friendly country' should not need an intermediary. The answer is twofold: the intermediary, because of vested interest, increases the size of contracts and the money resulting from the transaction goes to people the West uses for other purposes and wants to please. In other words, the deals have nothing to do with anything that might qualify as legitimate needs: the purpose is to sell more arms and to corrupt leaders who do the West's bidding.

The legitimate needs of Saudi Arabia should mean arming against Israel, a country with which it still maintains a state of war. But US arms sales to the country openly guard against American arms being used against Israel and the McDonnell Douglas F-15 aircraft supplied to the Saudis are of reduced range so as not to reach Israeli targets. Still, because Western governments continue to see a need to justify the size of the deals and the nature of the equipment sold, they go into the business of producing phoney dangers. For example, there is a Western insistence that Iran's purchase of $4 billion worth of Chinese arms with questionable electronic guidance systems poses a threat to Saudi Arabia. The size of the deal is condemned at a time when Saudi Arabia has $30 billion worth of military contracts outstanding with Britain and the United States and when Iran is manifestly looking inwards and wishes to avoid any problems or confrontation with the Saudis.

The phoniness of arming the Saudis and the Gulf states to deter would-be aggressors is exposed by two other factors. The security of these countries has been guaranteed by the West and the Gulf War has demonstrated that the sizes of these countries' populations and armed forces, and their obvious inability to use the arms they then had, renders them unable to resist invasion. And, according to Anthony Cordesman, a leading authority on the subject of Gulf armaments, there has been little effort to coordinate arms purchases and integrate the armed forces of these countries towards greater effectiveness.[44] In other words, the arms purchased would be almost useless if used against the people of these countries, or would at best provide a defending Western force with supporting troops.

To continue to use Saudi Arabia as an example of wasteful arms purchases, it can safely be stated that even before Saddam's invasion of Kuwait the latter had more arms than its small armed forces of 30,000 could use or master. After the Gulf War the situation got completely out of hand. An unprecedented shopping spree included contracts to buy Patriot Missiles; F-15s; laser bombs; a Hughes Aircraft aerial-defence system; Canadian Halifax frigates, French Hélec torpedo boats; British Tornado aircraft; and helicopters and boats from British Aerospace, Westland Helicopters and Vospers Thorneycroft boats. In the first six months of 1992 alone Saudi Arabia signed $17 billion worth of military hardware contracts and this is why, according to London's International Institute of Strategic Studies, the cost to maintain a Saudi soldier is five times the cost of maintaining an American soldier, not to speak of the lower costs of the British, French and German armies.

The House of Saud, Kuwait, Qatar, Oman and the Emirates share this position of pretending that they are buying arms to protect themselves. They continue to try to conceal their total, and to their people unacceptable, dependence on the West for the same protection which arms purchases are supposed to provide. Meanwhile every single deal carries a commission which goes into the pockets of intermediaries and their important pro-West sponsors.

The commissions realized by influential princes, sheikhs and generals amount to billions of dollars. This corrupt group decides what is needed and the quantities, attaches commissions to them and signs the orders. What is needed becomes what carries the highest commission, usually unique products available only from one source and not necessarily what is best to defend the country. On the other side, the West is happy with a policy which maintains its defence industry and which calls for these countries to pay for Western protection twice (the Gulf War cost Saudi Arabia $65 billion). The bond of the leaders who make commissions to the West is written in gold and in return they use their Western-equipped armies selectively, to perpetuate the pro-West policies of their countries. Minister of Defence Prince Sultan of Saudi Arabia is the man the world's press accuses of being one of the biggest skimmers in history, and, almost axiomatically, he is also the most pro-West member of a family which follows the West blindly.

Instead of the original use of arms to help leaders create and maintain states, the present sale of arms to Gulf rulers is aimed at buying their loyalty. The end result is to waste countries' wealth, impoverish the people and, instead of securing stability, create instability. Despite a precipitous decline in the Saudi annual per capita income in the past fifteen years, there are no signs that this policy is about to change. Nowadays the armaments business and cheap oil are the two ways of paying for Western protection against 'external and internal threats'. Because the money from both belongs to the people, these can be construed as direct acts against them, and this interpretation is supported by constant Western references to internal threats.

Beyond selling arms to make money and corrupt and control leaders, the West continues to use its monopoly of the trade to arm people who use them to destabilize unfriendly regimes and to further some divisive policies. The outstanding examples of this are the Kurds of Iraq and the Maronites in Lebanon. The supply of the Kurds has to do with undermining the central government of Iraq when it is unfriendly, and the supply of the Maronites with maintaining their control over Lebanon.

Arming and training of the Maronite Lebanese forces by the CIA is part of perpetuating the rule of a pro-West minority regardless of the feelings of the majority in a country. Lebanon is among the Arab countries where the situation created after the First World War hasn't evolved (see Chapter 6). The original need for Western support to guarantee Maronite predominance, despite a savage thirteen-year civil war, is the same now as when Lebanon was created.

In fact, the Western (CIA) response to the civil war which started in 1975 was to rescue the Maronites by providing them with arms and training.[45] It was analogous to supporting the Iraqi army against Shias and others in the 1920s and to arming Ibn Saud to defeat the Ikhwan. The arms the CIA gave the Maronites were used to attack Muslims, kill thousands of Palestinians and maintain a minority regime. The continuance of the present lopsided state of affairs favouring the Maronites is dependent on Western arms.

Supplying the Kurds with arms is an example of the crude use of a people, not to help them, but to undermine others. In the 1930s and 40s it was the British who intermittently supported the Kurds. From the late 1950s until now the CIA provided the Kurds with arms to rise against the central government of Iraq and always dropped them when that government was changed to Western liking, without much thought to the soundness of its grievances. This happened after the overthrow of Kassem, again in the mid-1970s, when relations with Saddam Hussein improved, and it is likely to happen if Saddam is replaced by a pro-West regime – even a cruel one which won't grant the Kurds any rights. During the Iran-Iraq War the Iraqi use of chemical weapons against the town of Halabja and the ensuing death of five thousand Kurds found the United States, then in the business of befriending Saddam, determined to put the blame on the unfriendly Iranians.[46] Since the Gulf War and the drastic change of attitude towards Saddam, the Iraqi Kurds have once again been portrayed as downtrodden people and supplied with arms to fight their central government. Unlike the entrenched Maronites, the Kurds are a disposable commodity to be used and abused in accordance with policies which have little to do with their national quest.

Arms kill. For over seventy years the West has used its position as the primary arms supplier to the Middle East to provide its deputy sherifs with the ability to kill their enemies. They have used this ability to create phoney states, to maintain them against popular forces, to enforce Western designs to divide Palestine, to pressure unfriendly regimes into cooperating with them, to make money and corrupt leaders, who become more dependent on them, and to sponsor minorities to stay in power and uprisings against unfriendly regimes or groups. Recently, because of widespread popular unrest in most pro-West Arab countries, there has been a marked increase in the West's supply of electronic gear for the security forces of these countries' unpopular regimes. The use of Western-made equipment in the Middle East to exercise power on its fate, though the type of equipment changes, shows no sign of abating. Even with the oil-producing countries of the region short of funds and suffering from economic crises, the direct correlation between the West's insistence on perpetuating this policy and the economic welfare of the people has become obvious. Because all the Western-armed regimes are minority ones without a popular base and because Islamic forces have assumed the mantle of political opposition, the coming confrontation in the Middle East is between Western arms and the sword of Islam.

4 · Coups For Sale

Coups d'état are a natural result of the inadequacy of the flawed minority regimes that the West established in the Arab Middle East after the First World War. There have been dozens of them and most of the Arab regimes of the 1990s are the direct or indirect descendants of military coups.

By the 1930s, because the colonial powers continued to ignore the average Arab and to support individuals, cliques and social élites, and created armies to maintain them, most Arab countries still lacked national cohesion and mature political movements. The dictatorships which followed and which ran the Arab Middle East showed no interest in broadening their narrow base of support or building state institutions, and their loyalties were to their creators-protectors.

As has happened throughout history, the armies that these governments created to protect themselves grew into a new force capable of exclusive assumption of power. Awareness of this prompted some pro-West rulers and ruling groups to reinforce their positions by securing, through various means, the support of their armies and sometimes sharing power with them. But more often the armies surfaced as a source of power on their own, became competitors of the deputy sherifs of the West and tried to wrest power from their hands. The armies' ability to compete with the original rulers was facilitated by the new higher level of education among Arabs and consequent increase in their determination to change the regimes imposed on them by the West after the Great War. There was a natural affinity between the armies and the people. An army capable of replacing an unpopular regime was more likely to respond to popular pressure calling for total change and, in turn, this encouraged its officership not to form alliances with the unpopular existing governments. The need for change became an impetus for change and the justification for change was the existence of an alternative.

This created a classic revolutionary atmosphere which threatened the system of indirect control developed by the West. But, aware that saving some traditional regimes from military interference was impossible, on many occasions the West was forced to try to use the military instead of opposing them. In most countries army officers inclined to cooperate with the West were found and this led to the creation of a new élite class, the clusters of army officers who were willing to be used to deter democracy and forestall the development of state structure in the manner of the old pro-West groups. After all, it wasn't ideology which bound the West to the rulers they created in the 1920s; it was their willingness to follow pro-West policies.

Conditions for army-led change were different from country to country. In Iraq, the army was created in 1921 to hold the country together. Initially officered by pro-British monarchists, it was the most cohesive force in the ethnically and religiously divided country and the non-acceptance of the monarchy and the Turkish-trained army officers behind it ensured that the army's eventual indirect or direct assumption of power was predictable, in a way inevitable. In Syria there was no army until the French granted the country independence in 1945. In 1949 the military wasted no time in overthrowing the government of the bourgeoisie which had followed the French. Egypt's army, though showing repeated signs of unease over the country's political direction in the 1930s and 40s, didn't enter politics openly until the Nasser coup of 1952, after British control of Egypt was loosened enough for the army to respond to the grievances of the people instead of following the orders of the pro-British monarchy. Because it was under direct British control until 1956, the Jordanian army's initial entry into politics took the form of an attempt by its Arab officers to remove their British superiors. And Saudi Arabia's army made its several unsuccessful attempts to overthrow the country's monarchy in the 1960s, after it became an organized, modern force and stopped being a collection of Bedouin irregulars who didn't subscribe to the most elementary command structure. In this case the army tried to act when the royal family's absolute ways led it to adopt unpopular policies and precluded accepting the army as a potential partner.

Although conditions were different in each country the reasons behind the armies' entry into politics were structural in a way which applied to all the Arab countries of the Middle East. The armies' political moves were anchored in a belief that they were entitled to run their countries. Either they were involved through obeying orders to maintain the status quo and this made them willing partners, or they responded to the people's dissatisfaction with the monopoly of power exercised by pro-West individuals, minorities or other ruling élites. In Jordan, Syria and Saudi Arabia the armies were the only organized group capable of changing the governments. In Iraq and Egypt there were other forces, political parties and occasionally functioning parliaments, but the armies were stronger and more capable of acting. Moreover, in all countries the armies were not only modernized in terms of their organization and training, but were perceived by most people as an expression of modernism and advancement and as such more capable of bringing an end to what the West had created or left behind.

The immediate motives behind every coup and attempted coup also differed, but they too had a common thread in the overall non-acceptance of the existing regimes. The 1936 Bakr Sidqi coup in Iraq, the first army-led movement to change a government in the modern history of the Middle East, was a rising of a new officer group against the old pro-British ones which had run the government in the name of the monarchy. The same reason lay behind the 1940–1 Iraqi coup led by Salluheddine Sabbagh, the one which produced an odd short-lived alliance with Germany and Italy. The 1949 Husni Zaim coup in Syria and the ones which followed it reflected an attempt by army officers to replace an abusive landowning and merchant ruling class and to elevate themselves to leadership status. Initially the 1952 Nasser coup in Egypt was a move by the most effective force in the country to stop the state from disintegrating and descending into a state of chaos. The 1958 Iraqi coup led by General Abdel Karim Kassem was an uprising against the unpopular, alien, Western-created monarchy and the select groups who supported it. Most of the Syrian coups of the late 1960s were sectarian in nature, aimed at placing the country under the dominance of the minority Alawi sect whose poor and disenfranchised members represented a popular revolt against the élite class.

But, even when there were immediate 'local' motives behind coups and unsuccessful coup attempts, when acting against established regimes the army officers and their supporters justified themselves by resorting to broader appeals acceptable to the majority of their people. Invariably, the communiqués announcing a coup spoke of the need to save the country in question from the tyranny of an abusive minority, the wish to strengthen the army to fight Israel and to protect the country against foreign dominance and interference, and the army officers presented themselves as the expression of a popular Arab will and the natural vehicle for change. Put together, the communiqués pointed out the unacceptability of the existing governments judged by Arab concerns and claimed that the army was better equipped to tackle the problems facing these countries. Because the popular declared aims were more Arab than, for example, Syrian or Iraqi, they represented a direct rejection of what the West had created and the people they installed in power.

The dichotomy between the declared Arab concerns and the narrower, often concealed and more real local ones behind a coup were either reconciled or led to new divisions within the army and further coups. More than anyone else it was Nasser who successfully merged the dual concerns of the internal problems of Egypt and the country's Arab position. Conversely, Bakr Sidqi's coup was undone when its purely Iraqi inclinations were discovered and the rest of the Iraqi army decided that the Bakr group was ignoring Arab problems, particularly that of Palestine. Husni Zaim was overthrown in a mere five months because he was exposed as a self-aggrandizing fool incapable of following his declared Arab aims of strengthening the army to fight Israel and start moves towards uniting with other Arab countries. His successors thought they could do better. And although sectarianism underpins the continuance of Syria's President Assad in office, his total adherence to pan-Arab policies and an anti-Israeli programme have overcome the local sectarianism factor as a source of weakness for his regime. In other words, Arab concerns always came before local ones and high among them was the wish to achieve an Arab union or unity of purpose and to fight Israel. Because the West was opposed to these two demands, the coups were either anti-West or had to pretend to be.

The communiqués which called for a response to the wish of the people to increase the competence of the armies, to form Arab unions or foster ties with other Arab countries, to prepare to fight Israel and to rid the countries of foreign influence amounted to declarations that the overthrown Western-sponsored regimes had failed to deliver what the people wanted. In fact, the wordings of army communiqués justifying any takeover of a government or direct interference in politics took the primacy of Arab considerations so much for granted that they amounted to an attempt to render null and void the nation states created after the First World War. Iraq and Syria, as countries created by the West, were paid less attention by their armies than the pan-Arab ideals of Hussein I. And even palace coups, the ones aimed at strengthening the hand of people already in power or at opening the door for army-led change, resorted to pretending to create new situations which incorporated all the elements inherent in all open anti-ruling establishment coups. Palace coups were no more than attempts to intercept the armies' desires to go it alone, an act of pre-emption using the same excuses.

If the ostensibly anti-Western and anti-establishment Arab nature of most coups is what made them acceptable to the people, then the eventual failure of some of the governments which followed resulted from the discovery that their claims were phoney or because their leaders changed direction and accepted Western hegemony instead of fulfilling their promises to oppose it. But were they and their leaders anti-Western from the start or was it a case of armies forestalling genuine anti-Western popular change by replacing a special interest civilian ruling minority by a military one? Perhaps they came about for no other reason than the discovery by the West that it is safer to use any army to create new leaders than to use it to support old discredited ones, while continuing to work towards the same indirect control of the Arab Middle East.

According to the historian Eliezer Be'er, there have been thirty-five coups and coup attempts in the countries under discussion during the past forty-five years,[1] and this does not include the pro-establishment ones manipulated by people like Nuri Saïd and King Hussein. However, only one of the successful ostensibly anti-establishment army coups came into being without Western involvement: the 1958 bloody coup which toppled the Iraqi monarchy. The rest of them were either Western-instigated, had indirect Western backing, expected Western support after the assumption of power or were the work of civilian manipulators who counted on or were capable of generating Western acceptance. And the nature of the connection with the West, how it was interpreted by the army officers and the West, was a determining factor in whether the army regimes which followed coups continued to receive Western support, were opposed or neutralized, and it also determined the consequent relationship between the army officers and the people of their country.

Nasser got CIA support for his 1952 coup because the Americans didn't want to see Egypt disintegrate. The CIA helped Husni Zaim take over Syria from a weak nationalist government because the agency thought it stood a better chance of controlling and manipulating him than of trying the same with a regime of the people. The man who overthrew Zaim, Colonel Sami Hinnawi, had British backing because he advocated a British policy aimed at uniting Syria with Iraq and creating a British-controlled regime in both countries. The Kassem regime which overthrew the Iraqi monarchy in 1958 was tolerated by the West until he depended on the local Communist Party for popular support, tilted towards Russia and threatened to invade Kuwait. This led the CIA to conspire with the Ba'ath Party and the Iraqi army to remove Kassem from power. Even Assad's 1970 coup had Western acceptance behind it because his rival, Salah Jedid, wanted to help the Palestinians' Black September confrontation with King Hussein and Assad did not. And the rest were no different.

Of course, not a single leader of any of these coups admitted direct or indirect Western involvement. Nor did the West claim responsibility for, or admit connivance in, any of them. In fact, in seeking popular support, the leaders of the coups hid behind the usual denunciations of Western influence and often the West helped them by pretending that the coup was aimed against it. By fostering this pretence, both the army officers and the West were admitting the existence of an anti-West feeling on street level, that the ordinary Arab opposed Western dominance, the policies it produced and the system of deputy sherifs. With this in mind, the results of many army coups can be seen as an attempt to replace the open connection of the traditional establishment to the West with an equally unsound, secret and very complex one between the West and an army élite. Western policy was concerned with producing the same results regardless of the nature of the West's relationship with the governing group.

There were other reasons to hide Western involvement beyond the wish to disguise the actions of small, undemocratic army groups with the same characteristics as the people they replaced. When Nasser overthrew King Farouk, the United States did not want to appear to be acting against a pro-West monarchy. This would have prompted other monarchies, including Saudi Arabia, to stop relying on America's ephemeral support and would have encouraged those countries' army officers to emulate Nasser. The American support for Colonel Adib Shaishakly, the man who overthrew the Hinnawi government of Syria in October 1949, had to be disguised because the CIA and Shaishakly were trying to keep Syria from uniting with Iraq, an idea which had considerable support among the Syrian people. Admitting that the CIA was behind the Ba'ath Party (and Saddam Hussein) in their successful effort to topple General Kassem in 1963 would have led to the coup's failure, and this made the United States pretend that it was opposed to coups in principle. Long before that, the British government supported Nuri Saïd's use of the Iraqi army to perpetuate its indirect control of Iraq, often in moves which were no more than disguised coups. To justify his actions, Nuri pretended that he represented Arab aspirations more than his opponents. Between 1939 and 1942 this claim was invoked four times, and when the truth was the exact opposite: the people undone by Nuri were more committed to Araby than he was. The British feigned innocence, in these and the more important previous happening which amounted to a coup, the 1939 murder of King Ghazi.

Most of the British use of armies was in support of the traditional élite and most efforts to elevate army officers to a ruling class were relatively new and largely American. Not only did the emergence of organized armies claiming to reflect a popular wish to change things coincide with an ostensible end to colonialism and America's assumption of dominant power in the Middle East, but the British and French were more inclined towards kings, sheikhs and landowners and subordinated their use of the armies to this inclination. Also, America's acceptance of army officers had a great deal to do with the armies' claim to modernity. Naked colonialism was un-American and relying on absolute rulers, despite the obvious commitment to Saudi Arabia, went and still goes against the grain. Meanwhile the claim to modernity created a natural attachment by the armies to American ways and made the officers seek American rather than other Western help.

Judged by its far-reaching and lasting consequences, one of the most neglected episodes in the modern history of the Middle East was the death of King Ghazi of Iraq. He was the son of King Faisal I, the first king of Iraq, who assumed his position with British backing in 1921. Ghazi became king on his father's death in 1933 at the age of twenty-one and died on 4 April 1939 at twenty-seven. The official story promoted by the British and Iraqi governments claimed that Ghazi died in a car accident, but the evidence is overwhelmingly against this. Ghazi was murdered by the pro-British élite which governed Iraq and which he opposed, perhaps with direct British participation or knowledge. Because it produced a major change in Iraq's political orientation, Ghazi's murder was a coup, a serious one.

Although it took nearly twenty years for the monarchy to be overthrown and for an Iraqi republic to be established, it was Ghazi's death which sealed its fate. The reason for this was simple: after his untimely death the Iraqi people started to believe that the British and their supporters, in particular Nuri Saïd, would never tolerate any king except one who followed British designs. Given the choice of a pro-British monarchy or none at all, the people opted to get rid of it.

Ghazi was the grandson of Hussein I of the Hijaz, the man abandoned by the British after he insisted that they fulfil their wartime promises to the Arabs. Indeed Ghazi was born in Mecca in 1912 and lived in that city long enough to see the humiliation administered to his grandfather when the British switched their support to the more manageable Ibn Saud. What happened to his grandfather was a humiliation of the noble House of Hashem which young Ghazi never forgot or forgave. And his anti-British feelings flourished after his father was made King of Iraq in 1921 and he was sent to Harrow in 1928. His one-year stay at the public school and a brief stint at Sandhurst were not to his liking; he didn't mix well with Britons and his less than impressive academic performance frustrated him and elevated his anti-British feeling to neurosis.

Indeed there was something odd about the diminutive Iraqi crown prince of the late 1920s and early 30s. His eventual graduation from the military college in Baghdad revealed a distinct lack of literary resources, but he had a mechanical aptitude, became a daredevil pilot and a sports car enthusiast and endeared himself to a whole class of young army officers. Nevertheless, he continued to live in the shadow of his celebrated father until 1932, when Faisal left Iraq for a lengthy visit to Europe and entrusted the running of the country during his absence to his crown prince.

Suddenly there was a rebellion by pro-British Assyrian Christians of northern Iraq against the central government. Historians are agreed that the British were behind it,[2] but there are differences of opinion as to whether the British were trying to weaken the monarchy as a whole, because it was demanding more concessions from them, or merely undermining the young crown prince, whose anti-British feelings were well known.

What is also of established historical record, beyond British support for the Assyrians, is how Ghazi reacted to the rebellion. Refusing to negotiate with the rebels or consider any of their demands, he unleashed the Iraqi army and air force against them. Whatever the British had in mind backfired. Instead of weakening the monarchy or the crown prince or both and making Iraq more dependent on them, the defeat of the Assyrians enhanced the credentials of the young royal with all sections of the Iraqi people except those totally beholden to Britain. In fact, he assumed the status of a national idol and from then on he was seldom seen except in the uniform of an army or air force officer.

In 1933 Faisal died unexpectedly in Switzerland and Ghazi succeeded him. The British and their Iraqi supporters, unprepared, were confronted with a popular anti-British king. In a short time, and the country had been subjected to repeated anti-British uprisings beginning in 1917, the nationalist forces coalesced around Ghazi and he became a threat to Britain's indirect rule through politician followers. The conflict between Ghazi and Britain and the political leaders of Iraq, to differing degrees all pro-British, was natural. The king, without planning it, became the symbol of the people's opposition to the forces installed in office by Britain and his mere existence exposed their vulnerability.

This was a strange situation indeed. The utter unacceptability of British hegemony over Iraq through a non-representative ruling élite was dramatized by a semi-literate king with prejudices but no political programme. Furthermore, to show how little it took to threaten the unpopular pro-British regime, Ghazi was a homosexual who was forced into marrying a first cousin in a country which considered people like him unfit for office. The unthinking boy-king, who for the first two years of his rule did no more than spend his time in the company of army officers, came close to undoing Britain's Middle East designs. After all, it was the army which held the country together on behalf of Britain and the army's love for Ghazi demonstrated that it could no longer be counted upon. Even more disturbing must have been Ghazi's elevation to the same heroic status by Arabs in Syria, Palestine and other countries, a solid confirmation of prevailing anti-British, anti-colonialist nationalist feelings of the times.

To the British and their followers this was an intolerable situation. They moved to subdue or remove Ghazi even though it would have reduced the effectiveness of the monarchy. The disadvantage of a diminished monarchy was preferable to living with uncertainty. Nuri Saïd began spreading word about King Ghazi's unfitness and demanding a regency council, and, as usual obtained British support for this.[3] Yassin Al Hashemi, Nuri's main competitor among the old guard, wanted to limit the king's direct contact with the army.[4] As early as 1934, one year after Ghazi took the throne, there was a British-backed tribal rebellion against Ghazi and his Prime Minister, Ali Jawdat Al Ayoubi.[5]

But it was Nuri, Britain's leading collaborator, who led the anti-Ghazi campaign. Ja'afar Al Askari's memoirs make a clear statement that Nuri wanted Ghazi removed and that he nominated Ghazi's uncle, Sherif Zaid, to replace him.[6] When that didn't work Nuri dispatched his son Sabah to Colonel Salluheddine Sabbagh, a popular nationalist army officer who figured prominently later, in the 1940–41 rebellion, to solicit his help in killing Ghazi.[7] He didn't stop there and tried to blow up King Ghazi's plane when he flew to Kut, a plot which might have succeeded but for the intercession of Minister of Defence Taha Al Hashemi.[8] The situation between the king and the solidly pro-British leading politician of the country, Nuri Saïd, was so tense that the two men carried pistols when they met each other.

The British, without whose approval Nuri never did anything, were not far behind. Initially they prevailed on Ghazi's Uncle Abdallah, the Emir of Jordan, to advise him not to oppose the wishes of the British ambassador, the man who until Ghazi's accession had acted as the uncrowned king of the country. Later their internal communications on the subject of the kingship of Iraq became more explicit. One such dispatch described Ghazi as 'an anti-foreign figurehead' (to army officers) and another, in 1936, asked for the creation of a regency council to replace him.[9] These followed a precipitous decline in relations between the king and Britain which led him to stop meeting the British ambassador in the mid-1930s, Sir Maurice Patterson.

In fact, by 1936 King Ghazi was boycotted by the leading politicians of Iraq and the British, who, until his assumption of power, had ruled without having to govern the country through the very same politicians. Isolated, fearful for his life but mentally incapable of developing concrete plans for his anti-British feelings, Ghazi reacted by fostering his relations with army officers and increasing his reliance on the military. This was followed by his adoption of the popular roles of advocate of the annexation of Kuwait and supporter of the Arab rebels in Palestine. To the British, these moves elevated him from nuisance to menace.[10]

On 29 October 1936 the opportunist army general Bakr Sidqi capitalized on the tension between Ghazi and the British to overthrow the government headed by Yassin Al Hashemi. There is little doubt that Ghazi had known about Sidqi's plans, and there is some evidence that he thought he was conducting a pre-emptive strike against the pro-British leaders, Al Hashemi included, who were trying to replace him. The consequences of this coup were considerable and eliminated the chance of any rapprochement between Ghazi and the British and their allies.

Among other things, the coup started badly. The leaders killed Minister of Defence General Ja'afar Al Askari, the one educated and sensible man among Iraq's pro-British leaders and potentially the one man who could have reconciled Ghazi's popularity with the armed forces with the demands of his opponents. This intentional move by Sidqi aimed at eliminating the chances of reconciliation threw Ghazi's opponents into a state of panic. Nuri was provided with an RAF plane to escape to Cairo and exile. Other leaders, disinclined to be adopted by the British in such an open manner, escaped to Damascus and Beirut. Sidqi, using civilians as a front, ran the country and made Ghazi his captive.

But Ghazi, having become the embodiment of anti-British forces in the country and the man who commanded the loyalty of most Iraqis, still demonstrated no inclination or ability to take things into his own hands and move the country forward. Meanwhile Sidqi proved himself a buffoon. Showing little understanding of the conditions around him, he adopted a policy of Iraq first which was in opposition to Ghazi's pan-Arab feelings and the reasons why the people initially backed the coup. Furthermore, Sidqi's lack of understanding of the forces arrayed against him and against Ghazi found him making overtures to the fascist regimes of Germany and Italy and, in a move which added to British determination to change things, planning to buy arms from them. The policy of ignoring the wishes of the king, underestimating his enemies and indulging in abominable personal behaviour led to Sidqi's assassination by army officers in August 1937, while he was on his way to Germany to conclude an arms deal.

With Sidqi gone, the pro-British politicians returned home to face the diminished king. And Ghazi stood alone, a simple, stubborn, uncompromising nationalist who followed his feelings without giving much thought to the results. It may have been a sense of frustration over his own inability to express himself by actually leading the country or developing a political programme which drove Ghazi to start something minor on the surface but with far-reaching consequences in 1936. His creation of a radio station committed to transmitting anti-British propaganda was akin to having a toy to which a child returned when he couldn't cope with his surroundings. But in political terms it was something more, as important as the special relationship that Ghazi had with his armed forces. Radio Kasr Al Zuhour, so named because Ghazi ran it from his Al Zuhour Palace, started operating in a serious way in early 1937. From the very start it concentrated on broadcasting appeals to the people of Kuwait to unite with Iraq and offered endless nationalistic support for the rebels fighting the British in Palestine. This remarkable development, a child-like king carrying his anti-British message directly to the people, was something neither the British nor their allies were willing to tolerate.

A government under the politician Jamil Al Madfai', one of the many pro-British premiers committed to controlling Ghazi, tried to get him to stop his radio broadcasts, but he refused. Once again Nuri began contacting army officers to convince them of the need to control the king, but they would not accept any of his criminal suggestions. Both Nuri and Madfai', as well as other members of the old guard, started a propaganda campaign to undermine the king. They went as far as accusing him of being party to the elopement of his sister Azza with a Greek waiter, a personal tragedy to the king because of the seducer's status and religion. But none of these things worked completely. In 1938 Nuri, making promises he never thought of fulfilling, managed to get enough backing from army officers to reassume the premiership against Ghazi's wishes.[11]

Meanwhile, the British Ambassador to Baghdad, Sir Maurice Patterson, met the king and asked him not to oppose British policy in Palestine and Kuwait. Member of the British cabinet R.A.B. Butler told visiting Iraqi politician Tewfic Sweidi, 'The King is playing with fire.'[12] And as usual, Nuri Saïd, once again in office, moved ahead of his British masters and, when his personal protests to the king were ignored, resorted to bribing workers at the improvised radio station to get Ghazi drunk at the time of the broadcasts.[13] Because Ghazi himself was doing many of the broadcasts this would have diminished his standing with his listeners, who, by 1938, were widespread throughout the Arab world. The issue got completely out of hand when, instead of bowing to these moves by the British and their clients and closing his radio station, Ghazi began making plans to set up two more.

The following is the sequence of events which culminated in the so-called automobile accident which ended in King Ghazi's death on 4 April 1939. At 11 p.m. on 3 April Ghazi received a telephone call from Sabah Saïd, the son of premier Nuri and the man who had tried to convince the army to remove him.[14] In response to the telephone call, at 11.30 Ghazi, accompanied by his manservant Ahmad bin Obeid Saïd and radio technician Ali bin Abdallah, drove his own car from the Al Zuhour Palace and headed towards Harithia Palace, just over half a mile away. Although many writers make the reasonable claim that he drove to Harithia to meet Sabah, this is impossible to verify.

At 11.45 telephone calls were made to the Prime Minister, army officers, politicians, the police department and dozens of other people claiming that the king's car was involved in an accident. Who started the chain of telephone calls is unknown and it is not totally clear who organized for the injured and unconscious Ghazi to be brought back to Al Zuhour Palace. He was suffering from a serious blow to the back of the head which had created a cavity the size of a fist. His manservant, slightly wounded, was admitted to a hospital; the radio technician suffered no injuries. The king never recovered and he died at 12.45 a.m.

With the Al Zuhour Palace teeming with dozens of people of importance, what immediately followed Ghazi's death bordered on the bizarre. Because Ghazi's son, Faisal II, was only four years old, the extremely unpopular pro-British Prince Abdul Illah, Ghazi's cousin and his son's maternal uncle, was declared regent. There was an attempt to pressure the doctors present when Ghazi died into testifying that Ghazi gained consciousness for a while and asked that Abdul Illah be appointed regent, but it failed. Among others, the doctor of the royal family, a Briton by the name of Sir Henry Sanderson Pasha, is cited as saying that he refused to lend his name to this move.[15]

Ghazi was buried in haste, the day after his death, without a post mortem or any other medical examination to determine the cause of the blow. The hundreds of thousands of Iraqis at the funeral, chanting slogans which claimed that the king had been murdered, tried to attack Saïd and other politicians, and Nuri was forced to flee the scene in panic. The same day Ali bin Abdallah disappeared, never to be seen again. At the hospital Ahmad bin Obeid Saïd made a statement that Ghazi had been murdered,[16] then he too disappeared for ever. Two weeks later, investigator Suleiman Duleimi, the man in charge of determining the cause of Ghazi's death, was dismissed[17] and went into hiding to save his own life.

Of the sixteen Iraqis interviewed by the author, including two former members of Iraqi cabinets under the monarchy, sons and daughters of politicians and army officers, prominent businessmen and others, only one, former Minister of Education Abdel Amir Ozrie, shied away from making a conclusive accusative statement and settled for an indirect one. He limited himself to 'there is a big question mark around Ghazi's death'. The rest cited considerable evidence supporting their claim that Ghazi was murdered, and everything they said was based on the word of parents or relations who were directly involved in the Iraqi government or Iraqi politics of the time.

There are other facts in addition to those already mentioned supporting the thesis that Ghazi was murdered:

1. The official report about the accident stated that the king's car, driven at high speed, hit a telephone pole which fell over and smashed his skull. Every single historian who has written about 'the accident' states that the car was undamaged, and available pictures support this. Neither do the pictures show that the car had veered, a natural consequence of such an accident.

2. Dr Saeb Shawkat, the one medical doctor who examined the king before his burial, remained adamant throughout his life that the king was hit from behind and that a falling telephone pole could not have caused his injury.[18]

3. Naji Shawkat, Minister of the Interior at the time of Ghazi's death, is cited as saying, 'He was killed and I had to cover it.'[19] Rifa'at Chederchi, the son of the prominent Iraqi politician Kamel Chederchi, told me in 1955, in an exhaustive interview on the subject, that Shawkat had confided the same thing to his father.

4. Historian Lutfi Ja'afar provides supporting evidence and says that the medical report stating that Ghazi died when the telephone pole fell on his head was prepared well after the fact.

5. Several historians report that an attempt by the leading Iraqi politician Mawlud Mukhlis to conduct a post mortem was refused.[20]

6. In his book *Iraqi Faces* the leading Iraqi politician and former Prime Minister Tewfic Sweidi states that Jamil Madfai', the man who became Prime Minister after Ghazi's death, refused to conduct an investigation into the accident.[21]

7. The dispatch from the British Embassy to the Foreign Office on the day of Ghazi's death, 4 April 1939, is missing. Only its title is known: 'Political Situation in Iraq'. So are several other documents from that period which could have a bearing on possible British involvement in Ghazi's murder.[22]

The list of documents and exchanges between the British Embassy in Baghdad and the Foreign Office, beginning in 1936, which dealt with the subject of controlling Ghazi or replacing him is too long to deal with in detail. One of them, FO 20 July 1936, PRO – FO 371/20017/E 3984 is titled 'Possible Alternatives to Present King of Iraq'. Subsequent ones, and I am acquainted with fifteen of them, addressed the same 'problem'.

Whether the British were directly involved in Ghazi's murder is likely to remain unknown. Only the appearance of missing documents or the unpublished memoirs of an old politician could shed light on this question. What is beyond doubt is the sigh of relief in London his death produced. The *Manchester Guardian* of 5 April 1939, the day after the king's death, summed it all up: 'Ghazi's death solved a problem for the British who were thinking of removing him.'

But the absence of evidence regarding direct involvement does not absolve the British. Their contribution to the atmosphere which made his elimination possible is evident. After Ghazi's death they hurried to reimpose their hegemony on Iraq. It is also true that they supported Nuri throughout the period of crisis before the king's murder, not only by helping him escape in 1936 when he was in danger, but by liaising with him constantly instead of working with governments appointed by Ghazi. And in 1939, as during the Gulf crisis of 1990, the British stood in total opposition to the popular Iraqi policy of wanting to annex Kuwait and to support the cause of the Arabs of Palestine.

With Ghazi's death, opposition to Britain's deputy sherifs was leaderless and unfocused. Ghazi's murder was a coup against the nationalist forces in Iraq and the Arab world. It contributed measurably to an Arab feeling of betrayal which continues to bedevil today's pro-West Arab leaders. To this day the Arabs see it as a simple case of the West resorting to violence to eliminate a popular leader. Ghazi's unworthiness notwithstanding, he still symbolized the wish of the Arab people to be independent and free of foreign control. In fact, the importance of his murder is enhanced rather than diminished by his simplicity. The need to kill a simple, meagrely endowed king because he opposed British hegemony over Iraq demonstrates beyond question the shaky nature of the Arab establishment-West alliance, which felt threatened by his presence.

As with Britain's implicit or actual complicity in the death of Ghazi, every coup instigated by America or aided by its agents had far-reaching consequences for the Middle East. Analysing all of them is beyond the scope of this book. However, the following examples of coups in Syria, Jordan and Iraq betray an inherent American belief that the Middle East can be run through the use of military élites, both to create new governments or to support existing ones or both. This belief reflects a more inclusive American one that 'democracy doesn't thrive in the Middle East because the economic and social basis for it doesn't exist'.[23] We're back to 1917 and how the British and French justified their control of the region. Only the native players are different.

In the 1950s, as now, Israel and Saudi Arabia were the twin pillars of American policy in the Arab Middle East. America was committed to supporting and protecting both countries against the wishes of the Arab people. Israel was viewed thus because of the influence of American Jewry and consequent Congressional commitment to protect and promote it and Saudi Arabia because America needed and controlled Saudi oil and wanted to protect its lifeline.

Both Israel and Saudi Arabia were opposed to the union of Syria and Iraq into one big country capable of threatening their security. The Israelis feared a militarily strong country to its east, while Saudi Arabia feared the same thing to its north and the possibility of a successful Arab unity scheme acting as a magnet for its own people. As a result, America's wish to accommodate Israel and Saudi Arabia meant opposition to all moves to unite Syria and Iraq.

The American position had two major elements against it. Unlike other Arab unity plans which came and went because they were essentially unrealistic, a merger of Iraq and Syria is economically sensible and historically justifiable, without taking into consideration the closeness of the people and the similar level of economic and social development in both countries. Britain was very much in favour of such a union but only under the Hashemite monarchy of Iraq which was beholden to it. The British believed they would control the direction of any country which emerged under the Hashemite monarchy and that they were capable of manipulating it to cancel the danger to the West's Israeli and Saudi allies. In fact, the British believed such a union would stop Syria from going radical and becoming a threat. Of course, the difference in approach as to how best to guarantee the safety of friendly regimes had behind it the selfish reason of each country wishing to spread its hegemony, and this led to secret confrontations between the two allied countries.

Between 1949 and 1958, before the anti-monarchist Iraqi coup and the Syrian union with Egypt which created the the United Arab Republic (UAR), the British made several attempts to incorporate Syria into Iraq under British hegemony. Simultaneously, the Americans tried to maintain Syria's separateness by promoting army officers beholden to it to Syrian leadership. On the Arab side, neither the British-supported Hashemites and Syrians who believed in them nor the American-sponsored army officers saw beyond controlling Syria in a way which pleased their backers. Both sides lacked coherent policy.

The Syrian people judged the many coups and countercoups taking place around them in terms of the claims of the army's communiqués. They didn't know that the CIA put Husni Zaim in power in March 1949, had little inkling that the British supported his overthrow and replacement by Colonel Sami Hinnawi in October of the same year or why Hinnawi himself was replaced by the pro-American Adib Shaishakly in December 1949. In carrying out their plans, Britain and the United States confirmed a Western willingness to kill, subvert, destabilize, misrepresent, forge alliances with villains and, above all, to guarantee the long-term instability of the Middle East through the use of assassins, incompetent colonels and corrupt politicians. Meanwhile the dizzying succession of Syrian governments was attributed to Syria's inherent social and political immaturity; the Western press attributed it to the Arabs' inability to cope with the idea of a modern nation-state.

There is no greater confirmation of the lack of solidity of governments which assumed power through coups and assassinations than the quality of the primary and secondary perpetrators of these activities, often men who are as lacking in political qualifications as simple fruit and vegetable vendors or even doormen. In July 1949 the Iraqi man entrusted with assassinating Syrian President Husni Zaim and, had it happened, paving the way for a Syrian army takeover that would lead to the country's union with Iraq and change the history of the Middle East was such a man.

Mahdi Saleh Al Najjar, a graduate of the Iraqi military college and a decorated veteran of the 1948 Arab-Israeli War, was a violent, enthusiastic Arab nationalist with limited horizons and the make-up of a gun for hire. Short, compactly built and with a manly moustache, he was a fearless crack shot with a history of superficial political involvement which produced a thick police file and frequent resort to subsisting by borrowing money from friends.

As stated before, Zaim was put in power by the CIA. His 30 March 1949 coup came into being under the supervision of Major Stephen Meade, the military attaché at the American Embassy in Damascus.[24] To all outward appearances, particularly the nationalistic communiqués, the Zaim coup looked like a strictly Syrian affair to reclaim the country's Arab identity. In fact, the Americans had plans to use Zaim to make peace with Israel and to intercept any moves to unite Syria with Iraq.

Monocled, overweight, sex-hungry and given to pompous overstatement and grand gestures, Zaim proceeded to behave in a manner embarrassing to his creators. Although a statement against Syria uniting with Iraq was among his earliest pronouncements,[25] he followed it by demanding bribes on all government contracts and spending most of his time with the leading Egyptian belly-dancer of the time.

The Iraqis, watching this with glee and seeing Zaim as an easy target, decided to act against the Americans and to eliminate him as a first step towards incorporating Syria into their country. But the solidly pro-British Iraqi Prime Minister, Nuri Saïd, was against a counter coup, though many Syrian officers were pro-Iraqi and pro-union. Saïd thought a second coup four months after the Zaim one would be too dislocating and difficult to justify. Instead, according to Nuri's logic, the simple assassination of Zaim could be followed by a smooth assumption of power by pro-Iraqi elements in the Syrian army and a call for immediate unity with Iraq.

What Nuri's plan needed was an assassin. The Baghdad police files produced a number of candidates, but none as qualified as Mahdi Saleh Al Najjar. During the 1948 War, Najjar had befriended many a Syrian army officer and he had been to Damascus on his way to Palestine and knew his way around the city. Also, since he was an army officer himself, his selection would impress the pro-Iraqi Syrian officers with whom he had to liaise, the people waiting to assume power after Zaim's death.

Najjar was a willing recruit. There was no need for training, just tips on how to behave once in Damascus and code-names to use to contact his Syrian army co-conspirators. As always, the operation was to be described as a nationalist one aimed at helping the 'Arab cause', the all-inclusive term used to suggest unity and fighting Israel. Najjar's final meeting before leaving for Damascus with £10,000 in his pocket, a small fortune to a destitute romantic, was with Nuri Saïd himself. Not only did Nuri approve of his selection, but Najjar later recalled Nuri's fatherly attitude and praise of his zealousness. It was a case of an unpopular pro-West leader entrusting an ignoramus with changing the map of the Middle East.

In 1949 the Americans were new to Baghdad and their local contacts were not as substantial as those of their British allies. Even so, they had a number of agents operating under ethnic cover, mainly Iraqis who had graduated from American universities, and one of them discovered the Iraqi plot. But the agent's report lacked one thing: he couldn't get the name of the would-be assassin.

The Baghdad CIA transmitted the news of the plot to Damascus for operatives Miles Copeland, Stephen Meade and Arthur Close to act on.[26] Though not enamoured with Zaim any more, the Americans still tried to intercept the unknown assassin (Najjar) through pro-American Syrian army officers without telling the Syrian president. They were unsuccessful: Najjar was nowhere to be found.

In fact, having discovered that Damascus was enveloped in a tense atmosphere which made carrying out his mission more difficult than expected, Najjar had decided to abort the whole operation. However, anticipating that Nuri and his police chief would not accept his reason for failure, he chose to go to Beirut instead, then an open city full of political exiles from throughout the Middle East.

Once in Beirut, Najjar could think of only one name, Abu Saïd Aburish, the news correspondent he had met in Jerusalem when Aburish worked for the London *Daily Mail*. Looking tired and in need of a shave, Najjar found Abu Saïd at the St George Hotel Bar, the centre for the foreign press corps. Initially Abu Saïd failed to recognize him, but later he listened to his tale with interest, particularly because Najjar claimed that he was defecting to avoid serving a regime which followed British designs.

Sensing that Najjar was telling the truth, Abu Saïd whisked him to his home and questioned him about the coup plot over endless cups of Turkish coffee. The more Najjar told him, the more the news correspondent became convinced that the whole thing was much too sensitive to be used as a news story.[27] Among other things, Abu Saïd feared what the Iraqis, and perhaps the British, might do if he exposed them.

But there was another use for the story. A committed Palestinian and long-time follower of the Grand Mufti, Abu Saïd asked Najjar to write everything down and transmitted the report of his God-sent discovery to the Grand Mufti in Cairo through his cousin and confidant Heidar Al Husseini. Abu Saïd wanted immediate instructions on what to do with the would-be assassin, who was hiding at his house and becoming more moody and unhappy by the minute.

After Cairo responded, there was a three-way meeting involving Najjar, Abu Saïd and Heidar Al Husseini during which the latter satisfied himself of the authenticity of the story. To Abu Saïd's genuine shock, Al Husseini instructed him to 'Find a way to get this information to the Americans as soon as possible. Only they can stop the British and Iraq.'

There were many ways of doing this, but rightly judging it to be a most unusual situation, Abu Saïd waited two days until Archie Roosevelt, the CIA station chief and grandson of Teddy Roosevelt, made one of his regular appearances at the St George, the Mecca of spies as well as journalists.

The polite, highly polished Orientalist Roosevelt listened to Abu Saïd attentively, then asked why Abu Saïd was favouring him with such valuable information. After some hesitation, Abu Saïd told him that he was acting on the Mufti's instructions. A smiling Roosevelt accepted the reason without any further questions. The Mufti, to the outside world the original Middle East ayatollah and terrorist, was known to be totally anti-Iraq, anti-British and against Syria and Iraq uniting. A Syrian-Iraqi union would create a strong state with negative consequences for the Mufti's leadership of the Palestinians. Allying himself to America, though its opposition to the proposed union of Syria and Iraq was partly aimed at pleasing the Israelis, was preferable to losing the loyalty of the Palestinians to a new country.

Roosevelt's only known action was to contact CIA agent Miles Copeland in Damascus to tell him to stop his search for the would-be assassin. Copeland managed to get the rest of the details of the plot in Damascus and passed the information to Zaim. Oddly, the arrogant, unintelligent Syrian president didn't believe him, but told Copeland that the whole thing was nothing more than a CIA fabrication aimed at making him more obedient to the agency. The Mufti sent Abu Saïd a warm 'well done' message, and the Mufti's people arranged for Najjar to travel to Pakistan on false documents to instruct groups of Muslim fighters training to renew the struggle against Israel.

But the failure of Najjar was nothing but a phase in the American-British struggle to control Syria, the Americans through its army and the British by making part of the country allied to them. Within a mere two weeks of this incident, a group of Syrian army officers led by Colonel Sami Hinnawi toppled the Zaim government and killed its leader. Hinnawi, pro-Iraq, pro-British and sympathetic to the idea of union between Iraq and Syria, established immediate contacts with Nuri Saïd to implement their common policy. It was as if all the excitement about Najjar had amounted to nothing.

With Syria and Iraq in earnest negotiations to unite and with Saudi Arabia and Israel agitating for the United States to intercept any such merger, the CIA once again went to work to find a Syrian colonel to stop the union and deputize for it. Luckily for them, Hinnawi, like Zaim before him, failed to capture the support of Syria's people, who lived in impatient expectation of their army delivering on the promises of fighting Israel that were contained in his takeover communiqués. The CIA made much of this and moved in for the kill.

Exactly two months after he took over power from Zaim, Hinnawi was overthrown by Colonel Adib Shaishakly, a man handpicked by the CIA to serve its purposes and those of its clients to keep Iraq and Syria apart. Hinnawi, though not guilty of personal stupidities, was operating beyond his level of competence. Unlike his two predecessors, Shaishakly was careful not to be saddled with assuming direct power; he installed a civilian government which followed his orders until November 1951. During this period, in 1950, Nuri Saïd made another unsuccessful attempt to change the Syrian picture. He dispatched another Iraqi gunman, Abbas Al Khassoun, to Damascus to kill Shaishakly and change the Middle East according to the plan Najjar had failed to carry out. But Al Khassoun, as deficient as Najjar, also absconded without completing his mission. Syria remained within America's political sphere of influence.

The considerable American help provided to Shaishakly and the incompetence of the civilians under him allowed him to come into the open and assume personal power from 1951 until 1954. His land reform programme, the creation of a political party to back the army and the purchase of much-needed, basic military hardware to strengthen the army came close to making Shaishakly popular and underwriting his continuation in power. But, despite these achievements, he too was overthrown by a coup. By then the Syrian army had become radicalized and divided into several factions, including a strong communist one, and this heralded the beginning of a power struggle between these groups which culminated in a Syrian decision to unite with Nasser in 1958, to save the country from a communist takeover.

This brief history of the Syrian coups and counter coups reveals several things. First, the old landowning and trading establishment which had assumed power after the departure of France was small in number and had no following and its main aim was to protect its primacy. The traditional élite proved incapable of confronting the cohesive power of the army. Secondly, there was never a shortage of army officers willing to front for outside powers to control Syria and, hiding behind popular slogans and disguises, to move it into a specific political direction dictated by these outside powers. Thirdly, Britain and the United States showed little interest or competence in selecting intelligent people to deputize for them.

Above all, the ease with which it was possible to change Syrian governments attests to a French colonial failure to create a working system to replace it the moment it left the country. The absence of a system or an acceptable governing group made it easy for the pro-American and pro-British army colonels to do what they did under disguise. But this too revealed the short-sightedness of Western policy, because elevating the army officers to power was easier than creating a permanent system to help them retain this power to serve their masters. It is the Western wish to follow policies unacceptable to the people of Syria which has always stood in the way of the success of their colonel clients, and before them of the old élite.

In relying on a discredited establishment and mainly incompetent army colonels, the Western powers revealed a commitment against accepting a popular leadership or a semi-democratic, responsive legitimate system of government at a time when the increasingly educated people were clamouring for both and when Syria had functioning political parties with acceptable programmes and popular leaders. But then why accept a leader or a party which reflected the will of a people whose preoccupations differed from those of Britain, America and France? By buying the loyalty of Syria's two cohesive forces, the old establishment and the army, Western actions not only thwarted the development of a legitimate system of government, but also contributed considerably towards Syria's becoming a divided, neurotic country. This is what Syria is today: an undemocratic land run by an army group reluctant to ease its grip on power for fear of a Western-sponsored army group replacing it.

To repeat, a *coup d'état* doesn't always mean the emergence of a new power group. Very often it could reflect the use of an army by one ruling faction against another to change the political direction of a country. This spacious definition includes the use of the armed forces by dictatorial heads of state to reassert their control of a country to intercept policies which resulted from temporary acceptance of the idea of a legitimate government, perhaps a parliamentary democracy.

According to this definition, Jordan has suffered more coups than any other country in the Middle East except Syria. King Hussein, for ever unable to decide between a parliamentary system in a democratic Jordan and one run by him as a royal dictatorship, has changed more governments through the use of the army than any man alive. Since the mid-1950s he has consistently used his army to overthrow governments which he allowed to come into being and which, responding to the people's wishes, acted independently of the royal will.

However, because all the governments Hussein has overthrown have been legitimate ones popular with the people, Hussein has always resorted to convoluted explanations and disguises to cover his anti-legitimacy changes of mind. His actions are invariably explained in terms of 'a communist threat', 'danger to the security of the state', 'outside powers' or 'misguided elements'. Whatever the explanation, Hussein has invariably needed and relied on Western support to carry out his plans. In fact, because his country is poor and dependent on outside assistance, and his mercenary Bedouin army requires financial support to continue to exist and carry out the orders of its master, it is through providing this army with money that the West comes to Hussein's aid. This background justifies the assertion that 'foreigners intervened [in Jordan] more than any other country.'[28]

King Hussein assumed power in 1952. In the mid-1950s Jordan was torn between a pro-Nasser population, two-thirds of which was made up of Palestinian refugees, and a king who owed his allegiance to the British creators of Jordan, who still officered its army under the leadership of the legendary Glubb Pasha (see Chapter 9). In 1956, bowing to public pressure, Hussein dismissed Glubb and replaced him and his sixty-four British officers by native ones. This was followed by free parliamentary elections which produced a pro-Nasser government under Prime Minister Suleiman Nabulsi. Briefly king and government worked together, but seeing his royal prerogatives eroded by a government of the people, the former reached for outside help.

In April 1957 King Hussein was twenty-two and the US government had already replaced Britain as his financial backer and protector. Having given up on Nasser and decided actively to oppose him and his plans to create an Arab front against Israel, the US government was determined to reclaim Jordan as a Western sphere of influence.[29] This meant replacing the freely elected government of Jordan and the re-emergence of Hussein's royal dictatorship.

Hussein, like the US, saw Nasser as the enemy. There was a built-in conflict between Nasser's ambition to create an Arab unity of purpose under his leadership and Hussein's desire to perpetuate a monarchical regime which, except for its use as a buffer state to further Western designs, particularly the creation and protection of Israel, was unsound, and most certainly unacceptable to the people of Jordan.

Initially the clash between the two forces leading Jordan in different directions took the form of a propaganda war. Nasser's relentless exhortations against the West and its clients appealed to the Jordanian people under the Nabulsi government. On the other hand, Hussein's opposition to Nasser and the Nabulsi government was secret. At first, Hussein and a small group of loyalists, including CIA propagandists (see Chapter 9 for more on the leading one, John Fistere) worked to discredit Nasser and Nabulsi by pointing out the discrepancies between their words and deeds, Nasser's dictatorial ways and his continued dialogue with the West and Nabulsi's failure to replace the Western financial subsidy. When this made no dent in Nasser's and Nabulsi's popularity, Hussein decided to use his army.

In 1957 the military attaché at the Jordanian Embassy in Beirut was a

British-trained Hussein loyalist, confidant and close friend of the king by the name of Colonel Radi Abdallah. Because the Beirut CIA station was responsible for Jordan, Abdallah decided to negotiate a deal with the CIA to save his friend and mentor.

Abdallah, an astute intelligence officer who was opposed to Nabulsi's pro-Nasser government and the then Jordanian Chief of Staff, General Ali Abu Nawar, took things into his own hands without consulting King Hussein. He found a willing partner in CIA agent James Russell Barracks. Between the beginning of 1957 and April of that year, the two men met at several locations in Beirut no fewer than six times.[30] Abdallah, having secured Hussein's approval to continue his efforts after the first meeting, kept journeying to Amman to brief the king on the plans that he and Barracks were developing. Because Jordanian intelligence reported directly to the king and a military attaché was an intelligence officer, Abdallah's activities aroused no suspicion.

The results of the Barracks-Abdallah conspiracy became news in August 1957 when, for a week, the Western press celebrated the derring-do of a twenty-two-year-old boy-king battling the forces of evil to save his throne. According to these stories, Hussein, using army units loyal to him, foiled a plot by Prime Minister Nabulsi and Chief of Staff Abu Nawar to overthrow him. Not only was he successful in leading his troops to victory, he also subsequently dissolved parliament and declared a state of emergency which consolidated all power in his hands. Throughout all this, Hussein added to the atmosphere of a military confrontation by donning the uniform of a general and behaving like one.

King Hussein, Harrow and Sandhurst-educated and speaking impeccable English, held a press conference three days after his final victory over the pro-Nasser forces in which he rehashed and embellished the history of the phoney plot against him. He heightened the drama by describing Nasser's so-called support for his conspiring Prime Minister and Chief of Staff as perfidy. After all, according to Hussein, he had trusted Nasser and joined forces with him to fight the common Israeli enemy.

The Western press, as usual, took the word of a pro-West monarch against an anti-West president. Nobody questioned Hussein about why he experienced considerable difficulty in finding a new Prime Minister to replace Nabulsi, because most politicians in Jordan resented Hussein's move against a freely elected government. No news correspondent made much of the fact that the new Chief of Staff appointed to replace Abu Nawar, General Ali Hiyari, defected to Syria rather than serve Hussein. Of course, nobody knew that Barracks had sneaked into Jordan and was at Hussein's side to direct operations against the popular government and the nationalist officers he and Abdallah had agreed should be replaced.

Essentially, what the Western press reported was a coup that never was, and it didn't know or failed to report the real coup that Hussein carried out against his own government. Nasser, Nabulsi and Abu Nawar were the bad guys and Hussein was a pro-Western knight. Not a word about how all three bad men were utterly opposed to any moves against the Jordanian monarchy because they knew Israel would carry out its threat to respond to Hussein's dethronement by occupying the West Bank.

The background to Hussein's coup against Jordan's popular government was a reflection of the West's determination to maintain deputy sherifs. Beyond the obvious dictatorial tendencies which Hussein retains to this day, there were practical, personal reasons of outright royal corruption.

Hussein had appointed General Ali Abu Nawar as Chief of Staff to succeed Glubb Pasha in 1956 against the advice of his senior army officers and the cabinet. Abu Nawar, until a year before a mere major, had been the Jordanian military attaché in Paris and it was there that the two had met and Nawar introduced Hussein to Paris nightclubs and other delights. Abu Nawar went into exile only to be recalled later and rewarded with the Paris Embassy. And Nabulsi, the clean and competent Prime Minister, was determined to curb the activities of King Hussein's arms and hashish-smuggling uncle, Sherif Nasser. Like the rest of the Middle East monarchs, Hussein placed family loyalty above all else and wanted to protect his uncle. Thirdly, Hussein himself was broke, for the promised Arab subsidy to replace the British one which stopped with the dismissal of Glubb never materialized in an organized way and the customary cut for the royal purse out of the money earmarked for his army had to be maintained.

King Hussein's coup against the Nabulsi government, distorted as it was by him and his CIA backers, had more corruption than ideology behind it. Hussein purged his army of 'all suspicious elements' (in reality popular officers) including all military attachés overseas, who had been summoned back to Jordan under false pretences by Barracks and arrested on arrival. Politicians were detained and some imprisoned without reason. Political parties were dissolved, except for Islamic groups which Hussein and the CIA wanted to use to combat Nasser's popularity. Jordan's Bedouin army was given a free hand in suppressing the particularly pro-Nasser population of the West Bank and this produced something akin to a reign of terror. With these things in place, the United States gave the royal dictatorship $50 million to renew its lease of life. Jordan, the fabrication which had always lived up to the reasons for creating it, to undermine the Arab position in Palestine, was refinanced to continue these policies.

*   *   *

Corrupt relationships breed corruption. The phoney reasons behind Hussein's 1957 coup, underwritten as it was by bundles of CIA money and open financial help to Jordan from the US government, encouraged him to tap the same source to make more money out of other phoney plots. The summer of 1958 was a particularly difficult time for Hussein. He was under pressure from Nasser to change direction yet again and to rejoin him in forging a common front against Israel. However, instead of responding to Nasser's call and his people's undoubted support for an Arab alliance, Hussein was once again hatching conspiracies.

On 7 July 1958, just a week before the overthrow of the monarchy under his cousin Faisal II in Iraq, a tearful, agitated King Hussein held a press conference in which he announced that Brigadier Radi Abdallah, the man who had conspired with Barracks to overthrow the Nabulsi government, had been placed under house arrest for plotting against him. Abdallah had been promoted and moved to Amman as the king's military aide-de-camp and Hussein's lament amounted to a complaint, boringly repeated throughout his reign, that there was no one he could trust any more.

The story was peculiar. Hussein never divulged the nature of the conspiracy, what kind of a coup Abdallah had been plotting, what its aims were or the number of people involved. Moreover, Abdallah was anti-Nasser and had always subordinated his personal ambitions to his loyalty to the young king. Even stranger was the fact that Hussein and his government refused to press charges against the would-be conspirator, or to set a trial date.[31]

In the end Abdallah was released after twenty-six months of house arrest in what resembled an act of kindness towards an old friend. The so-called conspiracy that Abdallah is supposed to have planned vanished without a trace. Stranger still was Abdallah's subsequent appointment to the most critical position of chief of intelligence, a confirmation that the original allegations against him were trumped up. But the image created by press stories about a beleaguered pro-West king stuck and no one chose to point out the king's obvious lie, not even after Hussein promoted Abdallah a second time, to the post of Minister of the Interior.

In fact, beyond the non-existence of a coup attempt by Abdallah, the man was a gentleman and an officer who would never betray his commander-in-chief. Not only was it another plot that never was, but in the process of organizing it Hussein used a loyal friend to cover his own need of money, his willingness to use corruption to take advantage of a gullible CIA, and rewards for his loyalty later. Abdallah, however, reaped the bankruptcy of his regime.

The real story behind this episode is an example of how corrupt pro-West leaders are and how they use the West's dependence on them to extend their corruption. The third party involved in Hussein's second phoney coup was none other than the CIA agent who had helped Hussein topple Nabulsi and regain his absolute control over Jordan: James Russell Barracks.

Earlier in 1958 the CIA agent, by now a close friend of Hussein, had given the king the sum of $2 million for covert operations against Syria, then the junior partner in the United Arab Republic founded by Nasser through a merger of Egypt and Syria. The CIA money was to be used by Hussein to sponsor anti-Nasser Syrian elements, to cause explosions and perhaps public disturbances, demonstrations and riots. The full amount was deposited in the Chase Manhattan Bank in Beirut, of which Suheil Abu Hammad was an officer.[32]

But Hussein had no people in Syria to sponsor and he spent the money on personal pursuits. When this became obvious after several CIA inquiries as to why nothing was happening, Barracks demanded that it be returned. He refused to accept Hussein's excuses that it takes time to organize such things. In July 1958 Hussein finally confided to Barracks that Abdallah, a co-signatory to the Chase Manhattan account, had withdrawn the money and gambled it away and promised to do something about his military aide-de-camp.

Knowing that he couldn't put Abdallah on trial for embezzlement, Hussein instead accused Abdallah of plotting a coup. He didn't stop there, but shamelessly implied that Nasser was behind it and got anti-Nasser propaganda mileage out of the episode. Abdallah, loyal as ever, knew that Hussein had spent the money, but said nothing. It was this act of loyalty which prompted Hussein to release him, then elevate him to his new posts in 1961, and to continue to point the finger at Nasser.[33]

There are endless variations on the dirty business of organizing unpopular coups. But all of them begin with a lie, distort their purpose and resemble an unholy alliance between Mafia families. When the CIA connived in fabricating a coup attempt to keep Hussein in power against the will of his people, they had little inkling that he would use their own disinformation methods to cheat them out of more money. But, despite the nature of the second phoney coup, the United States still wanted him to remain king and there was little the CIA could do but look the other way and place his eventual usefulness above his cheating. After all, he did point the finger at Nasser.

James Critchfield, the senior CIA officer and expert on communist infiltration appointed in 1960 to run the agency's operations in the Middle East and South Asia, describes the 1950s Middle East activities of the agency as 'the cowboy era'.[34] To judge from what followed in the 1960s, Critchfield's description is justified. From the early 1960s, the simplicity of the original CIA operations and resulting coups was replaced by highly complex planning and manipulations to confront communist penetration of the Middle East.

Critchfield was sent to the Middle East by CIA Director Allen Dulles, mainly to deal with one country, Iraq. Hardly an expert in the region, Critchfield, in addition to using his expertise in fighting communist infiltration and apply it to the Middle East, was entrusted with the secondary job of injecting more professionalism into the situation. Before appointing Critchfield Dulles had told the Senate Foreign Relations Committee on 28 April 1959, 'Iraq is today the most dangerous spot on earth.'[35]

To the CIA, republican Iraq under General Abdel Karim Kassem, the leader of the successful anti-monarchist coup of 1958, was endangering the balance of power in the Middle East. As already mentioned, Kassem's coup was the one in which Western intelligence services played no part, and Kassem was an odd outsider incapable of appreciating the necessity of an open or secret dialogue with the West. Moreover, the Iraqi leader's populist inclinations presented the West with a situation for which it was not prepared. This included the appointment of a collection of British-trained leftist bureaucrats to run ministries and Kassem's acceptance of a role for the local Communist Party, an unusual move which threatened to alter the nature of politics in Iraq and the Middle East.

Initially and superficially, the 1958 Kassem coup looked like a Nasser-inspired one directed against a pro-Western government and aimed at taking Iraq into the United Arab Republic of Egypt and Syria. But the British, with historical knowledge of Iraq and its independent character and totally committed to stopping the march of Nasser's Arab nationalism and unity schemes, knew better. Rightly, they saw the coup as an internal Iraqi affair and anticipated the re-emergence of the historical competition for leadership of the Arab world between Egypt and Iraq (see Chapter 8).

What ensued was a British effort to use Kassem's natural desire to maintain an independent Iraq to stop the march of Arab unity. But British support wasn't enough and, needing a popular base to oppose Nasser, Kassem began relying on one of the more organized movements in his country, the Iraqi Communist Party. Kassem followed this with a number of popular measures. He successfully pressured the British-controlled Iraqi Petroleum Company (IPC) into giving Iraq a greater share of the oil income, prevailed on the British to close their military bases in his country, encouraged the trade unions, built new cities for workers, distributed land to peasants, reduced rents, created the People's Militia and signed arms deals with the USSR. An Arabized Kurd of humble background, Kassem was an intense, unmarried man with a thin voice, who lived austerely and had no known outside interests except the building of a people's Iraq and a strong army.

Nasser and the Americans feared a communist takeover of Iraq and did not share the British notion that the Iraqi communists were not capable of assuming power in what the British considered an essentially tribal, sectarian and clannish country. Nasser, with a considerable following among Iraq's people and the officer class, time and again tried to topple the Kassem regime. All these attempts failed, some bloodily, and Nasser's concern and frustration showed when he served written notice on the USSR's Nikita Khrushchev that he would not tolerate a communist regime in Iraq.[36]

In the background, the Americans were fuming, unable to act. They were against Kassem and the Iraqi communists, but realized that over-throwing the Kassem regime would lead to a pro-Nasser one, the extension of the UAR to include Iraq and consequent destabilization of other Arab countries. They were having problems with Nasser and had already decided that Arab unity was against their strategic interests.[37]

Suddenly, in 1961, two things happened which changed this picture and the attitudes of both the British and the Americans. In September of that year Syria seceded from the UAR and became an independent country again and with that the Nasser threat to capture Iraq receded. The lessening of this threat coincided with two anti-British moves by Kassem. He nationalized part of the concession of the British-controlled IPC and resurrected the Iraqi claim to Kuwait; like King Ghazi in 1937 and Saddam Hussein in 1990, he considered it a part of Iraq separated from it through British connivance and wanted it returned to its mother country. With their oil interests inside Iraq and in Kuwait threatened, the British switched to an anti-Kassem stance and their position was reconciled with that of the Americans. Both sides knew that Kassem had to go.

The British resorted to something they had used in the past: they began to sponsor a new Kurdish insurrection against the Iraqi central government.[38] Dislocating and costly to the Iraqis as this was, it was far less effective than the comprehensive anti-Kassem plans developed and carried out by the CIA.

In developing the plans to overthrow Kassem the CIA wanted two things in place. The first was a confirmation that Nasser had ceased his efforts towards a union with Iraq and the second was to solicit his help in securing the cooperation of Cairo-based Iraqi exiles opposed to Kassem. The second aim was a more sinister one which coupled the overthrow of Kassem with a detailed plan to eliminate the Iraqi Communist Party as a force in Iraqi politics. This did not mean neutralizing the party or countering its appeal; it meant the physical extermination of its members.

Nasser, an avowed anti-communist despite his links with the USSR, accepted the American plan and acted on it. From 1961 until the overthrow of Kassem in February 1963, the Iraqi Section of Egyptian intelligence facilitated contacts between the CIA and Iraqi exiles in Cairo, including a then junior Ba'ath Party member by the name of Saddam Hussein. The Americans augmented these contacts by developing links between the Beirut and Damascus CIA stations and former police officers under the monarchy and Lebanese and Syrian Christian elements of the same pan-Arabist and anti-Kassem Ba'ath Party.[39]

The CIA wanted to determine the ability of the Ba'ath Party to overthrow Kassem and the willingness of its leadership, in return for CIA help, to undertake a 'cleansing' programme to get rid of the communists and their leftist allies. After lengthy deliberations there was an American decision to rely on the Ba'ath, both the exiles in Cairo and exiles and other elements in Beirut and Damascus.

This sinister alliance was not the well-kept secret it should have been. Malik Mufti, an assistant professor at Boston's Tufts University, has produced an excellent and yet unpublished report on this subject.[40] His efforts are a major contribution towards unravelling one of the ugliest episodes in the history of the CIA and the Middle East. In Mufti's report, former Kassem Iraqi Foreign Minister Hazem Jawad states, 'The Iraqi Foreign Ministry knew of the Ba'ath-CIA contacts.' This is dramatized by the recollections of former member of the Syrian cabinet Jamal Attasi, who asserts – without qualifications – that the Ba'ath Party in Syria confronted their Iraqi comrades with allegations of cooperation with the CIA. The Iraqi Ba'athists did not deny the accusation, but justified the contacts by describing them as an alliance of convenience. And the Iraqi Ba'ath leader and participant in the coup, Hani Fkaiki, told me that Yugoslavia under Tito also discovered the plot and saw fit to advise Kassem of the CIA-Ba'ath contacts. Why Kassem did not act on the tip-off remains somewhat of a mystery, but what ensued supports the theory that he believed he was too popular with the army and the people to be overthrown.

On 8 February 1963 pro-Ba'ath Iraqi army units moved to topple Abdel Karim Kassem. They were small in number -- they had a mere nine tanks under their command – and their immediate concerns were to isolate the larger army units loyal to Kassem, occupy the radio and television stations and eliminate some of Kassem's key supporters, particularly the charismatic commander of the air force, Jallal Al Awkati, and Kassem's aide and confidant Colonel Wasfi Taher.

Compared with other Middle East coups, apart from the meagre military units supporting the conspirators, this effort was neither highly organized nor was it a popular one aimed at overthrowing an unpopular leader. A major reason for an apparent lack of organization was the fact that the conspirators had moved the date of the coup forward after the arrest of one of them, Colonel Saleh Mahdi Ammash. A leader of the conspiracy and holder of all its secrets, this former assistant military attaché at the Iraqi embassy in Washington was the Ba'ath's contact man with William Lakeland, the assistant American military attaché in Baghdad and the man credited with masterminding the whole operation. According to Fkaiki, cooperation between the two men was total; Ammash is reported to have solicited Lakeland's help in delaying the return to Iraq of a group of Iraqi officers and fellow conspirators who were on a visit to the US. This group, headed by Colonel Muhammad Mahdawi, did not return to Iraq until the operation against Kassem was successful. This and other circumstantial evidence of constant meetings between Ammash and Lakeland is used by most Iraqis to support a claim that Ammash was recruited by the CIA during his service in Washington and that scheduling the coup for an earlier date than originally planned had to do with preventing him from revealing this connection under interrogation.

On the ground, the obvious lack of organization and absence of wide popular support precluded an easy and immediate success. Not only did some army units loyal to Kassem resist, but thousands of ordinary people flocked to his headquarters at the Ministry of Defence and demanded arms to fight alongside his troops. For twenty-four hours Kassem fought back, and throughout he behaved like a gentleman officer. He refused to arm his non-military partisans for fear of precipitating a civil war and adding to the already high toll of casualties. Also, he contacted the rebels and offered to surrender in return for a safe conduct agreement that would allow him to leave the country unmolested. His refusal to arm his supporters went unappreciated and his request for safe passage was denied.

On the morning of 9 February 1963, his headquarters under repeated aerial attacks, Kassem surrendered. His request to keep the insignias of his general's rank and to retain his side-arm were denied and he was led to Baghdad's television station and subjected to a summary trial which, in view of his command of army and street support which threatened the success of the coup, produced the expected death sentence. During his brief interrogation, he demanded to be tried in front of an open tribunal, but this request too was turned down and after that he refused to answer questions and admonished some of his aides for their unseemly pleadings with their captors. When the time to execute him came, he shouted, 'Long live the people' with a steady voice which betrayed no fear or remorse.[41] He was shot dead without a blindfold.

What followed the end of the only Arab regime this century which had no determining connections with the West came in three parts. First, there was the behaviour of the victors, what came to be known as the elimination campaign. Secondly, there was the official Western reaction to the rebellion against Kassem and to its success and his demise. And thirdly, there was the government which followed Kassem and the unexpected friendliness to the West that it demonstrated.

Writers on Middle East affairs, including respected ones such as Patrick Seale, Hanna Batatu, Muhammad Heikal, Marion and Peter Sluglett, Heather Deegan and Kassem's former Minister of Information, Ismael Aref, have confirmed that the elimination campaign took place and that the lists of those to be killed were provided by the CIA, some transmitted to anti-Kassem elements through broadcasts by a mysterious radio station located in Kuwait. But all the writers mentioned fail to provide more details. The number of people eliminated remains confused and estimates range from seven hundred to thirty thousand. Putting various statements by Iraqi exiles together, in all likelihood the figure was nearer five thousand and, with some effort, I have managed to gather over six hundred names.

The one thing my list shows, and regarding which all writers, former Iraqi politicians and observers of the country agree, is that the lists included some of the *crème de la crème* of educated Iraqis. There were many ordinary people who were eliminated because they continued to resist after the coup became an accomplished fact, but there were also senior army officers, lawyers, professors, teachers, doctors and others. There were pregnant women and old men among them and many were tortured to death in the presence of their young children. Saddam Hussein, who had rushed back to Iraq from exile in Cairo to join the victors, was personally involved in the torture of leftists in the separate detention centres for the fellaheen, or peasants, and the muthaqafeen, or educated class. And, tellingly, the eliminations were done mainly on an individual basis, house-to-house visits by hit squads who knew where their victims were and carried out on-the-spot executions. This explains the killing of seven out of the thirteen-man Central Committee of the Iraqi Communist Party – most after they were hideously tortured. The British Committee for Human Rights in Iraq, one of the few international groups to investigate what happened after the coup, confirmed all this in a 1964 report and compared the Ba'athist hit squads to 'Hitlerian shock troops'.

The accusation that lists of people to be eliminated were prepared by the CIA for the Ba'ath Party to act on has been confirmed by me. The lists were prepared in Cairo, Beirut and Damascus, in all cases with the help of Iraqi exiles. The American agent who produced the longest list was William McHale, who operated under the cover of a news correspondent for the Beirut bureau of *Time*. Most of his information came from a high-ranking officer of the Baghdad police under the monarchy.[42] In preparing the lists, McHale was acting under instructions from his own brother and senior CIA official, Don McHale.

The second source for the lists was a senior Egyptian intelligence officer. Among the Iraqi exiles Sidqi used to gather his list was Saddam Hussein. And the third source was two Christian officials of the Ba'ath Party in Syria, one with CIA connections which went back years.[43]

Violating all rules of diplomacy, the US State Department exposed the CIA's complicity in the coup hours after the start of the rebellion against Kassem and well before its outcome was a certainty. They instructed their chargé d'affaires at Baghdad to contact the rebels and to promise them recognition.[44] Later the official reactions to the coup in both London and Washington amounted to a deep sigh of relief. According to Malik Mufti, Robert Komer, then a member of the National Security Council, told President John F. Kennedy, 'the coup is a gain for our side'. James Akins, then a political attaché in Baghdad and later American Ambassador to Saudi Arabia, said, 'On account of the Ba'ath coup, we enjoyed better relations with Iraq.'[45] But it was Ali Saleh Sa'adi, the Minister of the Interior of the regime which replaced Kassem, who offered the unequivocal, 'We came to power on a CIA train.'[46] To the Egyptian writer Muhammad Heikal, King Hussein of Jordan confirmed the original reports that the CIA train included the elaborate setting up of a radio station in Kuwait, not only to supply lists of people to be eliminated, but one initially used to issue instructions to the rebels.[47]

Indeed King Hussein had reason to know what was happening. Until the CIA decision to rely on the Ba'ath, the agency had cooperated with him and the Shah of Iran in trying to find ways to topple Kassem. Throughout 1962 Jordanian intelligence headed by the already mentioned Radi Abdallah worked with the Shah's Iranian Chief of Intelligence, General Bakhtiar, towards Kassem's overthrow. These contacts stopped on CIA orders late in 1962.[48] Furthermore, the use of the CIA and Ba'ath of Kuwait goes a long way towards explaining Saddam Hussein's later 1990 paranoia towards the country and his reaction to the news that the CIA was using it to act against him.[49]

The British, relegated to observers of a highly complex CIA operation, celebrated Kassem's demise quietly. Amazingly, the Kassem threat to Kuwait had been successful and had produced an agreement for that country to federate with its powerful neighbour which entailed the creation of a single army and the ceding of the conduct of Kuwait's foreign relations and some control of its finances to Iraq.[50] After Kassem was overthrown the British moved with considerable deliberateness; they advised Kuwait to intercept any future threat to their independence by the new regime by bribing it. The Kuwaitis paid the new Ba'ath government the tidy sum of £50 million; the Iraqi claim to Kuwait was frozen. This too goes a long way towards explaining Saddam's attempt to intimidate Kuwait and force it to pay him money to meet his internal financial needs after the Iran-Iraq War.

The intelligence, political and economic moves which followed the coup reveal far-reaching cooperation between the CIA and the Ba'ath. Colonel Saleh Mahdi Ammash, the man whose imprisonment led to the anti-Kassem coup being moved forward, was released and made Minister of Defence. One of the first requests made to him by his American mentor and friend, William Lakeland, was to exchange much-needed American arms for Russian-made MiG-21s, T54 tanks and Sam missiles. The Americans wanted to assess the effectiveness of Soviet arms, particularly their aircraft.[51] The Iraqis gave the Americans what they wanted forty-eight hours after the coup and the Americans reciprocated by supplying them with military hardware and by building an air-bridge between Turkey and Iran and Kirkuk in northern Iraq within a day. The arms supplied by America to the Iraqi army were used to fight the Kurds.[52] Until Kassem's overthrow, both the British and Americans had supported the Kurds and provided them with arms.

In the commercial field, Shell, BP, Bectel, Parsons, Mobil and other British and American companies were allowed to re-enter Iraq to develop its oilfields. Robert Anderson, the one-time Eisenhower Secretary of the Treasury and later a CIA troubleshooter, came to Baghdad to negotiate a sulphur concession for the Pan American Sulfur Company. American companies began negotiations to build the Basra dry-dock facilities. The CIA-Iraqi connection was yielding economic benefits.

However, all this was short-lived. The first sign that the honeymoon between the Ba'ath and the CIA was coming to an end was an Iraqi request for the US to recall Lakeland, the CIA's chief field operative with troublesome connections to Iraqi army officers. This was followed by the deportation of Elie Zogheib, a Lebanese-American professor at Baghdad University who had acted as a CIA contact man. Curiously, the end of their roles was instigated by Nasser, the Egyptian president who had cooperated with the CIA against Kassem. Lakeland was one of the CIA agents in direct touch with Nasser when the latter overthrew King Farouk in 1952 and Nasser appreciated his ability and warned the new Iraqi regime against cooperating with him.[53]

The Ba'ath group which toppled Kassem was led by General Ahmad Hassan Al Bakr. Realizing the need for a well-known name acceptable to the Iraqi people as a replacement for Kassem, they selected Abdel Salam Aref, the army colonel who was Kassem's partner in the coup which overthrew the monarchy in 1958 and who, having fallen out with Kassem over the latter's refusal to join Nasser's United Arab Republic, had a following among the substantial pro-Nasser elements within Iraq and its army.

A firebrand with a religious bent, Aref was not party to the conspiracy and the contacts with the CIA, and he was to prove tougher than the Ba'athists who appointed him president and sought to reduce him to a front man. Using his old army contacts and Nasser's followers cleverly, he got rid of the Ba'ath in just nine months, installed a solidly pro-Nasser government behind him and elevated the haphazard contacts towards unity the Ba'ath had started with Nasser to serious negotiations.

What Britain and the United States feared most came to pass; instead of gaining protection for their strategic and oil interests through indirect control of Iraq, what emerged was an Iraq willing to follow Nasser's lead. It was this, the moves towards union with Egypt, under both the Ba'ath and Aref, which ended the period of cooperation between Iraq and the West.[54] Luckily for the West, Nasser had become careful about forming unions which had little chance of survival and reluctantly he turned down the Iraqi offers to join him.

The history of the Syrian, Jordanian and Iraqi coups leaves little doubt as to what constituted Western policy towards the Middle East in the 1950s and 60s. There was a clear pattern to American and British behaviour which showed what and who they supported or opposed.

The murder of King Ghazi is the simplest coup to explain. Coming as it did in 1939, it was a brutal extension of the colonial attitude which followed the First World War. Having appointed and controlled the heads of states of the Arab Middle East, the British thought they could still do the same in the 1930s. Ghazi's popularity was dismissed out of hand; the British were committed to the idea of deputy sherifs, people like Nuri Saïd.

The American and British differences which first surfaced in the 1950s were not of aims; they centred on how to achieve them. Both sides were one in their wish to install regimes in power which followed Western designs. The competition to control Syria, seen in that context, was nothing more than a British wish to carry out Western policies under its auspices through the reliance on a friendly Iraqi regime while the US thought using army colonels was a better way of controlling the same country. Their different attitudes toward Kassem were a reflection of their national characters: the traditional British belief that the Arabs are incapable of adhering to ideology and the American fear of communism. These differences vanished when Kassem threatened Western oil interests.

The West's willingness to corrupt its friends was a motivating factor in the Jordanian phoney coups which contributed to King Hussein's continuance in power and the consequent maintenance of Western hegemony over his country, supported by both sides. This underscored a Western willingness to be dismissive of attempts at legitimacy and the democratic process and to rely on dictatorships. To the West, Hussein combined the roles of a traditional monarch and an army colonel. Also, the West's willingness to accept the corruption of its friends was another by-product of the Hussein coups.

The anti-Kassem Iraqi coup of 1963 exposes Western opposition to populist Arab regimes. Moreover, cooperation between the CIA and the Ba'ath and Nasser supports my thesis that almost all Middle East coups took place with Western connivance. Certainly, the Ba'ath and Nasser accepted the need for American involvement.

However one analyses them, all these coups represent a Western commitment against any Arab unity except on the rare occasions when the British saw a union between Iraq and Syria as a way of extending Western influence under them. There is a total absence of concern regarding the effects of these coups in deterring the development of a state structure or democratic institutions. Opposing Arab unity and deterring democracy have governed the West's involvement in the Middle East throughout this century, and this is still true today. To judge from this, the Western belief that the Arabs are incapable of relating to democracy or of uniting is nothing more than an attempt at self-justification.

PART FOUR

The Deputy Sheriffs

5 · The Palestinians Against Themselves

More has been written about the Palestinians and their 'problem' than about any country, ethnic or religious group, or political movement in the history of the Middle East. Yet, despite some tiredness with the subject among sceptical book publishers and overwhelmed readers alike, an impartial, thorough and clear assessment of the Palestinian leadership and how its inherent pro-West policies contributed to the disaster which befell the Palestinian people has not been made.

Even the most courageous efforts – and Philip Mattar's *Mufti of Jerusalem* and Edward Said's *Peace and Its Discontents* are laudable efforts which deserve special mention – fall into a familiar trap. Namely, they place too much emphasis on the character of the Mufti and Yasser Arafat and do not accord the importance it deserves to the issue of their intrinsic pro-West inclinations and its effect on their relationship to the Palestinian people and their fate. Western writers erroneously see the Palestinians and their leadership as one and the same and Arab writers are fearful that exposing this situation would reflect poorly on their own beliefs in Arab-Western cooperation.

This is a major omission. Except when its position was threatened by its own people and it presented this threat as something else, the Palestinian leadership consistently followed pro-West policies or ones subservient to pro-West Arab considerations. This contributed in a major though immeasurable way to the unhappy outcome of the Palestinian problem.

To simplify matters, and because leaders such as Ahmad Shukeiri, who chaired the PLO from 1964 to 1967, produced no lasting influence, it is through examining the lives of the two men who decided the fate of the Palestinians for seventy years that this problem manifests itself. I refrain from writing 'led the Palestinians' because the Mufti of Palestine, Hajj Amin Al Husseini, and the leader of the Palestine Liberation Organization, Yasser Arafat, very often exercised their positions of leadership without the consent or support of the Palestinian people. Except for the recent poll confirming Arafat, neither man was ever elected to office. Their claims to leadership lack the credibility of a true democratic process and the necessary elements for legitimacy. Both men assumed their positions of leadership through circumstances beyond the control of the Palestinian people. The Mufti attained his position through British help and Arafat was elevated to it by the pro-West Palestinian élite and the Arab countries.

For most of their lives, to outside detractors both men are fanatics, terrorists and murderers. To their Palestinian and Arab supporters, they are heroes and paramount leaders. However, these labels produce the same result: the people described are perceived as the supreme champions of the Palestinian cause and the leading opponents of Zionism and Israel. The popular acceptance of these labels confirms them in their positions and eliminates the need to examine their validity.

A complete list of books which positioned the two leaders in accordance with these and similar descriptions would fill hundreds of pages. Yet on one thing most journalists and writers agree: the Palestinian problem has been so subordinated to the personalities of these two men that there is no way to separate them. In fact, the Palestinian people are very often seen as tools in their hands, obedient followers with little to say. Except for the two writers already mentioned, even the most well-intentioned of journalists and writers follow this formula. Other writers who have taken exception to this – and some, like Bernard Kimmerling and Joel Migdal, go further and identify much of Palestinian history with that of the fellaheen – do not leave a mark because they have very few followers.[1]

As we will see, the Palestinians possess a character which precludes subservience. They have an independent make-up and their belief in their rights as a people includes an attachment to the principles of democracy and a desire to express themselves freely, without relying on intermediaries. Yet, even when we question their claim to being the sole representatives of the Palestinians, the modern history of Palestine is the story of these two intermediaries. The Arabs and the world accepted them as the spokesmen for the Palestinians and they used this position to deal with the West in a manner which determined the fate of their people.

After defining the two men's positions *vis-à-vis* their people, the problem is reduced to how their hidden or overt pro-West behaviour affected the overall Palestinian problem. In particular, did the Palestinian leadership of these two men reflect the will of the Palestinian people or did they cooperate with the West and traditional regimes to assume and abuse their positions at the expense of their countrymen?

To judge by the content of interviews conducted with Palestinians in the occupied territories and throughout the world, the Palestinians believe that their leaders have failed them. The Palestinians think they deserve better than what the Mufti's and Arafat's seventy years of leadership have produced and what the future promises. The Palestinians, justifiably among the world's leading exponents of conspiracy theories, blame Christianity, the Western powers, Arab governments, their leaders and endless combinations of these elements for their misfortune. But the focus of our attention is the role of the leaders, their relationships to the Arab establishment and the West and what this produced.

The Grand Mufti of Palestine (1894–1974) was to the manner born. Muhammad Amin Al Husseini, as his last name suggests, was a descendant of the Prophet. Unlike other families who claimed this lineage, the Husseinis have successfully used it to attain positions of Palestinian leadership and paramountcy for centuries. Under Ottoman Turkey in particular, for more than three hundred years, the Husseinis were accepted as leading Palestinian notables upon whom the Turkish caliphate depended. In line with this policy, Istanbul appointed many Husseinis to a combination of religious or civil offices or both.[2] Their claim to holiness was enhanced by their belonging to the Hanafi school of Islam, the sect to which the Ottoman caliphs but not the mainly Shafi Palestinian people belonged. This bond, almost obsolete now, mattered until the First World War and the break-up of the Ottoman Empire.

Amin, who never used the Muhammad prefix, followed in the footsteps of many members of his family. He graduated from Al Rashidiya school in Jerusalem and went on to attend the Islamic university of Al Azhar in Cairo. For unknown reasons, he never finished his studies, but left Cairo and enrolled in the military college in Istanbul. Pictures of him in military uniform show a small, fair-skinned, moustachioed young man with an Astrakhan hat and a look of determination. With his blue eyes, often spoken of by people who knew him,[3] he must have been a handsome young man indeed. A slight, attractive lisp suggested shyness and was an added benefit.

The Mufti's involvement in politics was tantamount to exercising a birthright. His father and brother, Taher and Kamel, and several relatives had been Muftis of Palestine. In an essentially feudal society being a Husseini meant being a politician. In their case they possessed the two basic requirements for politics: they were both landowners and religious people. Amin had the added advantage of coming of age during the early part of the twentieth century, when the disintegration of the Ottoman Empire and what might follow created an atmosphere of uncertainty. This challenging period no doubt contributed to his early commitment to an activist life.

Whether, like so many Arabs in Cairo, Damascus and Turkey at the outbreak of the First World War, the Mufti joined any of the Istanbul-based or other societies advocating equality for the Arabs under Turkey or total independence is shrouded in mystery. What is known is that he wasted no time in joining the fray in Palestine at the end of the war. A.W. Kayyali, perhaps the foremost Palestinian historian of this period, states that in 1916–17 the hyperactive young man joined the Jerusalem-based Arab Club, Islamic Society and Brotherhood and Chastity Group.[4]

But vagueness continued to surround his activities even after he became president of Jerusalem's Arab Club, perhaps because there was nothing of note to report. However, in an omission which testifies to the continued reverence and fear that writing about the man generates, Arab historians shy from assessing the man's early years, even on whether he saw himself as a secular or a religious person or both. But on one thing practically all serious historians agree: Amin – contrary to the popular historical image of extremist nationalist leader – was pro-British.

In 1917, he recruited Arab volunteers to fight with General Allenby and the British to help them defeat the Turks and occupy Jerusalem.[5] But this and other minor activities are less significant than the favourable way the British viewed him four years later. Amin's dramatic emergence as a major figure in Palestinian politics, his election to the office of Mufti, had the British behind it. They made him Mufti.

In 1921 Amin Husseini's brother Kamel, the incumbent Mufti, died and the office became vacant. The Ulemas, the Muslim committee, held elections to choose a new one. The British High Commissioner, the Zionist Sir Herbert Samuel, was entitled to act in accordance with a law which gave him the right to appoint to this very important office one of the top three contenders. As it was, Hajj Amin came fourth, an automatic disqualification. But he wasn't rejected and instead the High Commissioner prevailed upon the third contender to withdraw. This done, Sir Herbert made the appointment of Amin Al Husseini to the position of Mufti.[6] Later he added to the importance of this position by creating and assuming the chairmanship of the Supreme Islamic Council.

This remarkable occurrence was the beginning of Amin Husseini's complicated relationship with the British. The decision which provided him with a springboard which he used slowly and most deliberately to assume the leadership of the Palestinians and place himself and his family ahead of the other families of notables, has been analysed many times, but its importance warrants further examination.

At the time of his appointment, the Mufti was twenty-seven. This and the fact that he hadn't finished his studies at Al Azhar should have disqualified him – at the least they represented serious drawbacks. And he had two additional strikes against him: he was known for his impetuosity and in 1920 he had been sentenced to a prison term of ten years for participating, to an unknown extent, in anti-British riots.[7] Interestingly, it was the same Samuel who had amnestied him.

Opinions differ as to what prompted Samuel to overlook the Mufti's shortcomings. Though the Husseinis' paramountcy was a factor, the other contenders for the job too came from prominent families. Because the British had just appointed Rhagib Nashashibi, the doyen of the Husseinis' main competitors, mayor of Jerusalem, many historians believe that the Mufti's appointment was part of a British divide-and-rule policy, an attempt to control the Palestinians through adding to the feud between their two leading families.[8] In fact, there is no need to accept this interpretation. Amin was appointed Mufti against competition from his own family, something which makes it possible to judge it as a personal appointment. The other Husseini contenders included Amin's nephew Taher and this supports a less-known contention that High Commissioner Samuel obtained specific promises from the future Mufti. Amin's subsequent behaviour supports this contention; despite popular pressures to do the opposite, his assumption of office under British tutelage was followed by a long period of open cooperation between the two sides. Clearly, the Mufti saw himself as Britain's representative to the Palestinians and the interpreter of Palestinian aspirations to the British, not to mention the fact that most of his salary was paid by the British Mandate Government. The situation was identical to elevating Hussein I and Ibn Saud to kings.

After 1921 the Mufti's career can be divided into three parts. The first, 1921–36, was a period of near-total cooperation with the British while keeping Palestinian demands under control. The second was 1936–48, when his balancing act came to an end and popular pressure forced him into going all-Palestinian and led him to assume a nationalist position against the British to the point of fomenting rebellion against them in Iraq and spending the years 1941–5 in Germany. And last was the period of the 1948 War and his eventual political demise in 1964, when the emergence of the Palestine Liberation Organization (PLO) rendered him obsolete.

Did the Mufti's behaviour during any of these periods reflect the will and desire of the Palestinian people or did relations and friendship with outside powers capable of providing him with support come first? There is little doubt that the national interest was subordinated to narrow personal and Husseini family interests, and that friendship with outside powers was used to promote both. The result of his selfish behaviour on the

Palestinian people's wish to retain their country and be free, independent and democratic was disastrous.

But the Mufti's relations with the British during the early 1920s cannot but be judged in terms of how other notables vying for the leadership of Palestine would have behaved. Not a single historian, Arab, Israeli or Western, denies that all leading Palestinian families were pro-British. Palestinian historians, in this case free to proffer inclusive judgement without offending a particular family and appearing dangerously partisan, concur in this judgement (Mattar, Kayyali, Hout, Shukeiri and others). In fact, Kayyali goes further and demonstrates that what existed between the various families was no more than an open competition between pro-British and very pro-British groups. He attributes this to the traditional relationship which existed between the leading families and Turkey, a beneficial bond of friendship which placed the notables in charge of the Palestinian people and which the British sought to perpetuate.[9]

This historical term of reference, however, is not an acceptable explanation or excuse. The notables, the Husseinis and Mufti included, may have subscribed to this tradition, but beginning with the 1922 disturbances in Palestine, the Palestinian people showed signs of coming of age and wanted them to behave differently and act on their behalf. Newspapers, often run by Christian intellectuals with admirable nationalist zeal, openly attacked the families through thinly veiled reference to 'self-interest groups';[10] and the fellaheen, never less than 60 per cent of the population of Palestine, were so desperate that they composed songs praising the days of Ottoman Turkey and lamenting its demise[11] or calling for a new caliphate. So, from the early 1920s, the families' and Mufti's cooperation with and wish to befriend the British was contrary to the wishes of a majority of an anti-British Palestinian people.

The British knew of this dichotomy but did nothing.[12] It suited their indirect rule plans which called for reliance on local chiefs. They also knew that the town notables, many of whose children were being educated in missionary schools, were the only people capable of registering land in their own names and encouraged this activity to allow them to grow wealthier and stronger. By appointing Amin to the religious position of Mufti, converting children to Western ways and aiding and abetting land registration in the name of a small number of abusive families, they were reconfirming their dependence on the accommodating élite. Amin, a Husseini who belonged to the main line of a family which operated under five branches, was the ultimate expression of this British pro-establishment policy. He had inherited a great deal of land and his appointment to the highest religious office in the land completed his qualifications.

The first test of the Mufti's position as the link between the British and the Palestinian people came in 1922, when anti-Jewish disturbances protesting against Zionist emigration and land purchases took place in a number of Palestinian cities. These serious events, which led to a disputed number of deaths, found the Mufti reluctant to take a position. The Palestinian people were restive, determined to start a protest movement or a rebellion against the British, but the Mufti turned down the prospect of leading either. Instead, his response to the troubles was to stay in constant touch with Sir Herbert Samuel, who used this friendly connection to nip the movement in the bud.[13] Not only did he follow a pro-British appeasement policy, but this was the first instance of his advocacy of cooperation between the various families of notables towards the same aim. He led the notables in calming the people and shortly after into talking the Palestinians out of non-payment of taxes. His instinct for self-preservation went further: in 1922 he turned down a promising British response to popular pressure, a proposal to create an elected representative assembly. Then and later, the idea of a representative assembly was against his thinking: it would have created an elected body capable of replacing him as the link between the Palestinians and the British.

Beyond acting as an instrument of appeasement and neutralizing both the people's passions and their passive resistance plans, the Mufti's activities between 1922 and 1927 appear to have centred on enhancing his position and that of his already powerful family. His traditional government-sponsored title and his chairmanship of the newly created Supreme Islamic Council allowed undisputed control of the *waqf* (religious endowments) and the Islamic courts, and the British allowed him to run both without hindrance. He controlled all religious appointments and the distribution of funds. The Mufti worked with Mousa Kazem Pasha Al Husseini, head of the purely political Arab Executive and a cousin, appointed another cousin, Izhaq Darwish Al Husseini as his chief of staff and brought in Sheikh Hassan Abu So'ud, a Shafi cleric, to enhance his religious position. He used the *waqf* money to buy support or silence would-be critics. It was a case of using the institutions of Islam in the service of the infidels.

Simultaneously the Mufti moved to control the hitherto neglected elements within the country which objected to the pro-Zionist British policies and represented a threat to his leadership. According to my late grandfather, Sheikh Mousa Shahine Al Izzarawi, the Mufti's special assistant for over twenty years, the Mufti proceeded on several fronts. To subdue the anti-Zionist educated Christians, he befriended some power-hungry sycophants among them, such as Emile Ghoury, a loud, unimaginative man who followed him blindly. He held constant meetings with newspaper editors and pleaded moderation and occasionally warned them against inflaming public feelings. But, above all, he tried to control the major source of possible rebellion by methodically appointing representatives who promoted his leadership in villages. Here he found fertile ground, for not only did many simple villagers derive special satisfaction from the unusual attention paid them by the leading notable of the land, but many of them, very much like the Bedouin sheikhs of Ibn Saud, were paid for their loyalty and proceeded to calm their flock. My grandfather's recollections, as I remember them, neglected another important move. Through his control of Islamic affairs the Mufti oversaw the appointment of *khatibs* (preachers) in practically all the mosques of the land and his appointees, in turn, preached his word to the faithful.[14]

In 1928 events were to test whether his elaborate efforts and his friendship with the British were to shape Palestine's future. A simple incident, in which a religious Jew placed prayer screens in a certain way against the Wailing Wall, led to questions as to who controlled it, released pent-up national and religious feeling and led to serious disturbances. Resenting what they saw as Jewish encroachment on the Mosque of Omar and the Dome of the Rock, both of which are situated over the Wailing Wall, Palestinians broke ranks with the Mufti and the Supreme Islamic Council and descended on Jerusalem with sticks, clubs and knives to protect what had hitherto been unquestionably theirs. The Mufti's balancing act, his inclination to befriend and please the British and to control the Palestinians at the same time, came under strain. The strength of Palestinian feeling left him little room for manoeuvre.

But once again the Mufti prevaricated until things calmed down, then threw in his lot with the British. The historian Bayan Al Hout writes of his fearing the loss of his position,[15] and Philip Mattar goes further by speaking of how this prospect made him distance himself from the disturbances which continued well into 1929.[16] Other historians offer variations on the theme of a man reluctant to do anything which might affect his friendship with the British administration, the source of his power.

Interestingly, this exposed another facet of the thinking of the man. Instead of reacting directly to what was happening, the Mufti's only response was to shift the focus of attention. He called for the convening of a Muslim Conference to discuss the issue of the Islamic holy places and went to work to convince the Palestinians of the far-reaching results that holding such a conference would produce. This was a clever, indirect response to the obvious unhappiness of the Palestinians, but it was also an attempt to use their misery to attain an elevated Islamic position for himself. Historians accept his action at face value. Little attention is paid to the fact that the British were more concerned with pressures from within Palestine than with any from outside, or to their approval of the holding of the Islamic Conference at a time when Palestinian gatherings and unfriendly political groupings were banned.[17] Unlike now, Islam was still safe.

In fact, while the Mufti was opting for an outside solution, a considerable amount of diplomatic activity and British-sponsored conferences and meetings to solve the Palestinian problem were taking place. The British, bowing to Palestinian demands, went as far as issuing a 1928 White Paper which promised to limit Jewish immigration and eventually hold elections. The Mufti accepted the White Paper and praised Britain for its impartiality while continuing to work closely with the British High Commissioners who followed Samuel, Lord Plumer and Sir John Chancellor.

However, his mind was set on convening the Islamic Conference, which was eventually held in 1931, shortly after the British government, headed by Ramsay MacDonald, had rescinded the White Paper by proclaiming its adherence to previous promises (the Balfour Declaration) to create a Jewish national home. The Islamic Conference was an apparent success; it was attended by 145 delegates from all over the world, and, as usual, proclamations and inflated promises of financial support were made but never fulfilled.

The Mufti's use of his dual role as a representative of the Palestinian people and a salaried official of the British crown to become an international Muslim figure is nothing short of remarkable. In dealing with Muslim and Arab leaders he was aware of their backgrounds and recognized their inherent adherence to pro-British positions. This posture, sold to the Palestinians as an attempt to expand support for their cause in the useless manner of today's Arab League meetings, took place well before the forced estrangement from the British in 1936.

Only two results of the conference are certain: he did try to use it to ease the pressure on the British in Palestine and he cherished his role as a major Muslim figure and an international one.

By 1932 the divergence between the Palestinian people's wish for palpable results on the ground and the Mufti's pan-Islamic posturing was challenged by a new and independent pan-Arab party of well-known personalities and intellectuals, Al Istiqlal. Initially, the party's leaders held several meetings with the Mufti and appealed to him to adopt an anti-British stance.[18] Not only did the Mufti refuse their demands, he so feared for his official and primacy positions that he increased his cooperation with High Commissioner Sir Arthur Wauchope.[19] Furthermore, in an act which betrayed his commitment to British-sponsored personal glory regardless of method and the damage to the Palestinian cause, he proceeded to accuse one of the Istiqlal's leaders, the honourable and committed Awni Abdel Hadi, of cooperating with the Zionists.[20] The Mufti's disinformation tactics, at which he was a master, and British pressure worked, and the Istiqlal's programme came to nothing.

But opposition to the Mufti surfaced again in 1933, and this time it was the other side of the coin: a violent movement of workers and peasants. Led by transplanted Syrian cleric Izzedine Qassam, a firebrand who preached an anti-British campaign based on a militant non-pliant Islam which resembles the fundamentalist movements of today, the Qassamites called for immediate armed rebellion and began attacking Jewish settlements. The Mufti was so alarmed by the mass appeal of the movement, particularly its religious nature, that he turned down their repeated offers of cooperation.[21] Characteristically, he entrusted his initial refusal to cooperate with them to my grandfather, a quiet, unassuming religious man whose normal duties precluded deciding on such weighty issues. Saddling assistants and followers with responsibilities for decisions that he was unwilling to assume publicly was one of the Mufti's trademarks.

Another act which reveals the unsympathetic character of the man was his reaction to the killing of Qassam and some of his followers by British forces in 1935. The Mufti's telegram of condolence was so lukewarm as to be rude. Shamelessly, the telegrams of the Nashashibis and other notables were no better. The Palestinian establishment, selfish and quarrelsome as its members were, was united in its non-acceptance of a popular leader who depended on workers and peasants to oppose Britain. Al Qassam was a bigger threat to them than following the British. (This is similar to Arafat's current relationship to Hamas and Israel.)

But what the Istiqlal and Qassami demonstrated was the existence of serious opposition to the Mufti's ways from both liberal intellectuals and the radical right. This, instead of serving notice on the Mufti to change his ways, made him sink deeper in his reliance on members of his family and other members of the Palestinian community who had little or no political following or principle.

For how the Mufti behaved before the inevitable 1936 rebellion, except for the known facts of the Istiqlal and Qassam opposition and the record of more British commissions and secret and open negotiations, a period shrouded in mystery, the writer is fortunate to have the recollections of his already mentioned grandfather and those of M. B., a Mufti follower and a member of the Arab Higher Committee, and the writer's father. My father, a young man in the 1930s, followed his father-in-law and became one of the Mufti's toughs at an early age.

All three are agreed that the Mufti depended more and more on members of his family, particularly Ishaq and Jamal (leaders of the Palestine Arab Party). Though ostensibly surrounded by advisers, the Mufti appears to have followed his own opinion without taking those of others into serious consideration. And there is little doubt that he was a snob who held the notables in high esteem to the extent of according those among them who opposed him greater respect than he gave to his followers from humble backgrounds. On the overall question of why the Palestinians did not produce an alternative leadership, the picture is less clear. As already mentioned, the traditional leadership, the notables, appear to have competed as to who was more pro-British (the Nashashibis and their National Defence Party), others who were intellectually inclined had little stomach for combat (the Khalidis and their Reform Party) and a third group of notables were outright collaborators (Hassan Sidqi Dajani, Haidar Toukan and Rashed Abu Kadra). Not only were these people unacceptable to the Palestinians, but British awareness of the poor state of affairs in Palestine led them to put their support behind the man best able to manipulate it, the Mufti.

This leaves unanswered the vital question of why no attempt to wrest the leadership appeared from non-establishment groups, from self-made intellectuals or educated villagers. There are three simple answers. As in the rest of the Middle East, tradition was against it, in Palestine so much so that the villages were often identified as 'a Husseini village or a Nashashibi village'. And no less important were the conditions of constant turmoil, which meant there was never enough time to develop an alternative leadership and which led to reliance on what existed. Naturally, there was also the British commitment to supporting the notables and their willingness, with help from their friends, to act against grass-roots movements like the Qassamites.

But neither the efforts of the British nor the wiles of the Mufti could delay the inevitable. Leaderless and certainly without the Mufti's support or approval, the Palestinians erupted in open and spontaneous rebellion in 1936. It had begun in small acts of violence in 1935, a short time after Al Qassam's death, and a year later turned into one of the most serious uprisings in the history of the British Empire. Yet the Mufti hoped to contain it until the last minute, even after the deteriorating conditions within Palestine forced him and his fellow notables to join forces and create the Arab Higher Committee, a political organization which pre-empted the need to incorporate new elements and form a national movement to face the coming storm.

The best way to judge the Mufti's attitude at this time is to examine his involvement, or lack of it, in the 1936 general strike – a total shut-down of all businesses which lasted six months and in which all levels of the Palestinian people participated. Not only was the far-reaching decision to strike taken under public pressure and without his sanction,[22] but initially he proceeded to try to end it on his own. When the strike's success became apparent and ending it proved immune to his efforts, he identified with it. The Palestinian people, simple and hungry for their leaders' support in order to continue their struggle, accepted this as an heroic act and confirmed the Mufti's primacy.

As with Yasser Arafat today, the Mufti's primacy position allowed him to operate on both an open and a secret level. If the Mufti's way of escaping the open 1936 Rebellion, which he couldn't stop and which was threatening his position, was to manipulate it, then what followed was no more than a slight change from his pro-British policies. His contacts with Arab leaders, cursory until confronted by the strike and the growing rebellion, became a regular affair. Agreeing with the pro-British leaders of Iraq and Saudi Arabia that the strike at least should be ended, he mistranslated their appeals and successfully presented them to the Palestinian people as guarantees that better things were on the way. He prevailed, and the Palestinians finally ended their strike.[23]

But time was catching up with the Mufti; he had misjudged the mood of his people, who were demanding more, and suddenly it was the loss of his Palestinian leadership which became the issue. He had expected the report of the Peel Commission (another British committee entrusted with finding a solution to the problem of Palestine) to contain a recommendation to partition the country and, late in 1936, rightly judging that this would push the rebellion beyond the point of no return, he hurried to Damascus to meet Palestinian and Arab leaders and declare his unequivocal support for what his people were doing.[24] This was the turning point: from then onwards the Mufti knew that only a totally anti-British stance would maintain him as leader. It was a decision which took a long time to make, obviously an unavoidable one which he had studiously avoided, but the Palestinians' hunger for an image to which they could attach their rebellion was so strong that all was forgotten and forgiven and they reconfirmed him as their popular leader. Sadly, his performance in the years which followed, his intrinsic commitment to use outside forces for personal glory, was to cause the Palestinian people more grief. His identification with another power, Nazi Germany, and his Arafat-like refusal to accept that his people had come of age, were as destructive as his original pro-British position.

Between 1936 and 1939 the Palestinians, poorly armed and without training or serious support, gave the British a hard time. The Palestinians' most important demand was that the British put an end to Jewish immigration to Palestine. They fought a British army of over fifty thousand men throughout the country and in the countryside engaged it in open and on occasion successful combat. In the cities there were strikes, boycotts, bombings and assassinations. It was a peasant-led uprising which produced innumerable acts of sacrifice and heroism and in spirit it was directed against the city effendis (notables) and their fezzes and silver-tipped canes as much as it was aimed against the British and the Jews. One of its signal victories, perhaps its most memorable one, was to bring the notables down a peg by forcing all Palestinians to wear the Arab head-dress as a sign of support for the rebellion.[25]

The British were taken aback by the strength of the rebellion and by the defection of their leading intermediary, the man who had kept a lid on things and whose failure had led him to change sides. Despite offers by the ever pro-British Nashashibis to step into the Mufti's shoes, the Mandate Government judged the strength of feeling of the Palestinians correctly and, realizing the futility of producing an alternative, dissolved the Arab Higher Committee, exiled some of its leaders and forced the Mufti to take refuge in Haram Ash Sherif (a holy area embracing the Mosque of Omar and the Dome of the Rock). There was no attempt by the British to violate the holiness of the area and arrest the Mufti and he managed to escape to Lebanon in 1937.

Here it is important to examine the Mufti's claim to leadership of the rebellion. That he became its recognized leader is undoubtedly true, but it is also true that he feared its anti-establishment tilt to the point of wanting to end it. Early in 1937, he did issue an appeal to the rebels to lay down their arms,[26] and, except for the involvement of Abdel Kader Al Husseini, a hero-cousin of whom the Mufti disapproved and was jealous, there is no evidence that he or members of his family supported the rebellion or used the funds available to them from Arab, Muslim and other sources to finance it. My father, a full-time participant in the rebellion and someone who had a direct line to the Mufti through his father-in-law, is utterly dismissive of the Husseini role. He speaks of discovering that would-be contributors to the rebels paid the Husseinis money which was pocketed and dramatically states, 'The Husseinis didn't suffer, we did.'

Yet, again very much like Arafat in Tunisia, the Mufti continued to run the affairs of the Palestinians from Lebanon. Operating from Al Zoq, a small village north of Beirut, he was the undisputed leader of a rebellion to which he contributed very little. At the height of the disturbances, in the middle of 1938, Abdel Kader's heroic deeds threatened to catapult him into a leadership position challenging that of the Mufti. But the Mufti, while often denying Abdel Kader help, claimed credit for the latter's deeds through emphasizing his Husseini name. In fact, Abdel Kader was a fighter, a magnificent field leader of men, but he had no political ambitions or time to pursue them. And there was nobody else.

The challenge to the Mufti was reduced to what he could do to reinforce his credentials as a revolutionary leader. Another conference, in London in 1939, and another White Paper gave him this opportunity. The British, particularly anxious to end the rebellion on the eve of the Second World War, agreed to partial stoppage of emigration and the eventual holding of elections to produce a proportional-representative body. The Arab leaders were divided in favour of accepting the offer; in fact, many of them were surprised at what the sacrifices of their peasants had produced. But the Mufti turned it down for fear of losing his new position; once again he opposed the creation of a representative body, because he was not sure he could accept it and stay leader.[27] Before that, he missed opportunities because of his desire to maintain his British-sponsored leadership; this time it was his wish to remain leader and sole representative of the Palestinians. Statesmanship had no place in his thinking. Majid Khadduri and other historians make a mild, circumstantial claim as to how the Mufti was forced into becoming anti-British.[28] This is a narrow interpretation of his solidly anti-populist performance between 1921 and 1935. He was forced into an anti-British position at gunpoint, the eruption of an angry rebellion with which, in order to survive, he had to agree.

A short time later, after British force of arms and lack of Arab help led the rebellion to fizzle out, the Mufti – unbelievably – reverted to form. According to the Briton Colonel Richard Meinertzhagen,[29] the Mufti, on 15 September 1939, offered the British cooperation during the Second World War in return for being allowed to return to Jerusalem. My father, by chance with the Mufti when the British declared war against Germany, recalls a subsequent conversation during which the Mufti admitted that the war was not helpful 'to the cause'. The merits or demerits of being pro-German and anti-British matter less than the exposure of a man wanting to return to Britain's fold to stay leader. So much for the Mufti's popular reputation as a man of principle.

The British refusal to have him back and the discomfort his presence was causing the French administration of Lebanon drove the Mufti to Iraq in October 1939. For almost a year he lived up to a promise not to interfere in Iraqi internal politics and to limit his anti-British activities, a pledge he had made to the Iraqi leadership upon arrival. It went further, and there is evidence that he still sought a settlement of his problem with the British to the point of soliciting the help of the Iraqi Prime Minister, his arch enemy, the solidly pro-British Nuri Saïd. He wanted Nuri to get Britain to honour the contents of the 1939 White Paper. But once again it was too late, and the British turned him and Nuri down.

His chance to 'resurface' came in April 1941, when a group of Iraqi army officers installed in office an anti-British government headed by the politician Rashid Ali Al Keilani. Suddenly he was totally anti-British again. Not only that, but he actively assumed the role of spiritual father of the Iraqi government at the age of forty-seven. With the substantial problems facing that government, mainly the uncompromising British demand for it to side with the allies, and the discovery that the Mufti had established secret contacts with the Axis powers during 1940,[30] the stage was set for him to become the undisputed leader of Baghdad. My recollections of conversations with my grandfather include stories of how the Mufti's home became a Mecca for Iraqi officers and politicians. Amazingly, little is known about what advice he offered them. That he advocated cooperation with the Axis against the British is assumed, but there is no solid proof of this, nor is there any record of him urging Iraqi military resistance to the landing of British troops in Basra in May 1941. What is a matter of record is in character: the Mufti relished every moment of his leadership role, he loved seeing the Iraqi establishment and army officers kowtow to him. He became bigger than Palestine, for he was the Arab leader standing up to Britain.

It was to be a short-lived elevation. Britain, determined not to give their Iraqi opponents time to establish themselves, sought Jordanian help, invaded Iraq and won an easy victory. The overrated Iraqi army collapsed. Most of the anti-British Iraqi officers behind the Keilani government were arrested and executed, but not the wily conspirator. He and Rashid Ali managed to sneak into Iran and after minor difficulties found their way to Turkey and established contact with Nazi ambassador Franz von Papen. By November 1941 the Mufti was ensconced in Berlin, soon to be joined by his ally Rashid Ali.

If confirmation of how the Mufti saw himself were needed, then it is the way he behaved in Germany. The Mufti's determination to be seen as the primary Muslim and Arab leader helping the Axis in their war effort was total, and he relied on his meagre religious credentials and embellished his political record to convince the Germans of his entitlement to both. Rashid Ali was his only competitor, and he feuded with his erstwhile host and reduced him to a minor also-ran.

Because of the hysterics which the various Jewish groups and agencies and the British press generated around the Mufti's person, his role while in Germany needs clarification. His anti-British and anti-Allies broadcasts during the war amount to understandable propaganda and are a matter of record, as are his efforts to recruit Balkan Muslims to fight with the Germans. However, there is absolutely nothing to suggest that he ever aided the German policy toward the Jews. Nor is there anything to suggest that the Germans, despite a meeting he had with Hitler and the several he had with Himmler, ever took him very seriously. His attempts at convincing them to pay the Middle East greater attention appear to have gone unanswered. However, Afif Tibi, a Lebanese-Palestinian journalist who saw him frequently during his time in Berlin, exposed two aspects of the Mufti's character which are little known. In 1961 Tibi told me, before an interview I was to conduct with the Mufti in Beirut, 'Don't be charmed like the ladies of Berlin.' Although he steadfastly refused to elaborate on this, he never took it back. Later, in a more serious vein, he told me that the Mufti's great asset was his success in recruiting people. 'He went out of his way to stay in touch with pro-Nazi Arab exiles, regardless of where they came from, to turn them into followers, to keep them on hold for whatever future he had in mind,' Tibi said with obvious admiration. This constant attention to creating an Arab following, though the German part of it is little known, is consistent. Except for the Hashe-mites and until the emergence of Nasser in 1952, the Mufti was the one regional leader with followers throughout the Arab and Muslim worlds.

There are several versions of how the Mufti escaped from Germany at the end of the war. What is clear is that the Allies had knowledge of his presence in France and it is conceivable that they helped him to leave to avoid having to try him and so inflame the Palestinians and Arabs. He arrived in Cairo in May 1946, asked King Farouk for asylum and, in line with Arab hospitality, his request was granted. Formalities out of the way, he wasted no time in assuming the leadership of the Palestinians. According to Collins and Lapierre,[31] the news of his safe arrival in Cairo produced spontaneous demonstrations of affection for his person throughout Pales-tine. Certainly the undisguised sympathy of the Allies towards the Jews following the war had exacerbated the Palestinian problem and created awareness of the impending dangers, even among the simplest people, but it is also important to remember that the man had followers throughout the country and that he successfully turned the negative results of his association with the Axis into a major asset − instead of blaming him for helping create pro-Jewish sympathy, the people admired him for seeing the perfidy of Britain and the Allies ahead of them.

With the approach of United Nations debates on the future of Palestine and the seemingly inevitable British withdrawal from the country, using the umbrella of the Arab Higher Committee, the Mufti set up the equivalent of a new government-in-exile in Cairo. Alas, according to both my grandfather and the then Arab Higher Committee chief accountant M. B., there was very little which was new in the enterprise.

Jamal, Izhaq Mousa, Raja'i, Munif, Haidar, Selim and the able Abdel Kader, all Husseini relations, became his chief advisers. Dozens of incompetents, sycophants and yes-men who had served him in the 1930s flocked to Cairo to rejoin him and were given jobs or money or both. The rest of the money that he was able to raise – and about that we know very little except that it came from Arab and Muslim sources – went to others within Palestine who were equally unfit. He wasted considerable time asking for people's opinion, about almost everything, but he never deferred to what they said. In particular, he always opposed Abdel Kader's suggestions, and the one sensible member of his family and entourage was often reduced to anger and tears. He still saw Abdel Kader as a competitor.

Reducing the influence of Abdel Kader wasn't the only thing the Mufti did at the expense of Palestine's national interest. His use of incompetents within the country was coupled with a total refusal to cooperate with Palestinian groups not beholden to him, including the Najada paramilitary organization, which was particularly strong in the key cities of Jaffa and Haifa. Beyond that, in the Arab arena, he opposed the plans of the Arab League to send troops into Palestine. He was adamant that the Palestinians were capable of fighting the Zionists unaided.

Everything he did, every single step he took on family, Palestinian, Arab and international levels, was aimed at attaining undivided control of the Palestinian and Arab side of the war that was on the way. Even the United Nations' decision in November 1947 to call for the partition of Palestine did not spur him into constructive action and he continued to devote more effort to perpetuating his personal control than to saving Palestine. By the time of the British withdrawal in May 1948, his hollow policies stood in stark contrast to conditions on the ground. The Palestinians were unprepared and the Arab entry into Palestine was poorly planned and coordinated. For all practical purposes, because of lack of plans and agreement on overall aims, Palestine was lost before a shot was fired. Abdel Kader fought bravely and died doing so; King Abdallah of Jordan conducted secret negotiations with Israeli leaders to partition Palestine and annex part of it to Jordan; some Arab leaders (for example, King Farouk) used the war to realize huge commissions from arms purchases and the rest of the Arabs made promises, including threatening oil stoppage, but did nothing. The only thing on which the Arabs, including the Mufti, were agreed was to refrain from asking Russia for help. After all, communism was a threat and an anathema to the Arab ruling classes.

The details of the 1948–9 fighting and its results have been told too often to bear repetition. What matters here is the Mufti's behaviour in the midst of all this. He appears to have been saddled with a Samson complex; every single step he took revealed his desire for things to be in his hands to the point of bringing the house down upon himself and everybody else.

In the middle of the 1948 fighting, following the death of the inspirational Abdel Kader, the Mufti appointed two fools to replace him, Khalid Al Husseini and Kamel Irekat. Their incompetence – Khalid spent his time drinking arak away from the battle and Irekat was a buffoon – demoralized Palestinian fighters. He didn't stop there, for at the height of the battle for Jaffa he refused to help the Najada defend it, although he had the arms they needed.[32] He also refused to communicate with Fawzi Al Kawakji, the leader of the Liberation Army, a force of Arab volunteers which had come to Palestine to fight. The services of able Palestinians, for example the exceptionally competent Musa Al Alami, were rejected. And he was dead set against dealing with the Arab League's appointed commanders, King Abdallah and the Iraqi General Ismael Safwat Pasha. He lived in a fool's paradise, like Hitler in his bunker.

The house came down. After the 1948 War the free Palestine that its people dreamed of was never to be. But the Mufti didn't give up. Late in 1948 he went through the motions of creating an all-Palestine government in Gaza, but he abandoned that and returned to Egypt after a few months. He went back to what he did best, backroom conspiracies and manipulations.

While he did nothing to alter our judgement of his overall character, the period from the end of the 1948 War to his replacement by the PLO in 1964 produced examples of how selfish and utterly behind the times the man was. In 1949 he cooperated with the CIA and fed them information, to foil a plan to unite Syria and Iraq under the Hashemites.[33] Paying little attention to the positive effects that such a union would have in terms of creating a powerful country to confront Israel, he acted in a selfish manner totally helpful to the Israelis. Much later, in 1959, he refused to accept Nasser's leadership of the Arabs, escaped from Cairo to Beirut and began working with Nasser's arch enemy, Iraqi leader Abdel Karim Kassem. To friends he claimed that Nasser was trying to settle the Palestinian problem through secret negotiations with UN Secretary-General Dag Hammarskjöld. While this may have been true, there is little doubt that he resented

Nasser's popular position. Beginning with the 1952 Egyptian revolution, leadership of the Arab masses had moved from the hands of the ultimate manipulator to the arena of open diplomacy, from the hands of the whispering Palestinian rebel to those of the President of the most important Arab country of all.

Unlike other Arab leaders, Nasser succeeded in neutralizing the Mufti. Not only was he the President of Egypt, he also took away the Mufti's Palestinian constituency, and by opting to cooperate with Russia, he had a superpower behind him. The Arab Higher Committee continued to exist, on paper, and there was the occasional attempt to find new backers within the Arab camp. But the Mufti had already become part of history. In fact, the 1952 Egyptian revolution had heralded a new age and the new Arab world which mattered was made up of Nasser, Kassem and other army colonels conducting new battles with old kings and clans. Both sides found the Mufti unacceptable; the new breed of leaders scoffed at his old thinking and the old guard were pro-West and disinclined against too close an association with him.

He still didn't accept defeat gracefully and his last major act was a year after the disaster of the 1967 War and seven years before he died. Forever a prisoner of old-fashioned thinking, he helped elect the establishment candidate, Yasser Arafat, leader of the PLO.

The Mufti is a prime example of the type of hollow member of the Arab élite that the British supported to control a country. It is true that the Palestinian people intercepted his alliance with the British, but what followed, including his alliance with Germany, had very little ideology behind it and was the result of a series of mishaps. British support was behind his rise to prominence and without it, without British reliance on him for a long period of time, the Palestinians would have fared better.

From its inception, the Palestine Liberation Organization was a child of the Arab establishment. The organization, whose acronym is inseparable from the name of Yasser Arafat and which he manipulated to assume the leadership of the Palestinian people, was born at Jerusalem's Ambassador Hotel in 1964. The PLO came into being after the Mufti had been marginalized by Nasser, to meet the need for a representative for the Palestinians in Arab and international forums.

All the Arab governments, including the traditional pro-West ones, either approved of or complied with its creation. Even Jordan, the traditional opponent of Palestinian independence and the country which then controlled east Jerusalem, accepted the decision. The election to the PLO's chairmanship of Ahmad Shukeiri, a Palestinian diplomat for hire who had represented Syria and Saudi Arabia at the United Nations, was another confirmation of the organization's conservative credentials.

Shukeiri was a braggart who made a lot of noise and issued a lot of unrealistic threats while basking in the company of the rich and famous. The 1967 War brought about his end. It is true that the war was an Arab-Nasser affair in which the Palestinians played a minor role, but its disastrous consequences called for a dynamic Palestinian leadership. This opened the door for Yasser Arafat.

The man's origins are so confused that no biographer has been able to unearth the true picture.[34] However, there is little doubt that he was born in either Jerusalem or Gaza in 1929 and that he grew up in Egypt. At what age and in what circumstances he went to Egypt is unknown, but his father appears to have been a small-time merchant with Egyptian connections, a modest and totally honourable man. On his mother's side, Arafat was related to Sheikh Hassan Abu So'ud, the already mentioned close adviser to the Mufti.

Although he was nineteen years old in 1948, the evidence regarding Arafat's involvement in the first Arab-Israeli war is confused. But there is considerable evidence, including many pictures, of Arafat's early 1950s activities in Cairo. It goes further, and his election as head of the Palestinian Student Association, a considerable achievement, attests to inherent leadership qualities. Cairo was a major centre of Arab student political activity and others who coveted this position had the benefit of more money and bigger names.

Arafat moved to Kuwait in 1958, after earning a civil engineering degree from Cairo University and after considering and deciding against emigrating to Canada. His personal life in Kuwait is as mysterious as his early days in Palestine. However, there is little doubt that an inherent nationalistic restlessness found him devoting more time to Palestine than to his small subcontracting business. Nowadays Arafat claims that he was a big-time contractor and a multimillionaire. This is not true[35] and amounts to an unfortunate misplacement of emphasis on his part. The demands of his 'revolutionary' activities precluded running a major company.

Furthermore, while nobody remembers the name of his subcontracting company everybody knows that he was instrumental in creating Fatah (in reverse, Harakat Tahrir Fallistinia, or Palestine Liberation Movement). Now, with the benefit of hindsight, its beginnings reveal a great deal about its eventual direction, and in reality it was a nationalist and not a revolutionary organization. Including Arafat, the five Palestinians who created Fatah came from backgrounds on the edge of notability; they belonged to the equivalent of upper middle class families and in the Middle

East such people usually try to elevate themselves by associating with and emulating the solid aristocracy.

The early political activities of the Fatah group reveal a clear conservative tilt. Arafat al Qudawa Al Husseini, despite the surname no relation to the Mufti, adopted the name of Abu Ammar after Ammar bin Yasser, a companion of the Prophet Muhammad. His chief collaborator Khalil Al Wazzir opted for the more Islamically suggestive Abu Jihad. This can't but have endeared them to the more religious and inherently conservative people of Kuwait and the Gulf. In addition, the Fatah group relied on well-established members of the Palestinian establishment, the Ghosseins, Kaddoumis, Abu So'uds, and others acceptable to Kuwait's pro-West government, for support. Acting as a group of equals, their quasi-establishment efforts met with success. They were able to operate freely, had powerful friends, including some royals, and they raised a lot of money, enough of it to travel freely and publish *Fillistunana* (Our Palestine).

And these untraditional heirs to Palestinian leadership chose Kuwait as the place from which to start. The other Palestinian movement of the time was centred in Beirut and it represented a cleaner break with the historical mould. A genuinely revolutionary one, the Beirut group was an extension of the Arab Nationalist movement which started at the American University of Beirut in the early 1950s and which counted George Habbash as one of its leaders. Distinctly left of centre, the intellectual Beirut group called for total revolution and the overthrow of the traditional Arab regimes as a first step in confronting Israel. And Beirut itself was closer to Palestine, the centre of Arab politics and the home of the free Arab press. But the popular Beirut-based leftists were unacceptable to both the Palestinian establishment and Arab governments, and they were short of money and unable to travel – and Habbash was a Christian. Considering that Jordan's brutal rule of the West Bank and Nasser's control of Gaza precluded the emergence of other groups, Fatah's advantage over Habbash and their Beirut competitors was overwhelming.

The creation of Fatah in Kuwait was followed by a period of expansion. A Qatari branch was established, and this meant more money from sympathetic Qataris and rich Palestinians working there. It went further, for Fatah concentrated its efforts on recruiting more rich Palestinians and gaining the support of the Arab élite everywhere.[36] Because Fatah, probably preoccupied with starting up, initially had no time for the Palestinians in refugee camps and the people of Gaza and the West Bank, and the Arab nationalists didn't have the money to undertake such an effort, run-of-the-mill Palestinians were ignored.

In noting the obvious similarity between the young Arafat and the

Mufti's early days in preferring members of the Palestinian establishment, pro-West Arab governments and rich Arabs everywhere, it should be remembered that the Mufti had operated on home ground and had greater room for manoeuvre. Yet, from his very early days as a leader, Arafat committed similar mistakes. Acting on his own, he appointed cronies to run the various Fatah offices, yes-men with connections whom he elevated more for their loyalty and contacts rather than their talent. Simultaneously Arafat sought and succeeded in controlling the purse-strings and determined who got financial support and who was denied it.[37] Everything he did showed signs of catering to a specific élite group, rejecting committee rule and an inclination towards personal glory. However, unlike the Mufti, Arafat had no family to depend on and there is evidence that his tilt towards the Palestinian élite and conservative regimes initially represented a genuine belief in the wisdom of using them.

His determination to take personal control of Fatah and the problems this created came to a head in Damascus in 1966 and led to his brief suspension as Fatah's military commander. The details are unclear, but Arafat was accused of giving considerable sums of money to his loyalists, the cronies with solid establishment connections but of questionable value to the movement, without the necessary authorization by his colleagues. The suspension was lifted after a few months, without a change in what led to it. This lack of concern for corruption and championing of cronyism dog Arafat to this day.

We know a great deal about Arafat's ways and inter-Palestinian dealings between 1958 and the removal of the incompetent Shukeiri in 1967, but there is very little which is illuminating about Fatah's attitude towards the West. Fatah's founders did resort to the usual condemnation of Western support for Israel, but this was no more than the rhetoric to which even the most pro-Western of the Arab countries subscribed. There was nothing in Fatah's pronouncement as clear-cut as Habbash's call for threatening Western economic interests or opposing the Arab regimes which befriended the West. Even Fatah's social attitude, its concentration on rich Palestinians and its relegation of the rest to a secondary position, revealed an inherently conservative bent. Fatah committed itself to wanting to continue the fight against Israel, to resort to guerrilla tactics to unbalance it and eventually defeat it. To judge by the atmosphere of the times, this was a conservative posture, compared with the demands of other groups a minimum Palestinian position which agreed with the policies of the pro-West Arab governments.

It is obvious that the Arabs saw Arafat as the lesser of two evils. Whether Fatah, like the Mufti, was committed to Palestinian rather than Arab primacy in the fight against Israel was never articulated, but Arafat's and Fatah's attitude reflects a mutuality of interest between them and their hosts. The Fatah group wanted to speak for the Palestinians, and the oil-rich governments in particular wanted a moderate Palestinian leadership which absolved them and didn't threaten them. Later Arafat advocated this openly and it helped guarantee him support from Arab governments looking for an excuse to disown the Palestinians. They settled for paying the Palestinians money to do their own fighting, and Arafat also got what he wanted: a Palestinian entity capable of keeping alive the aspirations of his people.

The decision to remove Shukeiri and replace him with Yasser Arafat, taken in steps, had considerable support from the Arab governments. Shukeiri's demise was sealed after the 1967 War; he had a tarnished image and he believed in the discredited pan-Arabism of Nasser. After an interregnum of committee rule, Arafat was elected chairman in 1969. And while he was elected to the post of PLO chairman by the Palestine National Council (PNC) – then as now it was an appointed body of mainly rich establishment people who were not selected by the Palestinian people – there is little doubt that the move had wide popular support. In fact, Arab leaders, including Nasser and King Faisal of Saudi Arabia, had a greater say and Arafat's election was a deliberate act in which Arab leaders were supported by conservative Palestinian businessmen Abdel Majid Shoman, Abdel Muhsin Qattan, Ziyyad Mayasi and Hassib Sabbagh. Moreover, Nasser's approval of Arafat and disapproval of the more popular but uncompromising Palestinian elements went beyond hosting the election meeting and supervising its predictable results: he ceded the command of several Palestinian armed units to Arafat and provided him with a propaganda outlet, the Voice of Fatah radio station.

This convergence of interest to saddle the Palestinians with determining their own fate falls considerably short of meaning that Arafat was a tool in the hands of the Arab countries. In this case, Arafat's claims and the facts are the same and it was his remarkable ability to please the leadership of each of the divided and feuding Arab countries which made them support him.[38] He went further: instead of competing with Habbash and others for leadership of the Palestinians, he prevailed on the bereft-of-support leftists to join the PLO under his leadership.[39] Suddenly the Palestinians had a new supreme leader – like the Mufti, an energetic, charismatic one, but sadly also a believer in personal glory who attained his position by discarding clear ideological colours.

But, unlike the old reticent leader, the Mufti who supported him from the comfort of the Riviera Hotel in Beirut, the new one loved the limelight.

Arafat devoted considerable time and energy to spreading stories about his early life and deeds.[40] Although undoubtedly a courageous man, he saw fit to inflate the number and nature of his forays into Israel. He hinted that he was related to the Jerusalem Husseinis. Naturally, the size of his Kuwait business was blown up out of proportion. And he began conducting business at night, also unnecessarily in view of his undoubted energy, as if this were most fitting for a revolutionary leader. Arguably, it was this larger-than-life character which was leading the Palestinians to victory. Indeed there is little doubt that he used this persona to keep the Palestinian issue alive in the world's media. According to an aide who spoke on condition of anonymity, Arafat did all this intentionally.

The propaganda campaign to inflate Arafat's image, indeed his election to the post of PLO Chairman, was made easy by what had happened in Jordan. Because it was simpler to infiltrate Israel from Jordan than to do so from Egypt and the chances of Israeli massive retaliation were less because of Israeli concerns for the regime of King Hussein, Arafat and several thousand Palestinian fighters had moved there in 1968.

There is little doubt that the Jordan-based fedayeen (as Palestinian infiltrators came to be known) caused Israel a lot of trouble. The Israelis found it difficult and expensive to respond to them because the Palestinians persisted, despite the fact that most infiltrators were either killed or captured. In March 1968 the Israelis decided to administer a lethal blow to the Palestinian forces encamped in Jordan; not only because of the dislocation they were causing, but because they were acting as a magnet for young Palestinians and other Arabs throughout the Middle East and their numbers were growing ominously.

The result was the Israeli attack on the town of Karameh, a major Israeli incursion across the Jordan with tanks and fighter aircraft and helicopter support. Luck, and a measure of preparation, were on Arafat's side. The Jordanian army had deployed its tanks and troops in expectation of such an attack and, acting on the orders of the local commander, who tried and failed to obtain authorization to repel the Israeli attack, the Jordanian army joined the fray against the Israelis and, with the Palestinians, gave the invading force a bloody nose. Colonel Muhammad Radi Abdallah, the Jordanian officer who ordered the Jordanian response and later Jordan's most decorated soldier, describes Karameh as Israel's 'first major defeat'. He speaks of the Palestinians bravely holding the line, and then 'we swung into action and did the rest'.

The Israelis admitted twenty-eight dead and seventy injured, but among others the seasoned journalist John Bulloch suspects Israeli losses to have been higher.[41] The Palestinians' losses were in the hundreds, and they themselves admitted 170 dead, but this was secondary to their obvious success against the Israeli army which had beaten the Arabs in the 1967 War. It was an undoubted victory for Arafat and his legend.

Victory on the battlefield endeared him to the Palestinian people, added to his other credentials and made his election to the post of Chairman of the PLO a popular as well as a governmental choice. The Palestinian fighter and conservative leader were one and the same. In electing Arafat to the PLO chairmanship both the Arab governments and the Palestinian people got what they wanted.

Arafat wasted no time; still committed to working with all Arab governments, he used his new position to ask Arab leaders for more money and diplomatic support. He got it in the form of direct aid and through the taxes they levied on Palestinians working in their countries. And there was an increase in voluntary Palestinian support. Further afield, a whole world tired of Israeli sledgehammer tactics celebrated the election of a new Palestinian leader with military credentials, and hundreds of young revolutionaries and adventurers descended on Palestinian refugee camps in Lebanon and Jordan to receive military training and fight shoulder to shoulder with Arafat's brave young men.

But, very much like an old-fashioned chief, Arafat failed to pay attention to organization or to the behaviour of his troops after victory. Dizzy with success, Jordan-based PLO fighters not only forgot that they were operating within the boundaries of an organized state, but went further and did everything to antagonize King Hussein, his government, his army and the population of Jordan. They refused to obey local laws, set up roadblocks, issued identity cards and collected money from willing or frightened donors. Arafat, unable to delegate, occupied himself with fostering his relations with Arab leaders and governments while his followers behaved like a leaderless rabble. The road to 1970 and the confrontation between the Palestinians and the Jordanian army, what later became known as Black September, started at Karameh and with Arafat's election as PLO Chairman.

The fighting in September 1970 between the Palestinians and the Jordanian army had the hijacking and destruction of three commercial airliners as its background. But it was inevitable, and Arafat's lack of involvement in the actual hijacking is not an acceptable excuse. For while it is true that the militants of George Habbash and fellow leftist Wadi Haddad carried out the hijacking, Arafat bears responsibility for not controlling them as members of his command and for allowing things within Jordan to deteriorate to the point where dialogue with the Jordanians wasn't enough to contain the consequences of this particular incident.

The Jordanians won after a week of bloody fighting which produced thousands of casualties. The Palestinians, outgunned and poorly trained and led, stood alone. Only Syria tried to help them, and it gave up after two days. The Arab house was divided as never before. For the first time since the 1948 War, the sympathy of the average Arab for the Palestinians was mixed with misgivings about their behaviour. Even officially, Arab dissent was so great that a meeting of heads of state chaired by Nasser to solve the Jordanian-Palestinian problem came close to producing fist-fights. Eventually there were the usual declarations of brotherhood and common purpose, but the business of producing an agreement was so taxing on the health of the already ailing Nasser that he died of a heart attack shortly afterwards, on 28 September 1970.

After that there was no enforcing the vague peace agreement brokered by Nasser. The Jordanians, with Western backing, were so determined to rid their country of all Palestinian elements that they forced some of them to flee across the River Jordan and seek Israeli protection. When no Arab country invited Arafat and a few thousand survivors to headquarter on its territory, he moved to Lebanon, the weakest of the Arab countries and one religiously divided between pro-PLO Muslims and mainly anti-PLO Christians. Shamefully, what followed in Lebanon was similar to what happened in Jordan, and Arafat confirmed his inability to control his followers and curb behaviour offensive to local sensibilities.

At this point, before detailing the Lebanese disaster which followed the one in Jordan, it is important to ask what else Arafat was doing within the Palestinian, Arab and international spheres. In fact, what was happening during and after 1970's Black September exposes a Mufti-like Arafat saying one thing and doing something else.

Openly the policy of the PLO called for creating a multi-ethnic state divided between Arabs and Jews and occupying all of Palestine. The total Israeli rejection of this naive dream was overlooked[42] and Arafat persisted in presenting it as an example of moderation to continue to woo the minority Palestinian establishment, the Arab states and, despite the obvious Western support for Jordan during Black September, to make an indirect appeal to the West. Even the Mufti continued to support him against Habbash and company, and joined Palestinian millionaires in praising Arafat's multi-ethnic plan and condemning his opponents. It was fear of these opponents, coupled with a natural sympathy for his fighters after the Jordanian débâcle and a wish to keep open the lines of communication with the West, which drove more rich Palestinians into his arms, mainly to protect their hefty incomes from the oil-producing countries.

This support, along with the void created by Nasser's death, strengthened Arafat's position *vis-à-vis* the Arab regimes. Nasser had been unassailable and, despite PLO objections, had accepted a 1968 peace plan by US Secretary of State William Rogers to solve the Palestinian problem in accordance with previous United Nations resolutions. Now there was no one strong enough, secure enough or interested enough to challenge the PLO's status as the decider of the Arab position in the Arab-Israeli conflict. The reasons behind the support of the establishment and the Arab governments were reinvigorated by Nasser's death and however opposed to the Rogers Plan he was, Arafat became the only person capable of protecting them against the rising threat from radical Palestinian groups.

But was Arafat really as rejecting of UN resolutions and as committed to a multi-ethnic state as he made us believe? The evidence is to the contrary. In 1968, when the PLO objected to Nasser's acceptance of the Rogers Plan, Nabil Sha'ath, to this day one of Arafat's closest associates, held secret meetings with Lova Elian, secretary-general of Israel's Labour Party and Israeli professor Moshe Mahover.[43] The plans for a multi-ethnic state were not discussed – the Israelis dismissed the idea out of hand – but there were wide-ranging explorations of the minimum demands of both sides at a time when Arafat's open position called for non-recognition of Israel. And secret talks with the United States started at the same time.

It was Ali Hassan Salameh, Arafat's favourite young Palestinian, who initiated important contacts with the CIA in 1970. (The novel *Agents of Innocence* is a stunning fictionalized account of Salameh's life.) But it goes further, and Samuel Katz's book *Soldier Spies* describes Salameh as a valuable CIA asset, a direct American channel to Arafat.[44] But neither the Sha'ath nor Salameh effort was as important as the secret negotiations between the PLO and former Pennsylvania governor William Scranton, which started soon after the latter visited Beirut as a special representative of President Nixon, or the contacts between Arafat's second in command, Abu Iyad, and the CIA's Vincent Canistrero.

Scranton was the brother-in-law of James A. Linen, the then chairman of Time Incorporated. Relying on the advice of his brother-in-law, he solicited the help of my father, *Time* correspondent Abu Saïd Aburish, to arrange a meeting with influential Palestinians who held sway with the PLO but were not associated with 'its unacceptable activities'. The person proposed by Abu Saïd was Kamel Abdul Rahman, a construction magnate and major financial supporter of Fatah. Abdel Rahman, wanting to put the best Palestinian face on the meeting, nominated his Christian partner, Hassib Sabbagh. Because of the impossibility of keeping a secret in Beirut, Scranton and Sabbagh met in Athens in 1973.

This was the beginning of a serious US–PLO dialogue which continued for over a decade. The US was anxious to know what the Palestinians would settle for and the Palestinians presented a list of complaints but, contrary to declared policy, discussed the notion of a small Palestinian state with little hesitation. Sabbagh always surrounded himself with intellectuals who shared his undoubted commitment and there is little doubt that – in international terms – his was a most sensible platform. Yet it was either a clear case of intellectuals and money-men representing Arafat and speaking for a people who knew nothing about what was happening, and who would have disapproved of negotiations with America, or a case of Arafat following a realistic policy but knowing that the time to sell it to his people had not arrived.

Meanwhile, during the early 1970s period of secret diplomacy, two anti-PLO developments were taking place. Having eliminated other contenders for Nasser's seat, Sadat began adopting an independent foreign policy, and the Lebanese were showing more signs of impatience with an uncontrollable Palestinian armed presence in their country. Beginning in 1971, Sadat put out feelers to the US towards signing a peace agreement with Israel. The initiative was turned down by Nixon on Kissinger's selfish advice: he didn't want his arch rival, Secretary of State Rogers, to succeed.[45] And the Christian Lebanese, as is now admitted by both sides, began negotiations with Israel towards evicting the PLO from their country.

The failure of Sadat's peace move led to the October 1973 War.[46] The PLO knew little about it until it started; it was an Egyptian-Syrian surprise attack on Israel, conceived and initiated by the leaders of the two countries. The Palestinians hurriedly joined the fight and, as usual, the Palestinian fighting men performed admirably, but the glory went to the chief planner of the only war against Israel which, in its early stages, came close to success.

Unlike his Syrian junior partner, President Hafez Al Assad, Sadat started the war to achieve peace. And although his partnership with Assad was short-lived and, despite the dismal eventual performance of the Egyptian army, which found the Israelis surrounding its Third Army on the Egyptian side of the Suez Canal, Sadat succeeded in his main purpose. From that time on, the United States focused its attention on him and moved to end the no-peace-no-war situation which had existed between his country and Israel.

At the end of 1973 Arafat found himself with the intransigent Assad on one side and the haughty, Egypt-first Sadat on the other. His adoption of an independent Palestinian policy cancelled his protests against Syria and Egypt; his reliance on the conservative oil countries, already his financial lifeline, increased; and he used the secret dialogue with the US to compete with Sadat (somewhat like Palestinian establishment families vying for British affection). But he still failed to take a definite position on the behaviour of his followers and the acts of terrorism of other Palestinian groups, or to tell the Palestinians what he had in mind.

In 1974 the acceptance by all Arab governments of the PLO as the sole representative of the Palestinian people, an act which ended King Hussein's absurd claim to Palestinian leadership, was trumpeted by Arafat as a great Palestinian victory. In fact, though the Arab countries had bowed to the obvious and Arafat had a hand in this, they did so because it suited them. The Rabat Declaration, so called after the Moroccan city in which the Arab heads of state met and accepted the PLO as something of a government-in-exile, was the culmination of many years of Arab leaders wanting but being unable to disown the Palestinians. Luckily for the Palestinian leadership, which unsoundly believed in confronting Israel alone, it was followed by a real victory, an invitation to Arafat to address the United Nations General Assembly. This was Arafat's crowning achievement and it overshadowed discussions of the consequences of Rabat. When he spoke at the UN in New York in November 1974, Arafat did indeed speak for a Palestinian people in need of solace, and in a legend full of mainly sad happenings his speech is remembered by every Palestinian in the same way most Americans remember the day Kennedy was shot. In his speech, Arafat offered peace based on UN resolutions calling for Israeli withdrawal from territories occupied in 1967. He didn't go further: an open assembly was not the place for presenting a comprehensive peace plan.

But Arafat's real or imagined triumphs have a history of being short-lived; they become undone, mainly because of the little attention he pays to proper management of his organization, his lack of ideological commitment and his reliance on discredited pro-West Arab leaders, incompetent aides and the wealthy Palestinian establishment. In this case, the festering Lebanese situation exploded in 1975.

The incident which ignited Lebanon, the wanton shooting of thirty Palestinians in a bus by Lebanese Christians, is hideous and sad, but judged against the wider picture it is still irrelevant. As in Jordan, Arafat's PLO had acted as a state within a state. The Lebanese political structure, already under stress because of Christian insistence on continuing to control the country with little regard for their Muslim compatriots, cracked. Whether it would have anyway is also irrelevant. Arafat's failure to control his people and to refrain from interference in Lebanese internal affairs is more to the point.

But, from the very start, the final results of the Lebanese conflict were destined to be larger than the elements which determined its outcome. Besides its inevitable and considerable effects on Lebanon, what was at stake for the Palestinians was their very survival as an armed movement in a geographic and organizational position to fight an Israel which had treated Arafat's United Nations offer with scorn.

The alliances and fortunes of battle during the fighting in Lebanon of 1975–82 changed constantly. The Syrians came to the aid of Lebanese Christians and fought the Palestinians to maintain a balance and avoid the emergence of a radical state to their West. Lebanese Sunni Muslims supported the PLO and fought with it. The Arab League sent a peace-keeping force which met with some success and then withdrew under pressure. The Shia Muslims, afraid of Israeli reprisals against them in southern Lebanon, opposed the PLO, then went militant and supported it, and finally opposed it again under Syrian pressure. Meanwhile the Syrians had grown exasperated with their erstwhile Christian wards and attacked them. In between, the US, Britain, France and Italy dispatched troops to keep the peace, but they too withdrew after several suicide bombings by Shia fanatics. And throughout all this, Israel provided the hard-core opponents of the Palestinians, the Maronite Christians, with material support and considerable military training.

Arafat was there, tirelessly dealing with everything himself – everything, that is, except the elusive business of disciplining his people and personally conducting the secret contacts with the US. He made several peace agreements with the Maronites, but none of them held. He attended Arab League meetings which produced one solution after another, and they didn't hold either. And while he changed alliances to face the new ones created to oppose him, he cleverly sought to re-establish secret contacts with the US.

During all this, Arafat never wavered on two things. His opposition to President Assad of Syria was rock-solid. The animosity between the two, often presented as a personality problem, is in reality a much more serious fight over who controls the destiny of the Palestinians. An anti-West believer in pan-Arabism to the point of considering Palestine a part of greater Syria, Assad was and is Arafat's direct competitor. And Arafat, never one to share, let alone cede, decision-making, knew this, wanted an open door to America and refused to co-operate with Assad even when it was beneficial to both. For example, during the early stages of the civil war Arafat insisted on acting alone at a time when coordinating with Assad might have produced a common Syrian-Palestinian front against Israel and its Maronite allies. His was an unfortunate decision which left him friendless and isolated when the Palestinians were in desperate need of any support.

Arafat's second commitment was to continuing the secret dialogue with the US. Because Sabbagh's commendable and quiet ways were also slow, he depended more and more on the loyal but incompetent Ali Hassan Salameh and on Abu Iyad. The gun-toting, whisky-drinking, skirt-chasing, charismatic Salameh may have been good at organizing terrorist raids, and indeed he is credited with organizing the Munich Massacre of Israeli athletes, but he was a man of no diplomatic and political quali-fications. Abu Iyad was made of different stuff, but his contacts with the CIA were through Vincent Canistrero, the agency's leading anti-terrorism expert, and they got nowhere because the latter wanted them limited to finding ways to stop PLO activities, or what the West considered terrorism.

Soon Abu Iyad gave up and the Salameh-US dialogue never got beyond everyday agreements which dealt with the subsidiary issues of protecting US interests in Lebanon and acting against hijackers. On the other hand, the dialogue between Sadat and the US was a much more serious affair which eventually, in late 1978, produced the Camp David Accord between Egypt and Israel. Arafat, despite justifiably shrill Palestinian cries of betrayal, joined the rest of the Arabs in condemning it and boycotting Egypt, but went no further. Radical Arab governments and Palestinian groups advocated direct action against Egypt, but Arafat held back, perhaps lest his own record of wanting to reach an agreement with America be exposed.

On 22 January 1979, four months after the Camp David agreement was reached, Salameh was assassinated by an Israeli hit squad. Arafat's despondency over the death of the man many describe as his adopted son evaporated before the end of the month, when Ayatollah Khomeini toppled the Shah and took over the leadership of Iran. Arafat, desperate to celebrate any success that would bolster his waning fortunes, threw caution and his established relationship with conservative regimes to the wind and hurried to Tehran to embrace the revolutionary mullah.

Interestingly, it was Arafat's chief rival for Palestinian leadership, George Habbash of the Popular Front for the Liberation of Palestine (PFLP), who had provided Khomeini's partisans with arms and training. However, because of his leadership position, it was Arafat who got the credit for this. But, that aside, the euphoria over the success of the Mullahs was short-lived. The Palestinian establishment and conservative Arab regimes, Saudi Arabia and Kuwait, threatened to withdraw their financial support and forced Arafat to backtrack.[47] Once again, pleasing pro-West financial backers took precedence over ideology and the feelings of the pro-Iranian Palestinian people.

The disavowal of Khomeini was but one of many contradictions in Arafat's behaviour in 1979. One of his close associates facilitated the kidnapping from Beirut of the well-known and pro-Palestinian Saudi writer Nasser Al Saïd and his repatriation to Saudi Arabia in return for a $2 million bribe. Arafat, though uninformed about this, made a point of ignoring the whole incident. On the diplomatic plane, the secret dialogue with the United States was going forward even during the first savage Israeli invasion of Lebanon, which produced hundreds of casualties and left thousands homeless. Openly Arafat made the usual condemnations and verbal attacks on the US, but behind the scenes he sent messages to the Carter administration and the UN accepting Resolution 242 and Israel's right to live within secure boundaries.[48] Ostensibly he was acting on the authorization of the Palestine National Council, which earlier in 1979 had authorized him to pursue a peaceful settlement. However, according to the Egyptian writer Muhammad Heikal, it was Palestinian money-men who prevailed on Arafat to adopt this position.[49]

But in reality, not for the first or last time, Arafat – regardless of the merits of what he was doing – was following his own instincts. The toothless, full-of-Arafat-loyalists PNC was and is a questionable source of legitimacy. What really motivated Arafat was his belief that the support of the Palestinian establishment and conservative Arab governments were indispensable. Most ordinary Palestinians were against disowning Iran, surrendering Nasser Al Saïd and making the huge concessions Arafat had made to America. Then and now the man's inclination to try to manipulate the Palestinian establishment and conservative Arab governments and to take the rest of the Palestinians for granted represents his greatest failing.

Yet, strangely, he must have known that he was out on a limb. Despite the contradictions and going further towards satisfying US and Israeli demands than his people wanted, he worked hard to justify this position. To Arabs and outsiders alike, Arafat began to pose as the only man who could deliver a peace agreement with Israel.[50] It went further, and cranked by Palestinian businessmen with solid Saudi connections, he succeeded in prevailing upon Saudi Crown Prince Fahd to present a peace plan at the Fez conference of Arab heads of state. In reality, the lazy, meagrely endowed Fahd had nothing to do with the plan, which was written by one of Arafat's trusted counsellors. It was a case of Palestinian leadership feeding its people unpalatable decisions by hiding behind an Arab façade; however justified as an example of realistic politics, it was a repeat perform-ance of the Mufti's call for the Palestinians to end the 1936 strike. But in this case the Arafat disguise failed when Syria's President Assad, rightly feeling that Fahd's plan had America's backing, boycotted the Fez meeting.

So the hectic activity of 1979–81 had the aim of determining which direction to take in the international arena. It produced nothing concrete or with Arab wrapping that Arafat could sell to the Palestinian people. But, however questionable Arafat's behaviour and motives, these moves produced a lot of pressure on Israel behind the scenes. Arafat's acceptance of Resolution 242 appealed to the Carter administration and the UN and hard-line Israelis were determined to foil Arafat's efforts. Prime Minister Menachim Begin of Israel, who came to power in 1980, decided not to take any chances. With hard-line Minister of Defence Ariel Sharon at his side, he began drawing up plans to eliminate the PLO once and for all. In this he had the full support of Ronald Reagan's Secretary of State, Alexander Haig.[51]

Using as a pretext the attempt to assassinate the Israeli Ambassador to London, Moshe Argov, by the anti-Arafat Abu Nidal terrorist group, the Israelis unleashed the so-called Operation Peace for Galilee on 4 June 1982. The invasion of Lebanon was indiscriminate, savage and without precedent. The Israeli air force reigned supreme, and despite disturbing television coverage which showed thousands of civilian casualties, the Arabs and the world fell into numb silence. Once again, only Syria moved, but it gave up after the Israelis destroyed more than seventy of its fighter aircraft in one day.

The start of the war caught Arafat in Saudi Arabia, but he hurried back to lead his men. In this case he was in his element. For eighty-six days he stood alone, a model of inspiration to his fifteen thousand ill-equipped and poorly trained fighters. The Israeli army fielded eighty thousand men and was unopposed in the air and at sea, but Arafat was everywhere issuing commands, redeploying men and putting up a brave fight. He had to contend not only with lopsided military balance, but also with spies who sent the Israelis signals of where he was, which led to repeated Israeli attempts to kill him.[52] By all accounts, he conducted himself like a courageous and tireless leader of men.

But it was no use. The Israelis, with considerable help from the Maronites, managed to encircle Beirut and subject it to barbarous air attacks. After considerable soul-searching Arafat and the PLO agreed to an American-brokered plan to leave Lebanon and disperse to far-away Arab countries. Arafat was the last to go. By holding out and fighting bravely, he had denied the Israelis unqualified victory. But the PLO which survived the Israeli invasion was a shadow of its former self and it moved to real exile in Tunis.

The period from his forced departure from Beirut in September 1982 until December 1987 and the intifada gives the clearest indications of Arafat's personal leadership style. It began with a success: Arafat finally got the message and his orders to his followers to behave themselves were clear, unequivocal and obeyed. But the rest remained the same. His Tunis office was run like an old-fashioned diwan of an Arab chief. There was no sense or appreciation of time and Arafat's aides, often to protect themselves against allegations about their personal and financial misbehaviour, improvised rules on who could see him and who could not. Arafat's control of money was total and he continued to use it to buy the loyalty of some worthy people and many others who were undeserving. His sense of organization was so lacking that all reports as to who followed him in the command of the PLO and who ran what were speculative. His relations with the Arab countries were very often entrusted to people who used their position for personal gain. He continued to show an old-fashioned lack of concern for the corruption of some of his closest advisers. And rich diaspora Palestinians, finding it easier to meet him in Tunis than had been the case in Beirut, claimed more of his time.

Arafat continued to massage the egos of all Arab leaders, but it was an effort aimed at attaining legitimacy with pro-West elements and financial survival. With Egypt ostracized by the Camp David agreement and out of the Arab picture, the only Arab countries capable of supporting him to the extent of offending the West were Iraq and Syria. But the former was preoccupied with its war with Iran and the quarrel with Assad precluded appealing to the latter. The remainder of the Arab countries, led by Saudi Arabia, were unwilling to go beyond giving money – in return for moderation which excluded offending their Western backers.

Dealing with America directly stopped being an option and became a necessity. As in the 1970s, Arafat relegated this to businessmen and trusted followers. The reliable Sabbagh was there and this time, because Secretary of State George Shultz had been an executive of the Bechtel Corporation, with which construction magnate Sabbagh had done business, his credentials as an intermediary were more solid. In addition there was Salameh's replacement, Bassam Abu Sherif, hyperactive but lacking in diplomatic skill or experience.

Why Arafat consistently followed this dual approach is a mystery. What is not mysterious is how he used it. Sabbagh, a shy man with no personal ambitions, operated like an old-world diplomat. A man with considerable business interests in Saudi Arabia and the Gulf, he tried to get Arafat to play the American card by accepting Shultz's demands for an open renunciation of terrorism and acceptance of Israel as a state. And Abu Sherif acted as Arafat's mouthpiece, the man who secretly or openly pronounced positions of compromise that Arafat could own or disown at will. What Arafat's real position was – and inevitably the two intermediaries must have reported back the same American position – remains another mystery. However, one thing is clear: discussions with the US never ceased and although there had been open ones which had been terminated after the *Achille Lauro* incident and there was talk of resuming official contact, this in essence had no bearing on what was happening. The indirect, secret contacts failed to produce results acceptable to the US and the PLO.

It was the intifada which saved the day and shifted attention from a diplomatic failure to the plight of the Palestinians. The spark which ignited the passions of the Palestinians of the occupied territories in December 1987 was spontaneous, broad-based and populist. Once again, as in 1936, it was the villages which led the way, but this time they were joined in equal measure by the refugees in Gaza and throughout the West Bank.

The PLO claimed and claims that the uprising was the work of Abu Jihad, one of Fatah's original founders. While this is not true,[53] it is definitely true that Abu Jihad's response was exceptional in its speed and extent. He ran after the intifada and adopted it and, under Arafat's direction, gave it the support it needed to continue. As in the period immediately after Karameh, the PLO was successful in a way which dazzled the world and captured the sympathy of millions of people, including many a hardened journalist.

In 1988 Arafat, trying to give greater content to what was happening, convened the PNC and declared a Palestinian state. This symbolic response to the intifada was accompanied by more secret diplomacy. The Palestinian writer Muhammad Rabi' reports that Palestinian businessmen were once again leaning on Arafat to accept Shultz's conditions; specifically, Sabbagh was joined in this effort by another millionaire, Munib Masri.[54] But it still didn't work.

Until the intifada, the silence from the occupied territories had suited both the Israelis and Arafat. But with hundreds dying and thousands injured and suffering Israeli detention and imprisonment, the people of the occupied territories were making their own claim. The pressure on the ground was coming close to demoralizing an Israeli army running short of effective responses to what was facing it. And even in America there was a discernible shift in public sympathy towards Palestinian kids and the strange emergence of Palestinian women as an important element in the resistance. On the Palestinian side, the intifada produced a leadership on the ground which included the non-establishment names of the remarkable Hannan Ashrawi, Elias Freij, Ziad Abu Zayyad, Radwan Abu Ayyash and many others. They joined establishment members Sari Nusseibeh and Faisal Husseini (Abdel Kader's son) in forging a leadership which paid tribute to the PLO while representing a possible alternative.

Suddenly there was pressure on both the PLO and Israeli sides to move. The longer the intifada continued – and it survived untold Israeli pressures and atrocities for five years – the more it vitiated Israel's position in the international arena. And the longer it lasted, the more of a potential challenge to Arafat's leadership it became.

This forced the hands of both sides. Peripheral, unimportant contacts, direct and indirect, between the Palestinians and Israel had taken place for years, but now they gained a new impetus. There were secret meetings in Geneva, Stockholm and even in Tunis. US Jewish groups, some genuinely committed to peace and others fearing the backlash from the erosion of the Israeli image, met Arafat and tried to overcome the obstacle of the PLO recognizing Israel without having something to show for it. It was a chicken-and-egg argument which eventually produced results in Stockholm in December 1988. Sitting next to Rita Hauser, a petite New York lawyer and the activist head of the Hauser Foundation, Arafat amplified his previous positions and accorded Israel unequivocal recognition. It was a triumph for the tireless Hauser, who had met, cajoled and pleaded with Arafat for over a year. And it was a merger of secret and open positions for Arafat, who had used his special adviser Bassam Abu Sherif to offer this recognition in a magazine article, but had stopped short of espousing it publicly himself.

The recognition announcement left Israel little room for manoeuvre. The major obstacle to dealing with the Palestinians directly was out of the way. Neither the UN, US, USSR or the rest of the world was willing to miss an opportunity for Middle East peace because of psychological factors such as Israel's refusal to deal with people whom it considered terrorists. The follow-up to this breakthrough was to be shattered by the Gulf War, which, disruptive as it was, added to the momentum.

Arafat, in a simple move which does not deserve the various complex interpretations some give it, sided with Saddam. The intifada and the emergence of local leadership in the occupied territories precluded anything else; he had to follow his Saddam-adoring constituency or lose it, and he had come to realize that his constituency was the people of the West Bank and Gaza and not the diaspora Palestinians with their unrealistic claims. His performance during the crisis was lamentable, and he came out of the whole thing with a diminished image. But he preserved the only

Palestinian constituency which had a direct say on any future settlement of the Arab-Israeli problem.

The pressure on both sides to reach a settlement increased. The Gulf War sent a message to the great powers to solve the Palestinian problem to eliminate it as a source of future regional discord. This translated into a desire on their part to adopt what was happening between the PLO and Jewish groups. After May 1991 the great powers lent a hand to secure clarification of some points. The chief one, the Israeli wish to deal with separate Arab delegations, out of the way, the US and the USSR prevailed on both sides to meet in Madrid in November 1991.

The road to peace was open. Tellingly, the Palestinian delegation included many people from the occupied territories and excluded Arafat. The leader of the right-wing and uncompromising Likud Party, Israeli Prime Minister Yitzhak Shamir, as intransigent as ever, attended the conference in a state of obvious unhappiness. The point-making between the two sides replaced regularly scheduled television programmes throughout the world.

Out of nowhere, the Madrid show was pre-empted by an announcement that the Palestinians and the Israelis had reached a peace accord through secret negotiations which had been taking place in Oslo under the auspices of the Norwegian government. The relatively moderate Israeli Labour Party had meanwhile replaced the hard-line Likud and the accord was reached between Israeli Foreign Minister Shimon Peres and Abu Mazen, a titleless Arafat associate. Caught by surprise, the US administration of Bill Clinton hurried to involve itself in the positive developments and share in the glory.

The accord, preceded by speeches by Israeli, PLO, US and Russian representatives, was signed on the lawn of the White House on 13 September 1993. It was one of the most celebrated occasions of modern times, probably the highest-rated television show of them all. Arafat was there, and he spoke for the Palestinians and shook hands with reluctant Prime Minister Yitzhak Rabin, the representative of Israel.

At this point it is worth repeating the three factors surrounding the Oslo accord and its signing in Washington. Above all, the 1990–1 Gulf War had forced Arafat's hand. He came out of the war ostracized by the oil-producing countries, his chief financial backers. The PLO's financial situation was so bad that some of its offices overseas were unable to pay staff salaries for periods of two to three months. Furthermore, the Palestinian millionaires who had backed Arafat were also unhappy with his Gulf War policies, which threatened their business interests in the oil-producing countries, and they too withheld money and went as far as wanting to replace him. Conversely, Arafat, who always pretended that he sought consensus, decided to go it alone to the extent of giving up on some members of the PLO's executive committee. The expected departure of Habbash and Hawatmeh was followed by that of Shafic Al Hout and the popular poet Mahmoud Darwish. For the first time ever, Arafat settled for a PLO made up exclusively of Fatah.

The results of the signing of the accord have been less than what even the Palestinians who supported it had expected. In May 1994 the Israelis allowed Arafat to set up an administration in the towns of Gaza and Jericho. The second phase of the agreement, which called for Israeli withdrawal from most of the towns and villages of the West Bank and Gaza, took eighteen months instead of the intended three months to sign and implement. The future of Jerusalem, vague and left until the last phase of the accord, is still pending. Even Hebron, promised to the Palestinians in accordance with the agreements which followed Oslo, has not been delivered to Palestinian control. In fact, with a new militant Israeli administration under Binyamin Netanyahu, the Israelis appear unlikely to cede real control of Hebron, a major Arab town with a few hundred Israelis in it. Also, a big question mark hangs over the future of the extensive network of settlements which the Israelis had established and continue to expand in the occupied territories and the extremely important question of water and Israel's wish to control its sources and who gets it.

This dismal picture has eroded Arafat's shaky popular base. While there are no exact figures which tell the story, there is little doubt that a great majority of Palestinians, though not well disposed towards Arafat's Islamic opponents, find the accord to be lacking in substance to the point of being left totally adrift. And, of course, the Islamic movements, chief among them Hamas, are opposed to the accord in principle, and have resorted to violence, including bombings of civilians, to stop it.

Arafat, regardless of occasional threats and theatrics, cannot go back on the agreement. With his relations with rich Arab countries still strained and with Syria refusing to make a peace with Israel except one stipulating total Israeli withdrawal from the occupied Golan Heights, Arafat's position is exposed. He continues with the agreement while going out of his way to try to control its opponents. In the process, his police have imprisoned and tortured hundreds of Islamists who oppose it – something which is unacceptable to his people regardless of reason or purpose. Bereft of friends in the Arab camp, he relies on Egypt and President Mubarak for support, another policy which doesn't sit right with his people. Furthermore, he has no alternative but to accept the overall umbrella of the US as the chief mediator between the two sides. This too is unpalatable to the

Palestinians, particularly under an unswervingly pro-Israeli Clinton administration.

The result of all this is an Arafat at the head of a Palestinian administration which does not represent what the Palestinians want from a peace settlement. Arafat's lifeline is in outside hands: the Egyptians who would like an end to the Palestinian problem regardless of cost; the Israelis who can preserve or undo the accord and who, having got the peace they wanted, are unwilling to recognize a Palestinian state and in no hurry to concede enough to the Palestinians to allow them to form one; and the Americans, who, as in other places, show little concern for the legitimacy of the regimes they support and are willing to back Arafat to stifle the will of his own people.

What the Palestinians have got as a result of the Mufti's and Arafat's seventy years of leadership is there for everyone to see: limited control under Israeli suzerainty of a collection of towns and villages and a restless flock. The issues of Jerusalem, water and the Palestinians throughout the world, are either relegated to the future or are not being considered.

As stated before, the Mufti was never elected to office and Arafat's recent election is clouded by his control of the mechanisms behind it. One was born to the establishment and the other emerged as its representative. Both men had the faults of ignoring the common man and surrounding themselves with talentless cronies who did their bidding. The open and secret positions of both men often diverged and very frequently they said one thing while doing the opposite. The dismissiveness of both men of the important issue of corruption, though Arafat personally is utterly clean, is near total. Both men used their control of the purse-strings in an antiquated way without proper attention to the modern requirements of national movement or an administration.

On issues of major policy, the Mufti and Arafat, despite the obvious weakness of their people, opted for a Palestinian rather than an Arab solution to the problem of Palestine. The Mufti needed this to assume his leadership position; Arafat could have remained Palestinian leader even within an Arab context. The Mufti began as the creation of the British and changed direction later; Arafat was a child of the Arab establishment who later accepted direct Western sponsorship. The Mufti joined the 1936 rebellion when he couldn't stop it and Arafat signed the Oslo accord in too much of a hurry, and his use of the unqualified Abu Mazen and Abu 'Ala, who speak little English, to finalize the Oslo accord, suggests that he did this to stop the able negotiators by then in Washington from reaching agreement. Arafat's final acceptance of American influence to settle the Palestinian problem, given his Arab and Palestinian establishment connections, was inevitable. And committed as one was and the other is to personal control of everything under them, to the point of totally ignoring the opinions of all others, both men are natural dictators.

But, however deserving of condemnation many of Arafat's ways are, there is little doubt that he was the one man who kept the image of Palestine alive. His persistence, ability to maintain among the Palestinians a measure of unity which rendered them more effective, the leadership he showed during the siege of Beirut and his speedy and effective adoption of the intifada are to his credit. In a way and very much unlike the Mufti, Arafat is a tragic figure. His shortcomings are a direct result of the strategic mistake of having always relied on the Arab establishment, governmental and otherwise. In the process he began to think like them. Because the establishment is beholden to the West, and because both show little concern for the feelings of the Palestinian people, there is no reason to believe that Yasser Arafat, however unwilling he is, will ever be anything but a tool in their hands. Now, as when he began, this is the danger to the Palestinians' aspirations – even the most modest one of having a state named after them – and this is what Arafat has always failed to understand.

6 · A Case of Religious Abuse

'How sad. I hear it was a beautiful country.' 'I know what a Christian is and have an idea what a Muslim is, but the Druze are new to me.' 'I think the Christians are entitled to a place of their own – after all the Muslims run the rest of the Middle East.' 'It's a country with 50 per cent Christians and 50 per cent Muslims and they don't like each other.' 'Goodness, all this killing and destruction – how can anybody benefit?'

Most people know of Lebanon as a result of the 1975–90 civil war. The statements cited above, even the one about the Druze, are essentially true. However, none of the speakers was making what he or she considered a final judgement and all of them followed what they said with simple questions which betrayed considerable confusion and a wish to know more.

The reason Lebanon confuses people goes beyond the inability to understand the indescribable butchery people saw on television. It is because Lebanon is not really a country. It has a flag, boundaries which are recognized by the international community and more than seventeen religious sects, but it has seldom had a government which provided a definition of sovereignty acceptable to all its people. So, even to the Lebanese, while most of them celebrate and exaggerate their country's scenery, food and modernism, Lebanon is an idea which is subject to interpretation.

In addition, what happens in Lebanon affects its neighbours and the rest of the delicately balanced Middle East, and this multiplies the ways in which Lebanon expresses itself. This possession of several identities is a problem that remains unresolved and is still a potential source of destabilization not only for Lebanon but for the rest of the Middle East.

Essentially, the country is viewed in two ways: the Christian-Western way and the Muslim-Arab way. To the Maronite Catholics, the historically on-and-off followers of Rome, and many other Christians, Lebanon is an outpost of Western civilization in the middle of a Muslim world, a provocative 'rose among thorns'. But to most of its Muslims, Lebanon is an Arab country, albeit one with a peculiar religious composition which affords a chance of bridging East and West. However, these broad perspectives subdivide to produce a plethora of political viewpoints. Indeed, every few hundred Lebanese share one.

Fundamentally, except for the very few who benefit from playing the two sides against each other, what the Christians and Muslims differ on is who is the seller and who is the buyer. Aware of their country's geographic location, their obvious economic dependence on the rest of the Arab world and the overwhelming cultural atmosphere surrounding them, most Christians admit the need for compromise and are willing to represent the West in the Arab world. But it doesn't work: the Muslims insist on the opposite, wanting a Lebanon which represents the Arab world to the West.

This is one of the most intractable political arguments in history. French and Lebanese Christian historians who maintain that Lebanon is unalterably Christian and indivisibly attached to the West go back variously to the Phoenicians, Charlemagne and the Crusades to dredge up support for their position. They award the Lebanon Phoenician ancestry and an unbroken and solid connection to Western Christendom. Muslim and other historians who hold the contrary opinion of an Arab Lebanon stress the fallacy of this position, pointing out the predominance of Arabic for over a thousand years, the centuries-old acceptance by the international community of Lebanon as part of Syria and the unsoundness of claiming a Phoenician ancestry and of creating a state where one religious sect, the Maronites, takes precedence over the others.

This is not an empty historical argument. Both sides are trying to legitimize their perception of the same small country which exists today and to gain control of it by presenting a winning case. Yet it is an essentially senseless argument which is not subject to solution. Impartial historians are able to agree that a Lebanon, half of what exists now, a mountainous region east of Beirut, has always had a distinct identity and a Christian character. Simultaneously, however, there is no denying its Arabness and that it has always been a component of the Middle East. What nobody can agree on is what the 1920 expansion of Lebanon has done to the original mountain-state and who should run the country.

Nowadays what we have is a minority sect, the Maronites, accounting for less than a quarter of the population, wanting to dictate their vision of Lebanon to the rest of its people even when it means overplaying their hand. Christians who belong to other sects, though somewhat marginalized by lack of intensity and a specific vision, accept the principle of a Christian Lebanon. But even their support isn't enough to guarantee Maronite supremacy; the country is over 50 per cent Muslim.

*   *   *

In 1919, shortly after the end of the First World War, the word 'Lebanon' followed the definition used by the Ottoman Turks and meant the already mentioned small, autonomous, Christian-run enclave in the mountains. This didn't stop a Lebanese delegation from visiting France with a view to creating a larger independent entity separate from its historical parent, Syria. The delegates visiting France for this purpose were led by Emile Eddé, later a president of Lebanon, and it comprised representatives of the Maronite, Sunni Muslim, Shia, Druze, Greek Orthodox and other religious sects which inhabited the proposed new bigger country. Determined to convince the French that all sects supported the creation of a self-sustaining Lebanon, the country we know today, Eddé prevailed on his fellow delegates literally to don the dress of their respective sects. This meant that Eddé and the Christian delegates wore Western clothes, the Sunni Muslim delegate wore a fez, the Druze was in baggy pants, the Shia was turbaned and so on.

The then French Prime Minister, Georges Clemenceau, must have thought he was facing a collection of circus performers, but he listened to them attentively, ordered his aides to get him a map and asked them to show him the Lebanon they had in mind. They drew a line around what we have today. On examining the area under claim, the Prime Minister pointed to Damascus and asked why they didn't want to incorporate it and what they had in mind: 'After all, it is only a few miles to the east.' 'That's the problem,' answered Eddé, 'we don't want to have anything to do with that city.'[1]

So the problem which faced the French occupiers of that part of the Middle East after the First World War had to do with the physical size and shape of Lebanon and its relationship to Syria, a country which never ceased to consider Lebanon part of its territory. There was a universal French commitment to protect and promote their co-religionists, the Maronite Catholics, but what this meant was not clear. The French had protected the Maronites since 1861, when a sectarian conflict with the Druze threatened their very existence. Ottoman Turkey, the sick man of Europe and the empire within which all conceptions of a smaller or larger Lebanon existed, was co-signatory to the Règlement Organique, an international agreement which recognized French protection of the Maronites *in their mountain redoubt*, but which still didn't dispute Turkey's suzerainty.

The confusion of Clemenceau, amusing as it must have been, underscored a very serious problem for France. It was much easier for the French to protect a religious sect with which they identified than to allow the sect to express its separateness and undoubted uniqueness by extending its territory and creating a much larger country which included other people who felt more Syrian than Lebanese. For, despite the presence in the Lebanese delegation of people from other sects, it was the Maronites who clamoured, lobbied and invoked religious affiliation to convince France that a Maronite-controlled Lebanon should come into being. And they were determined to expand the original autonomous but not totally independent Lebanon that France had protected in accordance with the Règlement Organique, because it was too small and economically unviable. The Greater Lebanon they had in mind incorporated areas which had been unarguably part of Syria and which were predominantly Muslim. Greater Lebanon included the districts of Aqar and Baalbek and the cities of Beirut, Tripoli and Sidon. Greater Lebanon was a spacious definition of whatever Lebanon had existed in the past.

After much vacillation, the French went along with the Maronites. Greater Lebanon came into being on 1 September 1920, a few months after the French conquered Syria and replaced its short-lived Arab government, an offspring of Lawrence's Arab rebellion, with a colonial administration of their own. The magnet for Lebanon's Muslims, the Arab government of Syria with which they wanted to unite, was no more and they had little choice but to accept the diktats of the French. So Greater Lebanon was formed to please the Maronites, without the consent of the Muslims. To take it further, by including unwilling Muslims in their territory, the Maronites became Lebanese and colonialists at the very same time.

For the next fifty years, even under the reformist President Fuad Chehab, from 1920 until the civil war of the 1970s, the Maronites perpetuated an unwholesome primacy in the country, with little regard for the feelings and welfare of other sects. The writer Wade Goria speaks of them having 'rights while the others had duties'.[2] And although no Lebanese government was ever brave enough to conduct the usual economic surveys, there is little doubt that in the 1920s and 30s the Maronites moved from the mountains into Beirut in great numbers and, with French help, took control of the governmental apparatus of the new country and its foreign trade and proceeded to prosper while most of their fellow countrymen lagged considerably behind.

In 1926, six years after the creation of the country, the French helped the Lebanese write a constitution. It was drawn up by a Maronite, Michel Chiha, with no Muslim participation, and was no more than a French-Maronite attempt to legitimize the control of the country by their sect. When Muslim agitation against the constitution threatened to get out of control, the French tried to defuse the situation by appointing a member of the Greek Orthodox Church, Charles Debas, as the country's first president. The election of a Greek Orthodox president was a temporary, phoney move which, judged by the rest of the French colonial behaviour, failed to prevent the total dependence on and favouritism to the Maronites. In the words of the eminent Lebanese historian Kamal Salibi, 'The Maronites secured themselves all other key positions in the government.'[3]

What happened under the French in the 1920s and 30s was nothing more than a slow, deliberate attempt to give Maronite political primacy an everyday content. The French, reeling under repeated Syrian revolts against their colonial rule, saw the Lebanese Muslims as too Arab and too allied with Syria to be trusted. Conversely, the Maronites, many of whom openly referred to France as our 'affectionate mother', were enthusiastic accomplices in French pressure against their country's Muslims. As a result, army and police officers, bureaucrats and most of the people who were given licences to import and export goods were all Maronite and the law courts used the French language, which most Maronites and very few Muslims mastered. The Maronites were succeeding in making Lebanon more Lebanese, and less Arab. Politically, Emile Eddé, who unashamedly used the word 'Bedouin' to describe the non-Christian people of the Middle East, went as far as joining Zionists in a spiritual alliance against the Arabs.[4] The Maronite refusal of an Arab identity went further and, fearing all acts which might undermine their dominance, they stopped taking a population census in 1932 and illegally naturalized Armenians, Assyrians and other Christians to perpetuate their control.[5] But then, as now, Christian emigration to the West and a higher birth rate among Muslims threaten seriously to tip the numerical balance in favour of the latter.

By the time the country was granted independence in 1943, Greater Lebanon was nothing more than Marounistan. Yet something was needed to compensate for the impending departure of France and the support they bestowed on the Maronites. But, instead of dealing with the obvious shortcomings of Greater Lebanon, the Maronites sought to have an equally lopsided system under their control. What emerged, the Lebanese National Pact, was ostensibly an attempt to bridge the gap between the Maronite and the Muslim perceptions of the country, but in reality it reflected the inescapable facts on the ground. It was not a compromise; the National Pact confirmed Maronite dominance without going beyond allaying the fears of the Muslims. Out of necessity, because writing a comprehensive document satisfactory to both sides would have been impossible, the National Pact was an oral agreement between the Christian leader Bishara Khoury and the Sunni Muslim leader Riad Solh.

To the historian M.E. Yapp, the National Pact was nothing more than a 'delaying mechanism'.[6] But what concerns us is what the National Pact produced, the emergence of a Maronite-controlled Lebanese state as a class maker. The Lebanon which presented us with daily horror stories in the 1970s and 80s, the country still licking its wounds without being seriously able to consider, develop or apply long-term solutions to its inherent problems, was the child of the National Pact, the oral and unquestionably vague agreement which purported to confirm the existence of a country where Christians and Muslims could exist in accordance with a live-and-let-live concordat.

The National Pact stipulated that the Greater Lebanon which the French created in 1920 should have a Maronite president and a Sunni prime minister. Representation in the Lebanese chamber of deputies also followed flawed sectarian lines: six Christian deputies to every five Muslims. The parliamentary speaker was to be Shia Muslim and the Greek Orthodox and the Druze merited lesser posts. The co-sponsors, Khoury and Solh, but with Solh in the lead, went further and tried to solve the problem of Lebanon's overall identity. The Pact accepted the country's Arab identity in return for Lebanon's recognition and acceptance by the rest of the Arab countries. This meant that Lebanon was to stop relying on Western powers as guarantors of its existence and to refrain from allowing the West to use the country as a springboard for controlling and influencing events in the Arab Middle East.

An unwritten agreement is subject to adjectival and adverbial interpretations. Not only is what it says subject to different explanations, but the application of the parts accepted by both sides demands constant vigilance. In this case what followed was another Maronite application of what they thought the agreement meant. They went beyond claiming as their exclusive property some important positions such as those of army chief of staff and chief of security. The rest of the senior officers in both services were Maronite and their French-trained bureaucrats perpetuated the hiring of their co-religionists to the point of totally excluding others. The Muslim Sunni Riad Solh, until his death in 1951 the country's perennial prime minister, managed to please his Beirut followers through patronage, and on occasion nobly held the line against the Maronites' attempts to monopolize all power, and some of the country's Shia and Druze leaders and others subscribed to the idea of Greater Lebanon because it made them ministers and chiefs. But, despite Solh's repeated attempts at rearguard action, the average Sunni, Shia, Druze and members of other communities were utterly neglected. In fact, the image of a prosperous, modern Lebanon reflected what was happening in Beirut and the mountain areas inhabited by the Maronites, the areas occupied by Khoury's people and what Solh managed to eke for his followers, and to a lesser degree the personal fortunes of feudal chiefs of other communities. The rest of the country, the Shia south, Druze mountain enclaves and even the Sunni city of Tripoli, which was led by Solh's competitor, Abdel Hamid Karame, did not benefit. Greater Lebanon became two countries soon after it gained independence: one led by the Maronites and a collection of Muslim collaborators, leaders who were enamoured with ceremonial positions, and another made up of the simple Muslims and Druze, who were relegated to second-class citizenship.

Khoury's and Solh's Lebanon lasted until 1952. In 1951 Solh was assassinated by a member of the Parti Populaire Syrien (PPS), a political party which considered Lebanon an integral part of Syria. Shortly before, in a sign of nervousness which underscored their concern over the solidity of Greater Lebanon, the two leaders had used a minor outbreak of armed rebellion as an excuse to execute the PPS's leader, Anton Sa'adeh. With Solh's death and the absence of the one man who was capable of holding the country together, there was no one to give sensible interpretation to the National Pact. Khoury wanted to amend the constitution, which forbids serving two consecutive terms, and to run for another six-year period. But the Lebanese chamber of deputies, the body which elects presidents, forced him to resign.

It is worthwhile examining the first Lebanese administration of Greater Lebanon. Khoury and Solh were chieftains of the old school and so cooperation between them was substituted for measures aimed at giving structural soundness to the National Pact. To appear successful, they inflated the importance of everything they did, adorned it and presented it to their followers as proof of the viability of the pact. For example, sincerely believing that what he had created was the best solution for his country, Solh used Lebanon's decision to join the Arab League in 1945 to appease the Muslims, who wanted a greater voice in the running of Lebanon and closer ties with the Arabs. Khoury extracted credit from the same event differently; he told the Maronites that belonging to the Arab League meant the acceptance of Lebanon by the rest of the Arabs without compromising its Christian identity. Meanwhile, neither referred to Syria's stubborn refusal to send an ambassador to the new country and the fact that Syrian-made maps showed no Lebanon of any size.

Like many another Arab leader, Khoury and Solh didn't think in terms of building a working system. They failed to institutionalize even the most widely accepted aspects of the National Pact. The background to what they did together was widespread corruption, both personal and of a more understandable traditional nature. Khoury's brother Selim and son Khalil had a finger in every business deal and every senior governmental appointment and realized money from both. Solh's was a more traditional and acceptable way; perhaps understandably, he insisted on relying on patronage to gain Sunni support for the Pact.

So Khoury and Solh misrepresented what they did, albeit for different reasons, and failed to understand the need for institutions which could outlive them while paying no heed to different forms of corruption. The alliance between the two totally failed to address what was happening in much of Greater Lebanon. Because they controlled most things which mattered, the Maronites were becoming richer. Meanwhile, beyond Beirut, the Muslims were becoming poorer. The religious division of the country was acquiring a destructive social dimension.

Khoury was succeeded by Camille Chamoun. A former diplomat, deputy and cabinet minister, Chamoun spoke impeccable English and French, wore Savile Row suits and had a penchant for big, monogrammed cigars. His worldliness and exposure coupled with an awareness of Maronite vulnerability led him to change sponsors. A France tired and weakened by the Second World War was replaced by the dominant power of the time, the United States.

Chamoun assumed office through using the big lie. He made several alliances with willing Muslim politicians which suggested a more even-handed approach to the sectarian problems of the country. In the Arab arena, he went as far as to question the 'Arab credentials' of his chief rival for office, Abdel Hamid Franjieh. But once in office, all alliances were forgotten and Chamoun began to behave in the most anti-Muslim and anti-Arab fashion. The United States, faced by a militant Arab nationalist movement, accepted Chamoun's abuse of power in return for his support of its regional policies.

Under Chamoun, within Lebanon the Muslims were no more than menial workers. The level beyond which a Muslim bureaucrat could not rise was lowered, pressure was put on Muslim army and security officers to resign and Chamoun so neglected Muslim neighbourhoods that even in Beirut many of them had no water or electricity for days at a time. Meanwhile, cynically acting as the middleman between the new, all-Muslim rich countries and the West, the Maronites were prospering.

In the field of foreign policy, Chamoun acted in clear violation of the National Pact. His commitment was to the West, with little regard for the Pact's constraints against using Lebanon as a springboard to further Western policy and interests. He was willing to entertain working with the West's Arab allies, while taking little notice of the wish of most Lebanese for a Lebanon that was neutral in Arab feuds. He threw caution to the wind and made it clear that he supported the British-French-Israeli Suez adventure against Nasser, a man extremely popular among his country's Muslims. Chamoun's policies cancelled Lebanon's middle position and left it vulnerable.

Chamoun's assumption of power in Lebanon coincided with the Egyptian army coup of 1952 and Nasser's emergence as the embodiment of Arab nationalism. Nasser, though acceptable to Lebanon's Muslims, had no designs on the country. But Chamoun saw Nasser's popularity among the Muslims as a direct threat to Lebanon and to himself. He should have known better, and probably did, but his hatred of the Muslims of his country and refusal to accept a modicum of Arab identity as called for in the National Pact produced an unreasonable man bent on confrontation. Chamoun, the leader of a fractured country which desperately needed stability to survive, began working against Nasser, Syria and all Muslim and Arab elements who didn't agree with him.

In the late 1950s the United States was unable to decide whether to woo Nasser or confront him, but the CIA, developing its own regional policies and alliances, made Chamoun's Beirut an extension of its headquarters in Langley, Virginia. American CIA agents and others operating under ethnic cover became the masters of the city. Bill Eveland, Archie and Kim Roosevelt, James Russell Barracks, James Eichelberger, Ghosn Zhogbi and Samir Souki, all friends of Chamoun, operated openly, and against Nasser, the most popular leader of the time. The convergence of interest between the Chamoun government and the CIA agents produced a bizarre atmosphere which altered Beirut's character. It became a CIA city where taxi drivers, bartenders, pimps, whores, members of parliament, cabinet ministers and religious figures bought and sold information to the highest bidder. Nasser competed, but the CIA had more money.

CIA agent Bill Eveland gave Chamoun money to use against both his Lebanese and Arab enemies.[7] Chamoun worked with the PPS, the same party which didn't believe in an independent Lebanon and which assassinated Riad Solh, to destabilize the Syrian government. He hosted and funded the former Syrian dictator Adib Shaishakly, a CIA darling, and worked with him against pro-Nasser regimes in Damascus.[8] He instructed chief of security Farid Chehab (cousin of the army chief of staff, and later President, General Fuad Chehab) to cooperate with the intelligence services of pro-US Jordan, Iraq, Turkey and Iran.[9] And in 1957 he readily accepted the anti-Nasser, anti-Communist Eisenhower Doctrine, well before the rest of the pro-Western leaders of the area had time to make up their minds.

The Muslims of Lebanon, and many concerned Christians, were

opposed to Chamoun's policies and attitude, but he was utterly disdainful of anything they suggested. And what Chamoun did within Lebanon was as sectarian and narrow as what he did in the field of foreign policy. He spent hundreds of millions of dollars building the Casino du Liban in a Christian area and nothing on desperately needed roads in Muslim districts. Little if any money was devoted to education. Banks wishing to open Beirut branches were granted licences when they partnered with Maronites and denied them when they had Muslim associates. Chamoun's son Dany became an arms trader and, with Israeli help, began arming tough Maronites before militias came into vogue.[10] And, blindly determined that his was the only way, Chamoun identified the mainly Muslim Palestinian refugees as the source of his country's problems and approved of moves against them by his security forces.

Because Chamoun was a classic case of power corrupting a leadership, he didn't know where to stop. In 1957, with his country still suffering because of the anti-Nasser stance he took during the Suez crisis, he went beyond the point of no return and used CIA money to bribe people and rig the parliamentary elections.[11] When some of the leading politicians of the country, for example Saeb Salam and Kamal Jumblat, failed to win their traditional seats, the issue was joined. The message to the Muslim leadership was clear: Chamoun wasn't happy keeping the Muslims down; he was dead set against any of their leaders who opposed him and he rigged the elections to replace them by a collection of hand-picked Muslim followers who were bribed to obey his orders. This major move was followed by the assassination of the Christian journalist Nassib Al Matni, one of many Christians who believed Chamoun's folly was leading the country to disaster.[12]

More than anything else, Chamoun became the symbol of Lebanon's schizoid soul, the possessor of an urbane, pro-West exterior and a tribal inside. The dapper handsome hunter who dazzled Westerners with his wit and charm was nothing but a skirt-chasing, narrow-minded tribal chief who saw nothing wrong in lying, stealing and murder. His claim to the Maronite tribe resembled that of a Mafia boss who wouldn't tolerate the existence of another family on his turf. In this case the other Mafia family was the Muslims.

A majority of the Lebanese people were against Chamoun: practically all the Muslims and, importantly, many a thinking Christian. The late Lebanese businessman and politician Emile Bustani saw the consequences of Chamoun's policies and tried and failed to move him in another direction. As army chief of staff, General Fuad Chehab feared for the unity of the country but kept his soldierly silence. And even the Maronite patriarch,

Butros Maouchi, took exception to some of Chamoun's acts and the rigging of the elections. Amazingly, the 'defection' of these important Maronite voices had little effect on the ground: by now a class as well as a religious sect, the Maronites supported Chamoun and, with unqualified help from the CIA, Chamoun steered the country towards disaster.

In 1958 a civil war erupted. Compared with what followed in the 1970s and later, it was a minor affair, a rehearsal. The Muslim streets exploded and forced the hand of its reluctant leadership, who, afraid of losing their positions, hurriedly ran after the rebellion and claimed it as their own. In fact, the Muslim leaders, including some advocates of equal sectarian representation in parliament and of rotating the presidency among the various groups, did more: they asked Nasser and the Palestinians for help.

Nasser, reluctant to get mired in Lebanon, afforded them the minimum amount of assistance to maintain his popular base while cautioning against the country's fragmentation. Moreover, he listened to the wise counsel of Maronite Emile Bustani more than he did to the opinions of Muslim leaders, who wanted to reduce or eliminate Maronite dominance once and for all. For the most part the Palestinians stayed on the sidelines, though some joined the Muslims in the hope of a government more sympathetic to their conditions and supportive of their wish to use Lebanon as a base for fighting Israel.

Chamoun's reaction to the protest resignations of several of his Muslim prime ministers and the outbreak of rebellion was in line with narrow Maronite thinking; he called on the United States for military help against the rebels. But, despite CIA support for his request, the United States, fearing regional repercussions and accusations of colonialism, turned it down. Chamoun was furious; his narrow-mindedness precluded understanding an American decision which placed regional interests above the interests of less than 2 per cent of the people of the Arab Middle East. His failure to talk the US into a military landing in Lebanon drove him to seek United Nations support. He lodged a complaint against Nasser, accusing him of conducting 'massive infiltration' of Lebanon's territory. The UN, though it discovered evidence of some infiltration, balked at the description 'massive' and decided that most of what was happening was an internal problem.

To Chamoun, the circle of betrayal of the Christians was complete. But luck was on his side. On 14 July 1958 the Iraqi monarchy was overthrown and replaced by a group of anti-Western officers headed by Brigadier Abdel Karim Kassem. Afraid that this might avalanche and threaten the rest of the pro-West regimes of the Middle East, the United States landed troops in Lebanon and Britain did the same in Jordan. Despite clear signs that regional rather than Lebanese considerations were behind the move, Chamoun gloated and felt vindicated.[13] Interviewing Chamoun about the landing, the famous Canadian journalist Blair Frazer complained to the present writer, 'Someone's got to tell this creep Lebanon isn't the centre of the universe. His talk of Lebanon being the guardian of Christian civilization is nauseating.'

Chamoun's deliberate misinterpretation of the landing of US Marines in Beirut perpetuated the destructive divisions racking the country. Although America kept its support for Chamoun to a minimum and prevailed on him not to seek an illegal second term, he and many of his Muslim opponents saw the landing as a sign of Western willingness to safeguard Maronite supremacy. Beyond eventually forcing Chamoun to leave office at the end of his term the rebellion produced very little. The abusive governmental structure favouring the Maronites survived intact. The presence of US Marines, the major aim of which was to maintain a regional balance, precluded the much-needed end to the religious abuse in Lebanon and briefly the unrepentant Maronites came close to vetoing the appointment of a reform-minded Muslim prime minister by starting a counter-revolution.

As Lebanon's luck would have it, the man who followed Chamoun in office had enough stature and foresight to stop the Maronite rebellion spreading. The Lebanese parliament, finally responding to the deep divisions eroding the country's chances of survival and threatening it with disintegration, elected as president the army chief of staff, General Fuad Chehab.

A descendant of the Chehab emirs who had ruled the original mountain-based smaller Lebanon, Chehab proved to be a wise politician, sensitive to his country's middle regional position and the needs of all segments of its population. Unlike Khoury, Sulh and Chamoun, he had no street following, tough men, militias or interest groups behind him. An army man all his life, he possessed both method and character and wasted no time in trying to heal the wounds of his country.

Chehab's presence ended the quarrel with Nasser. Because Chehab concentrated on Lebanon and didn't want to elevate the Maronite supremacy to a regional pro-West position in opposition to Nasser's Arab nationalism – a Western-Nasser war by proxy – the task of making peace with the chief political leader of the Arabs proved to be easy. Chehab's one meeting with Nasser, at the Syrian-Lebanese border town of Chtoura, eliminated the source of friction between Lebanon and the Egyptian leader. It proved that Chamoun was a liar inasmuch as Nasser had no plans to annex Lebanon. Chehab stopped the Americans from using Lebanon as a base for anti-Nasser activity and Nasser ceased his support for all Lebanese elements, particularly those calling for drastic change in their country's constitution and organization.

It was within Lebanon that Chehab faced insurmountable problems. First, the Maronites had accepted Chehab grudgingly. Because of his impartiality his Maronite co-religionists felt insecure. But there was more to it. The Maronites viewed his plans to build schools, hospitals and roads and to link the country with a telephone network as nothing short of an attempt to raise the standard of living of Muslims to their level. They dredged up every bit of religious hatred in their memory and refused to accept this as beneficial to all sides. They still wanted the money to be spent on promoting the tourist and banking businesses of Marounistan. Second, by trying to implement programmes aimed at direct help for the people, Chehab threatened the tribal make-up of the chamber of deputies, both its Christian and Muslim sides. With minor exceptions, the chamber had been closed to new contenders: members came from the same families and 60 per cent of them were feudal with no party affiliation and seats went from father to son, or to brother or cousin.[14] Not only did the feudal clans control the parliament, but the first ten cabinets of the country had been rotated among four families.[15] In fact, the feudal character of some Lebanese leaders contributed to Maronite paramountcy.

All this didn't stop the courageous Chehab from trying. Disdainfully referring to the traditional leaders as cheese eaters (*Fromagistes*), he embarked on a huge programme to tackle the structural and economic imbalance of the country.[16] Among his earliest acts was the banishment of his first cousin, the anti-Muslim head of security, Farid Chehab, whom he made ambassador to the Ivory Coast. He then tried and failed to introduce income taxes aimed at eliminating the poor-punishing Maronite-sponsored indirect taxation. He hired the French company IFRED to study the economic system of the country and to develop long-term plans to remedy the economic imbalance which underpinned Maronite supremacy. He tried to erode the importance of the sectarian school system which was perpetuating division within the country to the extent of teaching different versions of history. And he went for the obvious, a more even representation within the bureaucracy.

That Chehab was one of the rare happenings in modern Lebanese and Arab politics is undoubtedly true. But the odds were greatly against him and he did not succeed. It is true that he gave the country six years of internal and external peace, and towards the end there were many people who called themselves Chehabists and rightly agreed with his vision. But six years, the length of his presidential term, which he refused to extend by amending the constitution, was certainly too short a time to correct deep-rooted maladies, such as the suppressed IFRED discovery that hashish smuggling and prostitution were two major sources of national income.

Charles Hellou, a Chehab protégé, followed him in office in 1964. But he lacked the vision and strength of character needed to impose Chehabism on the country and Chehab was too much of a gentleman to run Lebanon by proxy. Lebanon began reverting to character and pro-West Maronites continued as if Chehab had never existed.

Lebanon under Charles Hellou was still an artificial state, but its inherent shakiness was concealed by a sea of ready cash which created the cosmopolitan Beirut of legend. Oil money was flowing into the city's more than seventy-odd international banks, and hundreds of thousands of oil-rich Arabs summered there, gambling and chasing blondes. There was a bar for every 140 people and the Casino du Liban claimed it had the biggest and best nightclub show in the world. Glamorous Beirut was Casablanca, Hong Kong and old Havana rolled into one. But despite the participation in its wealth by some Muslims, it was a Maronite city and it was corrupt.

The plans to build schools, hospitals and roads gave way to high-rise apartments and greedy landlords. Member of the Chamber of Deputies Raymond Eddé (the son of Emile Eddé), a perennial contender for the presidency, pushed through a banking secrecy Act to attract more money while sponsoring a rent control Act to help the poor. Others joined him and saw beyond the glitter and spoke of the needs of the poorer parts of the country. But what prevailed was something else; what triumphed was Maronite insensitivity.

Not only were the needs of large Muslim sections of the country, mainly the Shia south and the Sunni north, neglected, but the Maronites added indolence to their collection of unattractive qualities. Bureaucrats got four weeks' annual holiday and twenty-five days of official holidays. The Lebanese behaved arrogantly towards their Arab visitors; their manner suggested that they were doing them, the rich Muslim hordes from the Gulf, a favour by allowing them into their country. And following the usual Maronite convoluted logic, they perversely told their visitors that their Muslims' and Palestinians' calls for equality were nothing more than the work of misguided communists.

In the face of Maronite determination to have it all their own way, Hellou was helpless. He became ceremonial president of two nations divided by religion and socio-economic disparity. Two major events exposed and underlined his helplessness: the collapse of INTRA Bank in 1966 and the 1967 Arab-Israel War.

The challenge to Maronite hegemony over Beirut, which by 1966 had become the undisputed centre of Middle East banking, journalism and service businesses was INTRA Bank. The bank's chairman, Yussuf Bedas, was a Christian Palestinian, but the Maronites put his Palestinianism before his Christianity and saw his success as aiding the anti-Maronite forces of the country.

The bank controlled forty-two Lebanese companies, including Middle East Airlines, the Casino du Liban and the Port of Beirut. In 1965 rumours began to spread about the bank's finances; so prevalent were they that even the Emir of Kuwait demanded to see his multi-million deposits in cash. He and others were satisfied, but the rumours persisted. Suddenly, in April 1966, there was a run on the deposits of the bank and it collapsed.

Sheikh Najib Alummedine, the then chairman of Middle East Airlines, is adamant that the bank and its subsidiaries were solvent. *Time* correspondent Abu Saïd claims that the rumours against the bank were 'too well-orchestrated to be an accident, even by Beirut's rumour-mongering standards'. Paul Parker, a well-known and exceptionally talented American banker who was hired to give INTRA a more respectable face a few months before it collapsed, limits himself to saying 'the whole thing was unnecessary'.

Putting together the content of conversations and discussions with the three insiders (Abu Saïd was Bedas's close friend) and the results of interviews with many others, including former members of the bank's board of directors, who spoke on a non-attribution basis, it is easy to reach the conclusion that the collapse of INTRA Bank was engineered by the Maronite-controlled Lebanese Central Bank with considerable help from Maronite politicians and Israeli agents.

Not only is this a central thesis of Morris West's well-researched novel *The Tower of Babel*, but there are other facts to support this conclusion. The Lebanese Central Bank, despite the obvious huge damage that the collapse of INTRA would inflict on the Lebanese banking system, made no moves to save it. On the contrary, it withheld funds which would have averted the collapse when its governors knew INTRA was solvent. Furthermore, Central Bank orders were issued to managers of INTRA's subsidiaries to delay the delivery of financial statements which could have helped the bank secure backing from other sources. The concerted effort to derail INTRA was so organized that Bedas, its creative and iconoclast chairman, feared for his life and was unable to function properly and take action to prove the falsity of the rumours hounding him. Meanwhile, several Maronite Lebanese bankers and politicians became full-time anti-INTRA propagandists and encouraged depositors to withdraw their money.

The fall of Bedas served notice that the Maronites were declaring war on the Palestinians in their midst. Their efforts 'to purify' their country suited the Israelis, who saw in the bank a major source of support for Palestinian aspirations, an underpinning of these aspirations through economic attainment. This formalized the Maronite-Israeli alliance. Until then it had been a situation of mutual fear and resentment of the Muslim majority in the Middle East, a convergence of interest. After the demise of INTRA, cooperation between the two sides was through direct contact. The Israelis gained an ally within the Arab camp; the Maronites discovered a potential new protector. Above all, the Maronites demonstrated a willingness to destroy the country to maintain their supremacy.

As so often in their country's short history, Lebanese Muslim leaders joined forces with Maronite politicians to cover the true story of the bank's collapse; in this case not only did they fear loss of position, but some of them owed INTRA money. But confidence in the Lebanese banking system was undermined and many Gulf Arabs shied away from putting their money in Beirut banks. However, this was nothing compared with the crisis on the way. The 1967 War was the event which showed the extent of Lebanon's break from the rest of the Arab world.

Leaving aside the complicated history of the 1967 War, what happened in Lebanon was very simple. In the latter stages of the war, when Israel was making its final assault against the Syrian forces in the Golan Heights, Lebanese Prime Minister Rashid Karame ordered the country's army to commence hostilities to ease the pressure on the Syrians. Army commander Emile Bustani, the namesake of the well-known statesman, refused to obey the order. He didn't base his insubordination on military considerations such as the undoubted superiority of the Israeli army; he simply refused to take orders from the country's Muslim Prime Minister, Saeb Salam.

The issue of where Lebanon belonged in the Arab-Israeli conflict didn't stop there; the Maronites could hardly disguise their glee at the Arab defeat. In fact, with Nasser humiliated, they felt a closer kinship with Israel and stronger antipathy towards the Arabs, the Arab cause and the Muslim Lebanese, who identified with Nasser's ideas.

In 1968 there was yet another confirmation of this new Maronite attitude. Once again the Lebanese army refused to intercept an Israeli attack on Beirut's airport which destroyed thirteen aircraft belonging to the country's flag carrier, Middle East Airlines. And later, in 1973, the army refused to obey the orders of Prime Minister Salam, to intercept an Israeli hit squad which had landed in the country to eliminate three PLO leaders. The Israelis were in Beirut for fourteen hours and were allowed to finish their job while the Lebanese army looked on.

INTRA, the 1967 War and the 1968 and 1973 raids divided Lebanon as never before. It was no longer a case of religious and economic abuse. The Maronites were in open political alliance with the Israelis. Some of Lebanon's non-Maronite leaders, in particular the Druze leader Kamal Jumblat, decided in favour of an alliance between the disenfranchised Lebanese and the Palestinians. And the Palestinians, having assumed the mantle of Arab resistance to Israel after the 1967 defeat, were willing partners.

What began as French favouritism towards co-religionists to allow them to run their own country, albeit an exaggerated preference with questionable historical justification, became something much bigger. The Maronite determination to govern a Lebanon separate and distinct from the rest of the Arabs – while abusing their Muslims and living off these very same Arabs – became a major regional issue of Arab-Muslim against Maronite-Israeli forces. The ability of the Lebanese chamber of deputies, traditional leaders or the Lebanese government to undertake moves to extend the country's reliance on the National Pact was no longer possible. The march of folly became unstoppable: each side began preparing for war.

The 1970 election of Suleiman Franjieh to succeed the well-meaning but marginalized President Hellou exposed the hidden face of unattractive Lebanon. Franjieh, the representative of Maronite militancy, ran against the Chehabist Elias Sarkis. Chehab himself, though permitted by the constitution to run for a second, non-consecutive, term, declined to do so.

Refusing to settle for the silent defeat of their opponents, the Maronites elected Franjieh to prove their open assumption of undivided power. Franjieh was semi-literate, a tribal chief from the northern town of Zghorta, the butt of Lebanese jokes. His only previous claim to fame had been his involvement in the machine-gunning inside a church of twenty-two members of a competing Lebanese clan.

At election time, the building of the Chamber of Deputies, who elected the President, looked like an armed camp. Franjieh's followers filled the hall with people carrying shotguns, pistols and machine-guns. Deputies were threatened, others were bribed and a third group voted for Franjieh to avoid civil war. Behind him stood the figures of the zealously Maronite Chamoun and emergent Pierre Gemayal, the head of the Kata'eb, or Phalange Party, the Fascist Maronite militia. Solid relations with the only power willing to provide unqualified support for their religious supremacy schemes meant that both men had Israel behind them. Previously Israel had depended on the combative Maronites to support its anti-Palestinian and anti-Muslim designs; now it could claim the subservience of official Lebanon.

It was Franjieh who presided over the disintegration of the Lebanese state. His open championing of Maronite militias and refusal to use the authority of the state to control their fighting men produced an equal response on the other side. Lebanon became a military training camp. The Phalange, with Israeli military and financial support, trained thousands of young men. Chamoun's Tigers, another militia group, got similar help and support. The downtrodden Shias, having formed their own Supreme Islamic Council under the charismatic cleric Mousa Al Sadr, proceeded to create the precursor of their militia, Amal, or 'hope'. The Mourabitoun Nasserite movement was totally Sunni and its aims, though unclear, were Muslim and, like the rest, it was armed and trained and wanted to fight. The Druze leader Kamal Jumblat went back and forth on building and depending on a military group, but finally succumbed and created his own militia. The Parti Populaire Syrien, mainly Greek Orthodox, threatened as it was by Maronite militancy, began military training for its followers. Naturally the Palestinians fielded their own forces and decided the Maronites were as much of an enemy as Israel. The President himself refused to be outdone by his fellow Maronites, and built a militia based on his Zghorta constituency, the Zghorta Maronite Militia.

There were also armies within armies, small offshoots of militants, such as Father Cherbel Kasiss's Order of Monks, a group totally committed to the annihilation of the other side. Only two people stood aside and tried to make sense of the situation, Maronite Patriarch Boulos Khoreichi and politician Raymond Eddé. Khoreichi's advice was dismissed, because belonging to what had become a ruling class took precedence over pure religious affiliation. And Eddé honourably cancelled his own effectiveness by steadfastly refusing to build an armed gang around him. In fact, the gentlemanly Eddé, though a committed Maronite, saw the danger of what was happening before many an astute observer of Lebanese politics. His analysis of the war-by-proxy coming told him that whatever kind of Lebanon emerged would be a reduced version of its former self and he wanted an independent, Christian-Muslim Lebanon without enmity towards its neighbours.

In the final analysis, militias are armed gangs unconstrained by the rules of organized warfare of regular armies. Because they are created to fight dirty civil wars without rules, their inherent corruption extends to other aspects of what exists around them. Whatever is touched by militia leaders is corrupted by them. The corruption brought about by the existence of so many militias in Lebanon came close to redefining itself. People who accept the principle of killing innocent civilians suffer from an inclusive impurity of character which produces new names.

In the 1970s, the developing armed confrontation in Lebanon yielded a collection of militia leaders who deserve remembering for the corruption they created. There was Tony Franjieh, who doubled as a cabinet member and a militia leader. He was in his late twenties and as ignorant as his father, the President. He used his position as Minister of Post and Telegraph to realize bribes on contracts and licences and everything between. In a way, Tony could be described as an institutional militia leader: his father insisted on his membership of every cabinet formed under his regime.

A more important militia leader was Beshir Gemayal, the youngest son of the Phalange leader Pierre Gemayal. Beshir's killer instinct endeared him to his father, who placed him above his elder brother Amin and in 1969 appointed him military commander of the large number of Phalange fighters at the age of twenty-two. A pimply-faced, overweight hooligan who merits the teenage epithet 'greasy', Beshir was entrusted with dealing with the Israelis and developing joint plans to rid Lebanon of the Palestinians. In between, he gave interviews to lady journalists in return for a night of sex and deposited in numbered Swiss accounts a great deal of the aid money that the ever-present CIA gave him. The CIA was anti-Palestinian and pro-Maronite-Israeli cooperation.

Dany Chamoun was appointed by his father to head the Tiger's militia. Very much like him, he had a sophisticated exterior and savagely tribal inner core. He spent a great deal of time working with the Israelis and the CIA and, like many of the clients of the American intelligence agency, he claimed much of its sponsorship money for himself.

Cherbel Kasiss was a dangerous monk. According to him, Christian teachings sanctioned the killing of Muslims. In addition to his Order of Monks and Guardians of Cedars, Kasiss was instrumental in the emergence of several Maronite killer groups with sinister names: Knights of the Virgin, Sword of the Cross and Youth of St Maroun.

Not to be outdone, the Palestinians produced their own morally and financially corrupt counterweight, Ali Hassan Salameh. He competed with Beshir Gemayal as to the number of undone buttons on his shirt, spent a lot of PLO money chasing girls in discos and was Arafat's contact man with the CIA and the Maronite forces. He had the mental make-up of an Italian harbour boy and his emergence as a celebrated leader of Palestinian fighting men casts serious doubts on Arafat's judgement of men.

Kamal Jumblat, though he did have a militia, was made of different stuff. In the middle of all this, he actually worked to elevate his Progressive

Socialist Party to the status of a non-sectarian entity and, unlike other militia leaders, his aims were clear. He refused to accept the idea of Maronite dominance and proposed to replace it by a non-sectarian state. However, the realities of the Lebanese situation and the tribal traditions of the country stood in his way and he too ended up depending on his fighting men to be heard.

In examining the quality of leadership fielded by the various sides, it is easy to conclude that the complicated nature of the Lebanese situation was not helped by the mediocrity of the people who expressed the existing divisions in the country. As a matter of fact, nothing had done more to destroy the semblance of normality provided by Greater Lebanon and the National Pact than the absence of a Solh and the lack of substance among the Lebanese leadership of the 1960s and 70s. But it is important to remember that the emergence of poor leadership was not an accident and that it was the expression of centuries of hatred between Lebanon's two sides and the cynical use of this by outside powers. Had Lebanon been left alone, the chances of following the noble voices of Fuad Chehab, Emile Bustani and Raymond Eddé would have been considerably greater.

In 1969 there had been the Cairo Agreement, the Nasser-sponsored pact which attempted to satisfy the Palestinians by allowing them to raid Israel but to refrain from interfering in Lebanese politics. It failed; the problems of Lebanon went beyond the Palestinian presence. By 1974 Franjieh's mismanagement of Lebanon had become an accepted fact and many in the Chamber of Deputies, including the far-seeing Eddé, began advocating measures to force him to step down. The US, though a consistent supporter of Maronite ring policies, had belatedly become alarmed by the extent of chaos in Lebanon. Afraid that the Maronites were marching towards partitioning the country and creating greater problems, it expressed support for removing Franjieh.[17] But instead of producing positive results, the internal and external pressure on Franjieh prompted the Maronites into greater reliance on Israel. This cancelled the American support for change, increased tension within the country and led to the inevitable.

In April 1975 the level of violence, daily kidnappings and killings by militias out of control was elevated to the status of civil war. The Phalange ambushed a bus carrying Palestinians and murdered thirty of them. The Palestinians and their Lebanese Muslim allies responded with atrocities of their own. The killings, the formation of governments which came and went without leaving a trace, truces, more killings and increasing savagery climaxed on 6 December 1975, the day the Lebanese call Black Saturday.

Members of the various Maronite militias roamed the streets of Beirut killing Muslims at random, often after torturing them, and their unchecked rampage produced a death toll of over 300 people, mainly innocents who happened to be within reach.[18] It is a measure of the insensitivity of Maronite leadership that these acts of violence were taking place against a background of continued economic abuse of their Muslim countrymen. In February 1975 it was the pompous, pretentious CIA darling Camille Chamoun who tried to deny Muslim fishermen in the southern city of Sidon the source of their livelihood by awarding to the Proteine Co. an exclusive fishing contract beneficial to him. The confrontation between the poor Lebanese fishermen and the Maronite security forces who were sympathetic to Chamoun was bloody and it led to the death of Sidon's popular mayor, Ma'arouf Sa'ad.[19] To judge from the callousness shown by Chamoun towards the fishermen's genuine concerns and his militia's substantial role in the Black Saturday massacre, it appears that he was determined to eliminate the Muslims, either by starving them or by killing them.

Even by Lebanon's hideous standards, the end of 1975 and beginning of 1976 were bad times. It started with attempts by Maronites to end the Palestinian presence in some predominantly Christian areas. They succeeded in razing the Dbaye and Karantina refugee camps in December 1975 and followed this by laying siege to the larger one of Tel Za'atar. The latter camp remained under siege for eight months and its fall was followed by another orgiastic killing of over a thousand Palestinians: according to reporter Charles Glass and others, mainly women and children. Vowing to avenge Palestinian blood, Yasser Arafat and his Muslim allies attacked Chamoun's stronghold of Damour in January 1976, occupied then looted it and showed the world their version of how to slaughter people. Several hundred Christians, again including women and children, were butchered in cold blood. With their supporters invigorated by their Damour victory, Arafat and his chief Lebanese ally, Kamal Jumblat, decided to go for total victory. Their forces began to prevail over the Christians along a fifteen-mile front which cut across Beirut, and in other parts of the country.

The prospect of a total Christian defeat, particularly in view of the fact that the Lebanese army was fragmenting along Christian and Muslim lines, became real. Syria, afraid that this might lead the Israelis to intervene on behalf of their Lebanese clients, decided to move into Lebanon. The US, wanting to protect the Maronites and afraid of another Arab-Israeli war, sanctioned the Syrian move and the Syrian army was welcomed by none other than the Arab-hating Camille Chamoun.[20] The Phalange and other Maronite groups joined in celebrating the Syrian entry into their country and fought with them to defeat the Palestinians and their allies and to recapture some of their lost territory. Only Raymond Eddé saw the Syrian move for what it really was: the culmination of a desire to return Lebanon to its fold, to undo what Greater Lebanon and the National Pact had sanctified.

In September 1976 Syria stood as the enforcer of the *de facto* division of Lebanon: Israel was continuing to support the Maronites to the tune of $100 million a year[21] and it was time to elect a new president. The members of the Chamber of Deputies had elected Elias Sarkis in June to replace Franjieh, the man who used threats and bribes to defeat Sarkis in 1970. A colourless bureaucrat and former head of the Central Bank, Sarkis was much too weak for what confronted him and it was his inherent weakness, as well as the fact that he had been unable to resist Maronite pressure, which prevented him from making any moves to save Lebanon's and the Middle East's largest commercial bank, INTRA. And Sarkis, in a country where political support meant depending on young toughs to do the dirty work, was without a street following that could make a difference. In fact, he was elected to office with Syrian support for that very reason: that he had no popular following that could cause them trouble.

With Sarkis at the helm, it was as if both sides had committed themselves to a government incapable of solving the country's problems. The office of the president mattered considerably less than the word of the thugs running the streets of Beirut. And having used Syria to avoid destruction, the Maronites started speaking for partition and wanting their Syrian protectors replaced by Israeli ones.[22]

Two things stood in the way of the Maronites' desire to reduce Greater Lebanon to a totally Maronite smaller country under Israeli protection. Syria refused to budge and the United States supported Syria and rejected any moves aimed at creating another Israeli problem or expanding the already existing one.[23]

To detail the happenings between 1977 and 1982 is to make a list of the decline of sensibility. The Maronites attached themselves without shame to their fourth protector since independence. Their original protector, France, was out of the picture and, despite some attempts at mediation, did nothing beyond express shock at what was happening. The United States, to the dismay of the Maronites, viewed events in terms of its regional interests and refused to accept an exclusively Maronite solution. Syria, having achieved a tactical victory by temporarily forestalling an Israeli intervention and strategic victory by realizing its ancient objective of spreading its hegemony over Lebanon, had its own agenda, which precluded total alliance with the Maronites. Only Israel was willing to support Maronite intransigence and the subordination of the Palestinians and their anti-Israeli Muslim allies. And the Maronites, cynical and bloodthirsty as ever, allied themselves to Israel while continuing to live off jobs in the oil-rich Gulf and openly to seek Saudi financial support.

Within the country, the usual butchery assumed an added dimension. The Maronite militia chiefs, vying for the honour of raising a bloodied Christian flag over Mount Lebanon, began fighting among themselves. In 1978 the fighters of the Phalange killed Tony Franjieh, the infamous son of the former president, along with his wife, baby daughter and the family's pet dog. Members of the Phalange often kidnapped, tortured and killed members of the Tigers militia and the Tigers did the same. Occasionally, in a show of honour among thugs, they released some of their important captives.

By 1982 something resembling a balance of terror had emerged. Syria was still a presence in Lebanon, alone, without the help of the Arab armed contingent which had briefly gone there to help it, but the military cost and fear of Israeli interference prevented it from controlling the Christian area. Beshir Gemayal and his Israeli-trained and financed Phalange were confirmed as the dominant Christian militia. Despite the death of Kamal Jumblat, probably killed by the Syrians, who resented his militancy, the Lebanese Muslims and their Palestinian allies were still in full control of large sections of the country and West Beirut. The President and various functionary prime ministers acted as messenger boys between the warring factions, but they lacked the authority or power to do anything more. It was a shaky stalemate, within which violence was a daily occurrence, and it had to end.

Menachim Begin had become Prime Minister of Israel in 1977. He brought to office a considerable amount of messianic nonsense and a belief that, like the Jews during the Second World War, the Maronites were confronting the prospect of a holocaust. He accepted and expanded the Israeli relationship with the Maronites, and found the bloodthirstiness of Beshir Gemayal and his stubborn insistence on creating a Maronite state more to his liking than others. Gemayal became Begin's pet ally while other Maronite leaders were relegated to a secondary position.

In 1978, overreacting to the landing of a PLO hit squad near Jaffa and the consequent killing of several Israelis, Israel invaded southern Lebanon in force. The Carter administration responded angrily and pressured the Israelis to withdraw from most of the country, but not before hundreds were killed and thousands were made homeless and not until they had established a security belt of Lebanese territory to their north and manned it with their Maronite allies.

Between 1978 and 1982 Begin and Israeli Defence Minister Ariel Sharon watched Lebanese developments from a distance while lamenting the Maronites' inability to deliver what they wanted: the total destruction of the PLO and the creation of a Maronite state openly allied to Israel. In the meantime they refined their own plans to invade Lebanon and achieve what the Maronites failed to deliver.

On 3 June 1982, despite an effective truce between Israel and the PLO which had been secretly negotiated with US help almost a year earlier, the Israelis found their excuse. A Palestinian group opposed to Arafat tried to assassinate Moshe Argov, the Israeli Ambassador to Britain. Although the Israelis knew that Arafat wasn't behind the attempt, they unleashed their army and invaded Lebanon. This time there was no Jimmy Carter to cry foul. Ronald Reagan had been elected President of the United States in 1980 and his Secretary of State, Alexander Haig, was party to the Israeli decision to invade.[24]

It was what the Israeli penchant for misnomers called Peace for Galilee, one of the ugliest, most complicated, more widely reported and least understood military operations of all time. First, the Israelis kept contradicting themselves and misrepresenting their aims. Then the world, including the Arab states, were paralysed by inaction while the Israeli military machine, using jet fighters, cluster bombs and seven hundred tanks, rolled over everything in its way, again including women and children. Thirdly, Syria, though it switched sides completely and reassumed its more natural role as an ally of the Palestinians and Muslims, decided to avoid military confrontation with Israel after a feeble attempt at resistance which saw it lose over sixty aircraft in one day and despite repeated Israeli attacks against their armour. Fourthly, with little thought for the future, the Maronite militias openly supported the Israeli invasion.[25]

On 25 June, after the Israelis had subjected the surrounded Beirut to one of the most savage and indiscriminate aerial bombardments in history, Haig departed and minutes later the Israeli onslaught came to an end.[26] Reacting to mounting internal pressure in his country and throughout the Arab and Muslim worlds, King Fahd of Saudi Arabia had lodged a strong protest directly with Reagan, and a mere hint that oil supplies might be affected produced an about-turn in US policy and the firing of the incompetent Haig.

This was followed by a redoubling of US mediation efforts. The result was the departure of the PLO armed presence from Lebanon on 21 August 1982 and the election of Beshir Gemayal as president two days later. The

Israelis, in accordance with the agreement brokered by the US, had refrained from entering west Beirut. Meanwhile the Syrians had pulled out of Beirut and redeployed in the Baka' valley. But the respite was not to last long. President-elect Beshir Gemayal and forty of his followers were killed by a remote-control bomb at the Phalange headquarters in east Beirut on 14 September, a few days before he was to be inaugurated.

Even in death Gemayal represented the unattractive confusion of Lebanon. Nobody could tell who was responsible. The tribal Franjiehs had ample reason to kill him and avenge the death of Tony. The Palestinians had suffered so much at his hands that an attempt by them on his life would have been understandable. The Syrians, resentful of his alliance with Israelis, had reason to eliminate him. And the Israelis, as has become known since, also had cause to get rid of Beshir: they were beginning to resent signs that he was determined to follow an independent policy without deferring to them. Of course, as in all things Lebanese there could have been a convergence of interest or an individual acting on his or her own.

Speculation as to who killed Beshir didn't last long. After the murder the Israelis moved into west Beirut in obvious violation of their undertaking. They claimed that they were there to maintain law and order. On 16 September, with Beshir still unburied, the Phalangists, frustrated by their inability to act against other suspects, with Israeli connivance, moved into west Beirut and decided to punish the Palestinians. The massacre of over two thousand Palestinian civilians in a cinematic orgy of killing is one of the blackest pages of confessional conflicts. As the veteran foreign correspondent Robert Fisk put it in a newspaper article: 'THE CHRISTIANS DID IT'.

The Norwegian journalist Karsten Tveit and Tim Llewellyn of the BBC were among the first reporters to enter the camps after the massacre. They established Israeli culpability well before the international outcry which followed the massacres forced the Israelis to appoint a Knesset commission of inquiry, which admitted the same. To this day it is difficult for both Tveit and Llewellyn to describe what they saw and their conversations with some of the survivors. Without wishing to add to their anguish, certain things need to be repeated.

There were no arms in the camps and the Maronite entry into them did not follow combat. As such, this qualifies as a premeditated massacre of innocent civilians. In an operation which lasted over fifty-six hours, there was not one single act of mercy. People were tortured, particularly pregnant women carrying 'unborn terrorists', and the bodies of many victims were mutilated after they were shot. The Maronite troops seem to have derived particular pleasure from killing members of families in front of each other. Bayonets were used to draw crosses on the bodies of the dead or before they were shot. The names of Christ and the Virgin were invoked by the killers as they carried out their hideous work. The Israelis fired flares to guide the Maronites to their victims. Mainly because what was happening amounted to ritualistic slaughter and it took a long time, some Israeli officers finally tired and ordered the Maronites to stop. The guardians of Christian civilization in the Middle East wanted to continue until all ten thousand people in the camps were dead.

The world cried foul and hundreds of thousands of Israelis demonstrated against the massacre and demanded an inquiry. But the Maronites were unrepentant and the mother church, the Vatican, issued the usual mild condemnation of violence. It was the press – Robert Fisk of *The Times*, Tveit, Llewellyn, *Time* magazine's Roberto Suro, ABC's Chris Harper, *Newsweek*'s James Pringle and other foreign correspondents – who would not let go. Were it not for the press, Sabra and Chatila would have been relegated to another Beirut idiocy. But it was more, not because foreign correspondents made it more, but because the battle-hardened press corps could not but react to the savagery. Even by Lebanese standards, it was beyond anything they had ever seen or expected.

Meanwhile the tribal Lebanese hurried to elect Beshir's older brother Amin to replace him. It is worth noting that Amin had been bypassed because he wasn't tough enough, because the Maronites, again very much like the Mafia, had admired Beshir's killer instinct. That was essentially true, but Amin's commitment to a Maronite-controlled sectarian-tribal Lebanon was wholehearted. His disinclination to use the gun did not mean lack of belief in Maronite paramountcy.

Soon after Amin's election, as a result of the international outcry over Sabra and Chatila, a multi-national force of American, British, French and Italian troops was sent to west Beirut to protect its defenceless Muslims and Palestinians. It arrived a few days after the massacre, but its brief precluded involvement in a civil war and whatever survived of the pro-Maronite Lebanese army joined forces with the Phalange. Together they entered west Beirut, disarmed all Muslims and killed hundreds of them randomly; having learned their lesson, they did this on an individual basis or in small groups of five to ten people.

Not only did Amin refrain from stopping his constituents' dirty work, but he moved to formalize the Lebanese-Israeli alliance. In May 1983 he pushed through Lebanon's Chamber of Deputies a treaty of Maronite-Israeli cooperation, which, a year later, he rescinded to appease the Syrians. In October 1983 the multi-national force arrived and the Israelis began a slow, step-by-step withdrawal which involved considerable rearguard fighting. Overall, the Lebanese Muslims felt helpless.

Lebanese helplessness is a prelude to violence. In this case, the staged Israeli withdrawal saw the emergence of a new sectarian force within a country which needed anything but that. The downtrodden Shias, mainly responding to Israeli atrocities in southern Lebanon and undivided Western support for Amin Gemayal's administration, assumed the role of resisters of these two developments. The attacks on the Israelis, who in 1985 eventually left south Lebanon – all but a bigger security zone of some 400 square miles – were a daily occurrence; but the US became a new target.

In April 1983, in a prelude to things to come, a Shia suicide bomber blew up the US Embassy, killing sixty-three people. After Amin provoked them further by signing the treaty with Israel, in October 1983 Shia suicide bombers blew up the headquarters of the American and French multi-national force contingents, killing more than three hundred servicemen. A while later, another Shia suicide bomber blew up the Israeli army headquarters in Tyre. Once again, the world had another unattractive name to contend with: Islamic Jihad.

By early 1984 Amin's policies and US support had produced something similar to what had existed during the last days of Franjieh. The Lebanese army and Christian militias were joined in an alliance, but this time the opposition to them came from the Shia. For all practical purposes, Amin Gemayal, using a reverse route, became a Christian militia leader.

The absence of an army and a government left the multi-national force with no legal entity to support and it withdrew in July 1984. Things were changing for the worse in a new way. The era of kidnappings had arrived. And it began with an act of humiliation directed at the United States: the Shias kidnapped and killed Beirut CIA station chief William Buckley.

More abductions followed in 1985 and 1986. Shia determination to be the sole representative of the non-Maronite forces in Lebanon twice led them to attack Palestinian refugee camps to subdue their natural allies the Palestinians. Slowly the Syrian army moved back into Beirut and reassumed its role as the guarantor of the country's stability. In 1986 Terry Waite, the Archbishop of Canterbury's special envoy charged with negotiating freedom for many Western hostages, was himself taken hostage. The Lebanese civil war had been going on for eleven years, and many people, including some who were participating in the occasional flare-ups of fighting, could not remember how the whole thing started.

In 1988 and 1989 the country, now a shadow of its former glamorous self, faced a new crisis. The Chamber of Deputies set the ball rolling when it failed to elect a new president. Amin Gemayal decided to solve the problem by resorting to the totally illegal expedient of appointing General Michel Aoun, the army's chief of staff, to succeed him. Aoun, a true Lebanese, moved against dissident Maronite opponents and took his presidential position seriously. A conference in Taif, Saudi Arabia, in which most Lebanese sides except Aoun participated, produced a formula for a solution which included equal Christian-Muslim representation in parliament, reduced power for the Maronite president and placed greater power in the office of the Muslim prime minister. The Syrians, because they supported the Taif agreement, and because their presence stood in the way of Maronite hegemony, became the object of Maronite enmity. General Aoun declared war on Syria and fighting between the Syrian army and the Maronites became the new norm, until a heavy Syrian bombardment of Aoun's Christian army forced him to abandon plans for open battle.

In 1989 Aoun's unconstitutional presidency had a new sponsor behind it: none other than Syria's arch enemy Saddam Hussein. The Syrians' response to this was to force the Lebanese Chamber of Deputies to end the impasse and elect a president: René Moawad. Suddenly Lebanon had a Syrian-sponsored president and an Iraqi-sponsored one. With this act, except for the honourable Chehab, Lebanon had the dubious honour of having had presidents sponsored by France, the United States, Israel, Iraq and Syria. But the unfortunate Moawad didn't last long: in November 1989 he was blown to bits by a street bomb which totally destroyed his passing armour-plated car. There is suspicion that the Iraqis had a hand in his murder, naturally using the good offices of their Lebanese allies. The Syrians, who had become uneasy over Moawad's intentions to follow their agenda, were also suspect.

Angered and humiliated by the assassination of their original ward, or having found someone malleable, the Syrians sponsored Elias Hrawi to replace him and waited for their moment. In 1990, in return for their support for the anti-Saddam coalition in the Gulf War, the United States gave them a free hand to finish off Aoun and his supporters. While the world focused on Kuwait, and Saddam was becoming a household name, the Syrian army, heavily relying on its unopposed air force, bombed Aoun into submission, and he escaped to France after taking refuge in the French embassy.

Towards the end of 1996, Hrawi is still president and he runs the country with the assistance of a Muslim Prime Minister, Rafiq Hariri. The Syrian army is also still in Lebanon and Syria's presence, resented as it is by the Maronites, determines the behaviour of the Lebanese government. Of course, the West still supports the continued existence of Lebanon within secure boundaries and has little to say about the fundamental unsoundness of its governmental system.

The presidential term which was to end in 1996 has been extended. But there is still a need to elect a new Chamber of Deputies to choose a new president for a full term. Lebanon suffers the occasional small flare-ups of violence, but the people are tired and the Hrawi-Hariri government is trying to rebuild Beirut, reimpose its hegemony on all parts of the country and function as the government did before 1975. But is this possible?

Although holding a census comes low on a long list of things that need to be done, there is reason to believe that the basic situation is worse than in 1975, when the civil war started. Now the Shias account for more than 37 per cent of the population of the country. And because many Maronites have emigrated, their proportion of the population has sunk to around 20 per cent. Yet the Maronites will never forgo their claim to the presidency and refuse to settle for any situation which might deny them paramountcy. The West, although it has withheld support for the Maronites on occasions when regional considerations dictated it, still upholds Maronite paramountcy. Today, as on 1 September 1920, Lebanon is an absurd creation.

The long cycle of horror which began in 1975 has produced the opposite of what the Maronites wanted. Instead of having nothing to do with Damascus, Lebanon is operating within a Syrian sphere of influence. How long Syria's historical grievance will be satisfied by this indirect control depends on the Maronites' ability to obtain Western support to continue their age-old policy of religious abuse. As in 1920, providing this support depends on whether Syria accepts Western hegemony or rejects it, and, of course, on Israel.

7 · The Obedient Offspring

Jordan and Saudi Arabia are the two monarchies which have survived the constant turmoil of the Middle East since the arrival of the West after the First World War. Both were created by the West, and Western support is a major factor in their continued survival. Jordan was designed by Britain to satisfy King Abdallah and to undermine the Arab position in Palestine; Ibn Saud was allowed, and on occasion helped, to unite Saudi Arabia because he accepted Britain's regional hegemony.

Both countries have experienced massive threats to their survival. They successfully confronted the challenges of pan-Arabism, Nasser and internal attempts to change their governmental systems and loosen the royal grip on power. Nowadays they are both combating Islamic fundamentalism. Simultaneously, although there have been occasions when the rulers of these countries and the West disagreed, there has always been an overriding mutuality of interest between them. A Hashemite-run Jordan under King Hussein and the absolute rule of the House of Saud are essential to the West's desire to continue to control the Middle East indirectly, and both monarchies need Western support to survive against the wishes of their people.

King Hussein became King of Jordan in 1952, after his grandfather, Abdallah, the country's British-backed first king, was assassinated in 1951 and following the abdication of his mentally ill father. His forty-four years on the throne have been marked by constant attempts against his kingship and threats to the continuance of his country as an independent entity. Most of the dangers to Hussein and Jordan originated with its people, who have never accepted the country as a separate and viable entity. How and why Hussein managed to survive and continues as a major player on the Middle East scene, and how the West kept him on the throne, tell us a great deal about the Western commitment to perpetuate its indirect control of the Middle East to prevent moves towards Arab unity and the emergence of legitimate governments. In fact, one could argue that the challenges to Hussein are the result of his dependence on the West and not the other way around, and as such they are self-perpetuating.

Fahd bin Abdel Aziz, fifth king of Saudi Arabia, ascended the throne in 1982, after ten years as heir apparent and strongman behind his brother, King Khalid. His oil-rich country has never faced the severe threats to its existence which continue to bedevil Jordan, but there have been more external and internal attempts against the absolute rule of the House of Saud than is generally realized. Fahd assumed power at a time when the country's wealth allowed the House of Saud to buy the loyalty of its people and exercise considerable influence on the Arab and Muslim worlds and beyond. However, things have changed drastically since the 1980s. The decline in oil prices during the past decade, the squandering of the country's wealth by the House of Saud and the emergence of a strong Islamist movement have produced a slow but perceptible disintegration in the country's internal structure and this, coupled with a parallel inability to use money to buy the loyalty of people inside and outside Saudi Arabia, ended the Saudi era in Arab and Muslim affairs. But Saudi Arabia's security is guaranteed by the West, which continues to support Fahd and to overlook his and his family's abuse of power. It is another situation where Western support for traditional leaders precludes the enactment of reforms and the development of sensible Arab and Islamic policies and where the mutuality of interest between a repressive regime and the West heralds disaster.

King Hussein bin Tallal, to people and governments in the West the most popular Arab leader of our time, was born in 1935. His early childhood was an unhappy one. His father was a schizoid who tormented his mother and this led Hussein to transfer his affections to his grandfather, Emir and later King Abdallah of Jordan. To this day, he is full of affection and reverence for the memories of his grandfather and his mother but has little to say about his father.

To repeat, the British-created Jordan which King Abdallah ran from 1921 until 1951 had the twin purpose of satisfying the pliant Hashemite Emir and of acting as a buffer state which would facilitate British designs to create a Jewish state in Palestine. There is no disputing this, and it was Lawrence of Arabia at the 1921 Cairo Conference who summed up the British position by declaring, 'It would be preferable to use Transjordan [until 1950 the country's official name] as a safety valve, by appointing a ruler who would bring pressure to bear, to check anti-Zionism.'[1] And, according to Gerald de Gaury, 'Even its founder, Emir Abdallah, didn't regard it [Jordan] as a real country.'[2] It wasn't, and throughout its history the country, ill-designed and non-cohesive, faced structural economic problems and enough non-acceptance by its own people to create an identity problem. To survive, the Jordanian monarchy used two traditional tools, a Bedouin army and Western financial help, and an improvised one, a special relationship with Israel to confront external and internal threats to its being. The dependence on Israel for survival, which started in 1922,[3] is unique, but it should be judged as an expression of a Western policy aimed at guaranteeing the survival of both countries. In essence, the West was aiding the Arabs' enemy by helping to maintain an Arab non-sustaining entity that the Arab people never accepted.

Any realistic judgement of King Hussein's rule has to take into consideration not only the nature of Jordan but his own upbringing. His grandfather pampered him and oversaw his education at Victoria College in Alexandria, Harrow and the Royal Military Academy at Sandhurst. At all three establishments he proved himself a bright, active and popular student. He developed strong and lasting friendships with his schoolmasters and with Arab and non-Arab students and, according to all of them, he possessed that special qualification for leadership, charm. Moreover, as a Hashemite direct descendant of the Prophet, he was tutored in the ways of Muslim-Arab culture and he is the product of this traditional learning as much as of his Western education. He belongs to both East and West.

Whether Hussein manifested any political inclinations at an early age is unknown, but what was to him a tragic incident – the assassination of his grandfather while both of them were visiting Jerusalem's Al Aqsa mosque – hurled him into the vortex of Arab politics irretrievably. Legend has it that a medal on Hussein's chest was knocked off by one of the assassin's bullets, but witnesses deny this and it is the first of dozens of stories intended to enhance Hussein's life, achievements and standing, to make him a hero. In fact, it is through examining the real Hussein and comparing him with the distorted picture which exists in the West, one made up of press stories, that the differences between Western and Arab interests are exposed. The Hussein we know is a classic example of Western promotion of Arab leaders beholden to them, mainly at the expense of the truth and of Arab interests.

Nowadays the West sees him as a brave, wise and peace-loving monarch and, on occasion, even a believer in democracy. Is he? How do his people and the rest of the Arabs see him? More fundamentally, how do they view his dependence on Western and Israeli sponsorship? The issue now is the same as it was in 1921: whether or not the West should continue to support an artificial country, the existence of which serves outsiders instead of the interests of its people and the Arabs.

The Hussein who succeeded an ailing, unfit father in 1952 had a difficult time deciding what he and his country represented. He had spark, and those who attended him at the time speak of a youth embittered by the Arab defeat in 1948 and determined to reverse it. But the odds were against him. Glubb Pasha was still head of his country's British-financed army, the Arab Legion, and behaved like the chief of a native force, Jordanian in name only. The Palestinians of the West Bank, which had been annexed by Jordan after the 1948 War, resented him because of his grandfather's cooperation with Israel, as did the Palestinians who had fled to Jordan as refugees and made up two-thirds of its people. All this in addition to the inherent unviability of his sparsely populated and resourceless country and the wish of its educated people for it to disappear.

Nevertheless, the period until 1955 was the golden age of Hussein as an inspiring monarch. Until 1954 the Israelis were preoccupied with arguments about their fate, heatedly debating whether they should opt for immediate peace with their Arab neighbours or wait until their new state had a chance to mould its separate Jewish identity. Nasser was still busy vying with fellow officers for Egypt's leadership and paid little attention to Jordan and the rest of the Arab countries. Jordan was enjoying a period of relative quiet and the young king added to his stature by marrying an educated, popular cousin, Princess Dina Abdel Hamid, in 1954.

During this period Hussein was a popular king. His nationalist tendencies, though seldom articulated to his people, filtered through to them. Furthermore, his uneasy relationship with Glubb Pasha was to their liking, and Hussein, the born soldier, enjoyed visiting his army units and mixing with officers and other ranks in a manner which endeared him to them and to the rest of Jordan. But this populist posture had an inherent weakness. Whatever Hussein's feelings towards Glubb Pasha, the symbol of British hegemony over Jordan was not only there but was a living reminder of the structural weakness of the country, and his presence acted as a check on the behaviour of the monarch. Continuing the British subsidy depended on Glubb's archaic presence.

In 1955, although he never liked Glubb, Hussein demonstrated the uncertainty of his young years and an inherent pro-British attitude by announcing his acceptance of the British-sponsored anti-communist Baghdad Pact. However, when Chief of the Imperial General Staff General Gerald Templer visited Jordan to finalize Jordan's adherence to the pact, violent demonstrations broke out and Hussein relented. He didn't stop there: shortly afterwards he exhibited one of his many changes of direction and decided to support the enemies of the pact, the Nasser camp.

At this point Hussein's turn to popular politics and Glubb's lack of sensitivity to the changing times and the desire of Jordan's people to have

him leave their country combined to produce one of the most misunder-
stood acts of Hussein's kingship: the popular firing of the unwanted British
officers in 1956. Responding to Nasser's calls for a united Arab front
against Israel and drawn to young nationalist officers in his army, Hussein
rid his country of Glubb and his fellow British officers. The move was
overdue and had widespread support, but the consequent appointment of
Ali Abu Nawar as a replacement for Glubb and his elevation from the
rank of major to general in one step was a mistake. Not only were there
Arab officers in the army whose background and competence placed them
above him, but Abu Nawar was no more than a handsome playboy and
making him his army's chief of staff revealed a Hussein lacking in
judgement.

Hussein's Arabization of his army and his country's external policies
was followed by the laudable step of holding free parliamentary elections.
These resulted in a pro-Nasser government and, for the first time in the
history of the country, a popular Prime Minister, Suleiman Nabulsi. The
West's violent verbal reaction to these moves assumed concrete form when
the British cancelled subsidies to Jordan's army, its name now changed
from the Arab Legion to Jordan's Arab Army. On paper, Hussein had
planned for this; the Arab countries had applauded his moves and volun-
teered to replace the British subsidy.

But the Arab governments failed to keep their promises, and Nasser
was the darling of the Jordanian people, regardless of what Hussein did.
Despite this, Hussein held on to a nationalistic line, to the extent of
offering to fight alongside Nasser during the 1956 Suez War, something, as
explained later, the latter successfully convinced him not to do. Afterwards
Hussein's gentlemanly gesture went unappreciated while Nasser's defeat
increased popular affection for him. Suddenly Hussein was at a loss as to
what to do to maintain his army, country and throne. The response to
these problems came soon: not only did he change direction again and
decide to seek Western help, but this change marked a significant turning
point in his life, the beginning of disdain for fellow Arabs. Here it is
important to recall the underlying reason for this; as we will see, following
Arab policies diminished Hussein's status, while adherence to pro-West
policies invariably elevated him to centre stage in the Middle East
stakes.

The story of the CIA-Hussein conspiracy to remove his freely elected
government and incompetent chief of staff was detailed earlier (see Chapter
4), but there was more behind it than a need for financial subsidies.
Nasser's popularity and power had relegated Hussein to a secondary position within his own country and he resented that in the way he had

resented Glubb's presence and assumption of the role of uncrowned king. But, because he couldn't compete with Nasser, Hussein decided to replace Glubb as the representative of the West in Jordan. Moreover, the failure of the Arab countries to meet their promises left him free to assume this role. Perhaps Hussein had wanted to be a popular king and an Arab leader, but neither was possible while Nasser was alive. The Jordanian people judged what was happening in their country in terms of day-to-day events, but Hussein saw things differently, committed himself to the survival of the Hashemite name and resurrected the role of his grandfather as a reliable Western client.

Even internally, Hussein's dismissal of Abu Nawar and Nabulsi were more than coups: they signalled a complete change in direction. The Prime Minister who succeeded Nabulsi was one Ibrahim Hashem, a mild man of questionable qualities, but his Foreign Minister was Samir Rifai, a tried but unpopular pro-West politician. In addition to the uncompromising Rifai, Hussein surrounded himself with a new collection of mainly Bedouin officers who had been Glubb's allies, Habis Al Majali, Ghazi Arribyat and Radi Abdallah (the contact man with the CIA). He entrusted internal security to his uncle, Nasser bin Jamil, a man known for taking delight in cruelties which included drinking while watching political prisoners tortured. Martial law was declared in the country, CIA agents were everywhere, hundreds of people were arrested and all political parties were banned. Jordan reverted to being a royal dictatorship. Hussein stopped listening to the sounds of the street. The new Hussein who emerged believed that following an American line was the key to his survival and that, among other things, America wanted him to cooperate with Israel.

But the Arab pressure on Hussein intensified when Egypt and Syria merged to create the United Arab Republic (UAR) in February 1958. The people of Jordan wanted to join the UAR, or at least have close political and economic relations with it, but Hussein would have none of it and both America and Britain were determined to use Jordan to stop the march towards Arab unity. However, knowing that Jordan couldn't stand alone, they prevailed on Hussein to join Iraq in an anti-Nasser union, the Arab Federation. As far as the people of Jordan were concerned, this was adding insult to injury. Iraq, the senior member of the Federation, still belonged to the Baghdad Pact, which had been rejected by them through violent demonstration in 1955. Hussein showed little interest in what his people wanted.

On 14 July 1958 the Iraqi monarchy was bloodily overthrown by the country's army while an official Jordanian delegation was visiting Baghdad to finalize the union between the two countries. All members of the Iraqi royal family, including Hussein's second cousin, King Faisal II, were murdered and the out-of-control mobs in Baghdad killed the visiting Jordanian Prime Minister, Ibrahim Hashem, and several members of the Jordanian delegation. A revolutionary regime was installed in Iraq and overnight the saviour country became the source of additional threat to Hussein's rule.

Hussein, determined to follow openly pro-West policies, found no one to turn to within the Arab camp. Even Saudi Arabia couldn't afford to match his CIA-inspired policies and refused to oppose Nasser and the revolutionary governments openly. Hussein, with nothing behind him except Western support, asked Britain for direct military help to stay in power. Two days after the overthrow of the Iraqi monarchy the 16th Parachute Brigade of the British army landed in Jordan to protect Hussein. To him, 'The famous red berets in the streets made people realize we're not alone.'[4] This was an insult to his anti-British people, who had already reached the conclusion that their country was still a British colony and the Israeli connivance in the British landing operation was clear: the British force overflew Israel to reach Jordan. Naturally, financial help followed and the United States gave Jordan $50 million.

Hussein was intelligent enough to realize that there was no going back to being a popular king; that his rule continued courtesy of British bayonets and American financial help. Deciding that the amount of Western help he was receiving was in proportion to the threat facing him, he began scheming to exaggerate the dangers to his kingship and identified them as communist-inspired. But for by all accounts the Communist Party of Jordan was too small and ineffectual to constitute a threat and was never in any position to mount a coup, and most of Hussein's people were Allah-fearing Muslims.

But there were constant threats to Hussein's throne, and they came from the Jordanian people, who disapproved of his total dependence on the West. However, Nasser, though he exhorted them through Radio Cairo to pressure Hussein into following Arab policies, did not want Hussein toppled. Nasser feared that the overthrow of Hussein would lead to an Israeli occupation of the West Bank and he deliberately stopped short of organizing any conspiracies against Hussein or advocating his overthrow. In 1959, tiring of accusations that the UAR was plotting against Hussein, Nasser's Minister of the Interior Zakkaria Mohieeddine told Wilton Wynn of *Time* and Harry Ellis of the *Christian Science Monitor*, 'Gentlemen, we don't want to overthrow him [Hussein] and we don't want him dead – we know what the consequences would be. Some of our followers may act against him on their own, without our sanction, but if my government wanted him dead I'd have him killed without difficulty. I have people who're willing to do this throughout Jordan.'[5]

Hussein knew this, but he also knew that fabricating plots and attributing them to communism and to Nasser guaranteed him increased Western support. Above all, it intensified Western pressure on Nasser and made the CIA give him, Hussein, yet more money to indulge in plotting against the United Arab Republic.

One of the most remarkable of Hussein's efforts to perpetuate the legend of a beleaguered king fighting the evil forces of communism took place on 11 November 1958, four months after the overthrow of the Iraqi monarchy. According to Hussein, Syrian MiG fighters tried to shoot down his plane while it was overflying Syria on its way to Europe. The story continues with Hussein and his pilot ducking the Syrian aircraft and landing back in Amman, to be greeted by a massive demonstration of support.

This is an invented tale and pure nonsense. The Dove, difficult to manoeuvre, wasn't up to escaping a MiG, the royal plane didn't have clearance to overfly Syria, there is doubt that Hussein was aboard and the demonstrations celebrating the safe return of the king were too well organized and too large to be spontaneous. Moreover, immediately after the episode, CIA agents Bill Eveland and James Russell Barracks met several members of the Middle East press corps stationed in Beirut to confirm that Hussein had had clearance to overfly Syria and Lebanon. According to them, a certain Samir at Beirut's international airport gave them the details. The press carried the CIA agents' story.

The facts were much simpler. *Time*, with the advantage of being a weekly, investigated the incident more thoroughly than the rest of the press. The magazine's correspondents John Mecklin and Abu Saïd discovered that there was no Samir at Beirut's international airport, that the similarity between Hussein's and the agents' impromptu stories was too studied and that the whole thing was no more than an ordinary case of a plane invading Syrian airspace without clearance and being turned back. Smelling a rat, the *Time* team contacted the magazine's Amman stringer, Abul Hafez Bazzian. The latter confirmed that the demonstrations were organized by Jordan's security service well before the return of the plane.[6] The *Time* story detailed the new evidence, but it was too late. The world had accepted Hussein's version of events and the Western press had, once again, elevated him to a hero.

Soon after, in 1959, there was yet another so-called plot, this time an army-based conspiracy led by Brigadier Radi Abdallah. As discussed earlier (see Chapter 4), this represented nothing more than an attempt to blame

Abdallah for the disappearance of CIA funds that Hussein had used for other purposes. Abdallah was released and promoted soon after. There was a third plot in May 1959, when General Sadek Shara'a was imprisoned for conspiring to overthrow Hussein. A military man with an impeccable record, Shara'a insisted that he was innocent and repeatedly asked to be put on trial. He was never indicted and was released after a year. And, strangely, neither the Abdallah or Shara'a caper produced accomplices and thus, according to their royal accuser, the two men had planned the takeover of the government of Jordan single-handed.

Perhaps the strangest plot of them all was the one where someone was supposed to have put acid in the bottle containing Hussein's nose drops while the king was staying at the Amman home of an English friend, Maurice Raynor. Once again there were no consequences to this, and no one was arrested or charged. Logic would suggest that the people with access to the bottle of nose drops in Raynor's home were few and that such a serious attempt on the monarch's life would have led to a thorough investigation. Nothing of the sort happened.

Creating phoney plots was Hussein's own handiwork. It was part of building an image to guarantee Western support and reflected the uncertainty of his grip on power. Indeed, over the years, the perpetrators of these so-called plots change in accordance with the political climate of the times. In the 1950s and 60s Hussein foolishly used Islamic movements to gain popular support against Nasser's street following. Now that the West has identified Islam as the new enemy, Hussein has followed suit. The latest phoney incitement against Hussein took place early in 1996, when the Islamist Laith Shbeilat was arrested, tried and given a three-year prison sentence for being the mastermind behind it. Shbeilat, a deputy in the Jordanian parliament, opposes Hussein's pro-West and pro-Israeli policies and his trial was a mockery of justice. The whole thing is a sham, and the chances are that Shbeilat will be released as an act of magnanimity by His Majesty.

The mutuality of interest between Hussein and the West is far greater than phoney image-building exercises aimed at promoting and maintaining him. It covers fundamental policy areas: his relations with the Arab countries and his friendship with Israel. It is axiomatic that Hussein, dependent on the West as he was and is, follows its lead in these areas. But it isn't a clear-cut case and there is a second and often neglected influence on Hussein's political behaviour: his descent from the Prophet. A fortieth-generation Hashemite, he implicitly believes in a divine right of kings and feels obligations the meaning of which escapes others. Some of his deviations from a solidly pro-West policy, strange as they appear at the time, are easily understood when judged by this yardstick.

Hussein's contacts and cooperation with Israel began shortly after his 1957 decision that his survival and Arab unity, even interests, were mutually exclusive. During the first confrontation with the pro-Nasser elements in his country, Israel sent him several messages of support. But regular meetings between the two sides flourished beginning 1963,[7] when the pressures on Hussein to join an anti-Israeli Arab front were at their height. This was when the relationship, with Western encouragement, graduated from a political alliance of convenience and began to assume the perverse form of an anti-Arab pact, and when Hussein went as far as making a secret visit to Tel Aviv.

In the period preceding the 1967 War, Hussein performed several openly anti-Arab deeds. This was his response to the creation of the PLO, which wanted to replace him as the Palestinians' representative, and the efforts of its fighters to infiltrate Israel. Hussein's intelligence service, initially unable to act directly against fighters who were popular because they were battling Israel, passed on their names to the Israelis.[8] He didn't stop there, and the same intelligence service provided Israel with information about the rest of the Arab countries.[9] However shameful these acts, they were less damaging than Hussein's major one of contributing measurably towards the start of the 1967 War.

In 1966 and early in 1967, Jordan Radio was funded by the Americans, and CIA agent John Fistere had considerable say over what it broadcast. Obeying the CIA, and with input from the Israelis, Jordan Radio launched bitter attacks on Nasser accusing him of being a paper tiger. According to these broadcasts, Nasser – who was still trying to force Hussein into toeing an Arab line – was advocating a confrontation with Israel while sheltering behind UNEF (United Nations Emergency Force), the troops stationed in Sinai to separate the Israeli and Egyptian armies since the 1956 Suez War. The accusation undermined Nasser, forced him to call for UNEF's withdrawal and paved the way towards the 1967 War.

When things got out of hand and war became inevitable, Hussein, fearing the wrath of his people for not joining the Arab side, hurried to meet Nasser and placed his army under his command (United Arab Command) exactly five days before the start of hostilities. The story of the Arab defeat is too well known, but Hussein's conduct during this period typifies his behaviour throughout his life: he followed an outwardly Arab policy and a secret one of listening to the West and allying himself to Israel.

The perversity of cooperating with Israel against Arab and Palestinian

interests continues to this day. In 1970 there were several meetings with
Israeli Defence Minister General Moshe Dayan and with Israeli Prime
Minister Golda Meir.[10] Judged by Arab interests, this extensive period of
Jordanian-Israeli cooperation produced the most treasonable act of Hus-
sein's life, informing Israel of the impending Egyptian-Syrian attack of
October 1973.[11] And this time, despite the eventual desperate need of the
Egyptians and Syrians for military help, Hussein steadfastly refused to
join the battle and settled for the minor gesture of trying to repair Syrian
tanks damaged in the fighting.

Nor would this be his last act of obeying the West and promoting
Israeli against Arab and Palestinian interests. It was Hussein who, in the
mid-1970s, advised former Lebanese President Camille Chamoun to cooperate with Israel against the Palestinian presence in Lebanon.[12] Chamoun
and other Christian Lebanese groups followed his advice, got Israeli help
and inflicted untold damage on the Palestinians and their Lebanese allies.
This was in line with US policy, Secretary of State Henry Kissinger's
plans calling for the elimination of the Palestinians as a factor in Middle
East politics.

The secret alliance with Israel was an extension of Hussein's reliance
on the West and the continued threat to his throne. In the late 1950s, 60s
and 70s only Saudi Arabia among the Arab countries was capable of
providing Hussein with the support he needed to stay in power. But
although there was occasional Saudi help – to the extent of stationing
troops in Amman in 1958 – they shied from assuming responsibility for
Jordan and Hussein. Also, he himself felt more comfortable dealing directly
with the West and depending on it for financial support and to equip
his army, which he was using against his own people. This meant the
institutionalization of the original American efforts to save him, which
began in 1957, when financing and controlling Hussein and his army
became part of US policy for the Middle East.

Seen from the vantage point of Hussein and the West, regional political
developments justified this. Egypt under Nasser was against him, and
Syria, with or without Nasser, found him an uncomfortable neighbour.
All the regimes which followed the overthrow of the Iraqi monarchy in
1958 opposed him. But above all, in Jordan proper, even without the West
Bank, the mainly Palestinian people rejected Hussein and his policies and
wanted a change in government, even perhaps a replacement for the king.

Here it is well to recall that the West-pleasing contacts which Hussein
maintained with Israel were frequent and solid enough to produce personal
friendships. In the 1970s Hussein and Israeli Defence and later Prime
Minister Yitzhak Rabin became close friends. There was a similarity in

their thinking, and both men wanted the Palestinians out of the way and the re-creation of something similar to what had existed before 1967: a division of Palestine between Israel and Jordan without any consideration for the feelings of the Palestinian people.

After their defeat in 1967, the Arabs, including Nasser, ceded the leadership of the confrontation with Israel to the PLO. Until then, Hussein had dealt with a leaderless people and insisted on pretending to speak for them. So the emergence of the PLO and its acceptance by the rest of the Arab countries undermined this pretence. Nasser, tired and seeking a peaceful solution to the Arab-Israeli problem, no longer represented a direct challenge to Hussein and went as far as accepting the peace plan developed by US Secretary of State William Rogers in 1969. The Palestinians under Yasser Arafat rejected it, and the Palestinians were in Jordan, a popular presence because then they represented the true will of the Palestinian people and kept their hopes alive by carrying out frequent forays into Israel.

The bloody confrontation in 1970 between King Hussein and the Palestinians, later known as Black September, was a natural result of the assumption by the PLO of Palestinian leadership. There Palestinians armed and led by Yasser Arafat followed policies popular with the people. Sadly, they behaved like a mob which purported to be a state within a state. Unable to confront them openly, particularly after some successes against Israel, Hussein bided his time until their behaviour became intolerable. In fact, unforgivably, they played right into his hands.

In September 1970 Hussein unleashed his Bedouin army against the armed Palestinian presence in his country. This followed the hijacking and destruction in Jordan of American, British and Swiss planes by radical Palestinian groups. The fighting between Hussein's army and the Palestinians was bitter and there were thousands of casualties, but the well-trained army prevailed despite some major defections, including that of General Muhammad Daoud, a Palestinian appointed by Hussein as a caretaker Prime Minister.

The initial crackdown by Hussein was guaranteed success when the Arabs failed to support the Palestinians, partly deterred by the United States and Israel, which had placed their forces on alert to help Hussein if necessary. Later the Arab heads of state met in Cairo under Nasser's leadership and brokered a truce between the two sides. The day after the conference ended, on 28 September 1970, Nasser died of a massive heart attack and his death eliminated the one Arab leader capable of making the agreement work.

It was in the period following Nasser's death that Hussein's attitude towards the Palestinians and the PLO showed most clearly and brutally. From November 1970 until May 1971 Hussein carried out a savage campaign to eradicate the Palestinian presence in his country, both political and military. The PLO was already broken: among other things its fighters had no ammunition. Deals satisfactory to Hussein were offered time and again, but he would have none of it. Having once again replaced the Arab subsidies which had been cancelled in protest against his bloodthirstiness with American ones, he sought the physical expulsion of the Palestinians. More thousands were killed during the operation, Palestinian refugee camps were broken up and Hussein's Bedouin forces showed no mercy. They proved so pitiless that some PLO followers crossed the River Jordan into the West Bank and gave themselves up to the Israelis rather than fall into their hands. Unlike the somewhat justified initial confrontation, this was unwarranted and venomous. Only the anti-PLO United States and Israel were pleased.

But, to the surprise of Hussein and the architect of the American policy behind the crackdown, Henry Kissinger, the Palestinians lived another day. They moved to Lebanon, expanded their presence there and drew on the support of the rest of the Arab countries to continue and to thrive. And, despite a continued inability to behave themselves within a host country, they became an even greater source of dislocation to their Israeli and other enemies.

In 1971 the PLO assassinated Jordanian Prime Minister Wasfi Tel while he was attending an Arab League conference in Cairo. Tel had been one of the local architects of Hussein's plans to eliminate them. This was followed by a spate of assassinations and hijackings and many celebrated fedayeen forays into Israel itself. The nature of many of the PLO activities was highly questionable, the usual acts of desperation, but not so their purpose and their popularity. In the process of carrying them out they elevated the PLO and earned it the affection of the Palestinian and Arab peoples and the support of some Arab governments.

In 1974 another Arab heads-of-state conference, in Rabat, Morocco, declared the PLO the 'sole representative of the Palestinian people'. Hussein had no alternative but to accept this decision and the subsequent erosion of his regional and international standing. However, Hussein's recognition of the PLO's primacy in Palestinian affairs was disingenuous and his actions, like those of the West and Israel, continued to reveal a determination to undermine the PLO and reclaim his old position as leader and spokesman of the Palestinians in international forums.

Israel and America refused to deal with the PLO as the representative of the Palestinians. Hussein went further than that. He continued to pay the salaries of 18,000 West Bank civil servants who had been employees of his government before 1967. The poor economic conditions of the West Bank meant that he could use this as leverage to influence events there. He maintained a flow of funds to small groups who supported Jordan's return to the West Bank, old and corrupt family cliques with no constituencies. Moreover, with total Israeli approval, he sponsored West Bank newspapers and magazines which unsuccessfully tried to advance his leadership cause among the Palestinians of the West Bank.

It was a clear division which lasted for well over a decade: a PLO supported by the Arab people and grudgingly and otherwise by their governments and a Hussein secretly and openly supported by the West and Israel. There were secret PLO-US negotiations and moves by the PLO towards accepting UN resolutions, but Jordan was maintained as a fallback position, the country available to accept what the PLO and the Palestinians were refusing. Even Sadat's peace with Israel, the 1979 Camp David Accord, didn't change the nature of this balance. Egypt was ostracized and Hussein, more vulnerable than Sadat, continued to conspire, though too afraid to follow Egypt's example openly.

The Lebanese civil war, which started in 1975, and the 1980 Israeli invasion of Lebanon found Hussein willing to continue his campaign against the Palestinians. In addition to advising the Lebanese Christians to seek Israeli help, Hussein provided their forces with ammunition and training. In 1982 Sadat was assassinated and the PLO, using King Fahd as a front, promoted a comprehensive peace plan accepting Israel's right to exist within secure boundaries and other UN, American and Western requirements, but the absence of a positive US response to this opening torpedoed the whole effort and Fahd, hardly a determined leader, gave up.

It wasn't until December 1987 and the start of the intifada that the deadlock between Hussein and the PLO was broken. A spontaneous revolutionary movement led by children and women, the intifada was a totally Palestinian grassroots threat to the leadership of both the PLO and Jordan. Nevertheless, it still related to the PLO and tried to impose its will on the Palestinian movement in exile, while rejecting Hussein out of hand. Hussein wasn't only out of the running for Palestinian leadership: the strength of the intifada found him resorting to curtailing news coverage of its successes for fear that it might infect the people of his country. Moreover, it was the very same intifada which captured the imagination of the world, forced recognition of the Palestinian identity upon it and led an unwilling West to stop considering Hussein as a solution of the Palestinian problem. The intifada proved the need for a Palestinian state.

If Hussein's actions *vis-à-vis* the Palestinian question were determined by a wish to please his Western sponsors and Israeli allies, then his non-Palestinian relations with the rest of the Arab countries are the product of the same approach modified by his lineage to the Prophet. Most of the time merging these two determining factors of Hussein's life and actions is easy, but not always, and on occasion the discrepancies came very close to undoing the Hussein-West alliance.

Amusingly, recalling the way Hussein identifies his relationship with King Hassan of Morocco is one way of judging his strong feelings towards his ancestry. Hassan, another descendant of the Prophet, is addressed as 'cousin'. Very few Muslims and Arabs are impressed by this, but to Hussein and Hassan it is the source of their legitimacy and they take it very seriously indeed.

There are many examples of Hussein behaving in a manner compatible with the holiness with which his descent from the Prophet endows him. For example, he is intrinsically opposed to people rising against their kings and chiefs because the chiefs are, according to one interpretation of Koranic teachings, the deciders of all things. He demonstrated this in 1962, when he supported the despotic Yemeni royalists against the progressive republican regime, and in this case the West was in agreement with his policies. Later, he opposed Colonel Qaddafi's takeover in Libya, though he had little in common with the country's former ruler, King Idris. And throughout the Middle East, including the West Bank, he offered his support to old, established families and tribes who accepted the notion of his holiness, including the once-important pro-British Nashashibi family.

But the most important examples of Hussein's holy behaviour show in his attitude towards the Turko-Greek dispute over Cyprus, his support for Saddam during the 1980–8 Iran-Iraq War and his subsequent and near-fatal backing for Saddam Hussein's occupation of Kuwait in 1990. All of these had his belief in his holiness as background.

Although the act was relatively insignificant in terms of its effects on events in the Middle East, in the 1960s and 70s Hussein broke ranks with the Arab countries and supported the Turkish position in Cyprus. To him a descendant of the Prophet could not but support a Muslim country against Christian Greece, despite traditional Greek support for the Palestinians and a simultaneous Turkish acceptance of Israel. The Arab countries took a different view.

But the support for Turkey was nothing compared with Hussein's wholehearted support for Saddam during his war with Iran. America's desire to curb Khomeini and punish him for holding American hostages gave Hussein a green light to provide this support, but it was Khomeini's claim to holiness, his use of the term 'Imam', which annoyed the Hashemite monarch. Hussein saw himself as the Imam of the faithful and for Khomeini to assume the title and to pretend to speak for a resurgent Islam was a direct challenge to his traditional position.

In the case of the Iran-Iraq War, Hussein was able to merge his two positions: friend of the West and descendant of the Prophet. He fronted for Saddam and bought Western arms for him, sent a mechanized brigade to fight alongside the Iraqi army and never resisted a chance to promote the Iraqi position in Western circles. Jordan made a lot of money out of the Iran-Iraq War. With its outlets on the Gulf closed by fighting, Iraq used Jordan's port of Aqaba as its gateway to the world. And most of the arms trade was handled by a group of Hussein's personal friends, who realized huge commissions and took care of their mentor.

But giving diplomatic support to Greece and providing Saddam with total backing in his war against Khomeini were less significant than Hussein's pro-Iraqi stand during the Gulf War. Hussein threw in his lot with Saddam for a very simple reason: the original Iraqi claim to Kuwait was made by the Hashemite monarchy of that country, Hussein's relations, beginning in the 1930s. Hussein, the last Hashemite, felt an obligation to support a family claim. This time there was a divergence between his pro-West policy and his religious Hashemite obligations, and the initial Western hesitation and knowledge that Saddam's move was popular with the people of Jordan encouraged him to follow his familial-religious obligations. When the West finally resolved to force Saddam out of Kuwait, Hussein was caught in the middle.

A natural cooling of relations followed, and briefly Jordan was without friends in the West or in the Arab world. But it didn't last long, and Hussein hurried to mend his fences, first with the West and Israel and later with the rest of the Arab world which had opposed Saddam's invasion.

The period since the Gulf War has produced a Hussein set on pre-empting the position of the leading peacemaker in the region. Immediately after the September 1993 peace accord between the PLO and Israel, he signed a peace agreement with Israel which not only covered all border and other disputes, but also stipulated cooperation on security matters. He followed this by moving towards total normalization and now there are Jordanian-Israeli joint ventures in the areas of tourism, transportation and small industries. Whatever the PLO offers towards a lasting solution in its continuing negotiations with Israel, Hussein is willing to offer more. This has had the effect of producing a shameless competition between him and Arafat as to who could offer more to the Israelis in order to be accepted by them.

No Arab leader this century has held the two contradictory images Hussein holds. To the West, he is the ultimate attractive survivor against forces opposed to its Jordanian, regional and international interests. He is a polite, well-spoken man, with a pretty wife and good-looking children, a pilot and racing driver and a proponent of everything modern and appealing. His actions, opposing Arab nationalism, cooperating with Israel and maintaining Jordan as a buffer state, are celebrated, because ultimately they are expressions of Western policy.

The Arabs see Hussein differently. In personal terms, none of the qualities which endear him to the West holds much appeal except to a very small group of people. He is blamed for things which are dismissed and overlooked by the West: the corruption of his court, the behaviour of members of his family, particularly his brother Muhammad, and his family's involvement in the smuggling of arms and drugs and his obvious preference for Western ways. But it is in the political arena that Hussein fails the Arab test completely.

To the Arabs, Hussein's open amity with Israel, something which goes beyond making peace, is nothing short of treason. His total dependence on the West is rejected. Nobody accepts his continuing reliance on a Bedouin army to stay in power and people judge it as archaic and out of step with the times. The number of people who think his descent from the Prophet entitles him to a special political position is very small indeed. Except for an ability to obtain Western financial aid for a country which has never been self-supporting, Hussein has little going for him with his people. But the financial support he receives from the West and the reasons for it are seen as support for his person and not for his needy people, a situation similar to what the West did for his grandfather and for Ibn Saud. Hussein bin Tallal is not a modern king: he is the last of a dynasty created by the West for exclusively Western reasons. This is why Western people refer to him as the 'plucky little king' and the Arabs substitute 'perverse' for 'plucky'.

Fahd bin Abdel Aziz was born in 1922 with no expectations of becoming king. He is the eleventh son of Ibn Saud, the founder of modern Saudi Arabia, and both the succession process which existed and the mathematical odds were against him ever reaching his present position. Until Ibn Saud altered the succession process and decreed that his sons should follow him, power was expected to pass to one of his brothers. Even after the change, there were too many princes ahead of Fahd.

As a result, Fahd was never groomed for kingship. His father didn't pay him the special attention he bestowed on his brothers Saud and Faisal, the second and third kings of the country. Nor did Fahd have the benefit of a formal education; the somewhat confused record indicates that he attended the Princes' School in Riyadh for a maximum of four years. Islamically, and in terms of regular schooling, Fahd is an uneducated man.

But Fahd has always had an advantage over other members of the Saud family. He is one of seven full brothers, the sons of Hasa Sudeiri, who grew up in a small, cohesive family within the larger, fragmented Saud clan. Among the forty-one sons of Ibn Saud who survived him, there were several instances of two full brothers, but there are no cohesive groups to compete with the Sudeiri Seven, the ones who adopted their mother's name to denote their separateness.

Very much like Jordan, Saudi Arabia came into being as a creation of the West, a tributary state under a Bedouin monarch who depended on the support of his creators to stay in power. Ibn Saud, Fahd's father and the kingdom's founder, came to power because Britain wanted a 'disunited Arabia' which was easier to manage than a united one, and he knew that he couldn't survive as 'Britain's enemy'.[13]

However, the initial similarity with Jordan in terms of needing outside financial assistance to survive vanished when Saudi Arabia's oil potential was realized in the 1930s and 40s. After that the pro-West policies of the ruling House of Saud became voluntary, an alliance between a retrograde Bedouin monarchy and the West against the natural forces of advancement within the country and in the Arab and Muslim worlds.

This makes Saudi Arabia a clearer case study of the mutuality of interest between the West and a patriarchy committed to maintaining an absolute and obsolete system of government. Unlike Jordan, Saudi Arabia is in a position to choose a political direction more accommodating to the wishes of its people and independent Arab, Muslim and international policies. Even when we consider what cemented the closeness and interdependency between the House of Saud and the West – the country's position as the world's largest oil exporter and the possessor of 25 per cent of the world's known oil reserves – Saudi Arabia's reliance on the West need not be so total. In fact, it could have produced the opposite, a reverse reliance by the West on Saudi Arabia to utilize its Arab and Islamic positions. As it is, the mutuality of interest between the Saudi monarchy and the West ignores the rights of the Saudi people, contributes towards Arab divisions and ignites Islamic passions.

King Fahd is an expression and an extension of the pro-West policies adopted by the House of Saud throughout this century. The first phase encompassed the rule of Ibn Saud, the man who unified Arabia by degrees beginning early this century and who died in 1953. The second lasted from 1953 until 1975, the period of Kings Saud and Faisal. And the third started with the accession to the throne of King Khalid in 1975 and continues until today, the period of Fahd's rule, first as heir apparent and strongman under Khalid and since 1982 as King.

Ibn Saud's relations with the West are relatively simple to assess. Having received British assistance to wrest control of Arabia from its various rulers, particularly the Hashemites, he officially ceded the conduct of his country's foreign policy to Britain by signing the 1915 and 1927 treaties. Overall, he depended on British protection and looked inwards; beyond needing British subsidies to exist he devoted his time to prayer and to women.

But Ibn Saud couldn't remain aloof from Arab and Muslim entanglements. Saudi Arabia's position as the home of Islam's holiest shrines of Mecca and Medina, the problem of Palestine and his relations with his Hashemite enemies who – with Western help – had moved out of the Arabian Peninsula and set up monarchies in Jordan and Iraq, forced him to look beyond his borders. In 1929, responding to an outcry against his exclusive control of the holy places and the assumption of the title of king (in Islam there is no king but Allah), Ibn Saud convened a Muslim conference to justify his actions. The conference failed when the delegates refused to back him, but Ibn Saud continued to pursue Islamic support and legitimacy. In the 1930s he went as far as sponsoring a suspect Egyptian cleric, Muhammad Tammimi, to design a Saud family tree with a direct line to the Prophet.[14]

But it was Palestine which showed how Ibn Saud's pro-West policies were in direct conflict with the wishes, hopes and aspirations of the Arab people. The West's inclination to elevate the Arab chiefs it had sponsored as the final arbiters of Arab affairs meant relying on them to help with its designs to create Israel, and the Arab chiefs used this dependency to extend their influence and obtain more Western financial assistance. (As with Hussein and Arafat today, they competed as to who could concede more to be more acceptable.) With this in mind, in the 1930s Ibn Saud authorized his British adviser, Harry St John Philby, to negotiate an agreement with the Zionist leader and later first President of Israel, Chaim Weizmann, whereby Ibn Saud would support the creation of a Jewish state in Palestine in return for £20 million. Both Churchill and Roosevelt knew about this offer and approved of it, but it failed when Weizmann decided that the price was too high.[15] Later, when the Palestinians rose in rebellion against the British in 1936, Ibn Saud interceded with the Palestinian leadership to end it and to depend on 'our British friends'. Yet later, in 1948, he refused to participate when the Arabs sent their armies into Palestine.[16] Throughout, Ibn Saud's involvement in the Palestinian problem placed his relationship with Britain and America above Arab considerations. He undertook no moves which might conflict with the policies of his sponsors.

The broader issues of Arab nationalism and unity found Ibn Saud following divisive policies in line with those of the West. He was suspicious of the Hashemites of Jordan and Iraq as advocates of Arab unity and, having ceded his foreign relations to Britain, wanted it to continue to act as the final arbiter on all Arab problems, including the differences between them. In the same vein he supported republican rule in Syria to prevent it from uniting with other Arab countries.[17] Keeping the Arabs divided and weak so as to exercise indirect control over the Middle East was the original British policy which the Americans later adopted.

In fact, Ibn Saud's lack of responsiveness to things Arab extended to his people. There were, in the 1920s and 30s, dozens of rebellions against him which he put down mercilessly. Except for marrying women from the various tribes and turning these marriages into alliances, he was totally estranged from the people of the Arabian Peninsula. This showed in the composition of his Council of Advisers in the 1920s, 30s and 40s. It was made up of two Iraqis, two Lebanese, two Syrians, a Palestinian and a Briton (Wahbi, Damulgi, Awaini and Salha, Pharoan and Sheikh Al Ard, Husseini and Philby). There wasn't a single Saudi among them.

Nor did the discovery of oil change the backward despot who executed thousands of his people, used the stick on his children and servants, depended on foreign advisers and obediently followed the foreign policies of the country which controlled the purse-strings. The 1933 Saudi oil concession was won by the Americans because the British had oil in Iran and Iraq and wouldn't pay enough for it. During the Second World War, in 1943, realizing that Saudi oil would one day become critical to America's economic well-being, President Roosevelt issued an executive order which granted Saudi Arabia financial assistance under the Lend-Lease programme. With this, Ibn Saud's loyalty switched from Britain to the United States, and the weakness of Britain after the war and the emergence of America as the leader of the West in the Middle East confirmed this decision.

British imperialism was replaced by American neo-colonialism in the period between the end of the Second World War and Ibn Saud's death in 1953. The flow of oil money produced the first example of Western-aided and abetted overspending by the House of Saud. Ibn Saud leased the airbase in Dhahran to the Americans in 1949 because he needed money to augment his oil income and without much thought to the consequences.

In 1946 his garages cost £2 million to maintain while he spent a mere £150,000 on education.[18] He built a vast palace at Kharj at a time when his treasury was running a huge deficit. And this is when his sons started the family tradition of squandering the country's wealth in the unproductive and unattractive manner we know today. Ibn Saud's pocket and the treasury were one and the same.

A formidable budget deficit existed at the time of Ibn Saud's death. The people of his country, the only ones in the world to be named after their ruling dynasty, were more abused than ever. In 1953 there were no civil rights, law courts or a free press and certainly no political parties. The original British protection formalized by treaties was replaced by an American *de facto* one which presidents Roosevelt and Truman articulated. The world's most absolute feudal monarchy, the country which ignored Arab and Muslim interests, had one thing going for it: the guarantee of the United States of America to deal with external and internal threats.

In line with the amended succession process which invested kingship in the children of Ibn Saud, the eldest, Saud, succeeded his father. Saud was a simple man with attractive Bedouin instincts but, like his father, he viewed his kingdom as a piece of family real estate. However, the historical record needs to be corrected and Saud was never the useless figure portrayed by Western historians and the rest of his family. In fact, it is because he showed signs of responding to his people's needs and Arab political interests, and the consequent threat to the special relationship between the House of Saud and America, that the West and the House of Saud denigrate Saud and saddle him with the image of an utter incompetent.

The chief accusation against Saud is that he was a spendthrift who squandered his country's wealth and endangered its stability. This is a huge exaggeration and Saudi Arabia was in bad financial shape when he inherited the throne. His spending was similar to his father's and, within the country, he initiated the first development projects in its modern history and showed concern for the needs and welfare of the common man.

Saud ordered the building of the railway connecting Riyadh with the oil-producing eastern region, expanded Saudia Airlines, initiated the construction of highways and opened schools and hospitals. He elevated the civil service, a mere 4000 people at his father's death, into a functioning governmental apparatus, and there were very few, if any, beheadings for so-called political crimes during his years. He was benevolent and though he most definitely overspent, there was a human touch to what he did and he came close to undermining the abusive, vicious internal alliance between the royal family, the merchant class and bankers that his father had left behind.

Saud's first confrontation with America's indirect control of his country came one year after he assumed power, when he formed a partnership with the Greek shipping tycoon Aristotle Onassis to create a tanker fleet to transport his country's oil. To Saud it was a natural thing to do, but so incensed were the US oil companies that they turned to their State Department for help. American Ambassador to Saudi Arabia George Wadsworth and Secretary of State John Foster Dulles saw this as a first step towards nationalizing Saudi oil and issued explicit threats. At first King Saud resisted, but the propaganda unleashed against him finally succeeded; he had no support from within his own family. He was forced to give up the project.[19]

In 1955 Saud once again took a position inimical to Western interests by opposing the Baghdad Pact, the anti-communist alliance in which Arab Iraq played a dominant role. The traditional enmity between the Sauds and the Hashemites was behind this, but Saud added to Western displeasure by allying himself with Nasser and Syria – Egypt and Syria being the two countries opposed to indirect Western control of the Arab Middle East. This show of independence distanced Saud further from the West.

A year later, in 1956, King Saud's simple instincts led him to give Nasser moral and financial support during the Suez crisis. He went further and gave safe haven to Egyptian aircraft escaping the British-French-Israeli onslaught. His anger at what was happening led him to impose a partial oil embargo and to deny it to France, Britain and Germany. The United States had been against the invasion and helped Nasser at the United Nations, but it still joined other countries in seeing Saud's moves as the actions of an unreliable ally.

The scales tipped against Saud in 1957, when the United States finally decided to oppose Nasser. Saud could have resisted the pressure to have him follow this line except for the divided house behind him. Prince, later King, Faisal was Foreign Minister and heir apparent to his brother. There were jealousies between the brothers and Faisal wanted to be king. Most members of the divided Saud family supported Faisal and were pro-West and opposed to anything which might weaken their absolute rule. To save his throne, Saud saw fit to change direction, follow a totally pro-West policy and oppose Nasser.

When nationalist forces tried to topple King Hussein of Jordan in 1957, King Saud dispatched a brigade of troops to help the beleaguered monarch. This anti-Nasser move, aimed at pleasing the West and placating his family, was followed by the most destructive move of Saud's reign, the paying of a £2 million bribe to Syrian army officers to shoot down Nasser's plane as it was landing in Damascus.

The plot against Nasser was revealed by Colonel Abdel Hamid Sarraj, the Syrian to whom the payment was made in March 1958. Nasser and Saud's brother Faisal made the most out of it. Brandishing the cheque for £2 million in front of foreign correspondents, Nasser accused the West of conspiring against him and attacked Saud and Saudi Arabia relentlessly. Within Saudi Arabia, Faisal used the incident to accuse Saud of incompetence, claimed that he was undermining the future of their family and demanded that Saud cede power to him and become a figurehead king. Lacking family support, Saud bowed to the inevitable, and withdrew.

The period between 1958 and Saud's final abdication in 1964 was an eventful one in the history of the Middle East. Nasser accepted Syria as Egypt's junior partner in the United Arab Republic and became president of the union. The Iraqi monarchy was bloodily overthrown and replaced by a leftist army regime. Serious signs of unrest began appearing in Saudi Arabia and there were several army-based plots and some family members, led by Prince Tallal, who formed the Free Princes movement and declared his support for Nasser. The fires of oil nationalism were burning, fanned by Nasser's propaganda machine, and Saudi Oil Minister and Nasser follower Abdallah Tariki was leading the country towards confrontation with the oil companies and providing the newly created OPEC with the unqualified support of the world's largest oil exporter.

The Saudi monarchy was in trouble. Its need for outside support was greater than ever, and only the United States could provide the House of Saud with the substantial backing it required. And because the brothers Saud and Faisal were still feuding, each approached America and presented himself as the more reliable friend deserving of its help. After considerable hesitation, the United States decided to support the more capable Faisal. He was seen as being of greater use to the West in confronting Nasser's Arab nationalism.

The final act in Faisal's assumption of power was the Yemeni coup of 1962. The Yemeni government that the pro-Nasser officers overthrew was another absolute monarchy and the back door to Saudi Arabia. Faisal, deciding that a pro-Nasser Yemen endangered the security of his country, adopted the cause of the Yemeni monarchy and supported its surviving members to wage a civil war against the army officers who had overthrown them. This pitted pro-Nasser republicans against pro-Saud monarchists. Elder members of the House of Saud saw the danger and decided it was time to put an end to the family feud which was sapping their energies and endangering them and confirmed Faisal as King in 1964.

Faisal's governance is later discussed in detail (see Chapter 8), but the main outlines of his kingship, until his assassination by an irate nephew in 1975, merit brief examination here. Above all, Faisal did not end the family's corruption, the ostensible and still-repeated reason for forcing Saud to abdicate. He found a clever way of handling it by giving members of his family huge tracts of land which were gaining in value because of the oil boom. This allowed him to avoid dipping into the treasury to please them, and the country's finances looked much better. The camouflaging of royal greed, the giving away of land worth $40 billion dollars, mean that Faisal's governance was as corrupt, if not more so, than that of Saud.

In terms of Arab and Islamic policies, Faisal, again cleverly, decided to promote Islam as a counterweight to Nasser's Arab nationalism. In this he had the total support of a West which wanted an ideology to reduce Nasser's hold on the masses and to oppose communism. Faisal convened an Islamic Conference, adopted the issue of Jerusalem and worked towards better relations with Muslim countries throughout the world. The West overlooked the implications of the issue of Jerusalem to Israel because it liked the rest of Faisal's policies.

When it came to oil, Faisal was decidedly pro-West. He fired the nationalist Oil Minister Abdallah Tariki in 1962 and cancelled the Tariki-inspired demand for the oil companies to open their books for inspection. After the 1967 War he bowed to popular pressure and imposed a partial oil embargo which he lifted after a brief period – without achieving anything. He opposed the policies of the Shah and Qaddafi, which called for increasing the price of oil in line with growing demand.

It was Faisal and his Islamic movement which confronted Nasser, sapped his energies and contributed to his defeat by Israel in 1967. After this it was Faisal's day, and Nasser's death in 1970 left him without opposition. In 1973, to avoid the consequences of swelling popular pressure for action against the continuing Israeli occupation of Arab territory, Faisal conspired with Egyptian President Anwar Sadat to start the October War. His aim was a war of limited objectives and he imposed a partial oil embargo which almost got out of hand because of the actions of other Arab countries. Yet again, he lifted the embargo without achieving its ostensible purpose of pressuring the West into even-handedness. And he followed that by opposing, openly, all moves aimed at raising the price of oil and maximizing his country's income. He went as far as accepting a lower price for Saudi oil than was being charged by other countries.

On the surface, the Saudi Arabia that Faisal left behind in 1975 was a different country from the one he inherited and the one his father founded. But it was still a feudal monarchy and Faisal tolerated no dissent to the extent of personally ordering the execution of dozens of army officers and others who were accused of plotting against him, even when there was little proof of conspiracy. He reneged on instituting a Consultative Council, despite the promises he had made to President Kennedy to create one. He banned all organizations, such as clubs, which were capable of political activity, and took measures to exercise total control of his country's press.

Regionally, Faisal had little time for the Arab League and supported an Islamic approach to governance. He preached against communism as the enemy of Allah and of Islam, equated it with Zionism to make this view palatable to his people and bribed governments to sever their relations with the USSR. He supported traditional rulers, such as King Hussein in his bloody confrontation with the PLO in 1970.[20]

More importantly, despite having to impose the 1973 oil embargo, Faisal was solidly pro-American. He renewed the American lease on the Dhahran airbase, though the move was unpopular within his country. He made his financial aid to Egypt conditional on the country's ejection of Russian military advisers, something which weakened it against Israel. He depended entirely on Western military hardware to equip his army and on the Americans to train it. He entrusted the CIA with working with Kemal Adham, his brother-in-law and head of his country's internal security apparatus, to set up an elaborate internal security system. (According to former CIA agent Vincent Canistrero, in Saudi Arabia the function of the agency changes from an intelligence-gathering organization to one which protects a government.)

The country that King Khalid inherited in 1975 was rich, backward and the leader of the Arab and Muslim worlds. But Khalid, despite occasional flashes of decision-making, was a figurehead king who didn't want the job and accepted it only after his elder brother Muhammad had insisted on stepping aside in his favour. The power behind the Saudi throne was Prince Fahd, the heir apparent, to whom Khalid delegated most affairs of state. This was the beginning of the Fahd era, and whatever Saudi Arabia stands for today is Fahd's personal handiwork.

In judging King Fahd and the special relationship which exists between Saudi Arabia and the West, there is no avoiding the personal character of the absolute monarch himself. After all, Fahd bin Abdel Aziz is the head of state, chief religious personality, commander in chief of the armed forces and chairman of the family company which still views Saudi Arabia as its personal property.

But perhaps it is the way he is addressed which tells us most about him. He has dispensed with the unIslamic title of 'King' and replaced it with 'Guardian of Islam's Holy Shrines'. But he is also '*Al Muathem*', the one endowed with greatness; '*Al Mufada*', the one worthy of sacrifice; '*Moulana*', the holder of ultimate authority; '*Seydna*', our master; and '*Walye Al Amr*', the decider of all things. Nor does the vain man discourage the endless improvisations and variations which people use to flatter him.

The indignity which Saudis and Arabs go through to satisfy Fahd's ego is in character, and is confirmed by the way he treats foreign heads of state. In 1987 he was forty-five minutes late for a Buckingham Palace lunch with Queen Elizabeth. He has appeared late for meetings with President Bush, King Hussein and Japanese Prime Minister Fukuda. In a striking incident, his insulting constant unpunctuality prompted Argentinian President Carlos Menem to cut short his four-day visit to Saudi Arabia after two days. And in 1992, visiting Kuwait to celebrate its liberation from Saddam Hussein, he kept the Emir waiting to receive him in the airport lobby for an hour and a half while taking a nap in his parked plane.

And Fahd the lazy is also a gambler of renown. In 1962 the German *Stern* magazine and *Time* both ran stories about him losing $6 million in one night of fun in Monte Carlo. A Saudi citizen who used to gamble with him before he became king told me of how Fahd came to their gatherings followed by a servant with a briefcase full of money to meet his losses for the evening. He intended to lose, and whatever money was left he gave to the lucky briefcase carrier.

Fahd the womanizer and, until the 1980s, hell-raiser, isn't far behind. In the 1960s and 70s not only did he chase blondes in European resorts: he departed from the family tradition of marrying frequently and took to keeping mistresses. The wife of an acquaintance of mine was one, and he showered her with millions of dollars' worth of jewels and favoured her husband with trade concessions to make more millions. All his mistresses are wealthy.

The last of Fahd's striking personal characteristics is his drinking. Though he is reputed to have given it up, he was addicted to alcohol until the early 1980s. This, and overeating, underlie his weight problem. One result is an inability to move easily and it has led, among other things, to the building of an elevator in his personal Boeing 747 aircraft.

In addition to these shortcomings there is the question of Fahd's behaviour towards his family. His eldest son, Faisal, is head of the Youth Welfare Organization, Saud is the Deputy Head of Intelligence, Muhammad is Governor of the oil-producing Eastern Province, two are in the army and the youngest, twenty-four-year-old Abdel Aziz, is special adviser to his father with ministerial rank. Practically all of them have business interests. Muhammad, Chairman of Al Bilad Trading Company, is reported to have made hundreds of millions of dollars from telephone contracts and selling oil on the open market.[21] The list of business deals in which Fahd's sons are involved and which yield huge commissions is considerable, but the obscenity of it all is demonstrated by Fahd's apparent lack of understanding of what squandering the country's wealth means. His Al Salem palace in Jedda, one of seventeen palaces scattered throughout his kingdom, is reported to have cost $3 billion. (*Time* of 24 September 1990 gave Fahd's personal wealth as an estimated $18 billion.) During his official visit to London in 1987, Fahd personally complained to journalists Hajj Ahmad Al Houni and Ghassan Zakkaria that Abdel Aziz so overspent that he, Fahd, had to transfer $300 million into the fifteen-year-old's personal account. The statement, delivered as if this were an ordinary happening, reduced the journalists to speechlessness.

The granting of licence to members of the House of Saud to abuse the tribal monarchical system extends beyond Fahd's immediate family to cover the larger clan and its 8000 princes. In an interview with Lebanese journalist Salim Louzi, in *Al Hawadess* of 11 January 1980, Fahd defended his family's involvement in business as natural because 'with thousands of members, they can't all be employees of the government – they must make money'. Fahd neglected to mention that the influence of members of his family precludes commoners winning contracts and that the extended Saud family has over fifty billionaires.

Fahd's commitment to his family's supremacy is so total that even non-royal high officials are denied polite treatment. Ahmad Zakki Yamani, the famous former Oil Minister, heard of his dismissal by Fahd in 1986 on the radio. Muhammad Abdo Yamani (no relation), Minister of Information, Ghazi Al Ghoseibi, Minister of Health; Abdallah Al Jaza'ri, another Minister of Health, Ahmad Ali Abdel Wahab, Head of the Royal Court; and Abdel Munir Al Otteibi, Chief of Staff of the Army, were fired in a similar fashion. In addition, there was the summary dismissal in 1994 of members of the religious Council of Ulemas, and many other examples. This is Fahd at work; former Saudi kings seldom fired people and when they did it was done in a gentler Bedouin fashion.

But even the monstrosity of dismissing members of the cabinet in such an undignified manner doesn't match the hideous way in which the average Saudi is treated. Amnesty International, Middle East Watch, the Minnesota International Lawyers Association and other human rights organizations have documented endless cases of imprisonment, torture and elimination within the kingdom. Solitary confinement for years on end is a regular happening (former Saudi Ambassador to Switzerland Abdel Aziz Al Muammar), kidnappings and disappearances are common (Saudi writer Nasser Al Saïd and dissident Muhammad Al Fassi), political executions without proper trial are frequent (Abdallah Al Mutheif) and even women are not spared torture and humiliation (Alia Makki). In February 1996 a ten-year-old child was left in the sun tied to a rope in front of a police station. In six hours he was dead, the victim of the merciless desert sun. The boy had criticized the House of Saud.

Nor is punishment directed exclusively at individuals accused of political crimes. The Fahd government frequently metes out indiscriminate collective punishment. The Wahhabi sub-sect to which the House of Saud belongs considers the Shias 'outside Islam'. In 1993 Sheikh bin Jibreen, Deputy Head of the government-appointed Council of Ulemas, declared, 'The Shia is a heretic and idolater who should be eliminated.' So far we have been spared the elimination by official decree of this significant minority, but the Shias are denied the right to join the army and police and to study at some universities. There is no running water in their villages, they are not allowed to build mosques and their religious books are confiscated. They are second-class citizens.

The application of collective punishment extends to other groups. In 1995, by official count, 66 drug traffickers were beheaded, mainly without trial. Eight Turkish workers accused of importing aphrodisiacs were also executed. In May 1988 sixteen Kuwaitis accused of causing an explosion were executed despite strong appeals and later protests by their government. The wearing of crosses by foreign workers (no Christian can become a citizen of the country) is punishable by imprisonment for five years or more. Possessing a Christmas tree is against the law and conviction carries a long prison term. Even brewing or drinking alcoholic beverages can lead to public flogging and prison terms at a time when a considerable number of the royal family indulge to excess.

The government behind all this has no comprehensible definition. It is a xenophobic clique who run a country which they think they own, a feudal family with criminal inclinations. Fahd is the resident supremo, but the family is solidly behind him. Half of the cabinet portfolios are in their hands, including Defence, Interior and Foreign Affairs (Princes Sultan, Nayyef and Saud Al Faisal, respectively). The governorships of the fifteen provinces of the country are exclusively in the hands of the Sauds and their Sudeiri in-laws. There are family generals, ambassadors (including Ambassador to the US Prince Bandar), deputy ministers, chiefs of intelligence and police and no fewer than three hundred regular army officers. Nothing is beyond their reach: the number of male members of the family is increasing by a staggering forty or so a month and the royal budget is between $5 and $7 billion a year, augmented as it is by selling oil on the open market and billions of dollars of commissions a year from arms contracts. All this existed before Fahd, but the numbers were smaller, and there was some control to keep the level of abuse in check. Fahd has made an incredibly bad situation worse.

So Fahd and his family monopolize governance; realize billions out of corrupt practices; dismiss ministers at will; imprison, torture and murder their people and discriminate against Christians. It is true that much of this started with Ibn Saud, but things were never this bad. The House of Saud, huge in number as it is, has turned itself into a self-contained community insulated from the rest of the country and incapable of responding to even the minimum demands of the people. And, since the demands of the people have increased with the rising levels of education and expectations, the House of Saud and the country's citizens are moving in completely different directions.

Contrary to the prevailing picture in the West, Saudi Arabia has never been the sea of tranquillity we imagine it to be. The tribal rebellions against Ibn Saud of the 1920s and 30s were followed by direct challenges to his sons. There were labour disturbances during King Saud's time. In 1955 there was a pro-Nasser army rebellion in the city of Taif. In 1969 a serious air force mutiny occurred at Dhahran airbase. In 1975 Chief of Staff General Muhammad Shmeimri was arrested and executed for plotting against the monarchy. There was an open rebellion in Mecca in 1979 and the rebels occupied the Holy Mosque there until ejected by French paratroops. Sixty-seven of the rebels were later beheaded publicly. This was followed by an army-based attempted coup in 1983 and more executions.[22] In 1993 the students at the University of Riyadh rebelled and occupied the university for two days. In September 1994 religious zealots occupied the town of Bureida and declared an Islamic republic until the army went in. And there have been many more minor attempts against the government in between and since these events.

The Saudi government's failure to respond to these challenges in a sensible way is as interesting as the events themselves. To begin with, the House of Saud doesn't want to share power with the people. Ibn Saud didn't even understand the concept, and later, during the oil boom years, the family resorted to bribing people into silence. All this was made possible by the initial British support and the American support which replaced it. In both cases the Western governments accepted the House of Saud as it was and their support was unqualified.

The only acknowledgement of the wish of the Saudi people to participate in the running of their government came about in 1962, when Faisal was king. President John F. Kennedy confronted Faisal with demands for reform and forced him to announce a plan to convene a Consultative Council, half elected and half appointed, to help the royals run the country. However, subsequent US presidents paid no attention to this and after Kennedy's death Faisal chose to forget it.

Because of mounting internal pressures, the Consultative Council was finally convened in 1994, but it was different from what had been originally intended. All its members were appointed by Fahd; it was forbidden to discuss anything 'except matters referred to it by the king', the average age of its members was around seventy and the king is empowered to dissolve it at will and dismiss individual members in the same manner. The only response of the House of Saud and Fahd to their people's apparent unhappiness is an empty gesture, an outstanding example of the maxim 'too little too late'.

This detailed picture of the nature of the Saudi government under King Fahd is necessary to assess the country's Arab and Islamic policies and its destructive relationship with the West. What Arab and Islamic policies were pursued under Ibn Saud, Saud and Faisal are covered elsewhere (see Chapter 8); our concern here is how they evolved during the twenty-one years of Fahd's direct and indirect rule.

To begin with, Fahd was an unnatural leader of a country with pretensions to Islamic leadership. Unlike Faisal, his personal behaviour stood in the way, and he failed, probably through sheer laziness, to follow up Faisal's achievements. Saudi Arabia continued to provide Muslim countries with conditional financial assistance aimed at promoting a benign, anti-communist Islam. Even the 1981 Taif Conference of Muslim heads of state didn't produce anything concrete, only a deceleration of Islamic amity. Put simply, Saudi Arabia has nothing to show for years of pretending to lead Islam.

It was in the more immediate Arab arena that the Saudis shaped events. The first test of Saudi influence in Arab affairs came in 1975, when Lebanon erupted into a vicious civil war which pitted right-wing Lebanese Christians against the Palestinians and their Lebanese leftist allies. Unsurprisingly, in a move which pleased the West, Saudi Arabia backed the Christians because the Palestinians were considered leftists and anti-monarchist. The country's Islamic pretensions precluded open support for non-Islamic forces, but the Christians received substantial Saudi financial assistance.

This was followed by the 1977 Sadat visit to Jerusalem and its culmination, the Camp David Accord of 1978. Once again there was an open

Saudi position and a real, secret one. Fahd had been advised of Sadat's intention to end the state of war with Israel by his intelligence chief and intermediary Kamal Adham, but though he wanted to support Sadat, the Arab outcry which greeted Sadat's initiative made that impossible. Fahd joined the rest of the Arabs in condemning the move while secretly assuring President Jimmy Carter of his country's unequivocal support for Camp David. In fact, it was the rest of the Saud family which convinced Fahd that there was too much danger in doing otherwise.

The Iran-Iraq War, which started in 1980, was another test altogether. In this case American interests could be accommodated openly through being disguised and presented as an Arab effort to defeat Iran's Khomeini and his Islamic revolution. Fahd's support for Saddam Hussein was total and he provided him with loans and credits worth over $20 billion. Saudi Arabia went further and fronted for Iraq in the latter's efforts to buy Western arms, allowing it to use its ports to import goods and prevailing on Kuwait and other Gulf states to lend it additional financial support. It was a case of Fahd fronting for the West.

But the alliance of convenience with Iraq didn't prevent Saudi Arabia from capitalizing on the preoccupation of both combatants in the war and, with Western backing, creating the Gulf Cooperation Council. Composed of Saudi Arabia, Kuwait, Bahrain, Oman, the Emirates and Qatar, this rich countries' club was designed to protect its members against external and internal threats. In reality, because of these countries' small populations of between eleven and sixteen million, and the absence of serious efforts to coordinate their arms purchases and integrate their armed forces, this was nothing but a Western attempt to isolate Iran and Iraq. The West's support for the idea was natural: the weakness of the GCC members made them dependent on Western protection. Protecting them as a group had the consequent benefit of collective friendly oil policies.

The Saudi use, from 1975 to the mid-1980s, of the huge oil income to pretend that it was performing a leadership role in the Muslim and Arab worlds was not followed by a cohesive policy. An elementary examination of what this leadership produced exposes its utter unsoundness. It was based exclusively on money and this money was aimed at perpetuating the status quo and forestalling democratic development and the emergence of a counter leadership. Except for repeated resort to Muslim and Arab slogans, there was no organization or method to the Saudi era. Moreover, the countries which received Saudi financial aid never totally accepted the leadership of the donor and most of the time the grants went into the pockets of corrupt leaders who escaped being held accountable.

Arafat received hundreds of millions of dollars to keep his radicals in check, but went his own way. Assad of Syria was bribed to refrain from causing confrontation with Israel and to keep enemy Saddam off balance. Sadat of Egypt personally hoarded the money given to stop his country from reverting to radical politics. Pakistan's Zia Al Haq pocketed money intended to keep his country from disintegrating and to pay for troops that his country sent to Saudi Arabia to help protect the oilfields. Siad Barré of Somalia used Saudi money to stay in power against popular movements which objected to his corruption, and to keep Russia from the Horn of Africa. The massive financial help to Iraq was aimed at containing Khomeini and his Islamic revolution. Islamic groups in Algeria were provided with help to keep its left-leaning government weak. The Lebanese Christians were supported to prevent a much-needed change in the structure of the country which might have produced a more equitable sharing of power between its various sects. The Palestinian Islamic movement Hamas received money to keep Arafat from becoming too powerful. The Islamic movement in the Philippines, divisive and destructive in nature, was aided simply because supporting Muslims enhanced Saudi Islamic credentials.

Very little of the money that Saudi Arabia spent in the Muslim and Arab worlds was directed at sound economic programmes. And, except for the peripheral problem of the Philippines, the divisiveness that Saudi money generated accorded with the West's Middle East policy or contributed to it. Dividing the Muslim and Arab countries, keeping their corrupt leaders in power and limiting the influence of the USSR and leftist forces, the old-fashioned reliance on unacceptable pro-West leaders and a divide-and-conquer approach was what the West wanted. It wanted weak countries and leaders beholden to it and Saudi Arabia sought the same thing and stood in the way of Islamic and Arab unity. Saudi Arabia pre-empted the leadership role to protect itself and to serve the West, which provides it with this protection.

Without the West there would be no House of Saud. Ibn Saud came to power to guarantee Western hegemony, and he was successful. Saud, because he showed signs of independence, had to be subdued and eventually removed. Faisal was helped to face the internal and external threats against his country and provided with support to weaken Nasser and Arab nationalism and promote Islam as a substitute ideology. But it was under Fahd that the House of Saud's act of surrender to the West became total. Fahd made no commitment, unlike his father, to running a Bedouin kingdom; little or no inclination exists for independent action as appeared under Saud, and even Faisal's Islamic policies and the claim to Muslim leadership has been weakened. Fahd is a figurehead king, not a front for internal forces within his country or his family but an archaic presence who is completely manipulated by the West. Not a single example exists of Fahd doing anything in opposition to Western policies or interests.

The foundations of the Saudi-West relationship are relatively solid. Oil comes first, and the West cannot do without it and is committed to maintaining a Saudi regime which would guarantee its flow at a reasonable price. Next is the country's Islamic and Arab positions and the West's policy to use the country to deputize for it within these spheres. And finally there is the country's strategic position, the fact that it occupies a land mass equal to that of the United States east of the Mississippi and the possible effects on its neighbours should it fall to internal or external forces unfriendly to the West.

Until the late 1970s Saudi Arabia, Iran and Israel were the deputy sheriffs which promoted and implemented US policy in the Middle East. A hangover from the anti-colonial ideology which rejected direct interference in countries' affairs, the Americans' reliance on indirect control allocated different tasks to each deputy sheriff. Israel's role consisted of being available to render military help to protect the region against communist encroachment and it came to an end with the collapse of the USSR. Iran under the Shah was the pro-West country trusted with keeping the Gulf stable, and this ended with the downfall of the Shah. Saudi Arabia, though no longer threatened by communism or countries allied to the communist camp, is the one remaining country whose duties haven't changed, and the containment of Iran and Iraq has replaced the threat of communism as a reason for its strategic importance.

Western, mainly American, use of Saudi Arabia in this manner is totally understandable, but it is short-sighted. Providing the West with cheap oil despite contrary market conditions alienates the House of Saud from the Saudi people. Supporting corrupt Muslim and Arab leaders turns the Muslims and Arabs against it. And assuming an anti-Iranian and an anti-Iraqi stance is a gratuitous, unproductive policy. The adoption by Saudi Arabia of these policies has little ideology behind it. Providing the West with all the oil it needs at an unjustifiably low price flies in the face of the country's need to maximize its income and take measures against the depletion of its one natural asset. Deputizing for the West within the Muslim and Arab worlds is hardly consistent with the position of a backward country with a small population and a disinclination to lead. Responding to outside threats, be they communist or from Iran or Iraq, is not an issue when the threat isn't immediate. There were countries in the way of Russia's reaching Saudi Arabia, and both Iran and Iraq have denied any territorial ambitions against the feudal monarchy, and their actions have supported their words. The House of Saud accepts the reasons for its special relationship with the West for one reason and one reason only: in return for Saudi Arabia's assumption of the unnatural role of deputy sheriff the West provides the monarchy with total and uncritical support to maintain its present system of governance. Every American president since Roosevelt has renewed this commitment. This is the sum total of America's Saudi policy. This is what Fahd is all about.

Newsweek of 3 March 1980 detailed how Saudi Arabia sold oil at $18 a barrel at a time when the market price was $30 a barrel. Widely reported at the time, this was Fahd's idea of keeping the West happy. During the late 1970s and very early 80s Saudi Arabia not only set the price of oil, but often pumped more oil to force prices down to punish producers who wanted to increase them.[23] This was effective, earned the Saudis the enmity of Arab and other oil producers and, ironically, acted against its claim to leadership.

Under Fahd, the only time oil prices moved in a direction unacceptable to the West was when Saudi Arabia couldn't control them. Despite Fahd's efforts, this happened from 1979 until 1982, when market forces led to massive price increases. And it happened in reverse in 1986, when overproduction and the effect of conservation measures led to a price collapse which threatened the economic feasibility of producing oil in the continental United States. In the latter case, Saudi Arabia accommodated the United States by curtailing its production and increasing prices. The decisions behind these moves were taken by Fahd. His oil ministers were not consulted.

But the Fahd-Saudi wish to follow pro-West oil policies at the expense of the Saudi people, the Arabs and other oil producers went beyond pricing policies. The inevitable capital surpluses which resulted from the boom years were deposited, after Muslim and Arab leaders had been paid off, in Western, mainly American, banks at a time when they could have earned more money elsewhere.[24] In a less obvious move, Fahd chose not to pursue the downstreaming of his oil industry for fear of offending the Western oil companies and this has led to a serious lag in this area.[25]

Under Fahd there has never been a Saudi oil policy. It is solely a matter of responding to Western wishes. Successive OPEC meetings have produced efforts by Saudi Arabia to accommodate the users at the expense of the suppliers. Nowadays, with Iraq embargoed out of the oil market and Saudi Arabia and the rest of OPEC in need of greater income to meet internal demands, the Fahd policy still consists of replacing 90 per cent of the Iraqi production without trying to increase the price. And even pro-West producers are crying foul.

Despite the recent decline in Saudi government income to less than half of what it was during 1979–82, Fahd continued to use money to sponsor American policy beyond the Islamic and Arab worlds. If the regional and Islamic use of money represented a mutuality of interest between Saudi Arabia and the West, the use of Saudi money to support American designs in other parts of the world was no more than Fahd's way of making a direct payment, a bribe, to his family's protectors.

In 1978, Saudi Arabia, then flush with surplus funds, began to sponsor American policy in far corners of the world. It funded anti-communist Unità rebels in Angola, Contra rebels in Central America, despots in the Horn of Africa and provided oil to South Africa. The Saudi people didn't know where most of these countries were and there were more pressing needs for this money both within Saudi Arabia and regionally. Fahd was fighting America's wars while doing nothing about Israel, or towards building schools and hospitals.

But perhaps it is in Fahd's policy towards Iran and Iraq that the oneness of purpose with America shows most clearly and most seriously. Saudi Arabia continued to recognize the Shah as the legitimate ruler of Iran for some time after he fell, despite the fact that Saudi relations with him had never been cordial. The support for Saddam during his war against Iran and subsequent opposition to him after his invasion of Kuwait followed American lines. There is no evidence whatsoever that either country harbours designs against Saudi Arabia and its regime. Iran has studiously refrained from supporting the downtrodden Saudi Shias against their government. And Saddam signed a non-aggression treaty with Saudi Arabia in 1984 and refused to follow his occupation of Kuwait by a thrust into Saudi Arabia, despite the advice of his generals who preached the military necessity of such a move before the arrival of the American forces. Yet, through the Gulf Cooperation Council and by supporting America's twin-containment policy, the Saudis choose to turn the two countries into enemies.

The oil and other policies of Saudi Arabia are coupled with an outright and unproductive mutuality of interest in the area of building an army to protect the House of Saud. According to a statistical abstract of the International Institute of Strategic Studies, the cost of maintaining a Saudi soldier is five times that of maintaining an American soldier and hence, even by these high standards the Saudi army of 115,000 men is tantamount to an American force of 675,000 men.

Much of this inflated cost is the result of the huge sums of money spent on buying military hardware from the West, the natural extension of one of the roles assigned to Saudi Arabia by its Western backers. The country's pretence to Muslim and Arab leadership demands that it appear strong and there is the fabricated need to protect itself against external threats from its covetous neighbours Iran and Iraq. But there is another probably more valid reason for selling Saudi Arabia huge quantities of arms: until recently it was the West's way of recycling the oil money. This reason has been invalidated by the present low income of the country, but, to Western thinking, there are new and equally pressing reasons for continuing the breakneck pace of hardware acquisition. The end of the Cold War has meant a shrinkage in the arms market and a consequent Western need to maintain the Saudi market, underwrite the development cost of certain arms programmes and safeguard employment in the defence industry. And Fahd uses the greater dependence of the West on his country's purchases to enhance his position with his suppliers.

Analysing Saudi spending on military hardware tells many stories. First, according to a report by the Washington Institute, it has represented anywhere between 42 and 92 per cent of total government oil revenue for the past ten years.[26] In 1991 Saudi Arabia spent $23.5 billion on buying equipment from the United States, Britain and France.[27]

Secondly, the equipment-to-soldier ratio is lopsided and some of the equipment purchased is beyond the ability of the Saudi armed forces to master. For example, according to a statistical abstract published by the International Institute of Strategic Studies in London in 1993 the Saudi navy has four frigates, four corvettes, nine US-built Peterson patrol boats, three Jaguar-class patrol boats, eighty-two patrol boats of different types, four minesweepers, two replenishing ships, forty landing craft, three gun boats, four LCMs, fourteen tugs, two air rescue boats, and eight BH7 hovercraft. With the four royal yachts, this makes a total of 183 craft for a navy of 9000 people at the time. In addition, there are no fewer than thirty-two craft on order and several news stories have reported Saudi negotiations to buy eight submarines. Yet, in line with an overall policy of limiting the size of the armed forces, there is no plan to increase the existing thirteen naval bases or the number of personnel proportionally, and military experts insist that twice the number of people were already needed – in other words, some of it is not being used.

The stories of the air force and army are the same. The army has 1640 tanks and armoured personnel carriers, most of which are out of use and, according to *Flight* magazine of 24–30 July 1996, the air force has 665 fixed-wing aircraft. Nor can the Saudis use the sophisticated electronic gear on their F-15 aircraft, man the patriot missiles, maximize the potential of British-made Jaguar fighter-bombers or even fire the French-made Crotale missiles.

Thirdly, there are no attempts to integrate the multi-sourced equipment within Saudi Arabia or coordinate the Saudi purchases with those of the rest of the GCC. Anthony Cordesman, among the leading experts on this subject, states that 'little has been done in this area'.[28]

If the cost per Saudi soldier is five times the cost of an American soldier, then the effectiveness of a Saudi soldier is probably one-fifth of the American one. Not only does the army suffer from the obvious unpreparedness of the average soldier to master modern equipment; neither does it subscribe to the most basic rules of command structure – it is not an organization. Among other things, every brigade contains a member of the royal family who reports directly to his relation, the Minister of Defence and, in the process, undermines the chain of command. Furthermore, because of fear of coups, officers are rotated too frequently and most generals are retired at a very early age, just when they have learned the art of command. Finally, officers are promoted according to loyalty and not competence.

The West's reason for selling the Saudis more arms than they need is clear, and so is the reason why Fahd accepts this. Beyond that, there is the business of lining the pockets of members of the royal family through commissions. The *Observer* of 28 October 1985 detailed the pay-off of $300 million in commissions in connection with arms purchases from the UK. The *Washington Post* of 8 October 1990 analysed how the Saudi royals set up companies to handle defence subcontracts and how these companies realize exorbitant profits which cannot be made in the normal course of business. And, to repeat, Ronald Kessler, the biographer of arms dealer Adnan Khashoggi, has stated that Khashoggi realized $100 million from the Lockheed Company alone.

Saudi Arabia has run a deficit for thirteen consecutive years and has budgeted another one for 1996. The country is deeply in debt, but the size of the debt is a mystery. For example, it is accepted that the government has taken all the money from the social security system and replaced it with debt paper of questionable value, but we don't know the exact amount of money involved. The borrowing of government-owned companies does not show in the government's debt figures and some, like the electricity companies, lost around $2 billion in 1994 alone. The government's borrowing from local banks is a closely guarded secret and so are the costs of debt servicing. The government is in the habit of rolling over money owed to contractors and not showing it in the budget figures of the year when they are due for payment, and estimates indicate that over 400 contractors are involved. Overall, the figures of the World Bank's statistical abstract for 1993 merit repeating: the per capita income of the average Saudi declined from $14,600 in 1982 to $6400 in 1992, without factoring in inflation.

In 1982 Saudi Arabia's surplus was estimated at $142 billion, whereas nowadays its debt is somewhere between $60 billion and $120 billion. The wealth of the country has been squandered and mainly on the wrong things. The family and its spendthrift ways comes first, followed by expenditure on defence, support of corrupt Muslim and Arab leaders, sponsorship of US efforts against movements opposed to America and the staggering $60–$80 billion it cost to underwrite the Iran-Iraq and Gulf wars.[29] Meanwhile, according to official Saudi figures, from 1991 to 1996 the budgets for health and education have declined by an average of 5 per cent a year.

This financial disaster, which has already begun to produce the expected political consequences, is the work of Fahd and the West. To maintain Fahd as an obedient follower, the West refrains from criticizing the ways of the House of Saud. The foolish and expensive Saudi leadership of the Muslim and Arab worlds is a Fahd-sponsored Western policy, and so is paying for American adventures throughout the world. Selling the Saudis too much military hardware and *matériel* they cannot use suits the West and Fahd pays for this to keep Western support. And the costs of the Iran-Iraq and Gulf wars was born by Saudi Arabia at a time when the West claimed no involvement, or that they were fighting for a principle.

It is well to repeat and detail why Fahd chooses to buy the Western support which maintains him and his family in power. In 1979 there was the Mosque Rebellion in Mecca when Islamic zealots occupied Islam's holiest shrine for eleven days. In 1980 the Shias rebelled in the oil-producing eastern region of the country and the rebellion took weeks to subdue and cost dozens of lives. In 1983, according to the writer on Saudi Arabia Simon Henderson, there were army-based attempts to overthrow the government. The Saudi opposition in exile claims that this was followed by other attempts in 1984 and 1985. In 1986 army units at Tubuk and Khamis Mushit rebelled and 500 soldiers were cashiered. At the height of the Gulf War in 1991, two Saudi pilots defected to the Sudan and four more went to Jordan. In 1993 and 1994 religious Ulemas, academics and merchants petitioned the king several times, complaining about corruption and excessive Western influence in their country. On 24 September 1994 the open rebellion which took place in the town of Bureida was serious enough for people to occupy the town hall and declare an Islamic revolution. In January 1996 anti-House of Saud militants blew up the barracks of a US military mission in Riyadh, killing six and wounding over seventy. This was followed by the bombing of the American military compound in Al Khobar in June 1996, with the loss of twenty-one American lives.

Meanwhile anti-House of Saud audio cassettes have become best sellers and are available all over the country.

Saudi Arabia is not a cohesive society, and its geography and its huge numbers of royals are against the success of any coup attempt. But there are opposition groups and they are growing in strength and becoming more vocal. There is the Committee for the Defence of the Legitimate Rights (of the Saudi people), a Wahhabi opposition group; Hizbollah, a Shia party; the Committee for Islamic Reform; the Advice and Reformation Committee; the Reform Committee; and the Arab Socialist Party, among others.

Saudi Arabia's internal structure is disintegrating and its Arab and Islamic policies are a failure. Disorder is on the way. The days of cheque-book diplomacy are over. The Saudi people are demanding their rights. Fahd has no option except to deepen his dependence on the West. And the West, still pursuing short-term gains, foolishly guarantees the House of Saud against internal and external threats; it indulges in moral double-entry bookkeeping and contributes towards its bankruptcy. Not a single Western leader has even spoken about conditions inside Saudi Arabia and only Kennedy tried to get the House of Saud to change its ways. Clinton and Major support Fahd and Fahd supports them. The concordat is at the expense of the Saudi people, a situation almost the same as that which existed when Saudi Arabia was created under Ibn Saud and the decision was adopted by ARAMCO in the 1930s to treat oil payments as personal income.

Jordan exists because the West provides it with financial help. Saudi Arabia exists because it buys Western support. Neither approach takes the people into consideration. There is nothing to suggest that this picture will alter, or that peaceful change brought about by the populace is possible. Yet the people, drastically different from their 1917 ancestors, are determined on change. To judge from what happened in Iran when the Shah was overthrown, they will prevail despite Western support for their leaders. Because secular forces in both countries no longer exist or are weak, the only change possible is likely to assume a fundamentalist Islamic identity.

PART FIVE

Arab Leaders and
Their Makers

8 · Friends, Renegades and Revolvers

Permanent friends do not deviate. Renegades resemble angry teenagers who rebel against parents who don't understand them. Revolvers spin within finite orbits and cannot violate the laws of natural gravity. And so it was with the three leaders of Iraq, Egypt and Saudi Arabia who had the greatest impact on the Arab Middle East this century.

The late Nuri Saïd (1885–1958), fourteen times Prime Minister of Iraq, never did a thing contrary to the wishes of the country which adopted him during the Arab Revolt of 1914–18 and continued to support him until he was murdered and dismembered by an angry crowd after the coup of 14 July 1958 which toppled the Iraqi monarchy.

To his British sponsors, Nuri was a man with many credits to his name. He was among those who helped establish the Iraqi monarchy and who created the Iraqi army to maintain it. He bought the loyalty of the Iraqi tribes on behalf of the monarchy and its British backers by enacting laws which allowed their sheikhs to reclaim their feudal control of land and status which Turkey had revoked.[1] He was also behind the signing of the 1930 British-Iraqi treaty which gave Britain military bases in Iraq and afforded it special status and considerable say in the running of Iraq's foreign affairs. And until his death Nuri Saïd continued to follow Britain obediently and depended on it for support against his internal and regional enemies.

The other side of the coin was his use of this policy which placed Iraqi and Arab interests behind those of Britain and ensuing British support to embark on a number of dangerous and destructive moves which confirmed his primacy within the country. In the 1930s he short-sightedly encouraged the Iraqi army to interfere in politics by using its officers to sabotage the government of a political opponent, Yassin Al Hashemi.[2] He followed this by blindly opposing political and social reform and this included refusal to contemplate amending the faulty two-stage parliamentary election system. Later he endangered the unity of his country by undermining the authority of its young king, Ghazi, and used the army to force Ghazi's hand and appoint him Prime Minister.[3] Throughout his life, he was a committed anti-Shia who went as far as wanting to deny them normal education and relegating them to vocational schools in a country where members of this sect accounted for more than half of the population.[4] His cabinets had few Shia members, whom he accepted as an act of accommodation, and even when he died, in 1958, there were only two Shia members of Iraq's diplomatic corps, and neither attained the rank of ambassador. And, in an act of utter stupidity, in 1937 he delegated his son Sabah, at best an unintelligent bungler who couldn't keep a secret or organize anything, to talk to army officers about murdering the king.[5] He was the antithesis of a believer in democracy, openly scoffing at the idea, and his anti-democratic activities included expelling students from universities, sacking civil servants, banning newspapers, imprisoning politicians, eliminating opponents through implicating them in phoney plots and executing and banishing communists and leftists to brutal desert detention camps (in 1949 he ordered the execution of the communist leader Fahd while he was in custody and well after he had been tried and sentenced to a prison term). He went further, and the eminent historian Hanna Batatu accuses him of murdering two prominent opponents, Tewfic Khalidy and Abdel Gahaffur Badri.[6]

Beyond the hideousness of his internal policies, he followed equally flawed regional and international policies. In 1936 he advised the Mufti of Palestine to end the anti-British rebellion in that country at a time when both the Iraqi and Palestinian people wanted it to continue. During the 1948 Arab-Israeli War, he ordered the Iraqi army in Palestine not to go to the aid of beleaguered Egyptian army units reeling under the weight of an Israeli attack. After the same war he withdrew the Iraqi army from what was left of Palestine without much consideration for the consequences, which included an Arab inability to defend the territories his army was vacating. In 1955 he initiated an alliance with Turkey which eventually became the Baghdad Pact: the British-backed Central Treaty Organization against the Soviet Union, which was unpopular with his people, who wanted an Arab alliance against Israel. And he crowned his record of pro-West anti-Arab perversity by supporting the ill-fated British invasion of Suez in 1956, even though the British themselves were seriously divided on the issue and at a time when Nasser was extremely popular in Iraq.[7]

In fact, Nuri's personal behaviour was as abominable as his policies. Gertrude Bell, his Orientalist-agent friend and admirer, referred in several of her letters to his bad behaviour after heavy drinking. He humiliated his wife by openly having a long-term love affair with the Iraqi singer

Afifa Iskander. The writer James (now Jan) Morris claimed that Nuri had an illegitimate son who served in the Israeli army in the early 1950s.[8] Also, according to Iraqi writer Dr Saniha Zakki, Nuri found it so difficult to control his sexual urges that in 1953 he sent one Abbas Al Khassoun to Syria to assassinate that country's president in order to have an affair with his sister, Dr Fatmeh Al Khassoon (later executed by the Ba'ath regime). His corruption included the usual abuse of office and in 1936 he built himself a palace with money he received from the Iraqi Petroleum Company for extending its contract[9] and added to his wealth by allocating himself thousands of acres of public land.

What was most remarkable about Nuri Saïd and what reveals a great deal about how far the West, in this case mainly Britain, was willing to go in supporting unpopular leaders because they were friends, was his background and the fact that – despite his savage end and the undoubted damage his policies did to Iraq – he continues to be remembered kindly by Western governments, journalists and writers who hanker for the easy days when Iraq was administered by what amounted to a running dog. His contribution to the neurosis of his country and the consequences for the Iraqi people and the rest of the world are overlooked.

Above all, Nuri was neither king nor president: he was a strongman rather than a head of state. As is obvious from the brief description of his internal, Arab and foreign policies, he was an extremely unpopular and corrupt conspirator who stopped at nothing to stay in power and he had very little time for the Arabs and the Iraqis. However, by all accounts – including those of many of his opponents – the man had charm. It was a charm which appealed to women decades younger and which he used with tribal sheikhs, army officers, most members of the royal family, Iraqi politicians, Arab heads of state and Western leaders.

Somewhat implausibly, this is the underlying reason for his success. Other Iraqi leaders were willing to follow Britain – some to the point of trying to compete with his policies of total subservience – but Nuri won over them because he charmed Britain, the country which designed Iraq and continued to run it indirectly, into believing that his acts of servility were tantamount to statesmanship. This son of a junior Turkish official, a half-Turkoman half-Kurd member of the minor Qaraghul tribe, who lacked social background and who viewed the ways and traditions of his people with a disdain which earned him their hatred, was judged by the ridiculous yardstick of how engaging and cooperative he was. Western leaders were so taken by his ways that they depended on him to administer one of the most important and influential countries of the Middle East.

But the situation was not as mysterious as the preceding suggests, for in fact Nuri represented a whole personality type which exists in the Middle East. People with no claim to social background or who fall outside the social system are inclined to act along the same lines. Because they have no local social status and cannot compete with others who have it, they overcome this deficiency by developing compensating personal traits – in Nuri's case, charm. And it is easier for them to use such a quality with outsiders and thus attach themselves to them than with local people who belong – in Nuri's case, members of his country's establishment who never tired of pointing out his humble origins. Nuri went out to charm the British from the time he was an army officer during the First World War, and he never stopped. He had been an officer with the Turkish army, which favoured people without background and constituency, and his British connection started when they took him prisoner and used him to get other Turkish officers to defect. The British accepted him when his countrymen didn't, and he repaid them with total loyalty.

What Nuri had to offer the West during his forty-year career was improvised and never as substantial in terms of status as what other Arab leaders of the time possessed. Ibn Saud of Saudi Arabia was a Bedouin tribal chief with an exaggerated constituency, but a solid one nonetheless. The Hashemites were descendants of the Prophet and relied on this lineage to claim legitimacy. The Khedives and Kings of Egypt had been inherited from Turkey and kept in place in accordance with a better-the-devil-you-know policy. The Mufti of Palestine also came from an old family with lineage to the Prophet and there had been several Husseini Muftis before him. Even some of Nuri's fellow politicians in Iraq, Naji and Tewfic Sweidi, Taha and Yassin Al Hashemi and Rashid Ali Al Keilani, belonged to solid establishment families. Among the Arab politicians of his generation, only Nuri had no claim to tribal, religious or social standing and lived by wit, charm and an uncanny ability to manipulate the West – certainly not by creating a popular base for himself. Among the same generation of Arab politicians, only Nuri received the distinction of Britain's GCMG and DSO.

In dealing with the British, Nuri's charm showed in a curious way. He had a remarkable ability to listen to them and to read their minds. After re-forming this he would tell them what they wanted to hear and would disguise the whole thing as native wisdom. Britain loved Nuri's way of thinking and gave him room to carry out policies which amounted to nothing more than an extension of its own imperial designs. His was more than an instinctive reaction: agreeing with what the British wanted amounted to studied collaboration. This is what former Iraqi Prime Minister Tewfic Sweidi calls 'the complex of complexes', an inherent conviction on the part of Nuri that the Arabs were weak and unworthy of self-rule coupled with a belief that they must be allied to Britain.[10]

Nuri's fellow Iraqi politician and later brother-in-law, Ja'afar Al Askari, wrote of finding him, while in British custody during the First World War, consorting with Colonel Wyndham Deeds when the latter had summoned the then prisoner of war Askari for interrogation. The same memoirs tell of how Arab officers in the Turkish army who had become prisoners of the British believed Nuri to be a British spy. Tewfic Sweidi's memoirs claim that during the Arab Revolt Nuri never left T.E. Lawrence's side. Interestingly, Lawrence's *Seven Pillars of Wisdom* is replete with mentions and praise of Nuri, but there isn't much there to justify the praise. In a letter to her father, Gertrude Bell tells of how King Faisal of Iraq offered to name a brigade after her, only to be outdone by Nuri, who wanted to give her a whole army corps.[11]

This is a strange case indeed. What we have is a bird-like, moustachioed, blue-eyed, non-Arab-looking pipe-smoker who chased women, spoke several languages badly, was a poor public speaker, drank a lot of whisky (calories to him), played bridge and backgammon and never read a book. But Churchill, Eden, Lawrence, Sir Percy Cox (the first British High Commissioner in Baghdad), Gertrude Bell, Kinahan Cornwallis (adviser to Iraq, then Ambassador to Baghdad) and Macmillan all adored him. Later, after America's emergence on the Middle East scene, they were joined by CIA agent Bill Eveland, CIA chief Alan Dulles, Secretary of State John Foster Dulles, President Eisenhower and a slew of other officials.

To Western leaders, Nuri was 'our friend', one of us. To Western writers and journalists, in addition to being a permanent friend, he 'knew how to run Iraq' and 'was hand in glove with the British', while Lord Birdwood went further and elevated him to the level of an international strategist and compared him to Churchill. A year before he was killed by his own people, in 1957, *Time* saw fit to put him on its cover and crowned this effort with a long list of complimentary adjectives. References to whisky and wit came before all else.

Meanwhile the Arabs judged him differently. His original appeal to Britain during the formative period of the Iraqi monarchy in the 1920s was in accepting its hegemony over his country – something the Iraqi people detested. Later, his championing of feudalism generated some tribal support for Britain at the expense of the Iraqi people, who sought land reform.[12] In the 1930s and 40s he followed the British line on Palestine and other Arab issues when his people wanted a different, more Arab-oriented policy. Between 1950 and 1958 he followed an anti-communist line at a time when most Iraqis didn't see communism as a threat.

Throughout his time in office he rigged the country's parliamentary elections and saw to it that the Shias were underrepresented and tribal sheikhs overrepresented (the majority Shias never got more than 40 per cent of the parliamentary seats and often the tribes, no more than 15 per cent of the population, got 30 per cent of the membership of parliament).

The signs that Nuri's policies were a failure and that he was unacceptable to his people were everywhere and they began to appear early in his career. Not only were there districts of Baghdad that he wouldn't have thought of visiting, and student chants which compared him to a 'British shoe', there were also serious political manifestations of this unacceptability. There were the 1936 and 1941 coups, and rebellions by the Assyrians, Kurds and others. There were the bloody riots of 1946, 1948, 1952, 1954 and 1956, and those of 1948, 1952 and 1956 produced a large but unknown number of dead and wounded. Twice, after the 1936 Bakr Sidqi coup and the 1940 takeover by nationalist officers, the British helped Nuri escape from Iraq to avoid facing the anger of the people. And he had to do the same in 1939 after the funeral of the popular King Ghazi, when the mourners turned against him and he fled the scene in a river boat. On many other occasions, he took refuge in the British airbase of Habbiniyya to avoid the same prospect. Between 1952 and the successful coup of 14 July 1958 which brought about Nuri's end, according to the proclamations of his own government there were no fewer than six army-based attempts to overthrow the Iraqi monarchy and get rid of him.

Every escape, disappearance to London (and he was there frequently) or refuge in Habbiniyya was followed by a British-backed resumption of power which found him applying the sword to his enemies or imprisoning them without a second thought. On his return after the Sidqi coup he was determined to punish all those involved in it and he cashiered dozens of army officers. The officers behind the nationalist takeover of the Iraqi government in 1940–1, known as the Golden Square, were executed and left hanging in front of the Ministry of Defence building as a lesson to others. One of them, Salluheddine Sabbagh, was repatriated from Turkey four years later and met the same fate, despite appeals for clemency and fear of what the execution might do to Iraqi national unity. In the 1950s, though he was old, deaf and becoming senile, his criminal instincts still prompted him to imprison two of the leading politicians of the country, Kamel Chederchi and Muhammad Kubba, both able, decent and firm believers in democracy. He never tolerated dissent, nor was he capable of forgetting or forgiving.

In the absence of a clear policy towards an important country the West depended on one man, and no one thought of asking Nuri to change his ways or of responding to the wishes of the people of Iraq. The West simply refused to think of a replacement, or even a pro-West policy which took the Iraqi people into consideration. Even when other Iraqi leaders articulated constructive policies beneficial to the West and the Arabs, such as autonomy for the Kurds and a more equitable distribution of wealth in Iraq, the West stuck with him. Beginning with the Suez crisis, all the signs pointed to trouble ahead, but the West believed, indeed insisted on believing, that Nuri was secure.[13] They never saw beyond the banality and shallowness of the man. How could they conceivably turn their backs on a subservient and charming friend?

Perhaps Western leaders and intelligence services should have paid more attention to Nuri's personal behaviour. Even in his seventies Nuri always carried a gun. In July 1958, when the Iraqi army overthrew the monarchy, he took refuge in the home of Saddiq Al Bassam, an old friend. It was none other than Saddiq's young son who telephoned the army rebels with Nuri's whereabouts. Sensing danger, Nuri tried to escape dressed as a woman. But a mob recognized him, killed and tore him to bits and repeatedly ran over whatever was left of him with their cars. There was nothing left to bury. Unbelievably, he tried unsuccessfully to use the gun against his attackers.[14] Western policy towards Iraq amounted to this ridiculous act, a lonely old man trying to intercept the march of history with a six-shooter.

Gamal Abdel Nasser, universally known by his last name, was an amalgam of this century's most popular Arab leader and its towering renegade, a pro-West leader turning and going in the opposite direction. This was not by design: Nasser was the product of a historical, almost natural confrontation between the Arabs and the West.

By nature Nasser was not a revolutionary: he was a conservative with an intrinsic commitment to cooperation with the West. But – mainly circumstantially – he still became the embodiment of an Arab revolution against the West. In fact, he came to power with American help and this, along with his eventual emergence as the leader of the anti-West Arab camp, is what elevates any analysis of his career to the level of a study of whether Arab-West cooperation is at all possible.

To the Arabs, the image Nasser left behind is so overwhelming that a considerable number of them still use it as a yardstick of what is desirable, achievable and sensible. Conversations with taxi drivers in Saudi Arabia, government officials in Jordan, fellaheen in Palestine, men of letters in Syria, Yemeni workers in Cardiff, Wales, and descendants of Lebanese emigrants in Brazil produce endless refrains which amount to fulsome praise. Speaking of Saddam's Gulf War adventure, they resort to 'Nasser would have known better'; a reference to Qaddafi produces 'he would have behaved himself with Nasser at the helm'; and people who reject the recent PLO-Israeli peace agreement lament his absence with 'we would have done better had Nasser been alive'. In Arabs' hearts he lives in the company of Saladin, Tarik bin Ziyyad and Amr ibn Al As, Islam's military leaders of legend. This is strange company for a man who assumed power with CIA help and never won a battle in his life, a confirmation – if one were needed – that the Arab-West conflict is a state of mind, a structural cultural happening beyond simple solutions to transitory problems. Nasser symbolized this confrontation; accidentally, then willingly, he became, was, the confrontation. And if he is still so revered today, then this confrontation is alive, it lurks in people's hearts and, sooner or later, it will manifest itself and speak Nasser's language, in the absence of secular forces, under an Islamic banner.

Nasser had two things in common with Nuri Saïd: he came from a humble background and he had charm – in Nasser's case a natural, native one which left people breathless. I remember interviewing him with two colleagues and being smitten to the point of forgetting that he had said nothing worth reporting. And I remember *Time* correspondent James A. Bell saying, 'I don't know what it is, but he has it, loads of it.' He did have it; he was blessed.

Nasser was the son of a provincial postal clerk, born in 1918 in the village of Beni Morr with more strikes against him than could be analysed. His mother died when he was a young lad and his relationship with his father was lukewarm. He was a loner, an introspective youth who read a great deal and compensated for his lack of status by developing a considerable amount of inner discipline.

His love of books and the difference in their ages weren't the only things which separated Nasser from Nuri Saïd, until 1958 his chief enemy among the traditional Arab regimes. Unlike Nuri, Nasser was a family man and a devoted husband and father. He didn't drink alcohol, he observed Islamic rites and from school until his death of a heart attack in 1970, he worked more than twelve hours a day. But all this pales in comparison with more substantial differences: he abhorred violence, entertained no religious prejudice and believed in the rights and inherent dignity of the common man. Nuri believed in the supremacy of the West; Nasser responded to the voices of the street: he was a natural populist. It is this last point, his ability and wish to respond to the Egyptian and Arab peoples' desires which naturally and automatically distanced him from Western thinking. (In Eden's memoirs, *Full Circle*, there is not a single mention of the feelings of the Egyptian people towards the Suez crisis.)

There is little in Nasser's early life to suggest what followed. He entered cadet school after a second try and by all accounts he was a good if not a brilliant student. But it was here, through contact with students who were more politically inclined, that the first stirrings began. His earliest response to the pervasive political atmosphere of the times was a brief and somewhat distant (he never became a member) association with the Muslim Brotherhood, through a man by the name of Hassan Al Bakry.[15] We do not know what ideological differences kept Nasser from joining the leading opposition group of the early 1940s, but he left cadet school with no specific political association, only the friendship of many officers who later would become close associates in the Free Officers group.

It is interesting to note that the late 1930s, a turbulent period in Egyptian politics, provoked no unusual recorded response in the man, only an occasional participation in a street demonstration. Even later, unlike the impulsive Anwar Sadat, Nasser joined no pro-German, communist or Islamic army or civilian group. He met, listened and debated with people belonging to these groups, but he never became one of them. His biographer, friend, adviser and confidant, the writer Muhammad Heikal, claims that Nasser, Sadat, Abdel Hakim Amer (later Minister of Defence) and other Egyptian army officers formed the Free Officers in 1942, after the British, in an act of humiliation of the whole Egyptian nation, imposed a pro-British Prime Minister on King Farouk during the Second World War. It was this group which eventually overthrew the monarchy in 1952. But there is little reason to believe that, at this point, the Free Officers were an organized group with a political agenda.[16] From the little evidence available, it seems that it was the Egyptian army's defeat in Palestine which transformed this and other army groups from collections of concerned young officers disposed towards political discourse to a more cohesive entity capable of concrete action. The formation of the Free Officers occurred in steps.

Palestine, the issue which was to preoccupy Nasser for most of his life, prompted him into uncharacteristic action late in 1947. According to Jean Lacouture and other biographers, Nasser paid a secret visit to the Mufti of Palestine, then resident in Cairo, and offered to join the Arab irregulars trekking to that country to fight Zionism.[17] The Mufti had more volunteers than he could cope with and turned Nasser down. Nasser had to wait until the regular Egyptian army was ordered to Palestine by King Farouk in May 1948.

It was in Palestine that Nasser's true character began to reveal itself. He fought bravely: reports speak of a model, inspiring officer who was cool under fire. He was the second-ranking Egyptian officer of the Egyptian garrison at Faluja, a brigade-sized unit which was surrounded for over forty days by superior Israeli forces, but refused to surrender. It was during this period, with defeat staring him in the eye, that his thoughts crystallized. He became preoccupied with the dismal performance of the Egyptian army and what lay behind it: the rot consuming the Egyptian government. The historian Derek Hopwood quotes Nasser as saying, 'We were fighting in Palestine, but our dreams were in Egypt.'[18] After the 1948 Arab-Israeli War there would be no turning back; Nasser devoted himself to organizing and expanding the Free Officers movement.

At this stage the movement had no specific political colour. The officers were against feudal landlords because 6 per cent of the latter owned more than 65 per cent of the country's cultivated land. They opposed King Farouk and the political parties of the time, because they were corrupt and the parties drew their members from an urban élite which had little concern for the people or problems of Egypt. The Free Officers also resented the foreign control of commerce by Greeks, Jews and Armenians who spoke French and English, had special legal status guaranteed by the British and made a point of not identifying with anything Egyptian (most didn't even eat Egyptian food). And the officers held in special contempt the royal entourage, whom they rightly accused of profiteering from equipping the Egyptian army with faulty weapons and corrupt ammunition, a practice which led to the army's defeat and humiliation in Palestine.

The Free Officers had no Arab nationalist or Islamic dreams. The key word which represented what they stood for was reform. Bringing reform to Egypt meant replacing the people who controlled Egypt: the palace, the pashas and foreign parasites. However, since all these groups were solidly supported by Britain and because the Free Officers created themselves without outside help, then the officers were anti-British. This indirect anti-British stance was coupled with the simple, direct one of wanting the British to evacuate their troops from along the Suez Canal. Together, these positions may be seen as representing an anti-British policy.

Unlike the officers, King Farouk, who ruled Egypt from 1936 to 1952, depended on outside support to stay in power. He was in constant and direct contact with Britain and the United States and consulted them on everything. The pashas, like Nuri in Baghdad, accepted the corrupt monarchy and followed a pro-British line to such an extent that in 1951 Prime Minister Ali Maher conspired with the British Ambassador against Egyptian volunteers fighting to evict British forces from the Suez Canal Zone.[19] And the wealthy foreigners represented a pro-British class who had their own law courts, clubs and commercial monopolies. The enmity between Britain and the Free Officers was natural. Britain preferred to deal with known, corrupt quantities who depended on its protection for survival and followed its lead in foreign affairs.

But America was not an enemy. America had no troops or clients in Egypt. America was new to the Middle East: it arrived after the Second World War; its concerns of protecting the oil-producing Gulf and combating communism took precedence over Farouk's wish to befriend it and its interests were not threatened by the Free Officers. America saw the possible disintegration of the Egypt of Farouk and the pashas in the context of these interests at a time when Britain perceived any change in Egypt as a threat to its colonial hegemony.

The truest reflection of these differing attitudes – which eventually manifested themselves with stunning clarity during the Suez crisis – is in the thinking of the two governments in power from 1951 until the Free Officers' coup of 22 July 1952. According to the CIA agent Miles Copeland, both US Ambassador Jefferson Caffrey and superspy Kermit Roosevelt wanted the army to deal with the chaos consuming Egypt and take over the government.[20] Simultaneously, British Foreign Secretary and later Prime Minister Anthony Eden was thinking of something else; in response to the same problems and continued attacks on British occupation troops along Suez, he wanted to march on Cairo and occupy it.[21] The Americans prevailed.

The spark for change occurred on 26 January 1952, when British troops along the Canal Zone responded to Egyptian provocations by attacking an Egyptian police post in the city of Ismâ'ilîya and killing thirty Egyptians. Cairo exploded and mobs burned the heart of the city. More than 750 business establishments, including the legendary Shepheard's Hotel and the BOAC offices, were burned down, thirty people were killed and about a thousand injured. Police and army recruits joined the rioters, the government was dismissed and martial law was declared. In the words of Lacouture, 'It was the entire state which cracked.'[22] This chaotic situation gave the Americans their chance to move in.

If Miles Copeland is to be believed, the contact between Nasser and the CIA began four months before the 22 July 1952 coup and it took the form of meetings between Nasser and the CIA's Kermit Roosevelt. However, it is now established that an American Embassy officer, William Lakeland, and Frank Kearns, a CIA agent operating under the cover of a correspondent for CBS, met Nasser and some Free Officers before that time. Regardless of the exact time, what matters are the inherent pro-American inclinations of the officers and the nature of the contact. It continued – directly with Nasser himself – for several months and there is little doubt the Americans were fully aware of the plans of the Free Officers.

The coup itself was a non-event, aptly described by *The Times* of 24 July 1952 as 'a domestic affair'. The happenings on the day of the coup, which included the movement of troops to dismiss the cabinet, arrest monarchist army officers, send Farouk packing to Europe and establish a regency council ostensibly to safeguard things until the baby crown prince Ahmad Fuad came of age, amounted to very little. There was no resistance or violence, the radio proclamations were relatively moderate, the man appointed Prime Minister, Ali Maher Pasha, was an old name and for all anybody knew, the leader of the coup was a handsome, pipe-smoking general with solid conservative credentials, Muhammad Naguib.

In fact, Naguib was no more than the front man. The Americans accepted Nasser as the source of power and dealt with him through a multitude of CIA agents and Robert Anderson, an Eisenhower confidant and later his Secretary of Treasury. The British, seeing the coup for what it was, an American replacement of their hegemony over Egypt, sulked. On occasion, Eden resorted to threats and blackmail of an old-fashioned colonial type, but it was no use. On 27 July 1954, on the second anniversary of King Farouk's forced abdication, the British finally signed a treaty to evacuate their forces from Egypt. The most important article of this treaty, a solid confirmation that the Free Officers were essentially inclined towards the West, was one which stipulated the right of return of British troops in case Egypt and the Suez Canal were threatened by outside forces – that is, communism. And there was greater evidence of this pro-West tilt in the form of the personal connections of some of the Free Officers: Amer, Ali Sabir and Shukri Abbaza were related to and made use of anti-communist establishment families.

Nasser's anti-communism went further than accepting the return of British troops in case of attack. It was he who in February 1954 published the booklet *Communism As It Really Is*. And he did it during a busy time, three months before he finally replaced General Naguib after an internecine struggle for power. While these two acts reconfirm Nasser's Western inclinations – and there is suspicion that the Americans were behind the anti-Communist tract – the dismissal of Naguib presented Nasser with a new enemy. From then on, Nasser had to confront the Muslim Brotherhood. The organization which had backed Naguib saw itself as the natural heir to the monarchy and clamoured for elections. Confronted by the hostility of the leftists and communists whom he obviously opposed, the Muslim Brotherhood who wanted to replace him and the pasha class which saw him as a usurper and an upstart, Nasser had one source of support: America.

So Nasser was pro-West, anti-communist, against the corrupt pashas and opposed to Islamic movements. But, unlike many another Arab leader who depended on the support of outside powers to exist, he felt the need for something else, to respond to the wishes of the people. Moreover, he wrongly believed that he could reconcile his pro-Western policies with his commitment to the people.

This is when Nasser became ideological and, with considerable help from the journalist Muhammad Heikal, wrote *The Philosophy of the Revolution*. The book presented Egypt as the centre of the Arab, Muslim and African worlds, a country able to maintain good relations with the West while operating freely within its natural spheres of influence.

What separates Nasser from Arab leaders of his time and throughout this century merits elucidation. The others depended exclusively on Western support, regardless of source, and the absence of a countervailing power reduced them to simple followers incapable of independent action. But the voice of the people seemed to reside within Nasser's person. He felt a need to balance his anti-communist, pro-American stance, initially by responding to what the Egyptian people wanted and later to the wishes of the whole Arab people. As we will see, this duality, his inability to reconcile his two inclinations was to be his undoing. The West had little or no interest in the wishes of the people: only Western strategic concerns, the wish to protect Israel, and economic interests mattered.

In hindsight, the unsoundness of the US-Nasser alliance was built-in and its demise predictable. Nasser's assumption that, unlike Britain, America would accept his balancing act was wrong. However, the convergence of elements which came together in 1955 to undo his relationship with America and to create an atmosphere of suspicion which was to govern the attitude of both sides until Nasser's death in 1970, was a unique happening indeed. It all began with the Baghdad Pact.

The idea of the Baghdad Pact, though initiated by Britain, had American backing. It reflected Western preoccupations with communism and relegated more immediate Arab concerns, including the Palestinian question, to a secondary position. The West wanted to create a regional alliance of the Arab countries and Iran, Turkey and Pakistan against the USSR. Nasser haggled, demurred, then rejected the idea. In February 1955 Iraq and Turkey signed the first part of the pact, leaving Nasser and his wishes to concentrate on Arab problems in the cold.

Nuri gloated. In having the West to himself, he was undermining his upstart enemy. Nasser reacted furiously. To him, the pressure from the

West to go ahead with the pact exposed a neo-colonialist attitude which ignored the real problems of the Middle East and was a reconfirmation that the West was more committed to traditional friends than to cooperation. To him, putting the communist threat before the seething problem of Palestine meant a Western unwillingness to deal with the Arabs on a sensible basis.

A little later, in March 1955, the Israelis, using the presence of fedayeen bases in Gaza as an excuse, carried out a major raid which resulted in the death of thirty-five Egyptian soldiers. The Egyptian people wanted Nasser to respond, but he knew better; the state of preparedness and quality of armament of the Egyptian army precluded any military riposte. Coolly, and sighting the problem facing him, Nasser approached France and the United States with a request to buy arms. The West administered another humiliation: his request was turned down.

In April 1955, after meetings in Cairo with President Tito of Yugoslavia and Prime Minister Nehru of India, Nasser travelled to Bandung, Indonesia to attend what later became known as the Bandung Conference, a gathering of the heads of state of the non-aligned world. It was an encounter which changed the course of Middle East history. Nasser's discovery of an alternative to his relationship with the United States, the policy of neutrality which Western actions forced on him, was the second stage of his political career.

In Bandung, Nasser spent most of his time with Tito, Nehru and Prime Minister Zhou Enlai of China. Tito advised him not to trust anyone, Nehru counselled him to be cautious and Zhou admonished him for putting so much faith in America. Nasser accepted what they told him, but it was the exalted company of these men and their independence which affected him most. He returned to Egypt thinking of himself as a world leader capable of acting alone, without dependence on America. For him, it was time to put *The Philosophy of the Revolution* to work without deferring to America, to conduct a rapprochement with the Egyptian left, enact some land and labour reforms and resurrect in a more serious way the Palestinian problem, the magnet for Arab emotions. What better way to dramatize the change in his persona than finally to terminate the ongoing requests to purchase Western arms. The time for the big gesture to repay the West, the Americans in particular, for the Baghdad Pact and Gaza raid injuries had come. In September 1955, after long, secret negotiations with USSR Ambassador to Cairo Daniel Solod, Nasser carried out his first act of defiance and decided to buy arms from Czechoslovakia.

This was a huge gamble: the first contract to buy arms from the communist bloc by a non-communist country. It undermined the Baghdad Pact and Western defence plans. It was a slap in the face to the West and its clients and a commitment to Palestine which the Arab masses everywhere celebrated with undisguised glee. Eden and Britain's Foreign Office pointed the finger at the Americans. Too late, the United States sent emissaries to ask Nasser to cancel the deal. Israel used the whole episode to enhance its credentials with the West. There were pronouncements, disguised threats, secret offers of arms and other inducements, but Nasser didn't budge. When the dust settled the West and the world were confronted with a new Nasser. For the West, unlike permanent friend Nuri Saïd, Nasser became an evasive challenge. But the West still could not agree on what to do about him.

Britain and France, the latter reacting to Nasser's support of Algerian rebels against their rule, thought of colonial solutions, the use of force to subdue a bothersome native. But America wouldn't join them, fearing regional repercussions that included the disruption of the flow of oil. Above all, the CIA agents dealing with Nasser were convinced that he was 'controllable'.

This division among the Western powers showed itself in inglorious colours during the Suez crisis. Late in 1955 Egypt decided to go ahead with the building of the Aswan Dam, a project involving land reclamation and power generation. It was a huge, prestigious project which needed outside financing and Egypt applied to the World Bank for a loan of $200 million at a time when Nasser was basking in the glory of his newly defined post-Bandung position.

He was moving towards recognition of Red China; his propaganda machine was inciting the Arab peoples to reject Western influence and reject their pro-West leaders and he was preparing for a confrontation with Israel. Despite the arms deal, the fact that he forced King Hussein to dismiss his army's British Chief of Staff, Glubb Pasha, and the new attitude towards China, the United States knew, unlike Britain and France, that Nasser was not a communist stooge. But that was not what mattered. America was discovering that Nasser represented a popular power which had to be accommodated and this meant having to share the running of the Middle East with him. In principle, Secretary of State John Foster Dulles accepted this notion until he decided that Nasser's demands represented a larger piece of the pie than he was willing to cede, that Nasser's success with the Arab people, and his positions on Palestine and oil, were irreconcilable with Western interests. Dulles decided to cut him down to size.

On 19 July 1956, while Nasser was attending a non-aligned meeting at Brioni in Yugoslavia, Dulles, without notice, cancelled the offer to finance the building of the Aswan Dam. The act was bad enough, but the manner in which it was done was nothing short of an attempt to humiliate the leader of the Egyptians and Arabs. Nasser returned to Egypt in a hurry and on 26 July 1956, the fourth anniversary of King Farouk's departure, in a fiery speech delivered in Alexandria in which he singled out the United States for attack, he nationalized the Suez Canal.

The situation got out of control, suddenly all the players were confronted with new situations for which they had no plans. Nasser, despite the arms deal and still an American agent according to the official Soviet encyclopaedia, turned to Russia for financial help to build the dam. Britain and France, feeling somewhat vindicated, wanted to attack him. Nuri Saïd was for a direct attack on Cairo. The United States, perhaps more unprepared than the rest, started developing instant schemes which suggested international control of the Canal, directly or through a users' association. The Arab people were delirious with nationalistic joy. Nasser lived on potions of street chants.

This is when Nasser became the slayer of the Western dragon, the Zaim (leader), idol and image of an Arab uprising against the West. Never mind his CIA connection (unknown), never mind what brought about the nationalization, never mind the consequences; what mattered to Arabs was that he was expressing their anti-West feelings. And as with all dictatorships, the propagandists of the Egyptian state carried the leader's cry forward and amplified it every step of the way.

The West tried to mount a response. Official statements by Britain and France, and press reports everywhere, began creating the image of Nasser the monster. The *Daily Telegraph*, without providing proof, spoke of 'Nasser's Master Plan' to control the Middle East. The BBC Middle East correspondent openly compared Nasser to Haji Baba, a legendary joker. An official of the British Embassy in Washington referred to Nasser as public enemy number one.[23] *Le Figaro* resorted to the word 'dictator'. The CIA, probably acting on its own, as it often does, smuggled anti-Nasser pamphlets into Egypt itself. The *New York Times* and *Washington Post* followed *Le Figaro* and demanded that he be curbed. When the press in places like Canada, Australia and various European countries joined the fray, the whole affair began to resemble an East–West confrontation or, as far as many people were concerned, a Muslim–West confrontation.

For three months, until the Suez invasion by British and French forces started on 31 October 1956, the world was entertained by a comedy of secret and open diplomacy. The United States changed its mind constantly; Nasser believed his own propaganda and the various delegations which visited him, trying to reach a solution, found him haughtily rigid and unaccommodating. But it was left to Britain and France to commit one of the century's greatest acts of stupidity.

Still unable to accept the existence of a popular force and the fact that attacking Nasser or toppling him meant facing the people of the Middle East, they could think of only one solution: invasion. They didn't stop there: they compounded the problem, guaranteeing Nasser's eventual victory, by colluding with the Israelis. They still refused to take the feelings of the average Arab into consideration and to the average Arab the invasion of Suez was an act of hatred by people who wanted to enslave them for ever. In fact, Suez did more damage to the client Arab regimes than to Nasser.

The interlinked events went like this. On 21 October Jordan elected a pro-Nasser government. On 29 October the Israelis invaded Sinai and the British and French issued an ultimatum giving Egypt twelve hours to stop the fighting and guarantee free passage through the Canal. On 31 October the British and French, still pretending that they were acting on their own, began landing in the Canal Zone. On 4 November the Russians issued an ultimatum to the invading forces to stop. At about the same time, President Eisenhower and Secretary of State Dulles, having agreed that the ailing Eden, the mastermind of the invasion, had lost his sense of reason, decided to go public and oppose it. The United Nations, in constant session in an attempt to forestall the march of folly, voted against Israel, Britain and France and asked them to withdraw. Meanwhile, despite the dismal performances of the Egyptian forces, the Arab people supported Nasser, exaggerated his performance, blew up pipelines carrying oil to the West and challenged their pro-West governments and forced one of them, Saudi Arabia, to accept Egyptian military planes which needed a safe haven.

The most interesting aspect of the Suez crisis is the state of mind which governed it. For example, Britain and France were actually responding to the Arab street while refusing to admit that the Arab people mattered. The British turned Near East Broadcasting, a Cyprus-based radio station owned by them, into the Voice of Britain – as if anyone cared. French Arabic-language radio broadcasts bordered on the hysterical. Nasser told many friends of how Eden had tried to humiliate him during their one meeting in 1955, when Eden was on his way to a conference in the Far East. Even fifteen years later, in 1971, Heikal's book *The Cairo Documents* appears to be more concerned with how insulting to the Arabs Eden's wife Clarissa was than to the performance of the Egyptian army. She is supposed to have said, 'How dare this Egyptian challenge Anthony?'

The near-mad passion on both sides produced false claims and counter-claims. In fairness, in the middle of all this Nasser managed two coherent and intelligent moves. He told Jordan and Syria not to enter the war on his side, lest their armies be destroyed. And, being an instinctive propagandist, he made a film of the damage and killings carried out by the invading British and French troops and sent it to London with Emile Bustani, the Lebanese politician and construction magnate who never tired of supporting an Arab-West rapprochement. Bustani was successful in that the showing of the film in many countries helped change the image of the whole invasion from an attack on a dictator and focused attention on the suffering of the Egyptian people.

All this aside, it was within the Middle East that the most profound change of all took place. After Suez, the United Nations truce, the withdrawal of British and French forces and the abrogation of the British-Egyptian treaty, the Middle East belonged to Nasser. There was no middle ground: Arab leaders either joined Nasser against the West or came out in open opposition. Because Nasser had all the Arab people on his side, his Arab foes became the West's obedient servants more than ever before.

Once again, the Americans found themselves forced to act. The US administration, despite a greater sensitivity to Arab feelings than existed in Britain and France, proclaimed the Eisenhower Doctrine, an American pledge to protect the various regimes of the area against the penetration of communism or its agents – that is, Nasser. President Camille Chamoun of Lebanon was the first Arab chief to adhere to this policy and he was followed by Nuri in Iraq, the ever-changing Saud of Saudi Arabia and the master of full turns, King Hussein of Jordan. In essence, Nasser and the people were pitted against the traditionalists and the West. The clearest demonstration of the emptiness of the American post-Suez approach ('policy' is inaccurate) is to recall that the US very seriously considered the use of the semi-literate King Saud of Saudi Arabia as a regional counterweight to Nasser.

With America thus committed, even Nasser's surreptitious dealings with the CIA and Eisenhower emissaries in an attempt to reach an understanding with the West came to an end. He knew he couldn't face the West alone and was not willing to contemplate reclaiming America's friendship by disowning the Arab people. Nasser had no choice but to befriend the USSR. The country whose encyclopaedia still described him as a Western stooge was also interested. For both sides it was an alliance of convenience brought about by the actions of Britain, France and the United States.

But the alliance between the USSR and Egypt was never complete.

Because there was no ideological common ground, Nasser continued to oppose the communist parties in Egypt and throughout the Middle East. The then leader of the USSR, Nikita Khrushchev, was fascinated by Nasser's hold on the Arab masses but never trusted him. The only thing which bound them together was the presence of a common enemy and its influence.

In January 1958, Syria had a communist army chief of staff, General Afif Bizri, and the whole country was facing the threat of a communist takeover. Anti-communist Syrian politicians journeyed to Cairo and appealed to Nasser to save their country by uniting it with Egypt.

The advocate of Arab unity hesitated, then gave in. It was an anti-communist move by the ally of the USSR which the West didn't oppose. And Nasser's genuine hesitation to incorporate Syria into a United Arab Republic revealed two things: Nasser was still a conservative by nature and his calls for the Arabs to unite appear to have meant a unity of purpose rather than an actual act of merger. Still, he couldn't turn his back on any variety of scheme for Arab unity.

Nuri and his Western backers responded to the creation of the UAR by creating a new country of their own, the Arab Federation of Iraq and Jordan. The West, however thankful it was to Nasser for saving Syria from communism, needed a counterweight to save their friends from his growing popular challenge. The emergence of two Arab countries, one under a popular leader allied to the USSR and another beholden to the West and run by the most unpopular Arab politician of this century, led to an explosive situation. In this case the explosion came soon enough. The Iraqi monarchy was overthrown and members of the royal family were murdered on 14 July 1958. Nuri was apprehended and killed by the mob two days later.

As for this coup's potential for sparking a world war, it was no less critical than the Cuban missile crisis or the East–West confrontation over Berlin in 1960. Western reaction to it was swift. US Marines landed in Lebanon and British paratroops landed in Jordan. Lebanon was in the middle of a minor civil war between pro-West President Chamoun and Nasser's partisans. Jordan, having experienced a pro-West palace coup (see Chapter 4), had an unpopular government and was on the verge of collapse.

When the Iraqi coup occurred Nasser was visiting Tito in Yugoslavia. Worried about the Western troop landings, and a possible move against Syria or Iraq, he flew to Moscow and asked Khrushchev to issue a deterrent threat to the West. The latter refused, adamantly.[24] According to Khrushchev, the USSR was not ready to go to war to further Nasser's plans for

Arab unity. To Nasser, his inability to move the Russian leader came as a shock, the first one after the Iraqi coup. The second came when the Iraqi army officers who took over their government refused to allow him to land in Baghdad on his way back to Cairo.[25] Nasser read the situation right: the Iraqi coup might have been anti-monarchist and perhaps anti-West, but the leader of the officers who carried it out, Brigadier Abdel Karim Kassem, was not a Nasserite, nor was he willing to undermine his own position by playing second fiddle to a Nasser popular with the Iraqi masses.

This is one of the most important turning points in the history of the modern Arab world, in all likelihood the point at which the Nasser movement lost its momentum and Nasser his chance to control all of the Arab Middle East. Had the Iraqi army officers followed Nasser and joined the UAR, there would have been no stopping him. Instead, they went their own way and eventually provided a more viable opposition to Nasser than Nuri had represented.

Khrushchev's refusal confirmed that Russia too was not enamoured with Nasser's Arab nationalism. And Kassem's independent attitude owed much to the fact that the rebellious Iraqi officers had asked Nasser for help in carrying out a coup and had been turned down. In addition, there was the eternal rivalry between Iraqis and Egyptians and the fact that Iraqi officers looked down on their Egyptian counterparts. But there was something else as well.

Hani Fkaiki, a former Iraqi Ba'athist leader and a solid supporter of Arab unity, and Abdel Sattar Douri, a prominent Iraqi politician, insist that Britain had a big hand in the refusal to grant Nasser landing rights in Baghdad and what followed it. Kassem's later behaviour, his emergence as Nasser's competitor and the division of the Arab Middle East along new lines, which halted Nasser's Arab nationalism avalanche, support Fkaiki's thesis.

According to Fkaiki and Douri, Kassem held a meeting with British Ambassador to Iraq Sir Michael Wright hours after the coup. Kassem wanted to assure Wright that, however bloody, the coup was a domestic affair with no anti-British designs behind it. Fkaiki and Douri insist that the two men struck a bargain: Kassem agreed to continue to pump oil and made a promise not to join Nasser's UAR in return for a British promise of non-interference.[26] In other words, Wright told Kassem that the British and Americans would refrain from marching on Baghdad. There is circumstantial evidence to support the Iraqi politicians' statement, and they are competent and reliable sources.

The American troops who landed in Lebanon and the British troops who landed in Jordan were definitely equipped for a move against Iraq.[27] Furthermore, despite Kassem's extremely erratic record and occasional serious support for the Iraqi Communist Party, the British continued to support him as a counterweight to Nasser until he threatened to invade Kuwait in 1961. In fact, Kassem's anti-Arab unity stance was more to the USSR's liking and they too supported him against their unreliable ally. Arab unity was against the strategic interests of both sides. (Interestingly, this is the time when the double agent Kim Philby was covering the Iraqi situation for the *Observer* and *The Economist* and it supports a theory that he served the interests of London and Moscow with their full knowledge because they had the common purpose of promoting Kassem.)

From 1958 until 1960 Nasser tried to assume a neutral position in the Middle East that was acceptable to the major powers without endangering his popular standing. He argued with Khrushchev, personally and in correspondence, against communist infiltration of the Middle East and served notice that he would not tolerate a communist takeover of Iraq. Suddenly bereft of friends in the West, he developed a special relationship with Dag Hammarskjöld, the then Secretary-General of the United Nations. His open discourses with Hammarskjöld were sufficiently wide-ranging to include discussion of ways to settle the Palestinian refugee problem, and perhaps the whole Arab-Israeli conflict. This serious peace initiative was not to the liking of the Mufti of Palestine, who fled Cairo to Beirut and sought Kassem's help to stop Nasser.[28]

When John F. Kennedy was elected President of the United States in 1960, Nasser carried his diplomatic campaign further. For three years he conducted a highly personal correspondence with Kennedy in which both men discussed ways to end the turmoil in the Middle East.[29] Nasser wanted a neutral Middle East; Kennedy spoke of the West's strategic interests, which precluded that. Kennedy wanted Nasser to stop undermining the West's friends in the area; the latter agreed to do his best, but admitted that he couldn't control people 'who follow me'. The correspondence, though it did produce a period of relative peace between the Arabs and Israel, exposed the irreconcilability of Western and Arab interests.

In September 1961 the mercurial Syrians seceded from the UAR. In a statesmanlike gesture, Nasser refused to use force to maintain the union. And although the episode damaged his popular standing, it reinforced his belief in Arab unity without actual union. Two months later a pro-Nasser coup in Yemen compensated for the loss of Syria; the Nasser bandwagon was again on the road.

In Yemen the republican elements which overthrew the monarchy established a regime the make-up of which threatened conservative Saudi

Arabia and was opposed by it. This led to a Yemeni civil war which forced Kennedy into a delicate balancing act between a traditional friend, Saudi Arabia, and the man whom he recognized as the popular leader of the Arab world. Since neither Kennedy nor Nasser allowed the war to interrupt their communications, the opening to America continued.

Even on the Algerian question Nasser was showing signs of unusual moderation. He corresponded with President De Gaulle on the best way to extricate France from its Algerian predicament and the two men established good relations. However, throughout this period Nasser kept up his propaganda attacks on the West's friends and continued to buy Soviet arms. Whatever understanding of his position Kennedy, Hammarskjöld and De Gaulle manifested was based on their assessment of his popularity with the average Arab, and the security of his position as a popular leader depended an implicit ability to oppose the West, combat Israel and maintain the loyalty of the masses.

Kennedy's assassination in November 1963 brought a sudden and dramatic end to Nasser's efforts to occupy a middle ground acceptable to the USSR, United States and United Nations. His claim to this position required American acceptance of his attitude. But Kennedy's successor, Lyndon Baines Johnson, was the opposite of a big-idea man: he dealt with crude power politics. This precluded a successful dialogue with Nasser to reach an inclusive understanding of Middle East problems; in fact, the record of their brief correspondence reveals the opposite. Johnson was much more concerned with being elected to office, and quarrelling with Nasser, or the image Nasser had in the American media, was a sure vote-winner among Jews. The gate to the 1967 Arab-Israeli War swung wide open the moment Johnson became President.

Johnson and Nasser had an instinctive dislike for each other. Johnson thought accommodating Nasser was beneath the dignity of the United States, and Nasser thought Johnson was a crude, unthinking Texan. In the background, the problem of the civil war in Yemen was still there and so were Johnson's resentment of Nasser's attitude towards Western policies in the Congo and his neutralist anti-Vietnam War stance. Johnson's reaction to these problems was to withhold much-needed wheat sales to Egypt, then to agree to supply in instalments. Nasser interpreted this as blackmail, an attempt to coerce Egypt into changing its policies.

In 1965 things got worse. Johnson was courting Israel openly and to Nasser this upset the balance of the diplomatic even-handedness to which he had grown accustomed under Kennedy. Israeli Prime Minister Levi Eshkol, cleverly seeing an opening to drive a wedge between the two sides, spoke glowingly of US-Israeli relations and Johnson was not reassuring.

Johnson then went further and agreed to supply Jordan with arms at a time when it was conducting a serious quarrel with Nasser.

Although Nasser continued to try to mend relations, his dislike of Johnson showed in everything he did. In an attempt to explain the Egyptian position to Johnson, he dispatched Anwar Sadat to Washington and invited US Vice-President Hubert Humphrey to visit Egypt. But it was no use: the two leaders' antipathy towards each other was mutual. For example, a simple request by Johnson for a picture of Nasser to include in his gallery of portraits of world statesmen met with an intemperate rebuff. Johnson seethed with anger.

But it was a series of incidents in 1967 which made war unavoidable. It began when the CIA's Yemen offices, operating under the cover of aid workers, were attacked by Yemeni partisans of Nasser. Both the US government and the CIA were upset. In March 1967 the situation between Syria and Israel grew even more tense over grazing rights in the no man's land which separated the two countries. Simultaneously, USSR Premier Kosygin sent Nasser a message saying that Israel was about to attack Syria. While Nasser was considering what to do, Jordanian propaganda, controlled by CIA agent John Fistere, unleashed vicious radio attacks against him accusing him of being a paper tiger who wouldn't come to the aid of another Arab country and who hid behind the United Nations Emergency Force (UNEF), the troops stationed after the Suez War to keep Egypt and Israel apart. The Jordanian taunts persisted and they were successful in undermining Nasser's standing with the Arab people – one thing he never tolerated.

When the USSR's warnings of an imminent Israeli attack on Syria persisted, Nasser sent the Egyptian army into Sinai and asked UNEF to evacuate several posts along his frontier with Israel. In a surprising and stupid move, UN Secretary-General U Thant responded to Nasser's request by pulling out all of the UNEF troops. Confronted with the prospect of war, Nasser did two contradictory things at the same time: he dispatched messages to Johnson and De Gaulle stating that he had no intention of starting a war and he stationed Egyptian troops at Sharm Al Sheikh, the gateway to the Israeli port of Eilat. Israel claimed it was being blockaded; Nasser helped Israel by refusing to clarify the situation. The CIA, angry over the Yemen incident, obtained Johnson's agreement and told the Israelis to strike. On 6 June 1967 Israel attacked.

It took six days for Israel to achieve total victory over the combined armies of Egypt, Syria and Jordan – King Hussein had joined the fray to avoid being toppled by his pro-Nasser people. Israel occupied Gaza and Sinai, the West Bank and the Golan Heights. Humiliated beyond his worst dreams, Nasser first accused the West of colluding with Israel then offered to resign. Spontaneous demonstrations demanding that he withdraw his resignation erupted in Cairo and throughout the Arab world. He did retract his resignation and accused, then arrested, several officers and ministers and charged them with negligence. The defendants included his old colleague and comrade in arms, the commander of the Egyptian army, Field Marshal Abdel Hakim Amer. Later, he began to mend his fences with his erstwhile Arab enemies, in particular Saudi Arabia.

The 1967 War, tellingly and insultingly referred to as the Six Day War, ended the Arab nationalist movement. Nasser met, in Khartoum in September 1967, fellow Arab leaders, ended the Yemen war and made a declaration against any negotiations, recognition or peace with Israel. But the proclamation was an empty gesture; Nasser wanted out. This is when he, without much fanfare, agreed to cede the leadership of the confrontation with Israel to the PLO. It was the act of a tired, broken man who, having been defeated in his two objectives of uniting the Arabs and defeating Israel, was to become sad and despondent with time.

The Nasser who survived the 1967 War was a shadow of his former self. After the initial popular support, in Egypt, students and workers rioted and asked for the restoration of democracy. Regionally his crusade against the traditional regimes ceased because of his dependence on the oil-producing countries for financial support to replace his income from the blocked Suez Canal. The Palestinian problem was soon placed under the PLO and Yasser Arafat. The West, unlike after the 1956 Suez War, was united in wanting to see him diminished. The USSR, though it still supported him and supplied him with arms, knew that things could never be the same again.

He looked for a way out, but there wasn't one. In 1969, he started a war of attrition against Israel aimed at recovering Sinai and the reopening of the Suez Canal. Israel responded with ferocity and Israeli air force raids deep into Egypt humiliated him. Early in 1970, in an interview with the French journalist-diplomat Eric Roulou, he sued for peace with Israel.[30] Nobody responded, nobody cared. Then, in June of that year, he accepted the peace plan of US Secretary of State Rogers, a variation on UN resolution 242 and the 'land for peace' principle, against strong Arab opposition, particularly from the PLO's Yasser Arafat.

In late September 1970 he chaired a meeting of Arab heads of state to settle the problems between the PLO and King Hussein, the savage fighting in Amman which later became known as Black September. He succeeded, but the effort took its toll and he died of a heart attack on 28 September, the ninth anniversary of the break-up of the UAR.

With Nasser's death, the Arab masses lost their father figure. Millions of wailing Egyptians followed his cortège, every Arab government declared a period of mourning, radio and television stations repeated his speeches and eulogized him for days on end and among the people there were suicides, miscarriages, and endless expressions of despair. The common thread of grief amounted to the refrain 'How dare he leave us?'

It would be easy to describe Nasser as a failure whom popular history made a hero and leave it at that, but there is more to it. In terms of losing every war he fought, Nasser was a failure. His Arab unity schemes, be they calls for union or a united Arab stand, did not succeed. His efforts to free the Middle East from outside influences came to naught. Even his land and other reforms met with only marginal success and his Arab Socialist Union, the quasi-parliamentary body created to articulate his agenda for Egypt and the Arab world, never got very far. Despite all this, he was the most popular Arab leader this century. Why?

To me, it is because Nasser was the ultimate Arab, the one man who represented Arab dreams, complexes and foibles against Western hegemony. His quarrels with the West can be judged as an expression of the complex relationship between the Arabs and the West. The core of this relationship was an intrinsic desire on his part to be understood and respected and a consequent desire to be left alone and free. In this, he was the average Arab. And to this day the average Arab wants nothing more than a recognition of his or her rights against Western strategic interests and commitment to special interest groups.

Nasser's desire to do battle with Israel, if necessary, and his belief that only through attaining military parity could a just peace be achieved, were also the instinctive feelings of the Arab masses. It was and is the humiliation of defeat that the Arabs resent most, and this, along with the desire for unity and democracy, are sentiments the West refuses to understand.

Perhaps most importantly, Nasser came very close to breaking the back of the abusive pro-West Arab establishment. He was a humble family man who loved folk music, played chess and took pride in Muslim and Arab tradition. On the other hand, the Arab leaders who competed with him, even when they were not an extension of the regimes which followed the First World War, were an expression of the tyranny of the chosen few against the people. Their allegiance was to the West, their protector. Nasser's relations with the West failed because he refused to relegate the Arab people to nonentities. He represented the other option: an understanding with the West based on the will of the people. The West, even America, turned him down.

The journalist Wilton Wynn, a man who knew Nasser and wrote one of his earlier biographies, called his book *Nasser, The Search for Dignity.* I cannot think of a more apt description of what Nasser stood for. Regardless of success or failure, the Arab people are still pursuing this search and remembering Nasser.

If Nuri Saïd was the ultimate example of subservience and Nasser was the leading renegade of the century, then Faisal bin Abdel Aziz Al Saud, third king of Saudi Arabia (1964–75) and the self-appointed guardian of traditional Bedouin and Islamic values, is the man whose life reveals the effectiveness and shortcomings of the harmony between Western interests and those of the traditional Arab governing classes. Because the West's special relationship with the House of Saud is the only one which started early this century and continues to this day, examining it through Faisal tells us a great deal about the nature of these relationships and how they produced the Islamic threat which confronts us today.

Born in 1905, the third son of the desert kingdom's founder, Ibn Saud, Faisal grew up in accordance with the norms of his time. As a child, he wandered around barefoot, learned to ride horses bareback and started his day at the crack of dawn. But he was luckier than most children of his Bedouin monarch father; his mother's early death and the presence of many brothers and sisters found him living with his maternal grandparents, the Al Shaikhs, a distant branch of the House of Saud known for their Islamic learning. This gave Faisal an opportunity unavailable to other members of his family to read the Koran and the Hadiths of the Prophet, to acquire an Islamic education to add to the native, folk one he got from his father.

Beyond his Al Shaikh training and Bedouin upbringing, little is known about Faisal's childhood, but he appears to have caught his father's eye when he was in his early teens. In 1919 his father sent him to London to represent him in discussions about the kingdom's boundaries and regional position in place of his oldest surviving son, Saud. Faisal was a lad of fourteen, and most of the discussions with the British were conducted by his relation, guardian and travelling companion, Ahmad Thuniyan. However, the gesture of bypassing the heir apparent was not lost on his hosts.

Faisal's admirers, including many Western writers, are full of praise for his diplomatic skills and the degree to which he impressed his British hosts. In fact, the whole trip reveals nothing more than a smiling young man in full Arab regalia whose presence aroused curiosity and attempts at civil accommodation by his hosts, including the British monarch.

The same can be said of his ensuing reputation as a military leader, which started with the campaign to conquer Asir, the area north of Yemen, in 1923. Admirers insist that Faisal was a born strategist and leader of men, but there is not much support for this either. Nor, given his father's elevation of all his children to military commanders at an early age, did his assumption of informal generalship amount to anything special. Even his subsequent participation in the 1924–5 conquest of the Hijaz and occupation of the holy cities of Mecca and Medina produced very little of special note. Moreover, assuming responsibility for either campaign would have saddled Faisal with their consequences, which, among other crimes, included the butchery of hundreds of innocent people in the cities of Taif, Mecca and Medina.

Faisal's lack of achievement notwithstanding, his father still appointed him Viceroy of the Hijaz and Foreign Minister soon after he unified Saudi Arabia, in 1926, when Faisal was only twenty-one. This was a considerably more important move than the previous ones, for the Hijaz was home to the holy cities of Mecca and Medina, and Saudi Arabia was beginning to make an appearance on the world stage. But, once again, the reason Faisal was chosen for these two important posts is simpler than his admirers' interpretations allow. He was the second-eldest surviving son and the eldest, Saud, was meagrely endowed and busy assisting his father in his daily Bedouin chores in Riyadh. This is not to say that Faisal's informal education didn't place him above the rest of his brothers and in a better position to handle the representatives of foreign powers who continued to headquarter in the port city of Jedda and away from the Bedouin capital of Riyadh.

Indeed there is no dismissing the importance of the appointments which Faisal used to chart his future. Control of the holy cities meant contact with Muslims and the Muslim governments throughout the world and being Foreign Minister exposed him to the thinking of the Western powers. By the early 1930s Faisal was the only member of his family who could claim a solid Bedouin background, a measure of Islamic learning and knowledge of the thinking of the rest of the Muslim world, and an appreciation for the policies of the Western powers. He stood head and shoulders above the rest of his clan.

However, in reality, there was only one decision-maker in Saudi Arabia, Ibn Saud himself, and Faisal's emergence during the 1930s and subsequent elevation to spokesman for his country in international forums has to be seen in this context. Though his positions afforded him exposure, there is not a single event which suggests that Faisal had a policy or that he managed to move his father in any specific direction.

It is true that he toured Europe soon after he became Foreign Minister, visited the Soviet Union in 1932 and made an extensive coast-to-coast journey of the United States in 1944, but these trips produced nothing concrete. Yet there is evidence to suggest that the man had an inquisitive mind and was a fast learner. He impressed his European hosts with his interest in the consequences of the First World War, spoke with knowledge of the history of the Muslims in the Soviet Union and behaved in a non-committal and impeccable way towards the American oil men who guided him through the United States.

It was not until 1945 that the world, and the Arabs, got to know Faisal. His father was still alive and very much the sole decision-maker in his kingdom, but a new world was rising from the ashes of war, and the hitherto reticent representative of the desert kingdom had to speak at the United Nations conference in San Francisco. His country was a founding member of the new world organization and it was an occasion to introduce it to the world community. Faisal spoke in general terms of the wish for world peace and hopes for the United Nations Organization, and he spoke well. In addition, his colourful presence, his easy manner and impeccable presentation made an excellent impression on the world delegates attending the conference.

Here it is important to expand our assessment of the man making the speech by examining the country he was representing and Saudi Arabia's claim to a position within the world community. In 1932 Faisal married his fourth wife, Iffat Al Thuniyan, a distant relation who was brought up and educated in Turkey. Because of her background and relatively advanced views on the education of women, in Saudi Arabia she became known as 'the teacher'. There is little doubt that she represented an influence on Faisal's life, even if we base this judgement on the simple fact that he never married after her.

The country that Faisal represented at the UN conference and before it was an absolute feudal monarchy run by a brutal Bedouin ruler. Not only did it contain Islam's holiest shrines, but, beginning in 1939, it produced oil. It had been created with British help and the more advanced part of it, the Hijaz, had been taken away from the more sophisticated Hashemites when Hussein I quarrelled with the British over fulfilment of promises made during the First World War (see Chapter 7). Ibn Saud had no overt pan-Arab ambitions and he had signed several treaties with Britain in which he ceded the conduct of his country's foreign policy to them, beginning in 1915.[31] He accepted the hegemony of Western powers.

Faisal's emergence on the world stage should be judged against this background. He wasn't highly educated, polished or an exceptional speaker, but he was significant because he came from Saudi Arabia, a country which had accepted indirect Western control and the least advanced of the independent Arab countries of the time. The Iraqis and Egyptians fielded better people, but rightly they were judged by a different yardstick. Faisal was a star when judged by the standards of his country.

The celebration of Faisal as the impressive representative of a Bedouin kingdom took a different turn in 1947. Sent by his father to New York to participate in the UN debates over the future of Palestine, he experienced his first disappointment in Western policy and discovered the limits of the relationship which existed between his country and the West. The Americans, having secured the oil concessions in the 1930s against weak competition, had replaced Britain as Saudi Arabia's financial supporters and Ibn Saud had met President Roosevelt in Egypt in 1945 and obtained a promise of impartiality on, if not of support for, the Arab position on Palestine. But President Truman wasn't as committed to this notion as Roosevelt and he needed the Jewish vote to be re-elected president in 1948. At the UN, the Truman administration supported the Zionist plans wholeheartedly. The Arabs and Faisal were defeated, but Faisal saw the whole thing as a personal affront.[32] It was his first encounter with the hard facts of international relations.

In this regard Faisal's reaction was totally Bedouin. Dignity came before all else and it was the indignity of being betrayed by a country which he and his father considered to be a friend which mattered most to him. After all, the Kingdom was beginning to produce more oil and the existence of its vast reserves was already an accepted fact. The United States had negotiated an agreement to build the airbase at Dhahran and had a substantial air force presence there. However hurt Faisal was, what prevailed was Ibn Saud's policy and this meant continued cooperation with the United States and refusal to heed Arab appeals to use the oil as a diplomatic weapon.[33] Placing the overall US-Saudi relationship above Bedouin feelings and Arab interests was the approach Faisal himself followed all his life.

Ibn Saud died in 1953 and was succeeded by his son Saud. Faisal, as expected, remained Foreign Minister and became heir apparent. Because Saud was incompetent and had no experience in foreign affairs, everybody expected Faisal to stamp his imprint on the foreign policy of his country. To the Arab masses, Faisal was the brooding prince who was hurt most of all by the Arab defeats at the UN in 1947 and in the 1948 War.

American oil men, enamoured with the openness of his father and brothers, viewed Faisal's remoteness with unease bordering on fear. The United States and Britain watched his every move. What policies Faisal would follow became a guessing game for foreign and Arab journalists. Even Arab governments – and Nasser had just emerged in Egypt in 1952

– expected dramatic changes from the days of the desert warrior who founded the Kingdom. In fact, nothing happened.

In 1953–4 an opportunity presented itself to Faisal. Doing the right thing for the wrong reason, King Saud listened to greedy advisers who wanted to make huge commissions and created a tanker company in partnership with the Greek shipping magnate Aristotle Onassis to carry Saudi oil to the world. It was a move in the Saudi national interest which the Americans opposed strenuously. Faisal did nothing to help his brother against American pressure and CIA interference. The mystery man kept his secret; he refused to oppose America. The deal collapsed and Saudi Arabia was the loser.

But in the Middle East there is never a shortage of situations to force people to take positions that reveal their hands. This time it was the decision to create the Baghdad Pact which required a response. The inclusion of Iraq, an Arab country under the Hashemite foes of the Saud dynasty, prompted Faisal to act. He attacked the Pact, consulted its main opponent, Nasser, and declared that the Middle East should be free of alliances with outside powers.

This sudden exposure of a foreign policy merits analysis. The position taken by Faisal at this point was the one he followed for the rest of his life, and it governed his later behaviour towards Nasser and Arab nationalism, the question of reforms at home and the conduct of his country's oil policy. Faisal opposed the Baghdad Pact because he saw in it a threat to the House of Saud. His objection to foreign alliances was deceitful: Saudi Arabia itself was bound to the United States through secret agreements going back to 1947.[34] What Faisal objected to was Iraq's assumption of position as the West's primary client and friend in the Middle East. His *de facto* alliance with Nasser against the Baghdad Pact was one of convenience for, as Nasser was to discover later, the House of Saud always joined forces with people who afforded it direct or indirect protection. The difference of opinion with the West that his opposition to the Pact demonstrated was no more than a lovers' quarrel; as in future situations he wanted Western support and friendship exclusively for himself and Saudi Arabia.

Strangely, this act of cynicism gained him popularity among the Arab people. Few knew of the secret alliance agreements with the United States and most weren't concerned with the presence of a huge American airbase on Saudi Arabia's soil. What the Arab people accepted was Faisal's opposition to an anti-communist pact and they saw his amity with Nasser as a wish to confront Israel.

This misunderstanding in 1955 over the Baghdad Pact was followed by the Suez crisis of 1956, a much more serious affair which divided the Arab world between pro-Nasser and anti-West camps and the opposite. In this case, Faisal's decision to oppose the invasion chimed with that of America. It was a popular Arab move and it pleased his protectors.

This was a very shrewd move which kept the reaction of the pro-Nasser Saudi people in check. But it also undermined the leader of the Hashemite bloc and Baghdad Pact, Nuri Saïd, the man who urged the British to attack Nasser and vied with Faisal for Western affection. Thirdly, it improved Faisal's credentials with the United States, the country upon which Faisal and Saudi Arabia depended for protection. By opposing the invasion, Faisal had nothing to lose.

The late 1950s in Saudi Arabia were marked by competition between Faisal and his brother King Saud as to who ran the country and its foreign policy. Saud, though a kind man, was an ignoramus and a bungler who fluctuated between supporting Nasser and opposing him. But compared with Faisal, America considered Saud a more reliable ally and thought of backing him as Middle East leader against Nasser. Faisal's response to this was not to espouse Nasser, but to send the Americans messages declaring his allegiance[35] and, in 1957, to follow America in opposing Nasser by sending Saudi troops to Jordan to protect it against the partisans of the Egyptian leader. The American response to the messages and the Jordan move was positive: they gave up on Saud and began supporting Faisal. The Americans went further and proclaimed the Eisenhower Doctrine, the anti-communist, anti-Nasser declaration which gave President Eisenhower the power to respond to friendly calls to intervene militarily in the Middle East without consulting Congress. Faisal, the former ally of Nasser, followed America in opposing the Egyptian leader and accepted the Eisenhower Doctrine without reservation.

Nineteen fifty-eight was to prove a key year for Faisal, Saudi Arabia, the Middle East and Western interests in the area. That was the year of the emergence of the United Arab Republic and the Western-supported Arab Federation. Saudi Arabia felt isolated and threatened, even a pro-West union could turn into a magnet for advocates of Arab unity. Then suddenly, on 14 July 1958, the Iraqi army overthrew the monarchy and established a republic.

The elimination of the rival Hashemite dynasty was only a problem in terms of the possibility of republican Iraq joining Nasser's UAR. It took Faisal a week to recognize the new Iraqi regime, well after most Arab countries and Britain had done so. In this case, unlike in his opposition to Western-sponsored alliances and the invasion of Suez, Faisal supported the landing of American troops in Lebanon and British troops in Jordan for possible use against a pro-Nasser Iraqi regime. This was added confirmation that Faisal and the United States had designated Nasser as a major danger to their common interests.

It was then, between 1958 and 1960, that Faisal and the United States began exaggerating the communist threat to the Middle East. The CIA, with Faisal's full support, began promoting Islam as a counterweight to Nasser and Communism. The anti-Nasser Muslim Brotherhood was funded,[36] religious leaders were prodded to attack the USSR and Nasser's socialism, and small, CIA-sponsored Muslim cells opposed to Arab nationalism were created within Saudi Arabia itself.[37]

Faisal's promotion of his country's Muslim identity at the expense of its Arab one was another ill-conceived Western-sponsored move to keep the Arabs apart. He took this dangerous step because the Saudi identity, localism, was not a strong enough bond to confront Nasser. Horrified Arab writers and thinkers opposed this and spoke of its unsoundness as a long-term solution, but it was no use: Faisal and America adopted Islam as the way out.

Developments during the early 1960s reinforced Faisal's commitment to an Islamic direction. In August 1962 one of Faisal's brothers, Prince Tallal bin Abdel Aziz, a former Minister of Finance, defected to Nasser and formed the Free Princes (Saudi) movement. Then, in November, the Yemeni monarchy was overthrown and replaced by a pro-Nasser regime. The hiatus, a temporary Nasser eclipse, which followed Syria's secession from the UAR was replaced by a reinvigoration of Nasser's Arab nationalism. At this juncture Faisal's espousal of Islam took another form. With outside and internal threats undermining the House of Saud, he moved towards an overt confrontation with Nasser.

First, Faisal decided to deny Nasser hegemony over Yemen and tried to re-establish the country's monarchy. Finding that Imam Ahmad Al Badr had survived the pro-Nasser coup, he wasted no time in providing backward Yemeni monarchists with money and arms to undermine the new regime. And Faisal followed that by an attempt to promote his Islamic ideology by buying the loyalty of regionally influential Beirut newspapers and magazines and to wage a campaign against Nasser's Arab nationalism. Of course, support for the Muslim Brotherhood, Jama'yat Islam in Pakistan and other Islamic groups continued unabated.

But once again, as in 1947 and the American support for Israel, American and Saudi policy were not in full agreement. President Kennedy, while committed to the defence of Saudi Arabia and its security, was an admirer of the modern and progressive Nasser. Kennedy did not support Nasser, but he was for an American accommodation with Arab nationalism and dead set against some of the internal policies of the Saudi regime. In 1962, when Faisal was visiting Washington, Kennedy prevailed on him to issue a proclamation abolishing slavery and extracted a promise towards the creation of a consultative council as a way of affording the Saudis participation in the running of their country. This was followed by repeated impartial attempts by Kennedy to stop the Yemeni war raging between pro-Nasser and pro-Saudi forces.

Faisal was aghast. To him the Saudi-American policy of promoting Islam was all-inclusive. For Kennedy to point out the shortcomings of the regime behind them undermined this policy. Furthermore, this policy called for support of the traditional monarchist regimes in the Yemen and other places. Kennedy, while accepting the principle of Islam as a counterweight to Nasser, was trying to achieve a balance. Unlike Britain, America always suffered from a commitment to representative government and found it difficult to condone certain patterns of behaviour among its Middle East allies – something Faisal could not understand.

The inevitable accession of Faisal to the Saudi throne took place in 1964 after a foolish attempt by Saud to regain control of the country. At this point, the increasing American dependence on oil and the recent death of the far-seeing Kennedy produced a discarding of ideology and a reversion to uncritical support of the traditional regimes. In fact, it was the American dependence on Saudi oil which became a policy, a crude one articulated by Lyndon Baines Johnson. The Johnson years were the golden years of Saudi pan-Islamic policy.

The Secretary-General of a Faisal front organization, the World Muslim League, Muhammad Sabbah, was elevated to the post of minister. Saudi Arabia, with American support, invited Pakistani troops to protect the oilfields. Johnson equipped and trained the Saudi National Guard to protect the House of Saud. There was nobody to counsel Faisal against following retrogressive policies in Yemen. The attempts to get him to clean up his backyard came to an end and he allowed his brother-in-law and adviser, Kamal Adham, to realize a whole 2 per cent of the oil income of an oil concession that Faisal gave the Japanese in the Neutral Zone between his country and Kuwait.

It was back to 1917 and dependence on corrupt deputy sheriffs.

This was what existed in 1967. The Israeli victory in the Six Day War owed much to the fact that over 70,000 of Egypt's best troops were fighting Faisal-sponsored tribesmen in Yemen. Fighting Israel and Islam at the same time defeated Nasser and broke the back of the Arab nationalist movement. Nasser's battlefield defeat assumed a larger dimension: it amounted to a defeat of his secular policies.

The defeat was followed by a meeting of Arab leaders in Khartoum in September 1967. Ostensibly Faisal and Nasser made up and the oil-rich countries offered Nasser financial assistance. But it was Faisal's day, and being beholden to Faisal financially forced Nasser to stop his propaganda attacks against the traditional regimes, Islamic movements, and to settle the Yemen war. Even luck came to Faisal's aid, and in 1969 a crazed Australian Christian fundamentalist, Denis Michael Rohan, set fire to the Aqsa Mosque in Jerusalem and gave Faisal an opening to convene a Muslim heads-of-state conference in Rabat, Morocco, which allowed him to wrest the responsibility of Jerusalem from Arab nationalism and claim it as an Islamic issue. Western-sponsored Islamic fundamentalism was on the march.

The decline of Nasser meant that there was no one to stop the Faisal-West plans to promote Islam except the Saudi people. From 1967 to 1973 there were the greatest internal attempts to overthrow the Saudi monarchy in the history of the country. These failed, because America had succeeded in creating an elaborate internal security system and provided the country with personnel, including the seconding to the Saudis of the local CIA station chief. But, despite Nasser's death, these manifestations of internal unrest and the failure of Sadat to recover Sinai from Israel meant that Faisal was still vulnerable and exposed to accusations of failure. This, inadvertently, led to the October 1973 War and the oil embargo which followed it.

The question about the oil embargo in the West: How could a friendly government do this to us? ignores the facts of what preceded the actual happening. Faisal needed to show that his Islamic policies were producing results. He believed that doing nothing about the Arab-Israeli problem would lead to serious internal and regional turmoil. He tried to defuse the situation resulting from the continued Israeli occupation of Sinai, the Golan Heights and the West Bank and Gaza by providing the West with reasons to solve the problem.

In 1973 Faisal prevailed on Sadat to reduce his links with the USSR and to follow a more pro-Saudi and pro-American policy. Sadat accepted the plan and expelled Russian advisers and distanced himself from the USSR. Sadat went further and sent several messages containing peace offers to America. But America did nothing (see Chapter 5). Faisal, afraid that Egypt might revert to radical politics time and again pleaded with America, directly and through the press, to apply pressure on Israel. He went as far as using ARAMCO's Frank Jungers as an intermediary. There was no response; America, which would have responded to the same moves by Nasser, took its friends for granted.

Radicalism was being reignited and this and rumblings within Saudi Arabia were endangering Faisal's position as a Muslim leader. When Sadat, severely under pressure because of his many promises to his people to regain Sinai, told Faisal of his decision to go to war Faisal had no option but to promise to support him.

What followed, the actual embargo, was the result of a series of mishaps and not the product of a clear-cut Saudi policy to strangle the West economically. The war started on 6 October and Faisal immediately offered Egypt $200 million worth of aid. On 12 October, hoping to intercept an American decision to come to the assistance of Israel, Faisal and other Arab oil producers announced a 5 per cent reduction in their output. On 16 October this was increased to 10 per cent, and there was a promise of a further 5 per cent cut every month.

In the middle of all this a Saudi envoy, Omar Saqqaf, was dispatched to see President Nixon to ask him to make a statement pleasing to the Arabs to help Faisal avoid a confrontation. But Nixon was in the middle of the Watergate scandal and needed internal support. Instead of helping Faisal to get around the pressures building up on him and to revert to his natural pro-West position, Nixon decided to supply Israel with $2.2 billion worth of arms. Faisal's response was forced on him.

It was Sheikh Zayyed of Abu Dhabi who answered Nixon by announcing a total oil embargo. The pressures on Faisal to follow suit came from every direction, from within his country, the Arab world and the Muslim world. He was caught; he had to follow Zayyed's lead.

The Saudis went to work to lift the embargo the moment it was in place. Faisal was not only against harming the West and America economically, but was convinced that high oil prices were good for Russia. The records of the Kissinger–Faisal meetings during the three months which followed the embargo reveal a desire for a face-saving formula to end it as soon as possible. Simultaneously, in February 1974, Faisal had no problem in journeying to Pakistan to attend the Islamic conference and be received as a hero of the embargo.

Soon, with popular passions down, and deciding that the embargo had already served his Islamic leadership, Faisal ordered its lifting in March 1974. He got no American concessions for the Egyptians or the Palestinians. What he got was the semblance of a Muslim leader able to stand up to the West and a quadrupling of the oil price.

Faisal was assassinated in March 1975 by an unstable nephew who was avenging a Muslim zealot brother whom Faisal had executed. Despite the personal nature of the act, Saudi propaganda labelled him a martyr and made veiled references to the oil embargo and Faisal's statements about wishing to pray in Jerusalem. In fact, it was America and the West which lost a valuable ally and viewed the future of the kingdom with unease.

Faisal's relations with the West must be judged in terms of the issues which joined them and appeared to separate them: Palestine, the Yemen war, internal reforms, oil and the confrontation between Islam and Arab nationalism. How Faisal responded to these issues and what his policies produced differed from what appeared to be happening, and this includes the oil embargo. Unlike those of Nuri and Nasser, Faisal's policies eluded people.

Faisal's Palestinian policies were a failure. From 1947 until the end of his life, his commitment to avoiding confrontation with the West came before his commitment to the Arab position on Palestine. He and his father refused to use the oil weapon in 1948; Saudi Arabia consistently declined to send troops to fight on the Arab side and his eventual resort to the oil weapon was forced on him and he used it reluctantly and lifted the embargo before it could produce results. Above all, by opposing Nasser when the latter was allied to the USSR and had a chance to achieve military parity with Israel, resulting in a just solution, Faisal demonstrated that his feudal pro-West preoccupation with confronting Russia mattered more than Palestine.

The Yemen problem differed substantially. In this case, it was Kennedy's obvious sympathies with the republican regime which created a crisis between him and Faisal. The detestable monarchy and what it stood for were supported by a Faisal who, seeing himself as the spokesman for the traditional establishment, sought total support from America and the West. Both sides wanted regional stability but differed as to how it might be achieved. Unfortunately, Kennedy's death and Johnson's succession eliminated the need for the United States to make a decision on a balance between its wish to please the Arab people and blanket support for traditional regimes.

When it comes to internal reforms, the West failed to move Faisal in the right direction. Corruption continued unabated, though he used the sophisticated method of paying his family and friends indirectly, by giving them huge tracts of land worth billions of dollars, and he made no attempt to curb the behaviour of members of his family. His response to Kennedy's demand for involving the people in the business of governance was short-lived and vanished under Johnson. As in Yemen, what the West wanted were minimum reforms to enable Saudi Arabia to continue strong, but Saudi absolutism prevailed.

Faisal's oil policies, despite the 1973 embargo, were solidly pro-West. His forced use of the oil weapon was brief and without results. He resisted the increases in the oil prices advocated by the Shah of Iran and others because high oil prices were good for the USSR and bad for the West. He went further; he instructed Oil Minister Ahmad Zakki Yamani to engineer a decline in the price of this commodity and deposited his country's huge surpluses in Western banks and certificates of deposit when other oil producers were realizing greater benefits using their surpluses differently.

Above all, it is Faisal's rejection of Arab nationalism and adoption of an anti-communist Islam which produced the greatest effect on the Middle East. In this, except for differences of detail, Faisal and the West were one. They used Islam to oppose communism and destroy the secular forces calling for change in the traditional structure of Middle East governments and society. The Faisal-West efforts succeeded, but the Islamic movements helped and created by this effort were always unaware of why they were supported, and they are now making their own militant claim without reference to it. These are the Islamic movements which have replaced the secular forces and which now represent a greater danger to Western interests than Nasser ever did. This proves that the clash between the West and popular movements is built-in.

In deciding on the issues of Palestine, Yemen, internal reforms, oil and supporting Islam instead of nationalism, Faisal's policies were those of a Bedouin chief who agreed with the West and did not reflect the feelings and attitude of his people. His quarrels with the West were on how to implement the same policies, and were no more than minor differences of opinion.

There are several conclusions to be drawn from examining the lives and policies of Nuri, Nasser and Faisal. Nuri's policies of total subservience and subsequent total Western support were a failure. The difference between the interests of the Iraqi people and those of the West and their deputy produced a disaster: the overthrow of the monarchy and the continuing instability of Iraq. Nasser represents an attempt at reconciling the conflicts between Arab and Western interests. He failed, and his failure renders questionable all attempts by the two sides to overcome what separates them. Faisal fell somewhere in the middle. His pro-West position assumed the existence of Western policies which supported the establishment in a subtle way which required providing the Arab people with a traditional ideology acceptable to them and not in conflict with the West. In a way, Faisal's was a much more serious failure than even Nuri's because the West has seen fit to oppose the Islamic ideology it created the moment this ideology began responding to the wishes of the common man. Taking those points together, one may conclude that the West remains more committed to those who do not respond to their people and opposed to anything which takes the Arab people into consideration.

9 · The Players

No understanding of the relationship between the Arab Middle East and the West is complete without an appreciation of the human factor, the British and American individuals who, through acts of omission, commission or sheer lack of understanding or talent or both, contributed towards its structural unhealthiness and its present sad state.

The historical enmity between the Arabs and the West began with the rise of Islam. Unlike Oriental religions, Islam could not be ignored because it shares and challenges some of the tenets of Christianity and Judaism, and this includes demoting Christ to a secondary position after Muhammad. The Crusades, though in essence expressions of greed, a spirit of adventure and the competition between European princes and kingdoms, were justified by the inherent differences between Christianity and Islam. However, the Crusaders failed to wrest control of Christian holy places from the hands of the infidels and in the sixteenth century this failure was followed by Ottoman Turkey's Islamic penetration of Europe and the Siege of Vienna. After the Crusades and Turkish encroachment on Christian Europe confirmed Islam as the enemy, the conflict between the two sides lay dormant until the First World War. In the intervening period, for various reasons to do with maintaining the Ottoman Empire in order to keep a precarious balance between the European powers, the West kept in abeyance its natural inclinations to control the Arab Middle East.

As we have seen, the leaders and generals who claimed the Middle East for the West early this century recalled the historical enmity between Islam and the West to justify their conquest. This state of mind superseded the practical considerations of the area's strategic importance, immediate though minor commercial interests and the prospect of discovering oil. In fact, it was this inherent anti-Muslim attitude which defined the practical considerations and the behaviour of the West after its conquest of the Middle East.

With time this attitude contributed towards the evolution of a policy, an amalgam of historical prejudices and the colonial state of mind of the time. This policy took shape at a time when the Arab Middle East was emerging from Ottoman Turkey's control and hundreds of years of socio-logical, economic and political decay. In most places local conditions were used to support the Western contention that the Arabs were incapable of managing their own affairs and to justify their resort to using or creating local leaders beholden to them to guarantee stability and their hegemony over the region.

It was a new, unique approach aimed at indirect control which differed from the purely colonial one employed in other parts of the world and which came into being after the British and French had already occupied the region. The process of arriving at this policy involved a relatively long period of trial and error which included the need to locate local pro-West leaders. This delay produced a situation which afforded the Western officers and agents on the ground considerable room to interpret their missions in a highly personal way. This is why so many more field opera-tives left an indelible personal imprint on events than would have been the case had there been a clearer line from the start, or had they been restricted by precedent.

Among other things, the ability of officers on the ground to follow their own interpretations as to what should be done explains the contradictions between the promises they made to local leaders and what eventually happened. For example, the importance of the correspondence between Hussein I and Sir Henry McMahon, in which the latter promised to make Hussein King of the Arabs in return for help against Turkey, goes beyond the contents of the letters exchanged. It should be judged in terms of whether McMahon was acting on his own, making unauthorized, unbind-ing and illegal promises or whether his letters reflected official policy in London. The same is true of the work of Captain William Shakespeare, the officer sent to liaise with Ibn Saud, and whether he exceeded official policy through constant disregard of his instructions. This penchant for making on-the-spot decisions was certainly true of St John Philby when he represented the British to Ibn Saud and when he later represented Ibn Saud to the British.

Considering the consequences of the personal inclinations and behaviour of the various officers and agents, one concludes that examining the record of these men, and woman, is as revealing as analysing the policies of their governments. Would the British have disowned Hussein I if he had not turned against them for failing to fulfil McMahon's promises? Indeed, did Gertrude Bell's obvious lack of belief in the Arabs as a cohesive cultural group capable of assuming a national identity influence her attitude towards the creation of an inherently unstable Iraq under a questionable government and the consequent behaviour of the latter? Was Glubb Pasha a mere British officer who followed his government's policy or did his religious belief in the redemption of Israel lead to his anti-Arab behaviour during the 1948 Arab-Israeli War?

The answers to these questions are conclusive: because of the lack of clear policies and a natural tendency to accept the word of its own, most of the time Britain trusted its agents and officers to follow their initiative. And even when they were following the official line, as in the case of Glubb, poor communications and the fluid situations on the ground meant that their prejudices still mattered as much as the policies they purported to implement. What the British did in the Middle East was as much the creation of McMahon, Shakespeare, Bell, Philby and Glubb as it was of Whitehall.

Strangely, this was true too of the Americans who became instrumental in shaping the Middle East of the 1940s, 50s and 60s. The United States also arrived on the scene without a clear practical policy towards the region. In the background there was America's commitment against colonialism, but it proved easier to advocate from a distance than to apply on the ground. The freedom of field officers to give personal interpretations to weighty matters, and the absence of experts in the State Department and in the higher echelons of the CIA, produced a situation where field officers pre-empted the policy-making process, either *de facto* or after what they did was adopted by their superiors in Washington. Judging that what the field people proposed or implemented was as good as anything it was capable of producing, the State Department discarded the traditional ideological commitment and sanctioned the unsound *realpolitik* proposals and actions of its operatives and often extended them.

It was the Damascus CIA station which decided to change the government of Syria repeatedly until the whole thing resembled a bad habit. It was the CIA agent Bill Eveland's penchant for high living which drove him into the arms of Lebanese President Camille Chamoun and a disastrous US policy towards that country. And nobody but the meddlesome James Russell Barracks would accept the wisdom of having an unpopular King Hussein foment trouble for Nasser in Syria and staked US policy and credibility on that unsound notion. Bent on leaving their personal imprint on events, the unqualified American agents had little time for traditional American ideology.

In both cases the inability of the British and American governments to develop coherent long-term policies towards the region was the key to what followed. Even when these governments were not particularly impressed with their field people and their abilities, they still followed them because they offered a way, even when it was invalid, out of a muddle. This is attested to by Churchill's accusation to Gertrude Bell that each Oriental agent had his or her 'Arab pet'.[1] Nor can we see the description by former CIA Middle East chief James Critchfield of the 1950s and 60s activities of some of his colleagues and subordinates as 'the cowboy era' as anything but condemnatory.[2] But neither assessment led to change. Churchill still followed the recommendations of his Orientalist-agents and Critchfield's rebuke had more to do with the unacceptable personal behaviour of some of his agents and produced no fundamental change in the attitude of the CIA or America towards the Arabs – only a more methodical way to replace and implement equally questionable operations.

The British and American traditions which formed the behaviour of their field people differed substantially. The thinking of the British agents and officers who appeared on the Middle East scene early this century was a continuation of the scholar Orientalists of the previous century. Most of the major players, certainly T.E. Lawrence, Harry St John Philby, Gertrude Bell and General Sir John Bagot Glubb, possessed literary talents. All romanticized the Arab in a semi-scholarly but often elegant way and in the process identified him with the pure, simple Bedouin. This was the only way they saw the Arabs, and this is why they disliked those who didn't fall within this definition, the great majority of the Arab people. It was a narrow historical vision, recently ably examined and found wanting by the Arab writers Edward Said and Rana Kabbani (in *Orientalism* and *Imperial Fictions*, respectively). Beginning as pretentious scholars with the British Empire behind them, they became larger-than-life agents who personalized a popular cult of romanticism, and the freedom of action they were allowed – or which they assumed or earned – elevated them to imperialists.

The Americans came to the Middle East scene differently. Their original presence was as missionaries, and it was extensive and covered Syria, Lebanon, Jordan, Palestine, Egypt and Iraq.[3] But their lack of success in converting local Muslims left them preaching to the converted Christians and led them to a change of direction in favour of becoming educators. From the early 1950s, after oil was discovered and commercialized, and America assumed responsibility for the West's regional strategic position, it was the descendants of the educators and missionaries who merged their original roles with agenting and became the protectors of American interests. It was the Blisses, Closes, Eddies, Penroses and others who combined the two functions and became the first American intelligence agents in the Middle East, originally working for the Office of Strategic Services and eventually for its successor, the CIA.

This first group of Americans suffered from a conflict which didn't exist among the British, in that their country's historical anti-imperialism implied some commitment to the people of the countries where they worked. But this version of American populism never flourished because, as with the British, but without concentrating on the image of the Bedouin, the American field operatives were more comfortable with the local people who provided them with what America wanted, the ruling classes who accepted that there was a communist threat to the Middle East, offered them oil concessions without taking the interests of the common man into consideration, and who were willing to accept American-sponsored solutions to the Arab-Israeli problem. And the second-generation American agents, the upstarts with no missionary or educational credentials who followed the first group, appearing on the Middle East scene in great numbers as a result of America's expanding world leadership role, inherited all the faults of the original group and none of their style, manners and kindness of heart.

I know of no British operatives or American agents who played a major role in determining the shape of the Middle East during the past century who really liked the Arabs. Setting aside the six subjects of this chapter, most British agents continued to see the Arab as a Bedouin and most Americans never formed a clear picture of what the Middle East needed, which went very far beyond a simple, genuine and foolish belief that America's ways were good for everyone.

The subjects of the six case-studies which follow, three Britons and three Americans, are people whose behaviour and actions contributed towards the problems of the Middle East as we experience them today. Gertrude Bell, Harry St John Philby, General Sir John Bagot Glubb, Miles Copeland, William Crane Eveland and John Fistere were people who either created, manipulated or maintained some countries of the Middle East. The acts of creation, manipulation and maintenance needed the cooperation of local chiefs, kings or colonels. It is through the interaction between the unprepared, twisted or self-serving players and their local unrepresentative and ill-equipped deputy sheriffs that we see why the relationship between the West and the Arabs hasn't worked. In fact, if one is permitted a dash of cynicism, the wonder is that things aren't much worse than they are.

Gertrude Margaret Lowthian Bell (1868–1926), the daughter of a rich ironmaster, was a linguist graduate of Oxford who wore Paris frocks and had Mayfair manners, an inveterate letter-writer and a bad judge of men. She was the leading female Orientalist-agent of her or any other time and, by all accounts, the major field contributor to the creation in 1921 of modern Iraq under a pro-British Hashemite monarchy.

It is for her notable contribution to creating one of the most important countries of the Middle East that Bell is best remembered. To this day, members of the Iraqi establishment shy from using her surname without reverentially prefixing it with 'Miss'. And collections of her letters are still in print, a source of satisfaction to admirers of turn-of-the-century romantic Orientalists as well as to students of Iraq. However, it is indeed the consequences of what she created, modern Iraq, which occupies and haunts us today. And this achievement, particularly for a female in that time and place, has to be judged not only in terms of the obvious lamentable results, but in accordance with what was available and possible at the time.

There is no doubting Bell's literary talents, spirit of adventure or energy. In the late 1880s, still in her early twenties, she travelled to Istanbul and became such a fixture of the city's diplomatic social circle that she managed to meet the visiting German Kaiser. But soon afterwards her restlessness drove her to Tehran, where she mastered Persian and translated the works of the fourteenth-century poet Hafiz. Travels to Syria, Mesopotamia, the northern parts of Arabia and Jerusalem followed, and she established contacts with local leaders and many a Western expert on the area. She coupled this with a successful attempt to learn Arabic. Interestingly, wherever Gertrude Bell went and whatever she did, there were two things she would not forgo. Even in the middle of the desert she insisted on using silver cutlery and sitting for a meal as if she were enjoying a soirée in London or Paris. Moreover, she demonstrated a special devotion to her guides and treated them like native objects of art, with the utmost deference and affection.

Her Syrian experience produced – in addition to her letters – her most important literary achievement, *The Desert and the Sown*, to this day the classic study of the towns and people of that country at the end of the nineteenth century. To the people she studied, to the gentry of Syria, she became known as '*Sit*', or 'the lady', and they relished her presence and good company. But the obvious literary achievement and ostensible interest in archaeology concealed other pursuits. On her way to the Middle East, she had met and followed the guidance of an Orientalist family friend David Hogarth, a man with high connections in imperial circles and a talent for using archaeology as a cover for his agents. (It was Hogarth who sent Lawrence of Arabia to his first archaeological dig and who later hired him as a full-time agent when he, Hogarth, became head of the Arab Bureau in Cairo.)

While the evidence that Hogarth, directly or through the intercession of friends, was responsible for Bell's espionage activities is circumstantial, what followed leaves little doubt about her new role as an agent, and she quickly moved into the fray with ease. Her tour of archaeological sites in 1905 found her paying special attention to Ottoman military facilities. And there is a record of her hobnobbing with spies who, in 1911, gathered at the Victoria Hotel in Damascus to check on what the Ottoman Turks were doing.[4] Everything she did smacked of intelligence work.

But if all this served to prepare her for her future role as one of the great brokers of the modern Middle East, then it was a personal tragedy which concentrated her natural passions on Iraq as an outlet for her energies. In 1915 the married man with whom she had had an illicit relationship, Colonel Charles Montagu Doughty-Wylie, was killed while leading an assault on Turkish positions in Asia Minor. She was never the same again, and the reduced human being which survived devoted herself to creating Iraq and manipulating its fate to compensate for the loss of the man she so dearly loved.

The obsessed traveller, writer, archaeologist and twittering socialite arrived in Basra in southern Iraq in 1916 as a representative of the Arab Bureau, which handled the affairs of the Middle East from Cairo. Initially a political officer with an inexact brief, she later became the Oriental Secretary to Sir Percy Cox, the chief political officer designated to Iraq from the India Office and eventually the British High Commissioner in the new country which emerged. Cox was the quiet man who figured prominently in the shaping of political Iraq, delineating the borders between the various countries which came into being after the First World War, and in establishing and expanding Britain's relationship with Ibn Saud of Saudi Arabia.

It was in Basra that Bell showed the first signs of a lack of judgement and confirmed her commitments to the superficial, the two elements which determine any assessment of her career. Her constant lavish parties, mainly paid for personally, were expressions of snobbery which didn't belong to a place rising from the ashes of war. But she couldn't and wouldn't do without them. More importantly, her characteristic high-handedness showed in the condescending way she treated Arab women; her intense dislike of them unless they were modern, adoring of her person and 'of the better classes'.

Considering what existed in post-First World War Basra, this attitude cannot but have isolated her from most of the women there. Moreover, her treatment of the men of Basra, the occupiers of her unnatural milieu, scarcely differed except for a more pressing need to communicate with those of them who belonged to the 'better classes' she obviously adored. In essence, what we have is a snob with strong opinions, using native contacts selectively and applying a social attitude to conditions which required different judgement.

Nor was she all that sensitive in her treatment of Arab leaders. Her protégé and fellow Orientalist in Basra, Harry St John Philby, of whom more later, recorded how she insisted on calling Ibn Saud by his first name, Abdel Aziz, at a time when the British were redoubling their efforts to befriend and elevate the man.[5] Years later, Ibn Saud was fond of imitating her shrill voice while shouting his name and constantly, like a nervous housewife, asking his opinion of one thing or another. In fact, this behaviour was seriously flawed and no Arab chief, particularly at that time, could have enjoyed being called by his first name without a respectful 'sheikh' or 'emir' as a prefix.

But Bell continued to move ahead, and it was her arrogance, which would have placed insurmountable hurdles in the way of others, that helped her succeed in British circles. Consistently, she played up to the high and mighty among her British superiors. She used her haughty demeanour to exercise considerable influence on Sir Percy Cox and to manipulate him, both politically and socially. Her every word was his command. Moreover, it was this very attitude of hers, which imbued her with a sense of power, that prompted her to 'adopt' people beneath her and to become the key to their advancement, and this she used effectively with the younger Philby. It was a simple case of relying on family background and social origins to claim status among the detached field people, and Bell had both, adding to them as she went along. Her social credentials created arrogance and enabled her to overcome its results.

Yet there were those who saw beyond the social graces and ability to confound superiors and who rejected her status and objected to her influence. Among them was Mark Sykes, the infamous co-author of the plan to divide the Levant between Britain and France. Discarding all attempts at diplomatic language, he described her as 'a silly chattering windbag of conceited, gushing, flat-chested, man-woman, globe-trotting, rump-wagging, blithering ass.'[6] It didn't stop her; the power of her admirers was greater than that of her detractors.

The period after the defeat of Turkey in 1917 and the consequent creation of an Iraqi monarchy in 1921 found Bell devoting her social energies to winning over local Iraqi chieftains through what she was best at, giving parties. She and Sir Percy Cox were trying to give substance to the Iraq stitched together by the British from the *vilayets* of Mosul, Baghdad and Basra, but they still hadn't decided what form the government of the new entity should take. Initially, they were in favour of creating a republic under the Naqib, the spiritual leader of the Sunni Muslims, the country's more advanced but minority sect. But they also considered placing at its head, in whatever form, Sayyid Taleb, a corrupt firebrand from Basra who was part of the class of people Bell was nurturing. Later they decided in favour of creating a monarchy and, with little attention to the desires of the people of Iraq, demography or geography, produced a list of seven candidates for king including the former Sultan of Turkey and the Aga Khan.

Two things occurred which brought the Iraqi situation to a head. Bell herself used her undoubted energies to produce a massive document entitled *Review of Civil Administration in Mesopotamia* (under Turkey). This detailed and impressive piece of work was to act as a guide for the British to develop political plans for the country, the yardstick by which they judged what was possible and what was not. The second development was the appointment of Winston Churchill as Secretary of War.

Churchill was determined to ease the burden on Britain's Treasury created by the 1920 rebellion in Iraq. He wanted to produce conditions conducive to the withdrawal of much of the British army. But, lacking in first-hand knowledge of the country, he used Bell's study of the civil administration of the country as a guide. These factors, and the natural sympathy between the two believers in taking the high road, provided the background to their meeting in Cairo and the momentous developments which followed it.

It was at the Cairo Conference of March 1921 that the two met, and their friendship blossomed. The conference had as its purpose the settling of the disputes arising from the various promises and counterpromises made by the British during the war. All the participants in the mishmash were there, including Lawrence, and Gertrude arrived in the company of Sir Percy and Lady Cox and proceeded to convince Churchill of what she had in mind, both directly and through the pliant Cox.

The Bell-Cox plan on which the attendants at the conference agreed called for the instalment of Faisal, the second son of Hussein I, Britain's original client in the Hijaz, as King of Iraq. A pro-British monarchy in Iraq would ease the financial burden on the Treasury. The argument in favour of Faisal was supported by his credentials as leader of the pro-British Arab revolt against Turkey, his lineage to the Prophet, Iraq's need for a person to unify its ethnically and religiously diverse people and the important fact that Faisal was more 'manageable' than his older brother

Abdallah, who – with British sanction – had already declared himself King of Iraq.

This was the Bell plan adopted by Churchill. And, even then, all the reasons behind her decision to make Faisal king were either wrong or their importance was exaggerated or misjudged. Faisal's credentials as a leader of the Arab rebellion had been eroded by his tacit, though vague, acceptance of a Zionist claim to Palestine and his dismal performance as King of Syria, before the French threw him out of that country in 1920. His descent from the Prophet never carried the weight Bell and other Orientalists attached to it. Furthermore, he was unacceptable to the majority Shias of Iraq, who considered him a member of the Sunni sect. Lastly, his pro-British policies and acceptance of British hegemony over Iraq and obvious relegation to deputy sheriff did not endear him to most of the religious and educated people of the country, both Shias and Sunnis, who had already risen in rebellion against the British occupiers and who wanted independence. Moreover, although an essentially decent man, Faisal did not have the strength of character to mould a new nation, let alone a country suffering from the colossal religious and ethnic diversity which existed in Iraq.

Even after the British decision to make Faisal king was adopted, Bell and Cox continued to pretend that the Iraqis would be allowed to decide their own fate, including whether they wanted a monarchy or a republic. This contradiction (in fact they were lying) was similar to the ones the Cairo Conference had been convened to reconcile. The British, while pretending a final decision had not been made, went further and made a considerable effort to guarantee Faisal a popular reception in Iraq and ignored the other contenders for kingship. As it was, Faisal's reception at Basra in June 1921 was so embarrassingly unenthusiastic that the pro-British Arab leader entrusted with organizing it was compelled to shout to the crowd, 'For Allah's sake, cheer.'[7] And, to complete the picture, Faisal arrived in the company of Kinahan Cornwallis, the arch imperialist who was to replace Bell as the ultimate misjudge of the dynamics of the newly created country and the man who perpetuated an unpopular Hashemite dependence on the British which guaranteed the monarchy's eventual downfall.

Like most people who make inexcusable mistakes, Bell and Cox responded to the obvious coolness towards Faisal of the Iraqi people by resorting to more lamentable errors which made the original situation worse. Bell began to dismiss the word of the Iraqi politicians who proffered advice on how to salvage the situation and arrive at a *modus vivendi* acceptable to Britain and the Iraqi people. And the odd couple capped a long list of actions offensive to the Iraqis by arresting, after inviting him to tea, the leading claimant to Iraqi leadership, Sayyid Taleb, and deporting him to Ceylon.[8] After that, they administered the *coup de grâce*: they ended all hopes for a legitimate system of government by rigging a plebiscite which approved Faisal as king by over 90 per cent of the vote.

They went further than eliminating Faisal's political opponents in open, ungentlemanly and unattractive ways and rigging elections. They moved to create an unacceptable base of support for their client-king. Among their reactions to the unpopularity of what they did was the resurrection and reinvigoration of the tribal system by reimposing old laws which gave state land to sheikhs. This move to win the loyalty of the tribes was followed by a studied use of the old sheriffian officers to run the new country, the defectors from the Turkish army who had joined the British during the war and worked with Faisal in Damascus to run the short-lived Syrian government.

These were two direct strikes against the Iraqi people. Feudalism, ugly and abusive, began reasserting itself. But most tribal chiefs failed to carry their restive flocks with them because the people wanted the land for themselves. And the sheriffian officers, though most were originally Iraqis, were unpopular and more beholden to the British than to the people. Meanwhile, most educated Iraqis saw the monarchy as an alien, British-supported presence and wanted to get rid of it. In addition, the democracy which was supposed to start functioning with the establishment of the monarchy didn't function at all. The sheriffian officers, Saïd, Madfai', Askari, Ayoubi, the Hashemi brothers and others competed as to who could win favour with the British, tribal sheikhs held sway, pro-British minorities were favoured and the common denominator, the people, were ignored.

So the Iraq which emerged was the worst possible expression of Bell's original flawed plan. The wishes of the Shias and Kurds were neglected, moderate politicians were ignored, the country was saddled with an unpopular king, feudalism was given a new lease of life, members of minorities were recruited into special forces, the Levies, who guarded the British interests in the country, and a cabal of former Arab officers in the Turkish army, who owed their allegiance to Britain, ran the country unopposed. Because the King and his officers were Sunnis who favoured and relied on their co-religionists, the Sunni primacy in the country was complete and it showed in the composition of the army, the force which was entrusted with holding the country together. High positions within the armed forces became the exclusive domain of a small group of Sunni officers and, along with refusal to allow entry into the military college to

Shias, this eventually led to the predominance of certain Sunni groups, including one from Saddam Hussein's town of Tikrit which, to this day, underpins his hold on power.

But all this was in character. Bell had no interest in the Iraqi or Arab people or in democracy; her interest was in a special group of people and in being a king-maker. She had been totally dismissive of Arabism in *The Desert and the Sown*, stating 'there is no nation of Arabs'. She had viewed what she did in Iraq as a birthright, to the extent of writing to her father about how tiring king-making was. She consistently invented ways to establish her primacy, a case of a Western aristocrat running native aristo-crats, as when she convened the Council of State in her house. She visibly cherished the name given her by the local nobility, '*Khatun*', an archaic Turkish title of respect. And she went into a state of girlish ecstasy when the Iraqis tried to honour her by naming army units after her. In the middle of all this, she was visited by the Lebanese writer and traveller Amin Rihani. The astute Rihani's judgement summed her up: 'She can't manage her kingdom.'

Rihani was right. Bell's activities in managing 'her kingdom' led her to devote more and more time to appearances and less and less to substantive issues. Having created a monarch, she proceeded to try to endow him with totally Western and locally alien trappings of power. She accompanied Faisal on most of his junkets, saw to it that the band played 'God Save the King', acted as a power-broker in the selection of his ministers and organized cultural exhibitions and museums which reflected British taste more than Arab culture. But all this wasn't enough and, when Iraq began maturing and slipping out of her hands, she reverted to being a lonely, chain-smoking, floor-pacing insomniac. Miss Bell died of an overdose of sleeping pills in July 1926.

That Gertrude Bell deserves study, that her activities had a profound influence on the Middle East, is undoubtedly true. But even the renowned *The Desert and the Sown* can be judged as nothing more than the work of an educated socialite who had an eye for local behaviour. Her success with the British government and her political decisions concerning Iraq are an extension of the same social person. She could write, and well, but her judgement was seriously flawed. Every move she took, from the imposition of an unpopular king to ignoring the Shias and Kurds and recreating the feudal system, was narrow, short-sighted and foretold future problems. There were Iraqis who wanted to cooperate with Britain on a more sensible basis. There was a chance of attaining legitimacy or even introducing democracy. The British presence need not have been so intrusive; the Shias could have been satisfied and integrated into the system and the abuse of the sheriffian officers could have been curtailed. She did not see the need for any of this. Silver cutlery and 'God Save the King' came first. Her end was the final judgement on her unfitness.

Harry St John Badger Philby (1885–1960), the man whose name is inextricably entwined with those of Saudi Arabia and its founder, Ibn Saud, was the social opposite of Gertrude Bell. Born in Ceylon in 1885, he was the son of a coffee plantation owner and adventurer who lost everything he had in one bad season and whose subsequent poverty left an indelible mark on his son.

But Philby was an intelligent lad and his family's colonial attachment to betterment pushed him towards scholarships at Westminster and Trinity College, Cambridge. In both institutions, and later, he harboured an explicit hatred of the rich and famous while competing with them to attain what he ostensibly rejected. And, throughout his multi-faceted career, his background stood in the way of his developing an appreciation of the workings of the corridors of power and, unlike Bell, how to endear himself to men of power when the opportunity presented itself.

His lack of background, and consequent prejudices, went beyond an inability to appreciate the nuances of power politics within the British government to affect his assessment of people and politics in the Arab world. Like Bell, it was the consistency of a definite social attitude which was key to Philby: what he did and how his behaviour affected events in the Middle East.

Philby's career divides easily into three parts. There is the very early period of a colonial officer sent to the Middle East by the India Office and the reasons why he was noted and promoted. Secondly, there is the confident Orientalist, with his own opinions and stubbornness, who developed a personal though suspect attachment to Ibn Saud and adopted and promoted his cause. And thirdly, there is the celebrated but bitter traveller-Orientalist who felt unappreciated by the British government and Ibn Saud and proceeded to criticize both.

Philby came to Basra from India in 1915 to reinforce the civil side of the new British administration there. In India, he had been a minor official, but in Iraq his addition to the small British group running the country was met with more than the usual welcome, and Bell in particular appreciated his keen mind, energy and command of colloquial Arabic. In fact, it was his superior command of that language which moved Bell to become his mentor.

But Philby showed early signs of rebelliousness and he quarrelled with Bell and others openly when they began to consider the imposition of a monarchy on Iraq. Philby wanted a republic and he was shrill about it. And though his opinion was ignored, his undoubted value meant overlooking his behaviour and precluded ostracizing or firing him.

Philby's big break came in 1917, when he was sent to the Nejed to re-establish British contact with Ibn Saud in order to reintegrate him as part of the British plans for the Middle East. Philby's ultimate boss, Sir Percy Cox, had been happy controlling Ibn Saud from a distance with 'gifts of gold, perfume and aphrodisiacs',[9] but Philby's mission was of a higher order, to reinvigorate a relationship which had been neglected because of the British reliance on Hussein I. And he was entrusted with giving Ibn Saud the then handsome sum of £20,000.

The money was enough to guarantee Philby a good reception, and the reasons for sending it cannot have failed to add to the aura surrounding the visitor. It was to help Ibn Saud remove Ibn Rashid, the contender for supremacy in central Arabia, and to establish the first British political agency in Ibn Saud's capital of Riyadh. Ibn Saud was in favour of both moves; he wanted to settle his tribal feud with Ibn Rashid and he welcomed the opening of a political mission because it signalled the end of years of being relegated to the sidelines by the British.

The unsurprising enthusiasm of Ibn Saud was more than matched by the behaviour of the visitor. Bell had briefed him on what lay ahead of him, but it was Philby's own quirkiness of mind which drew him to the Bedouin chief. He had wanted a republic in Iraq because he had objected to the candidates for the kingship, who were members of the Arab and Muslim establishment, sherifs, agas and emirs, and he took to the raw, physically imposing, flea-bitten Bedouin who had no airs and graces. If, as all his colleagues had insisted, the Arabs were not ready for a republic then Philby settled on the next-best thing, a real native, the embodiment of a populist. That was what mattered to Philby, and his mastery of Arabic aside, and very much like most Orientalists, he never developed any appreciation for city Arabs or enthusiasm for what they wanted, even when it coincided with his own thinking.

The 'love affair' between the two men flourished. To Ibn Saud, Philby was the symbol of his reinstatement. Meanwhile, Philby went back and forth, always bringing money with him, and he bombarded his superiors with reports about the wisdom of sponsoring Ibn Saud and placing him ahead of other chiefs, including the then recognized sheikh of sheikhs, Hussein I of the Hijaz. In 1919 Philby got his chance to match words with deeds and he was with Ibn Saud when the latter attacked and occupied Hael and brought an end to the Rashid dynasty.[10]

With the Rashids gone, the contest to control the Arabian Peninsula was between Ibn Saud and Hussein I of the historically more substantial Hashemite dynasty. The British, though already quarrelling with Hussein over interpretations of the promises made to him during the war, still viewed him as Ibn Saud's superior. Among the Orientalists, initially only Philby supported Ibn Saud, and, as with his espousal of a republic in Iraq, nobody listened.

In 1919, after the defeat of Ibn Rashid, Philby had his first chance to promote the cause of 'his pet' in London itself. The visit of Prince Faisal, Ibn Saud's second son, to Britain was an occasion to promote Ibn Saud as a replacement for Hussein. Faisal, though only fourteen, was received by ministers of the crown and the King himself, and Philby acted as guide and mentor. But there is no record of his obvious partiality to Ibn Saud seriously affecting what the British government already had in mind. His pleas went unanswered and this chance to participate in open diplomacy frustrated him further, and confirmed the official opinion of him as a braggart and a meddler.

In 1921 Philby had another chance when the Foreign Secretary, Lord Curzon, sent him to mediate a settlement of the skirmishes between the forces of Hussein and Ibn Saud. He hurried to Jedda, but, in a happening which reveals the type of confusion of the times, Lawrence beat him to it, and by the time he arrived one of the many truces frequently reached between the two men was already in effect. This was a serious blow for Philby; he had counted on using the new assignment to foster his connections with Ibn Saud. Another failure, more frustration and histrionics.

With things going against him and with a burning desire to return to the Middle East to be in the midst of things, Philby tried and failed to get a job in the administration of Sir Herbert Samuel, the pro-Zionist British High Commissioner in Palestine.[11] This cancels the legend of Philby's supposed anti-Zionism and underscores a lack of commitment except to his career; it is also a solid indication that his sponsorship of Ibn Saud was perverse in nature and based in essence on his penchant for outsiders. Future events were to confirm that Philby's attachment to things Middle Eastern had little to do with love of the Arabs, or even of a specific person.

In fact, what followed his failure to win favour with Samuel is more to the point. Churchill himself had an eye for the odd and perverse, and he appointed Philby Political Agent to the new court of the Emirate of Jordan. The writer Mary C. Wilson speaks of him 'being jubilant'[12] and he got along with the Emir Abdallah, though the latter was a Hashemite and an arch enemy of Ibn Saud. Eventually Philby and Abdallah, irascible as they were, quarrelled, and Philby left Jordan in January 1924. However, the quarrel had nothing to do with Philby's preference for Ibn Saud and what continued to attract him to Arabia proper was twofold: a feeling that it mattered more than other territories and the fact that it afforded him a greater opportunity for advancement.

Indeed there was no stopping the man. After Jordan, and a brief stint at Whitehall, he reappeared in Jedda late in 1924, at a time when the Foreign Office was backing Ibn Saud against Hussein. There he tried to spy on the Hashemite forces on behalf of the man who would give him his big chance. Disposed to act even more independently than the free-wheeling Orientalists of his time, he raised fears among his masters in London that he might spoil their carefully designed plans and they instructed Reader Bullard, the British agent in the Port of Jedda, to intercept his activities. This took the form of an official letter reminding him that he was still a servant of the crown[13] and the reluctance to adminis-ter a more severe punishment suggests that it was his manner, loud support for Ibn Saud, rather than his basic activity which was opposed by London.

Once again, we are confronted with an anomaly, a servant of the crown out of control to the extent of having to be reminded of his official status. And once again, the legend, which tells a different story, and which shows Philby as refusing orders, is proved incorrect. He obeyed Bullard and returned to London empty-handed but still officially acceptable, to do what most Orientalists did: devote his time to book and article writing, giving presentations and holding seminars.

But that was short-lived and he returned to Saudi Arabia in 1925, just in time to associate himself with Ibn Saud's conquest of the Hijaz and ejection of its Hashemite rulers (Hussein I and his son Ali). The Saudi writer Nasser Al Saïd alleges that Philby not only fought alongside Ibn Saud, but participated in the massacre at Taif,[14] a massacre that Philby himself laments in his books without mentioning the personal factor. Whatever his involvement, his presence confirmed his peninsular cre-dentials.

But, yet again, the contradictions appear, and instead of being the pliant servant of Ibn Saud, Philby considered promoting the leader of Ibn Saud's Wahhabi forces, the religious fanatic Faisal Dawish, to replace his osten-sible protégé.[15] When nothing came of this, he reverted to supporting Ibn Saud. After that, he never deviated.

When he visited London in 1926, Philby revealed a new but important aspect of his personality, an interest in business. His reputation as an iconoclastic Orientalist and writer was in place and he received enthusiastic endorsements to join the Athenaeum, the pukka headquarters of Oriental men of letters. He made much of being the 'discoverer of Ibn Saud', and he relished it as a singular success in registering a social protest; but now he was preoccupied with commerce. His so-called socialist inclinations did not deter him from bringing with him a list of products and services the new country needed and contacting companies and individuals who might help him with procuring them and appointing him their agent. He succeeded, and returned to Arabia as the official agent for the Ford Motor Company and Marconi Radio.

The relationship between Philby and Ibn Saud which followed was a curious one indeed. Because there were no external political problems facing Saudi Arabia, Philby intermittently toyed with the idea of promoting Ibn Saud as king of the Arabs. Though there is evidence of the idea having some ephemeral appeal to the wide-ranging Churchill, nobody else took it seriously. But the meddler wouldn't be stopped, and when the Palestinian problem moved to the forefront in the 1930s, Philby tried to promote this idea by describing Ibn Saud as the one Arab capable of solving the major regional problem.

In 1937 Philby supported the recommendations of the Peel Commission to partition Palestine, something the Arabs totally rejected. The following year he attended the Round Table Conference held in London to settle the Palestinian problem, and once again he supported plans to divide the country between Arabs and Jews. This is when he went further and approached the Zionist leader Chaim Weizmann with an offer to guarantee him Ibn Saud's support for partitioning Palestine in return for £20 million, an offer which Weizmann refused.

Philby's Palestinian activities, anti-Arab as they were, leave unanswered the question of what really prompted them. Was Philby promoting British policy, Ibn Saud, or both, or was it a case of a restless Orientalist incapable of sitting on the sidelines? The record is unclear. Whether Ibn Saud was party to Philby's original machinations is unknown, though he is – after the Weizmann rejection – on record as being insulted by the idea of cooperating with the Zionists. And although there is little doubt that Philby's connection with the government in London was still in place, there is little evidence that he was adhering to official instructions. In all likelihood this was a merger of what Philby stood for, and was: a case of going along with British plans, trying to use them to promote his protégé and the usual Philby penchant for meddling and self-aggrandisement. Whatever the motive, as in previous situations, his activities had no effect. It was in other areas of endeavour that he succeeded and made a name for himself.

There is little doubt that Philby managed to establish a firm friendship with Ibn Saud. But, by all accounts, it covered more personal than official matters. Robert Kaplan, author of *The Arabists*, and others have written of how the two men shared girls,[16] mainly slaves whom Ibn Saud passed on to Philby after deflowering them. Furthermore, Ibn Saud went out of his way to protect Philby against the criticism of religious people in his country who objected to the presence of an infidel at his court, until Philby ended the problem by undergoing an opportunistic conversion to Islam in 1930. And it was Philby who responded to Ibn Saud's poverty by finding a Western company to prospect for oil in Saudi Arabia.

Getting involved in the concession to prospect for oil in Saudi Arabia was a merger of Philby's commitments to business and to Ibn Saud. The original concession to the British Eastern and General Syndicate had expired without producing oil. Ibn Saud was broke and oil was being discovered in neighbouring Bahrain. What better way to line his own pockets and serve his friend than to grant the concession to a new group? But the British oil companies had too much oil on their hands and were inclined to accept the results of the Oriental and General search. They were reluctant to spend money in Saudi Arabia. This is when the person and reputation of Philby came to Ibn Saud's help.

Having crossed the Empty Quarter in 1932 and established a reputation as one of the great explorers of the time, Philby staked this reputation on a beneficial granting of the oil concession. But the manipulator was always there, and in the end he got himself appointed agent for the two competing parties which expressed interest in the country's oil prospects, Standard Oil of California and Anglo-Iranian, the British consortium. With Anglo-Iranian acting half-heartedly, the Americans won the greatest prize in commercial history for a mere $250,000. Philby and his master were in the money, and the scheduled payments to Ibn Saud which followed found Philby benefiting through exercising a virtual ten-year monopoly on the automobile business in the Kingdom.[17]

Philby was becoming rich, and his reputation as an explorer was established. But, although he was instrumental, circumstantially and almost accidentally, in granting the oil concession, political achievement still eluded him. As we have seen, his scheming regarding the Palestinian problem never worked and his plan to elevate Ibn Saud to leadership of the Arabs was never taken seriously. This is when he decided to try for a seat in the House of Commons.

His foray into British domestic politics was plain foolish. He had done no groundwork and it was obvious that he was suffering from lack of direction and appreciation of how things worked back home. He seriously expected his reputation as an Orientalist adviser to Ibn Saud to provide him with the platform for elective office. It was 1939, and war was on the way; and the last thing on the British people's mind was Arabia and exploration. He ended up losing his deposit and for the umpteenth time returned to Arabia a dejected man.

With the outbreak of the war, the urge within, the endless quest for status, reasserted itself. In Saudi Arabia he began issuing anti-British statements which described the war as an ill-conceived venture. Nobody paid much attention to him or what he said; the news of war overshadowed his empty declarations. However, when, in 1940, he decided to travel to America to pontificate against the war, the British government intercepted his trip and arrested him in Bombay.

Philby was released in 1941, after an incarceration of a few months. His continued wish to travel to America was turned down and he began a life of isolation in Wales. But there is a solid record of cooperation between him and Donald C. Downes of the Office of Strategic Services (OSS was the CIA's predecessor) between 1942 and 1943, and there is little doubt that during the war his expertise on the Arabian Peninsula was put to use.[18] Once again, this points to a Philby who had solid official connections but whose personal behaviour was unacceptable. In this context his arrest can be seen as nothing more than curbing the behaviour of a troublesome official.

Philby returned to Saudi Arabia in 1945, yet again with Foreign Office assistance. He tried to reassume his previous position of trusted British adviser to Ibn Saud, but as usual his judgement of the conditions around him served him ill. The American presence in Saudi Arabia precluded tolerating an old-fashioned British Orientalist-agent and his attempts to endear himself to ARAMCO, the company which had supplanted Standard Oil of California as the oil concessionaire, made no impact on the Americans.

With the end of the war Saudi oil began flowing in prodigious quantities and the contrarian in Philby rose to the occasion. This time he began objecting to the way the oil revenue was being spent and to the corrupt ways of the Saudi court. In fact, the ways of the court were the same as before, and Philby was doing nothing more than protesting against the diminution in his personal position.

In 1951 those protests led to his estrangement from Ibn Saud and he left Saudi Arabia and took up residence in the town of Ajaltun in Lebanon. Although he used his time to finish *Arabian Jubilee*, his celebration of fifty years of Ibn Saud's rule in which he compared him to the Prophet Muhammad, by 1956 things were never to be the same again. Ibn Saud had died in 1953, and Philby had a new king to cultivate. Continuing to protest in order to be noted, he was once again exiled by the new King Saud in 1957 and this time he moved to Lebanon never to return. He set up home with his famous spy son Kim and died on 30 September 1960. According to Kim, the last words he uttered were 'I am bored.'

I knew both Philbys in Beirut of the late 1950s. Philby *père* was still his old contradictory self. He used to appear at the St George Hotel, the centre for journalists and spies, with his Saudi wife, Rozy, supposedly a present from Ibn Saud. Though he continued his pretence of adherence to Islam, he would leave his hapless wife in the lobby of the hotel while he drank in the bar. And he continued to preach virtue and the return to pure Arabian ways and sought to publish articles on the subject which most publishers rejected, including a 'Whither Arabia?' missive which he tried to place in *Life* magazine. The more people ignored him – and most found him an intolerable loud-mouth – the more bitter he became. Furthermore, it was this period which writers analyse for clues to his relationship with his spy son.

Having watched the two together, and read most of what has been written about their effect on each other, I have come to the conclusion that their relationship was a normal if strained one. Philby had had three daughters and Kim and then there were his sons by Rozy, Khalid and Faris, Kim's half-brothers, but there is little doubt that the attractive Kim was the apple of his father's eye. The old man had been a bad husband and father, and his meddling always came first, but the relationship was hardly perverse and father and son were nothing more than a mutual admiration society. They were an awakened father who in old age wished to make up for lost time and a son who was attached to the larger-than-life image of a father whom he was getting to know for the first time.

But any serious examination of St John Philby must concentrate on his achievements elsewhere. His record as a bad family man and an annoyance to outsiders, a cruel man who wrote to his first wife of his various escapades and sexual inclinations and spoke of them to others, is there for all to see. However, this must be seen in the context of what preoccupied him. The central point of Philby's life was his pursuit of fame. He tried to achieve that by taking an individual road as an agent, and that didn't succeed. There was no republican Iraq and the populist regime of Saudi Arabia was something which existed nowhere except in his mind, even though he did everything to overlook its cruelties and endow it with an aura of Bedouin benevolence which it didn't deserve. His constant scheming to make Ibn Saud king of the Arabs and to promote him to centrality in the Palestinian problem also failed. It is after taking these factors into consideration that what and who Philby was matters.

We do not know when Philby stopped being an agent or, judging by the help accorded him by the Foreign Office after the war, if in fact he ever did. The perverse behaviour he manifested, including his activities in the Second World War, do not preclude agenting and there is no reason to discount the possibility that he still sought a role which was beyond his brief and which led him to misinterpret his times and to misbehave accordingly. In other words, his supposedly treasonable activities could have taken place within a framework of someone operating inside the ranks of government, just as other players on the Middle East scene did.

Philby's achievements are in his explorations and his role as a businessman. He was an explorer of note, a good writer and a successful entrepreneur. He deserves study more for what he represented than for his political legacy or influence on events. He was the dark failure of the imperial spirit because he couldn't shed the prejudices of his background; to Robert Kaplan he was 'a conceited, irascible and thoroughly perverse' individual.[19] If Gertrude Bell was an example of the empty socialite managing to misjudge everything in her way and creating havoc in her aftermath, then Philby was the upstart contrarian who was bent on creating noise. Even the most unsuccessful of British agents – and, judged by his failures, that is indeed what Philby was – is still worthy of study. It is enough to say that what he claimed to have created, Saudi Arabia, is a perverse creation, and his half-Saudi sons have seen fit to change their last name.

General Sir John Bagot Glubb (1897–1986), to this day better known as Glubb Pasha, was free of the complexes of both Bell and Philby. The man who commanded Jordan's Arab Legion from 1930 until his unceremonious dismissal by King Hussein in 1956 was the embodiment of the old-fashioned colonial army officer, a solid servant of the British crown who never saw very far. He deserves analysis for two reasons: because he was a primary example of the type he represented, and for his central role in the 1948 Arab-Israeli War. Glubb Pasha died without understanding or admitting the nature and degree of damage he inflicted on the Arabs' military chances in 1948.

Unlike others who followed the lure of the desert and the legend of the Bedouin, John Bagot Glubb went to the Middle East by accident. The son of Brigadier Sir Frederick Manly Glubb, a colourless officer of Danish descent who pursued military careers without ever making an impact, young Glubb was brought up to continue the tradition of his forebears. His preparation was Cheltenham College and the Royal Military Academy at Woolwich.

Glubb produced nothing of note at either place. But he demonstrated two qualities which explain the rest of his life. He was a loner, and he was religiously minded. His religious inclinations he inherited from his mother, a descendant of Irish gentry with an interest in little except the ordinary graces of a home life. In fact, it was Jack, as his family called him, who reflected the quiet ways of his family, while his sister Gwenda May was drawn to a more activist life of volunteer work during the First World War and a later interest in the budding feminist spirit of the times.

Glubb was a member of the generation whose horizons were expanded by the experience of the First World War. By all accounts he was a model officer and he was wounded twice and awarded the Military Cross. His second and serious wound, at Henim in June 1917, did away with the lower part of his jaw. Much later, during his service in Iraq and Jordan, the Bedouins called him Abu Huneik, 'father of the little chin'.

Jack Glubb wanted to go to India, where his father had served, but because the British needed officers to put down the 1920 rebellion in Iraq he was sent there instead. It was to be a temporary assignment, so much so that he needed no interview to obtain it. And, according to his biographer Trevor Royle, 'he knew nothing about the history and culture [of the people of Iraq] before he arrived'.[20]

The first phase of Glubb's Middle East service, the Iraq period of 1920–30, provided some everyday excitement for a young officer, but he was a minor player. Major Glubb was entrusted with putting down the rebellion of Azo Bedouins, and later with stopping the incursions of Ikhwan religious followers of Ibn Saud who were raiding Iraqi territory to spread their particular Islamic message.

Glubb performed well, taking his orders from the British, who still had responsibility for protecting the Iraqi monarchy. He bought the loyalty of some Iraqi tribesmen and, combining this with the superior fire-power available to him, he managed to subdue the rebels. Later, from 1927 until 1930, he expanded his recruitment activities and successfully used the tribes to drive off the Ikhwan. His success in both efforts owes as much to the presence of the Royal Air Force as to his organizational and leadership abilities. Neither opponent was up to fighting an air force.

His achievements were no more than what a good regular officer would have attained, but two characteristics of the man manifested themselves clearly. First, unlike Philby and others of an independent bent, he obeyed orders unquestioningly. Secondly, and more importantly in terms of his future role, he studiously shunned the company of educated city Arabs. The loner enjoyed the company of the Bedouins and spent his time with them. He took to wearing Arab dress, learned Arabic, told desert stories and didn't object to being called Abu Huneik. But there was little importance attached to this, and he is not mentioned in the many memoirs of the Iraqi officials and senior British military or civil officers who ran Iraq at the time. This reinforces the judgement of Glubb as being nothing more than a simple British officer who consorted with the Bedouins with ease and who managed to use them as mercenary troops, something many others did with equal competence.

Glubb's big chance came in 1930. The tribal skirmishes and Ikhwan forays had come to an end, and Colonel Frederick Peake (Peake Pasha), the man who founded the Arab Legion, was retiring. This is when the British decided to move Glubb to head Jordan's Bedouin army. With his experience of Iraq, Major Glubb was the man for the job, a perfect choice as commander of a mercenary native force which continued to be officered and financed by the British. The Arab Legion's ostensible purpose was to protect Jordan, which had been created in 1921 to please the Hashemite Emir Abdallah, and to ease the pressure on the British in Palestine to allow them to help create a Jewish state in Palestine.

Glubb's appointment to his new post was an entirely British decision in which Abdallah had to acquiesce.[21] He arrived in Jordan wearing the Order of the Rafidain medal which had been awarded him by King Faisal I of Iraq, Abdallah's brother. In a strange way, his transfer from Iraq to Jordan is a footnote to the bigger picture of Britain's support for the Hashemites in their role as its deputy sheriffs.

Glubb always described his appointment to Jordan as mysterious, but this is to endow it with more than it deserves for it was nothing more than the transfer of a promising British officer between two entities run by the British, a regular colonial administrative move. In fact, the transfer order also appointed him assistant district representative in Palestine, to protect his British pension.

From his arrival in Jordan in 1930 until 1941 Glubb devoted himself to training and expanding the Arab Legion and the Jordanian Frontier Force. He was determined to keep the larger Arab Legion purely Bedouin and in the process established new direct relationships with the tribes of Jordan. Indeed he was careful to balance his recruitment and use it to further these relationships, regulating how many people came from each tribe. The Frontier Force, although it had many Bedouins who wore skirts and became known as Glubb's Girls, was a mixed bag of a mercenary force and there were Palestinians and Bedouins from other countries who crossed the border to join it.

A substantial British military mission existed to assist Glubb in his efforts with the Arab Legion. Senior officership of both forces was exclusively British, but it was Glubb's legendary ability to win the loyalty and the confidence of the average Bedouin which mattered most. There is no evidence that he was ever close to the sheikhs of the Bani Sakhr, Huwaitat or Hadid tribes from which he recruited his men. He dealt with the sheikhs, but he was uncomfortable in their company and preferred, perhaps because they were awed by his colonial presence, the simple Bedouin. This reluctance to deal with chiefs also governed his relationship with Emir, later King, Abdallah and many of Abdallah's advisers and prime ministers. Glubb and Abdallah got along but were never close, and Abdallah didn't defer to Glubb in the way he did to the British High Commissioner, Sir Alec Kirkbride. In short, in his dealings with the king, tribal chiefs and city Arabs, Glubb remained a man apart.

Yet there is little doubt that his position made him privy to Abdallah's various conspiratorial meetings with Jewish leaders during this period, the ones aimed at partitioning Palestine between the Zionists and Abdallah. These meetings had begun in 1922, well before Glubb's arrival and a mere year after the creation of Jordan. But in the 1930s the secret meetings continued under Glubb's eyes, including the important ones during Palestinian disturbances in 1932 and 1936.[22] The amity between the two conspiring sides was so total that in a meeting Abdallah and a Jewish envoy discussed ways of eliminating the Mufti, the leader of the Palestinians and the enemy of both sides.

There was no way for the Zionists to enter and leave Jordan on such missions without one of the two forces of the country knowing about and facilitating their visits. But Glubb was doing more than obey Abdallah's orders; the partition plan had the blessing of the British, and the connivance of the obedient Glubb was unsurprising. Moreover, there was more to this than secret meetings, and the first involvement of the Arab Legion in the politics of Palestine came in 1936, when Glubb used it to intercept Arab irregulars from Syria and Iraq on their way to join the Palestinian rebels fighting against the British Mandate Government. Supported by British secret service funds, which he received for this purpose, Glubb's action contributed to the failure of the 1936 rebellion.

Glubb's writings, however, contain nothing of value on these issues. He saw no contradiction in what was good for Britain and what was good for the Arabs, and in this case, and always, to him and to the Foreign Office, the Arabs who mattered were the wise kings and emirs appointed to positions by the British, and the romantic Bedouins. Unlike Philby, Glubb wasn't promoting an outsider or arguing a particular case: he was following clear British orders. After all, an independent Arab Palestine would want to reclaim Jordan and do away with the local British-sponsored Abdallah.

Despite his reluctance to befriend chiefs, by 1941, Glubb had become a king within a kingdom. James Morris cites a British official describing Glubb's proprietary behaviour at the time as tantamount to 'thinking he's the King of Saudi Arabia'.[23] His undoubted hold on the Legion was beginning to inflate his sense of self-importance. But there was no problem with the real king, Abdallah, who saw everything British as acceptable. It was the local politicians of Jordan who resented Glubb's establishment of a kingdom within a kingdom, but they could do nothing.

After his efforts to support its policies in Palestine, the first important test of the usefulness to the British of Glubb and his Legion came in 1941. Iraq had been taken over by a nationalist government which allied itself with Germany and the control of Syria had been transferred to Vichy France. The British wanted both administrations removed and Glubb put his forces at the disposal of his country and participated in planning its invasion of Iraq. But when the time came to carry out his invasion plans in April 1941, he was confronted with a surprise. Members of his Jordanian Frontier Force mutinied against fighting the Arabs of Iraq. He quickly put down the disturbance and his Legion of Bedouins followed his orders blindly, but it is remarkable that the event left no psychological mark on the man. To him a genuine refusal by Arabs to fight fellow Arabs was not important, and that it is the way the incident is presented in his memoirs.

Glubb showed greater concern in wheeling his forces from Iraq back into Jordan to join the allied forces trying to eject Vichy France from Syria. His Legion figured less gloriously in this effort than in the Iraqi campaign, but he still cherished the role. The British-controlled native force was doing what it was created for. Its first purpose, guaranteeing Jordan's existence, was merged with the second one of serving Britain's regional hegemony.

Nonetheless, Glubb's participation in the invasions of Iraq and Syria was relatively unimportant compared with what followed. It was later, during the period leading to the 1948 Arab-Israeli war, that his particular position began to have an important bearing on regional politics. When Abdallah's acceptance of the various schemes to partition Palestine failed in the face of Palestinian and Arab opposition, Abdallah's determination to cooperate with the Zionists against Palestinian interests bordered on the perverse. In 1942, he openly asked Moshe Sharret, later an Israeli foreign and prime minister, for money to continue with his anti-Arab plotting.[24] Later, time and again, he instructed Glubb to facilitate Golda Meir's secret trips (some while she was disguised in Arab clothes) to Jordan.

As the British were still committed to the idea of a Jewish state, this meant a convergence in the attitudes of Glubb's real bosses and his native chief and Glubb became an instrument of the designs to further Jewish plans. His belief in the redemption of Israel was part of his Christianity and Abdallah's and Britain's interests gave him the chance to give it substance. And Britain, seeing that an Arab-Israeli war was on the way, decided to use the Arab Legion in the manner for which it and Jordan had both been created, to help the Jews.

In 1946, two years before the outbreak of hostilities, Glubb, acting in a political role, accompanied the Jordanian Prime Minister Tewfic Abul Huda to a meeting with Britain's Foreign Secretary, Ernest Bevin. In this meeting Bevin instructed the Jordanian Prime Minister and the commander of the Arab Legion not to use the best Arab fighting force of the time to invade territory allocated to the Jews by the various partition plans.[25] The acceptance of this by the pro-Zionist Christian Glubb and perverse Abdallah meant that the Arab Legion was to be used in a role supportive of the Jewish forces in Palestine.

Glubb's behaviour during the 1948 Arab-Israeli War ranks as the greatest betrayal of Arab interests in Palestine by any non-Arab figure in history. There are many facts to support this claim, but I will limit myself to listing some major ones.

1. Glubb constantly referred to Palestinians fighting the Jews as terrorists and gangs and refused to work with them.[26] He went further and intercepted shipments of arms to them.

2. Glubb deliberately refused to send reinforcements to save the Palestinian city of Safad because it had been allocated to the Israelis by the UN.[27]

3. Glubb, though he eventually did so under duress, was reluctant to have the Legion enter and later defend the old city of Jerusalem.[28]

4. Glubb refused to go to the aid of the beleaguered Egyptian army in 1949 and allowed the Israelis to occupy the southern part of the Negev.[29]

5. Glubb conducted his own negotiations with the Israelis through Colonel Desmond Goldie. His aim, an extension of British policy, was to avoid bitter fighting between the two sides so as to prevent the derailment of common plans to award most of Palestine to the Jews.[30]

6. Glubb, following what Bevin had asked for, instructed the British officers of the Arab Legion not to fire into areas allocated to the Jews by the United Nations.[31] These orders were obeyed against compelling strategic considerations.

7. Glubb's willingness to cede Palestinian cities and areas to the Israelis exceeded the terms of Bevin's instructions from London. His withdrawal from Lydda and Ramle, justified by him on the grounds of lack of ammunition, led the Jordanian Prime Minister, Abul Huda, to accuse him to his face of lying. Phoney lack of ammunition was something he constantly invoked.

8. After the 1948 War ended – and I am an eyewitness to examples of this – Glubb looked the other way while his beloved Bedouin Legionnaires imprisoned and tortured former Palestinian fighters in the West Bank, the area ceded to Jordan through the secret agreements between Abdallah and Israel.

In 1951 Abdallah, who had been elevated to king in 1946, was assassinated by a Palestinian while visiting Jerusalem. He was succeeded by his son Tallal, a schizophrenic, who was forced to step down after nine months. King Hussein, Abdallah's grandson, ascended the throne in 1952, at the age of seventeen. When Hussein's initial attempts to accommodate the British while following policies pleasing to his anti-Glubb people failed, he bowed to Nasser's and internal pressures, fired Glubb Pasha and gave him twenty-four hours to leave Jordan.

This was the end of the military career of a man who prided himself on never entering the home of a city Arab and who spoke of Jordan being a happy country until the 1948 War. The British government, foolishly refusing to accept Glubb's dismissal as the beginning of a new era, treated it as an affront. Glubb returned home to be knighted, fêted and celebrated. Hussein bore the brunt of hostile British propaganda. But more to the point is Glubb's later behaviour.

Shamelessly Glubb went on to make money out of the misery he had caused the Palestinians. He devoted himself to lecturing and writing, becoming a pro-Palestinian Middle East expert in the manner of many self-appointed spokesmen who represent no valid or acceptable point of view. To any thinking Arab, he became a practitioner in the big lie.

In his books and lectures, Glubb continued to describe the Palestinian fighters of 1948 and before as gangs and terrorists. In offering his justification for the defeat of the Arabs in that year he ignored them completely when tabulating the figures of Arab forces which fought the Jews, and he went further and also refused to include the 10,000-strong Arab Liberation Army. He defended King Abdallah and the plans to partition Palestine, and justified both biblically. But for his Bedouins, he manifested no understanding of the Arabs and was so opposed to the Arab nationalist movement that he lamented how Nasser was chasing Britain out of the Middle East 'with words'. Even years later, when I visited him in Hove, he still spoke with a colonial voice which was part of a history long gone and there were no signs that he understood why he had been dismissed.

Glubb was a narrow-minded Bible-thumper who didn't even know what a real Arab was. The only Jordan he understood was not a country: it was a colonial outpost, an army with a country. His contribution to the Arab defeat in Palestine cannot be concealed, and it is made doubly painful by his acceptance in the West as an authority on the Middle East and by Western insistence on seeing him as a friend of the Arabs. The man was nothing more than a rigid British officer whose dispatch by accident to the Middle East generated, and still generates, bitterness and furthered the misunderstanding between the Arabs and the West.

Until the Second World War, American involvement in the Middle East was confined to the work of missionaries and educators and the odd commission which appeared on the scene to investigate specific political problems. In the 1920s and 30s the Americans were popular. Their inherent anti-colonial attitude was articulated by President Woodrow Wilson's policy: open commitment to democracy and lack of involvement in the inner workings of the region were in their favour.

Whatever love affair the Americans had with the romantic Bedouin was subordinated to their efforts to educate the townsmen and, furthermore, the American Orientalists of the first half of the twentieth century didn't create their country's ensuing attitude towards the Arab Middle East. The Americans' serious entry into Middle East politics had immediate commercial and political considerations behind it. America needed Middle East oil, wanted to stop the spread of communism and felt an obligation to participate in determining the outcome of the Arab–Israeli conflict. The Americans on the ground appeared in a supporting role; they were the only experts America had to implement some or all of these policies.

Because France was being forced out of Syria and Lebanon and Britain was tired and financially unable to cope with the problems of the area, there was an urgent demand for America to appear on the scene and it did, without being limited by historical involvement or preparation. At first, there were only a few with knowledge of the area, descendants of missionaries and educators, but soon the expanding American presence called for more people and this opened the door for those without background, attitude, expertise or preparation for the task ahead of them. Unlike with Britain and its Orientalists, the American players of the 1950s and after, the ones who followed the missionaries and educators, were a new breed with no background or educational qualifications to recommend them.

Miles Copeland (1913–92), was a leading representative of the new generation of Americans who arrived in the Middle East in the late 1940s. His career included official stints in Syria and Egypt, a long period of residence in Beirut and continued meddling in Middle East affairs from New York and London until his death. That he was a senior CIA operative who organized *coups d'état* in Syria and liaised with Egyptian President Nasser on behalf of the agency is established and accepted.

Despite his celebration of his own activities in the books *The Game of Nations*, *The Game Player* and *The Real Spy World*, there is considerable doubt regarding Copeland's various roles and further doubt about his performance. These doubts are supported by his overall attitude towards the Arabs and his involvement, before and after the fact, in the disappearance to Russia of Kim Philby.

Copeland's character and the fact or fiction of his various claims are not easy to separate. In 1961 *Time* correspondent Wilton Wynn gave voice to the misgivings of the Beirut-based press watchers of Copeland by describing him as 'the only man who ever used the CIA for cover'. Years later, in London in 1991, former *Washington Post* correspondent Jesse Lewis listened to Copeland recall some important events in the Middle East, then administered a devastating judgement which extended Wynn's original condemnation: 'Miles, you're full of shit.'

In between, the number of people who have accused Copeland of being a loud-mouthed liar include Egyptian journalist Muhammad Heikal, former Egyptian Intelligence Chief Ashraf Marwan, former Egyptian Prime Minister Zakkaria Mohieeddine and dozens of others. I know of some people who are inclined to forgive his lying and emphasize his other talents, but I know of no one who denies it.

In fact, I can attest to the fact that the man lied. But what concerns us is not the simple lies aimed, as most of them were, at enhancing stories – and he was an outstanding and charming raconteur. What is of concern is the lies that affected his work and others, which were aimed at hiding the truth or twisting the record of important historical events. Unravelling some of these might help us to judge Copeland's contribution correctly and to understand the behaviour of a whole CIA generation and American activities in the Middle East of the 1950s and 60s.

Copeland's father was an Alabama physician, but he appears to have had greater attachment to his mother. Why he never attended college is shrouded in mystery. He was an extremely intelligent man and, according to him, in March 1941 he achieved 'the highest ever recorded grade in a US military IQ test'. The same curriculum vitae details a musical career as a trumpeter and arranger with some of the most famous jazz bands of all time, including those of Stan Kenton, Glenn Miller and Benny

Goodman. This is supposed to have happened between the ages of seventeen and twenty-eight, but the move from provincial Alabama to the pinnacle of the jazz world, like his lack of formal education, isn't explained.

According to him, Copeland's entry into the world of espionage was at the highest level. His first contact is said to have been with 'Wild Bill' Donovan, Head of the Office of Strategic Services, America's first intelligence service. This led to his stationing in London, his elevation to specialist in counter-espionage, his supposed entry into Paris ahead of Allied forces and his assignment to the group which converted the OSS into the CIA immediately after the war. There is exaggeration here, but also a measure of truth. Whatever his achievements during this period, he arrived in Damascus in 1947 to join the American Legation.

The question to be asked about Copeland's Damascus appointment is the simple one of what qualifications he had for the post. What was it that a jazz aficionado from Alabama had that led the State Department and the CIA to send him to the Middle East? Nothing, nothing except his intelligence, and this indeed is a good enough reason. After all, it was the only qualification of most of the CIA agents of his time, and they possessed no particular expertise in things Arab.

But Copeland asserts that he was sent to Damascus to meet Syrian President Shukri Quwatly 'to liberate the political system of the country'.[32] If this is true, then it was a serious mistake. Quwatly was an astute, accomplished politician who had led Syria for two decades and one would have expected America to dispatch a more qualified diplomat to liaise with him. But the questionable claims go beyond the exaggeration of Copeland's role within the Damascus Legation, for he also asserts that while in Damascus he wrote a dictionary of colloquial Arabic which earned him the epithet, 'the Dante of the Arabic language'.[33] This too is hard to accept, and my personal recollection – and others support me – is that his command of Arabic wasn't particularly good.

What Copeland did in Damascus was much simpler than the claims suggest. The American Legation had a number of enterprising young officers who managed to infiltrate the Syrian army and purchase the loyalty of many Syrian army colonels. Copeland was a member of this group, which included Stephen Meade and Arthur Close and who – very much like their British counterparts, but for different reasons – acted with the minimum amount of supervision and encouraged Colonel Husni Zaim to overthrow the Syrian government in April 1949. When the British responded to the American-supported coup by organizing a successful countercoup of their own, the Americans bounced back with a third coup in October 1949.

So in 1949 there were three Syrian coups, two American and one British. Little doubt exists that Copeland was friendly with the man who headed the first, Colonel Husni Zaim, and the leader of the third, Colonel Adib Shaishakly. But even when we consider that the third coup established a government which lasted four years, these efforts have to be judged as ill-conceived and short-sighted because they frustrated the development of democratic institutions in a country where the level of advancement and education could have produced them.

Moreover, the American group behind these efforts had no interest in substantial issues such as a government acceptable to the people. In *The Game of Nations* Copeland tells how Colonel Husni Zaim became pompous after assuming power and objected to Copeland addressing him with the familiar French *tu* instead of the formal *vous*.[34] Later in the same book he devotes considerable time to showing how close he was to Colonel Shaishakly, and how his son Ian was given Adib, Shaishakly's first name, as a middle name. Political gossip and intrigue were what engaged Copeland, and there are juicy tales of confrontations and close escapes in everything he wrote or told. But there is little about why these things happened and what the coups tried to achieve; indeed there is very little about how these coups affected Syria and the Syrian people.

If Copeland is to be believed, his second term as a power broker came when he was sent to Egypt as a representative of the management consultants Booz, Allen and Hamilton. He goes further and denies that this was a cover for his CIA work, but refuses to give us a credible explanation of how a consulting job positioned him to see 'more of Nasser than any other Western person'.[35] Nobody believes either statement.

That Copeland had occasion to see Nasser frequently is true, but was he the primary mover of events, the adviser to Nasser, that he always pretended to be? Copeland does a great deal to disqualify himself as a confidant of Nasser. There are many instances to support this, but two are enough for our purposes. Copeland states, 'Nasser isn't an Arab.'[36] Then, with a characteristic turn of phrase, he tells of how he began the search for a Muslim Billy Graham to replace Nasser.[37] How Nasser is supposed to have trusted someone who did not accept the very basis of his intensely Arab political philosophy and sought to replace him with a Muslim cleric is never explained. Moreover, there is little doubt that Nasser's ubiquitous secret police would have found out about Copeland's activities and surely this would have made him *persona non grata* with the Egyptian leader.

The anti-Nasser attitude which underlies Copeland's statements about Nasser's Arabness and the plan to use Islam against him are supported by other seriously anti-Arab statements. Throughout his books Copeland speaks of advocating cooperation with the Mossad, the Israeli intelligence service. Also, he condemns the average Egyptian and refers to his idleness and lack of interest in anything. He goes further and tells of how the Syrian security system was inherently anti-Christian.

We don't know whether Copeland was sounding off or whether he actually believed these statements. But, even if he did, they betray an obvious lack of understanding of things Middle Eastern. How could a man who, in his own words, was entrusted with improving Arab-American relations, advocate American cooperation with the Mossad? How could a friend of Nasser who prided himself on calling him by his first name seek to replace him with a Muslim cleric? The accusation that Syrian intelligence was anti-Christian is the work of an uneducated middle-class mind bent on making statements which appeal to kindred uneducated people. The Syrian intelligence service was a secret police which worked against everybody and there was no reason to single out the Christians. But accusing it of being anti-Christian sells more books. Furthermore, there is no record anywhere of Copeland's dictionary of colloquial Arabic. Despite all this, the CIA continued to use and rely on the man.

Copeland was in Beirut when Kim Philby left that city and defected to Russia on 23 January 1963. According to Copeland, he was no longer with the CIA and he had returned to Beirut to consult for Gulf Oil and other American companies with concessions and agencies in the region. Questioned by a fellow journalist about why, during this period, he spent so much time with known CIA agents and entertained known and major CIA operatives such as Kim Roosevelt and Robert Anderson, Copeland answered that the agency 'still gave him funds to entertain' but 'I was no longer part of them'. Among other things, this is an insult to the interviewer.

There is little doubt that Miles was still with the CIA during this period, and there is even less doubt that watching and reporting on Philby was among his activities. In fact, the former head of the CIA station in Beirut, Ed Applewhite, confirmed this to the writer Anthony Cave Brown and distanced himself from Copeland by saying that Copeland reported directly to Washington. But this well-known fact pales in comparison with the really big lie he produced about Kim Philby.

The defection of Philby was followed by an avalanche of stories and keen competition to unravel the defection among some of the finest journalists of the age. Among those who came to Beirut to do 'the real Philby story' was the celebrated freelance American journalist and former diplomat Edward R.F. Sheehan. The result of Sheehan's meticulous research over a period of several months was an article in the *Saturday Evening Post*.

The usually reliable and undoubtedly honourable Sheehan produced a number of questionable statements. A year after the article appeared, Sheehan admitted to me that 30 per cent of the article was untrue, that he had been 'misled' and he regretted the fact. My probing made Sheehan admit that Copeland was behind the errors in his article.

More curious in view of the Sheehan admission was the inclusion of the story in former CIA chief Allen Dulles's *An Anthology of Great Spy Stories*. It is safe to assume that Dulles knew the facts as well as Sheehan did and that the inclusion of the story was no more than an attempt to perpetuate a CIA lie. But what was the purpose?

The lie had to do with the manner of Philby's disappearance, how he had been monitored by the CIA, found the circle closing in on him and managed to escape Beirut just in time. Many details of Sheehan's story are untrue. The American circle around Philby was not closing in on him, Copeland was not the close friend of Philby he pretended to be and the Americans had no knowledge that the British were confronting Philby with evidence of his treason. Much more interesting is the simple fact that Philby's disappearance was followed by the firing of Copeland from the CIA.

In 1964, a year after Philby's defection, Copeland was in New York, broke. So broke was he that he borrowed money from Webb McKinley, an editor with Associated Press, to pay the school fees of his daughter Lennie, who was attending Vassar College. Having seen him regularly during this period, I can testify to the fact that he was short of funds. Furthermore, a senior *Time* editor with impeccable CIA connections but who spoke on a non-attribution basis confirmed to me that Copeland was fired over the Philby disappearance and that his dismissal had been abrupt.

But, two years later, Copeland was operating a consultancy service from posh offices at 1 Rockefeller Plaza. His partners in the consulting firm were James Eichelberger, a former CIA operative in Cairo, superspy Kim Roosevelt, Robert Anderson, former Eisenhower Secretary of the Treasury and CIA troubleshooter and one businessman, Jack McCrane. Interser, as the consultancy company was called, specialized in helping large American corporations with their Middle East business. There is little doubt that it was a CIA front organization, though the businessman in the group may not have known this.

This suggests that Copeland's estrangement from the CIA was brief, though it most definitely took place. The details of what lay behind his firing and rehiring are unclear, but there is evidence of conflict within the CIA in the wake of the Philby defection. If, as Applewhite and others have asserted, Copeland reported directly to a branch of the CIA in Washington without going through channels in Beirut, then it is easy to assume that whoever controlled him was unhappy with his performance *vis-à-vis* Philby's disappearance and whoever reinstated him felt the opposite.

Given that Allen Dulles promoted the Copeland allegations on the disappearance, then Dulles was a Copeland supporter. It is also safe to assume that James Jesus Angleton, the CIA's chief of counterintelligence and the man who funded Copeland's entertainment in Beirut and whose preoccupation with Philby drove him into paranoia, was behind the firing. Sheehan and others are silent on this subject, though nobody disputes that Copeland faced serious financial difficulties in the period following Philby's defection. Given Angleton's inclinations, the question becomes one of whether he expected Copeland to stop the defection and whether Dulles thought everybody was better off with Philby in Moscow rather than on trial and in a position to expose their overall incompetence.

Though it is obvious that Copeland was reinstated, things were never the same again. From the early 1970s until his death he moved from one 'consultancy' function to another. Outwardly denying a CIA connection, he did everything to create the opposite impression, to lead people to believe that he was still part of the agency's Middle East set-up.

According to him, one of the most controversial of his activities was an attempt to bribe the PLO not to hijack the planes of Pan American Airlines. However, an investigation of this claim by me and *Mail on Sunday* journalist Chester Stern produced no evidence of this, and the PLO in particular made it clear that Copeland was the last man with whom they would cooperate on anything. In fact, the PLO was convinced that he was working against them and wanted to interrogate him.

Another Copeland effort bordered on the ridiculous. In a supposed move to foster Arab-American relations, he prevailed on the city fathers of Birmingham, Alabama, to declare it a sister city of Jedda, Saudi Arabia. According to Copeland, this would lead to much business between the two places. However, because there was no business to transact between the two cities, it came to nothing.

Every time there was an American presidential election, Copeland made much noise about going back to Washington from London, where he had headquartered, to help the incumbent. The last effort in this regard was supposed to be George Bush's 1988 campaign. Once again there is no record of anyone wanting him in Washington or caring about his presence or support.

The one area where Copeland met with success was in assuming the media role of an intelligence expert and talk-show guest. Here he was in his element: charming, intelligent, knowledgeable and with a gift for words. He could outscore anybody who took a contrary view and relished his new role and came close to becoming a household name.

But, for other experts, Copeland's faults were greater than his assets. His books, some of which he produced during this period, were full of misleading mistakes. For example, he referred to the 'People's Front for the Liberation of Palestine', whereas the real name was the Popular Front for the Liberation of Palestine, and extended the mistake by accusing this organization of being Maoist when it wasn't. He went further and told Edward Sheehan of a meeting with former Egyptian Premier Zakkaria Mohieeddine, only to have the latter state categorically that he hadn't seen Copeland for years.

But the most important aspect of Miles Copeland's involvement in the Middle East was his lack of understanding of what the area and its people are all about. Towards the end, he took to spending time with arms dealer Adnan Khashoggi, seeing this as a new way into Middle East affairs. This betrayed a striking lack of judgement. It was the work of the mind of the man whom the United States sent to liaise with Quwatly and Nasser and who, among others, was allowed to help change the government of Syria at least twice. His work in Syria and Egypt cannot but have contributed to a superficial appreciation of both countries and an ensuing misunderstanding of the Middle East by America. Copeland missed his calling, for he was a natural showman, a talented writer, a remarkable storyteller, an enchanting companion and a revolving liar.

In glittering Beirut of the late 1950s and early 60s, he was called the co-chairman of the Ten AM Club, whose members gathered informally at that hour to drink at the St George Hotel Bar. Wilbur Crane Eveland always arrived on time in a black chauffeur-driven limousine, the type reserved for diplomats. But though he was a major CIA operative who figured prominently in many vital developments in the Middle East for nearly twenty years, drinking and the pomp of having a chauffeur interested him more.

Tall and with a purposeful look, Bill Eveland, 1918–92, was born in Spokane in the state of Washington. In his autobiography *Ropes of Sand* he recalls the difficulties of growing up during the Depression, but his attribution of his family's poverty to the Depression was untrue. In fact, his attempt at disguising his poor background extended to his insistence on using his Crane middle name and falsely claiming a relationship to Charles Crane, the American diplomat who figured in the Middle East earlier in the century. Both claims were attempts at psychological and social compensation.[38]

During his youth Eveland appears to have moved from one insignificant job to another without leaving a mark. Going to college was beyond his family's means and his enlistment in the Marine Corps Reserve in 1939 is what white people from humble origins did. In 1940 he joined the army and was promoted to officer in a short time. He caught the eye of his superiors, was recruited into security work and, in 1949, was sent to the Army Language School at Monterey, California, to study Arabic. Why he was selected is unknown, but it is curious because he had an utter lack of interest in the Middle East. However, it merits repeating that, unlike the British, the Americans were short of talent and bright young men became instant Middle East experts.

Eveland's first trip to the Middle East was to Dhahran, Saudi Arabia. Murmurs of labour unrest among Arab workers in the oilfields produced a need for security experts and the oil companies which owned ARAMCO called on the US government for help. Eveland was among the officers dispatched to remedy the situation. As with so many of his assignments, little is known about what he did, but whatever it was it still earned him another promotion, this time to the rank of major.

Eveland's serious involvement in the Middle East began when he was appointed military attaché at the US Embassy in Baghdad in 1949. Again, though, even he is unable to claim that much came of this; despite the importance of his position and a background of political turmoil in the country, what Eveland achieved in this post was what he was best at. Undoubtedly he established lasting relationships and friendships with establishment Iraqis, many of whom held the name Crane in reverence. Iraq was still within Britain's sphere of influence, and the activities of the American military attaché were to inform Washington of what was happening rather than to control actual events, which suited Eveland.[39]

But, as always, Eveland parlayed this undramatic performance into something bigger. On his return to Washington in 1952 he was made a member of the OCB (Operations Coordinating Board), the very important intelligence arm of the National Security Council. Whatever he did for this body, which reports directly to the President and Secretary of State, soon afterwards he was seconded to the CIA.

For someone without an educational and social background this was already a remarkable track record of advancement and it reflected the inherent presumption of the man, and his natural ability to consort with and please those in power. From the very beginning he was given to calling important people by their diminutive names and he showed a talent for drinking and socializing with them in a way which pleased them. As a matter of fact, his lack of background appears to have produced the opposite of the expected reaction: instead of limiting him it endowed him with a strong, studied desire to overcome it through pretence and arrogance. He understood the weaknesses of powerful people for loyal followers and hooked into it. In this regard *Ropes of Sand* tells a true story.

After three years of participating in the work of committees and groups and expanding his social contacts in Washington, Eveland was sent back to the Middle East to work with CIA veterans Kim and Archie Roosevelt, Miles Copeland, James Eichelberger and others. In 1954–5 his first mission was to assist in improving relations with Nasser, whom America was trying to stop buying arms from the USSR and depending on the communist bloc for diplomatic support.

Eveland – and in this case his claim is supported by others – promoted the idea of creating a regional alliance of Arab and Muslim states, with Egypt and Nasser as founding members. But whether this was his own idea or his usual way of expressing the thoughts of his superiors and supporters is unknown. And though the regional alliance he advocated eventually became the Baghdad Pact, Eveland failed when Nasser not only refused to join it but opposed it vociferously and unleashed a huge propaganda campaign against the only Arab country which did, Iraq.

On this, Eveland's memoirs are contradictory. At one point he mentions the Arabs' lack of interest in participating in anti-communist alliances, and speaks of their preoccupation with confronting Israel; but later he attributes Nasser's stand against the alliance to the fact that Iraq, his competitor for Arab leadership, had joined it. The contradictions – after the fact – are understandable. What emerged from Eveland's and other recommendations was a shadow of what had been intended, and the eventual collapse of the Baghdad Pact after the overthrow of the Iraqi monarchy in 1958 diminishes the importance of the original idea.

Failure to induce Nasser to join a Western-sponsored alliance and to prevent his plan to equip his armed forces with military hardware from the communist bloc weakened the West's position in the Middle East and contributed towards the Nasser-West confrontation which followed. It was Nasser's decision to buy arms from Czechoslovakia which led Secretary of State John Foster Dulles to cancel the American offer to finance the Aswan Dam and the consequent nationalization by Nasser of the Suez Canal and the Israeli-French-British invasion of Suez.

Strangely, Eveland was not affected by this huge failure. Years later he spoke openly of there being no success like failure. What mattered to Eveland most was using the opportunity of dealing with Nasser to develop special relationships with important people in Washington. Almost disrespectfully, he referred to Secretary of State Dulles as Foster (and, of course, CIA Director Alan Dulles was Alan) and he cherished his ability to hobnob with the CIA's Roosevelt cousins Kim and Archie.

So the Eveland who was promoted and sent to Beirut in 1956 had a signal failure, contacts in high places and no achievements behind him. Officially he was never an employee of the CIA, still a member of the OCB, but he was sent there to complement the agency's work and to report directly to Washington, without deferring to the local ambassador. His penchant for consorting with the high and mighty, which had served him well in Washington, represented his approach to his new areas of operation, Lebanon and Syria.

The problems of the two countries Eveland was sent to render safe for American and Western interests differed. Syria was torn between factions which were anti-West and wanted to follow Nasser, and others with a pro-West orientation. Eveland was entrusted with supporting the latter groups while making sure that a pro-West Syria would stop short of uniting with Iraq and threatening Israel and Saudi Arabia. In Lebanon, he was to work towards perpetuating the pro-West Maronite-led orientation of the country by strengthening sectarian elements opposed to Nasser and his Arab nationalist and seemingly pro-Soviet policies.

In 1956 Eveland's idea of creating a pro-West Syria consisted of conspiring with anti-Nasser and anti-communist elements in that country. But instead of finding reliable ones, he took the easy way out: he dealt with the people he could bribe. Who those people were and the levels of their popularity or acceptability to the Syrian people wasn't part of the thinking of a lazy alcoholic. It went further, and he paid little attention to their ability to stay in power or run Syria should they have succeeded.

Eveland's main Syrian contact was a Christian Syrian merchant-politician by the name of Michel Ilyan. Old-fashioned and without a personal following, Ilyan was honest and he repeatedly made it plain to Eveland that the most he could do was to bribe pro-West army colonels, but Eveland didn't care. Eveland's second contact was a more substantial Syrian politician by the name of Rushdi Kihya, but he also was too weak and unpopular to be effective. Thirdly, Eveland paid huge sums of money to a small Syrian party, the Fascist Parti Populaire Syrien, a political entity which depended on the support of minorities for its very existence. In other words, the need for popular leaders or solid political entities escaped Eveland, or was considered an interference in the many hours of the day he spent drinking. There isn't a single word of appreciation of this in his memoirs or in the recollections of people who knew him at the time.

In Lebanon, Eveland conducted himself with similar unawareness of and lack of interest in what mattered. Between 1956 and 1958 the country faced one of the most serious crises of its short history. The then President, Camille Chamoun, utterly dismissive of the feelings of his people, saw himself as deputizing for a West desperately in need of friends, just the way post-First World War leaders did. Chamoun not only saw Lebanon as an outpost of Christian-Western influence in the Muslim area, but tried to use the mutuality of interest between himself and the West to amend the Lebanese constitution to allow himself a second consecutive term in office.

Eveland was happy working with Chamoun and Chamoun alone. He loved calling the colourful president by his first name. The wish of the Lebanese to live in peace with their Arab neighbours, Chamoun's gratuitous work to elevate himself to the level of a regional leader to compete with the very popular Nasser, the threat to the delicate structure of the country and its traditional neutrality in Arab affairs this created and Chamoun's personal corruption – none of these mattered to Eveland.

What did matter was that he was dealing at the highest level of government and his consequent ability to bribe the President, Foreign Minister and Prime Minister at the same time.[40] And he didn't stop there, for he provided Chamoun with funds to rig elections, alienate the traditional leadership of the country and thereby contribute directly towards the outbreak of the Lebanese civil war of 1958.

But if Eveland concentrated on a handful of people whom he successfully promoted in Washington, then it is only fair to ask what he did with the rest of his time. Part of the answer to this question, that he spent a great deal of it drinking, has been given, but he also organized press support for his so-called policies.

Eveland wasn't called the co-chairman of the Ten AM Club for nothing, for he spent no less than four hours a day drinking at the St George Hotel Bar. And there, using his friendship with Sam Pope Brewer, *New York Times* Chief of Middle East correspondents and co-chairman of the infamous club, he planted stories in America's leading newspaper which purported to prove the soundness of his important activities. Deliberately Eveland gave Brewer enough for a daily story and the latter, once an outstanding foreign correspondent, obliged and wrote supporting Eveland's words and indirectly making Eveland a hero. Eveland went further and used the connection with Brewer to feed stories to *New York Times* correspondents Cyrus Sulzberger, Kennet Love, Hanson Baldwin and Homer Bigart. The man running the US policy in Syria and Lebanon had America's leading newspaper promoting his policies.

But the emptiness of the man has more to it. Undoubtedly inadvertently, Eveland in his memoirs makes no effort to hide most of what he did as having taken place over glasses of White Label whisky. Next in importance to whisky came staying at fancy hotels everywhere, chartering private jets to make trips and assigning the people with whom he dealt importance through a detailed retelling of their inherent social graces. His judgement was thoroughly superficial.

To add to his erroneous dependence on Chamoun, Eveland befriended chief of Lebanese surety Farid Chehab, an extremely unpopular believer in Maronite supremacy. Eveland was close to journalist Samir Souki and claims the man was a CIA agent, and Souki was an anti-Muslim who saw popular movements as an Islamic threat to Middle East Christianity. Eveland's blindness was so total that he cynically, and given his record, unbelievably, accused Galo Plaza, the UN envoy sent to Lebanon to determine whether the country was being undermined by Nasser, of being an untruthful drunk. Even his lack of knowledge was there for everyone to see and in his book he described the pan-Arab Ba'ath Party as 'dedicated to an independent Syria' when it was the party most committed to Arab unity and the merging of Syria into a greater Arab country.

Eveland's assignment to Lebanon and Syria, although it was aimed at guaranteeing the existence of both countries under pro-West regimes, produced the opposite results. Chamoun, after contributing measurably to the start of a civil war, was forced to step down. The lie behind his stand was exposed when his successor, Fuad Chehab, managed to establish good relations with his neighbours, including Nasser, without compromising Lebanon's independence and its inherently pro-West position. And Syria, after many turns, joined Egypt in forming the United Arab Republic under Nasser, exactly what Eveland was supposed to thwart. Even what happened later in Lebanon, the bloody civil war which began in 1975, was influenced by Eveland's efforts, which suggested that the West would always support Maronite control of the country.

From 1958 until 1960 Eveland was one of the promoters of the Eisenhower Doctrine, the American policy designed to protect pro-West regimes against external threats and internal upheavals. This too failed when the most solid pro-West regime, the Iraqi monarchy, was overthrown by nationalist army officers. But even that left Eveland unfazed and he continued to attach more importance to White Label whisky, posh hotels, calling important people by their first name and pretending that he possessed social credentials. By the early 1960s, after twelve years of his destructive activity, the US government woke up to Eveland's shortcomings and moved him out of the Middle East. He was sent to Rome, from where he was supposed to do intelligence work in Africa under the cover of a representative for construction companies.

But it didn't work. His alcoholism got the upper hand and he no longer made much sense. Transferred to the Far East after several incidents of drunken behaviour, he still managed to get into trouble. Finally, the US government gave up on him and he was fired in the mid-1970s.

What followed borders on the tragic. The various business jobs he managed to get produced nothing but legal suits. His employers always fired him after discovering his addiction to alcohol and high spending. He always responded by suing them.

By the late 1970s Eveland had become a destitute drunk. He used the credit card of the widow of his friend Sam Pope Brewer to pay his bill at London's Hilton Hotel. He borrowed money from most people he knew and couldn't pay it back. He pathetically tried to sell the writer a couple of gold cuff-links because he needed 'money to eat'. In 1978 he retired to California to write his memoirs, *Ropes of Sand*.

The CIA tried and failed to stop the book. They shouldn't have. There is a great deal about bribing people, drinking in the company of famous men, his friends Foster and Alan and a long list of the fancy hotels where he stayed and the number of times he chartered private planes, but there is nothing to suggest any understanding of the Middle East and its problems. It isn't that he was an exaggerated case of American bumbling and reliance on people who no longer mattered; the US policy in the Levant during the late 1950s and early 60s was called the Eveland Era. No greater proof is needed of the emptiness of it all.

In terms of the nature of his assignment, John Fistere, 1908–92, resembled the British players of the Middle East game more than he did the Americans. Initially, unlike most CIA agents with open-ended briefs which forced them to operate beyond their level of competence, Fistere devoted himself to one country and one man, Jordan and King Hussein. In fact, judged by ordinary human terms, there was nothing wrong with Fistere the man and the problem has to do with his being circumstantially elevated to a role for which he was unqualified and unprepared, something tantamount to placing America's Middle East policy in the hands of amateurs.

Despite the original nature of his assignment, Fistere was thoroughly American in most ways. As with others, his emergence on the Middle East scene followed America's replacement of Britain as the guardian of the West's Middle East interests, and in fact he arrived a little later than most of them. Unlike Copeland and Eveland, Fistere was competent to handle what he was supposed to do until he was – and this must have been a deliberate decision – thrust into uncharted territory.

Fistere was of German descent and, according to him, his last name was a simplification of Fisterer. He was born near Pittsburgh, Pennsylvania, to a modestly successful businessman, attended Lafayette College and became a reporter on the *Detroit Free Press*. There was nothing special in his upbringing, schooling or his career achievements until the Second World War.

Having moved from the *Detroit Free Press* to *Fortune* magazine in a business rather than a reporting capacity, Fistere, like Copeland and Eveland, became a member of the Office of Strategic Services, the CIA's predecessor, through joining the army. In 1944–5 he was sent to Egypt. Still young and entrusted with minor duties, he did a regular tour which left him with a taste for things Middle Eastern.

After the war Fistere returned to a comfortable job with *Fortune*. His performance was average, but having joined Time Inc, the parent company of *Fortune*, at an early stage he was part of the original inner circle of the larger publishing empire which emerged and, accordingly, his financial attainment exceeded his business success. Eventually, in the early 1950s, he became the magazine's promotion director, a relatively important job.

In 1955 Fistere took a year's leave of absence from *Fortune* and went to Beirut to act as a public relations officer for the United Nations. Although the UN was responsible for feeding and educating the Palestinian refugees, it was also blamed for partitioning Palestine, and Fistere's job was to promote the organization's humanitarian image. He appeared to do that well and once again returned to *Fortune* when his one-year stint was over. Whether this assignment had American intelligence behind it is unknown, but there is little doubt that he used the year to establish high-level contacts throughout the Middle East.

In 1958 Fistere severed all connections with *Fortune* and returned to Beirut to set up a public relations firm. He rented a large office with a staff of eight and out of nowhere became King Hussein's PR man, confidant and political adviser. He had other clients, including major corporations such as IBM, but work for Hussein came first, took more of Fistere's time and provided him with status in Beirut's socio-political community. He was King Hussein's front, the man entrusted with promoting the image of a pro-West Jordan and through that guaranteeing it the political support of America and warding off any questions regarding the king's popularity.

That Fistere served King Hussein under the CIA's auspices has been confirmed by many a journalist in the late 1950s and early 60s. His role in creating an image for the king, promoting Jordan's tourist potential and attracting American investment to the country was essentially political and everything he did was aimed at maintaining American political support for Jordan. Later, after the start of the Lebanese civil war in 1975, Fistere gave up all pretence of being a straight PR man and honourably went out of his way to secure US visas for many a needy Lebanese friend. According to some people who benefited from his intercession, his referrals to the American embassy were tantamount to orders.

The background to Fistere's emergence as King Hussein's chief political adviser is important. Glubb Pasha, the West's *de facto* representative in Jordan, had been fired in 1956. King Hussein faced a hostile people enamoured of Nasser's Arab nationalism and determined to force their country and king to follow his lead. Jordan, unable to support itself, was dependent on outside subsidies to survive and America had replaced Britain as the country's chief financial backer. The issue at hand was keeping Jordan independent and pro-West and foiling the march of Arab nationalism.

Fistere went to work to create a positive image for Hussein in his country, regionally and throughout the world. Within Jordan this was aimed at increasing Hussein's popularity with his people. Regionally its purpose was to show that traditional monarchies were preferable to movements which wanted to unite the Arabs. And further afield, presenting King Hussein as the guardian of a pro-West position had the twin purpose of guaranteeing the flow of Western financial aid and the necessary political backing for the boy-king's policies. In other words, the overall purpose was to maintain Jordan as an independent country under an acceptable pro-West king.

This is similar to what Gertrude Bell tried in Iraq, to Philby's promotion of Ibn Saud and to the creation of leaders from army colonels by the CIA station in Damascus. It was old-fashioned king-maintaining using different tools which Jordan's particular situation required. The Jordanians were more advanced than the Arabs of earlier in the century and the competition differed. Nasser and Arab nationalism represented a viable alternative and Fistere, entrusted with helping Hussein, worked from behind the scenes instead of openly and used recognizable PR methods. Instead of a British officer with a swagger-stick, Jordan's continuance depended on an American with a button-down shirt.

Within Jordan Fistere used a two-pronged attack. He worked closely with Wasfi Tel, then Director of Information and later Prime Minister, to improve the effectiveness of the country's propaganda apparatus. This included control and improvement of the quality of radio programmes, methodically preparing for the introduction of television and establishing direct relationships with local newspaper editors and telling them what to say and how to say it. In these efforts, Fistere had the backing of the CIA and experts who visited him regularly, mainly people from the Voice of America. But, having known him, I have little doubt that his narrow understanding of what he was doing found him transplanting sophisticated PR techniques to the wrong place.

The second part of Fistere's local approach consisted of creating a feedback apparatus, and this was pure intelligence work. He recruited people in refugee camps, the Bethlehem municipality, the security forces of Jordan, managers of Palestinian refugee camps and others, who fed him with information about conditions on the ground and spread rumours helpful to his client. His chief retainee was one Abul Hafez Bazzian, who probably knew nothing of Fistere's purpose, a strange owner of a flower shop and a supreme storyteller who had the ear of many of the country's politicians,[41] and there were the mayors of two important West Bank towns.

Fistere's regional work was carried out from the comfortable surroundings of his posh offices along the Golden Coast of Beirut. He liaised with and befriended Lebanese editor Ghassan Tweini, editor-owner of *An Nahar* and a man who opposed Nasser for ideological reasons. He did the same with Kamel Mroweh, the editor of *Al Hayyat* and another ideological opponent of Nasser. His relations with Beirut's two leading newspapers, aimed as they were at spreading anti-Nasser stories, were augmented by contacts with others. While Tweini and Mroweh had ideology and not money behind them, others accepted bribes or retainers and I have established that Fistere enticed many Lebanese newspaper editors to follow the line of Tweini and Mroweh.

But the local and regional efforts paled in comparison with his efforts to promote Hussein internationally. I myself was among twenty-two foreign correspondents taken to Amman in 1959 to meet King Hussein and to get his story first hand. The story was nothing more than a straightforward attack on Nasser and the forces of Arab Nationalism, with the usual inclusion of communism to appeal to Western readers. The accusations against Nasser were mainly false; the communist elements were no more than local people wanting a voice in the running of their country and Jordan's Arabness was subordinated to the pro-West position of the king. Junkets similar to the one in which I participated were frequent: there were at least eight of them, and they were complemented by individual work with important journalists and feeding them more pro-Hussein stories. The spy Kim Philby, nominally a correspondent for the *Observer* and *The Economist*, used Fistere to get an exclusive interview with Hussein and so did William McHale of *Time*, Webb McKinley of Associated Press and dozens of others. It was a successful effort.

Except for recruiting people in Jordan to do intelligence work, this was all regular public relations work aimed at selling King Hussein as a good man whom the West should support. But, as with Bell's and Philby's promotional efforts, the facts on the ground told a different story and support for Hussein meant forestalling the development of a legitimate system of government. Hussein was unpopular, particularly among the 60 per cent of his people who came from Palestine. The Jordanian security apparatus, with which Fistere worked, was among the most criminal of such forces in the world and advocates of democracy were frequently imprisoned and tortured. Above all, Jordan's rule of the West Bank produced nothing less than a reign of terror against the Palestinians. Again, what the smooth-talking, well-connected Fistere was doing was similar to what Gertrude Bell and others had done: endowing an unacceptable regime with a façade of acceptability and respectability that it didn't deserve. But was it as simple as it appeared? The answer is no. Unlike colonial Britain, the United States of the 1950s, 60s and after was divided between advocates of following popular leaders or promoting democracy and others who pursued a traditional line of depending on 'friends'. Fistere was with the agency, the source of support for dictators like Hussein, and judging from the considerable amount of work he did in Washington, he was selling Hussein to the US government as much as he was to others.

But however questionable Fistere's activities in these fields – and he did spend a considerable amount of time talking to Congressmen, Senators, State Department officials and think-tank gurus – it was still public relations work. Selling Hussein to his people, the rest of the Middle East and the world and promoting him within American government circles was entrusted to a Madison Avenue expert. And, as usual with people like Fistere, it didn't stop there. It was when Fistere involved himself in higher affairs of state that his unfitness for his function became a serious political issue and the lack of substance of the US government's policies merged with the bungling of field agents to produce a particularly destructive situation.

There was no way of getting involved with Jordan and its survival without getting involved also in its relations with Israel, and here Fistere was manifestly unequipped for the task. To King Hussein the survival of Jordan and his own continuance in power always came before pleasing his people and Arab interests (see Chapter 7). This created a mutuality of interest between him and Israel, which was happy to support a Jordan opposed to taking into account the wishes of its anti-Israeli people, accepting Arab unity schemes or to lining up behind Nasser's leadership to combat it. In practical terms, this meant a secret alliance between Jordan and Israel against the Arab countries.

From the early 1960s King Hussein held secret meetings with Israeli leaders to develop plans to help Jordan hold the line against the feelings of its people and the plans of the rest of the Arab countries. Some of the meetings took place while skirmishes between Jordan and Israel produced Jordanian dead and wounded, a case of the head of state consorting in a friendly fashion with an enemy who was killing his soldiers. From the late 1950s until the early 1980s Fistere was a participant in most of these meetings.

This bordered on the sinister, and many meetings are recorded in books about Israel's intelligence services, including *Israel's Secret War*, *Soldier Spies* and *Every Spy a Prince*.[42] But, to reduce things to essentials, the question is, what was Fistere doing there? He was there to help Hussein carry out an anti-Arab policy. He was with Hussein during some visits the latter made to Tel Aviv. He was with Hussein in October 1960 when the King flew over Israel on his way to the United Nations to give a speech attacking Nasser. The instances of Fistere's presence at Hussein-Israeli meetings are too many to list comprehensively.

Fistere, undoubtedly obeying orders, worked against Palestinian and Arab interests. And it didn't stop with Israeli meetings; Fistere was always there during Hussein's anti-Palestinian crackdowns, including the major one in September 1970 which sent the PLO to Lebanon and resulted in the emergence of the terrorist Black September movement.

In July 1959 Beirut's *Al Hawadiss* magazine ran an article lamenting Fistere's influence over King Hussein and comparing him to Glubb Pasha. There is a great deal to this. Both men were servants of their governments and performed their functions well. And both men were endowed with simple thinking and had no appreciation for what mattered in terms of the future of the Middle East, the development of legitimate governments and what ignoring these things might produce. But it isn't Fistere who should be judged: it is the government which sent him to facilitate an alliance with a king against his own people. It is the government which reduced its handling of a major Middle East theatre of operations to a public relations exercise. Very much like Glubb, Fistere thought Jordan was a happy country, happy, that is, until people spoke of human rights, press freedom, democracy, their Arab identity or the Palestinian problem.

It is hard to argue against the results of Fistere's work when King Hussein is still in power and is still being presented to Western audiences as the ultimate survivor against the forces of evil, originally the socialists and communists and nowadays the Islamic fundamentalists. But will Jordan be a happy country while continuing to ignore the wishes of the majority of its people? Indeed, will Jordan survive? The policy of depending on men instead of institutions, on depending on Madison Avenue PR to obliterate any news about what the Jordanian people want is behind many of the problems of today's Middle East.

The Fistere case is a sad example of the widening divide between how the West and its clients see things and what matters. Bell, Philby, Glubb and even Copeland and Eveland dealt with pure politics. However misguided the policies behind them or the ones they developed, they were still more substantial than solving the problems of the area through a public relations effort carried out by a man with superficial judgement. Relegating serious Arab problems to this level proves that Western thinking towards the Arab Middle East has taken serious steps backwards. Madison Avenue is not the answer.

PART SIX

A New Slave Class

10 · The Beirut-on-Thames Syndrome

On 17 January 1996 a large gathering at London's Natural History Museum encapsulated the strange relationship the Arab establishment maintains with the West today. It was an unofficial event which did not merit press coverage, but, because it was an extension of the behaviour of today's Arab governments towards their Western protectors, it was an occasion which complemented and explained the behaviour of the existing Arab leadership, the conclusion of what has happened between the West and the Middle East this century.

A classic Middle Eastern event instigated by Arabs to present their point of view about important issues to their Western friends, the meeting typified gatherings of Arab and Western kindred spirits, the people who through word and deed, instinctively or in a studied manner, reflect the spirit of the relations which exist between the Arab Middle East and the West.

The occasion was a lecture by a leading Palestinian intellectual entitled 'Islam, the West and Jerusalem', a discourse about one of the most intractable problems of our time, one which is likely to determine the success or failure of the Arab-Israeli peace process and influence the future of the Middle East. Jerusalem comes first in the long list of contentious problems which continue to bedevil the peace process.

By any ordinary standards, the highly publicized affair, sponsored as it was by a new publishing house created to generate interest in Arabic literature in the West, Hood Hood, was a resounding success. But judged by the realities of happenings in the Middle East, the lecture was no more than an elaborate show directed at a specific audience and the show and the audience misrepresented both the conditions existing in the Arab Middle East and the concerns and attitude of the average Arab. The whole affair was tantamount to a pretence, an extension of what has been happening for most of this century; a pre-emptive effort by establishment pro-West Arabs to represent their people, a grand delusion emitting a false impression that those present were contributing to the solution of one of the major political problems of our times.

The lecture was given by Professor Walid Khalidy, a Senior Research Associate at Harvard University's Center for Middle East Studies. A learned Jerusalemite descendant of one of the city's oldest and most prominent Arab families, Professor Khalidy has been an outstanding voice of Palestinian moderation for more than four decades, a celebrated academic who has also taught at Oxford and Princeton. In addition, he has been the Chairman of the Center for Palestine Studies, an author, lecturer and adviser to several Arab governments. Professor Khalidy is a leading authority on the Palestinian problem.

The lecture itself was a stunning performance, a combination of erudition, verve, showmanship and mastery of subject matter. The audience of several hundred people sat mesmerized as Professor Khalidy wrapped the history and significance of Jerusalem in elegant language with the right degree of emphasis and detail. There were former diplomats, journalists, academics, publishers, politicians, businessmen, socialites, Middle East groupies and professional lecture-goers. They were Arabs and British with a sprinkling of Americans and other Europeans, mainly people known to each other, all well dressed, well-spoken and worldly. At the end, Professor Khalidy received a rapturous ovation and many, including several Arab ambassadors, lined up to shake him by the hand.

But what was happening at the Natural History Museum that day was drastically wrong. Above all, the audience was wrong. The Arabs in attendance were rich expatriates, ambassadors of pro-West Arab countries, writers, academics, businessmen and pretentious hangers-on. They were a special group of wealthy, secure and powerful people and, as such, the Arab group least affected by recent Middle East events. And, as usual on such occasions, their Western friends in attendance shared their enthusiasm for what was being said and they too failed to realize what was missing: ordinary Arabs. The lecture was aimed at fostering the good feeling of oneness between the two segments of the special audience, and it succeeded.

In concluding his impressive presentation, Professor Khalidy stated, 'And that is why all those committed to an honourable solution [to the problem of Jerusalem] must get together to stop in their tracks the forces of fundamentalism – Muslim, Christian, and Jewish – slouching towards their rendezvous in Jerusalem.' So the purpose of the lecture was to move the audience to prevent a slouching towards Jerusalem by the destructive forces of fundamentalism, and the audience, feeling complimented, loved it.

But nobody is slouching towards anything and the forces of which

Khalidy spoke are, in one form or another, already in Jerusalem. Jerusalem, run as it is by Likud mayor Ehud Olmert, is in the hands of Jewish fundamentalists. A zealous Zionist, Olmert never misses a chance to identify Jerusalem as 'the eternal capital of Israel'. Nor has any Israeli government been far behind Olmert. The late Prime Minister Yitzhak Rabin, his successor Shimon Peres and the recently elected Binyamin Netanyahu have all used Olmert's uncompromising language and declared the status of Jerusalem to be non-negotiable. The Israelis are hardly slouching, the Muslim fundamentalist counter-claim is violently expressed through occasional bombings and the Christians, their numbers reduced by emigration, have been marginalized. In essence the lecture did not deal with today's Jerusalem, certainly not with the concerns of its Arab residents whose land is being confiscated on a regular basis. It presented a Jerusalem whose problem could ostensibly be solved by this audience. It anticipated the problem and identified the way to solve it when it is already with us, visibly and disturbingly so.

This is why, to an élite audience of privileged Arabs whose thinking precludes acceptance of the attitude of real Jerusalemites, and to their Western friends who accept this privileged group's interpretations of Middle East events, Professor Khalidy was a voice of reason. And Walid Khalidy did not pretend to speak to anyone else. An average Arab or a suffering Jerusalemite would have rejected the basis of his lecture. Both sides, the speaker and the audience, got what they wanted. By merging an appeal to save Jerusalem with one against fundamentalism, they confirmed that they live in a world of their own, a world where the problems of the Middle East are solved through discourse between moderate establishment Arabs and their Western partners and that they, the sensible lecturer and his listeners, take precedence over Olmert, Rabin, Peres, Netanyahu, the Arab masses and Islamic fundamentalist groups on the ground, and are even able to represent the disappearing Christians of the city. Admitting the realities of Israeli control, the nature of Arab feeling and the Muslim fundamentalist claim and how it is expressed, as well as the marginalization of the Christians, would have cancelled the value of the lecture and rendered it a non-event. In this way was maintained the unwritten concordat between the Arab and Western sides, based on a shared pretension that they are the voice of the Middle East and that what they think and do contributes towards solving the problems of the area.

This concordat between the Arab élite and the West, in essence a commitment to settling Middle East problems between willing partners without incorporating the wishes of the majority of the Arab people, is in effect whenever Arab leaders and their Western counterparts 'solve' the problems of the area. This has been the case since the First World War. The concordat was behind the creation of states to satisfy individual leaders after that war and its rules determine the behaviour of President Husni Mubarak of Egypt when he visits America and declares, 'The beacy brocess will continue becausy our beople want beace.' Mubarak is another voice of reason, in this case one which falsely 'bretends' to speak for his people.

What would have happened had Professor Khalidy asked the audience to help Jerusalem's Arabs to rise and resist the ceaseless Israeli expropriation of their property? What would have happened had he taken an overt Arab-Muslim position and stated that the Arab-Muslim claim to Jerusalem, the one accepted by Arabs and Muslims everywhere, precludes compromise over their rights to their holy places? What if he had said that there was one Muslim attitude towards Jerusalem and that it is shared by fundamentalists and non-fundamentalists alike? What if he had refrained from loosing his audience-pleasing broadside against fundamentalist forces and stated instead that Islamic fundamentalism is the only movement which is resisting Israeli plans to Judaize Jerusalem and that it is a popular one which expresses the general Arab will towards Jerusalem? Admitting these points or others which follow naturally from the title of the lecture would have broken the link between the speaker and the audience; at best, it would have been a different meeting. A minority incapable of solving any of the Middle East's problems, and hugely less involved and affected by what is happening in Jerusalem than the Jewish and Muslim fundamentalists on the ground, the people who attended the lecture flocked to listen to a leading member of 'the club', someone who speaks the voice of reason. And Mubarak's voice of reason too precludes telling an American audience that the people of the Middle East no longer believe in the peace process, that it has already failed.

It is difficult to criticize the work of a learned man and a gentleman such as Professor Khalidy when it is well intentioned and totally honourable. But the reasons for my harsh criticism are more important than my wish to avoid offence. Members of the Arab establishment, and that is what the speaker and the audience were, have appealed to the official West and to Western groups using the same voice of reason throughout this century and there is nothing but misery to show for it. The advocates of civilized discourse, whether leaders or other pro-West Arabs, have failed. Lacking the support of their people, those in power have had to become more dictatorial and the intellectuals, once a source of hope, are no longer listened to. Together they are still a minority who represent and present a minority opinion which, because it is not acceptable to the people, cannot solve anything.

It is the people committed to a specific cause, Olmert and Hamas, who will decide the issue of Jerusalem and not a collection of people dressed for a night at the opera. It is true that many members of the Arab expatriate establishment who attended the lecture, like Professor Khalidy himself, love Jerusalem. But history and today's facts are against them. The appeals to save Jerusalem through combined Arab-Western action without incorporating what the people immediately concerned think have been made by every pro-West Arab leader, intellectual and journalist this century. The city, against the undoubtedly honest hopes of Professor Khalidy, is already the battleground of extremist elements who, however unattractive, represent the will of the Israeli and Arab people, the ultimate deciders of its fate.

Two weeks before Professor Khalidy's lecture, the British Home Office announced its intention to deport the Saudi dissident and human rights activist Dr Muhammad Al Mas'ari. The Home Office admitted that Mas'ari's continued presence in London endangered British-Saudi political and trade relations. It was the second attempt to deport the outspoken Mas'ari and he responded by proclaiming that he would fight the deportation order to the Caribbean island of Dominica and claimed entitlement to remain in London under the right of asylum as defined by the United Nations. The heated debate in the British media which followed the attempt to deport Mas'ari elevated him to the status of a household name.

Unlike the urbane Professor Khalidy, Dr Al Mas'ari is a bearded Islamist, a member of the Committee for the Defence of the Legitimate Rights (of the Saudi people). A hyperactive, Western-educated physicist, Mas'ari is no match for Walid Khalidy – on any level. Indeed, and despite his PhD in physics, he is unworldly, naive, given to making serious linguistic mistakes and exaggerating simple facts and often guilty of unclear thinking.

However, what Mas'ari and his group advocate is a serious matter. They are calling for substantial political change in Saudi Arabia, an end to the absolute ways of the House of Saud. Whether this is a call to reform or replace the House of Saud is not clearly articulated, but either way, CDLR's plans, if successful, would change the internal, regional and international policies of Saudi Arabia in a way which would affect the flow of oil, the balance of power in the Middle East and the relationship between the Arab and Muslim worlds and the West. And, importantly, Mas'ari, though he may or may not represent the Saudi people, reflects their general dissatisfaction with their government and hence can be seen as a legitimate expression of what they think.

Regardless of how much its leaders try to disguise it, the hundreds of messages that CDLR faxes every day from London to Saudi Arabia through an elaborate electronic command centre and which are distributed throughout that country through internal re-faxing are both revolutionary in nature and suffer from a distinct lack of polish. This means that CDLR's audiences, inside and outside Saudi Arabia, differ considerably from those who attended the Khalidy lecture. Within Saudi Arabia they are simple people with grievances, who are concerned with real problems, and outside it they are people who think things are not well in an important country.

Even press conferences held by the expansive Mas'ari have revealed some jarring crudeness which offends his listeners. Asked about beheadings as a form of Islamic punishment, he answered that no one has come back to tell us whether it is cruel or not.

Immediately following the order to deport him, Mas'ari held a press conference at the House of Commons. The aim was to present his case, and the Saudi story, to the media and to prove that he had done little beyond disseminate information, peaceful appeals against the crimes of an evil regime. The press conference, held on 5 January 1996, was attended by some forty reporters, two politicians, about a hundred members of Islamic groups which operate in Britain and some Middle East watchers. The press corps covering an exciting story and the politicians aside, the audience had little in common with the people who flocked to the conference. It was obvious that most of them were unsophisticates who earned a living the hard way. There were no British people who mattered, no former diplomats or British establishment members like the people who attended the Khalidy lecture. This placed Mas'ari and his Muslim audience at a disadvantage. Even the two British politicians who attended the conference to support him, the Labour MP George Galloway and the Liberal peer Lord Avebury, are considered outsiders with small followings.

So Mas'ari did not speak to the 'people who matter', the wealthy, educated and self-appointed deciders of the fate of the Middle East. However, because of the obvious cynicism behind the British government's decision to deport Mas'ari, the wide press coverage of his case produced more support for his petition to stay in the country than had been expected. But the great majority of the press which supported Mas'ari did so because of editors and journalists who believed in the right of asylum and not because of what he himself represented. What he represented remained alien and somewhat incomprehensible, part of a built-in refusal in the West to understand representatives of popular movements, regardless of their individual merit. This was true when Nasser and Arab nationalism threatened Western hegemony, and it is true today of any political movement the label or programme of which suggests the same danger, and here

Islamic groups are a prime example. In essence, Mas'ari's acceptance by certain segments of the British press and public had little to do with his ideas and more to do with protecting their institutions. Except for being a news story, he was totally unacceptable.

When it comes to Mas'ari and his advocacy of change in Saudi Arabia, which is what the Saudi people want, there was no voice of reason to celebrate. This is the consistent attitude towards people like Mas'ari of the important Arabs who attended the Khalidy lecture, Western people involved in the Middle East and establishment Arabs everywhere. And while both sides who attended the Khalidy lecture followed the Mas'ari case from a safe distance, their lack of interest didn't come as a result of knowledge of the many serious shortcomings of Mas'ari or members of his group and their programme. The man and what he stood for were rejected out of hand. Whether Mas'ari is the wave of the future, a mere braggart or an eventual example of the revolution devouring its infants mattered less than his obvious Islamism. After all, Islam, whether organized in political movements or as a popular force, is seen as the representative of the people's wish to oppose the established Arab regimes. Axiomatically, Islam is also a threat to the Arab establishment, including the one overseas, and to its Western supporters. The important thing to remember is that Mas'ari the Islamist was unacceptable even to many who supported granting him asylum.

In fact, acceptability or rejection by the expatriate Arab élite and their influential Western friends has very little to do with individuals. Walid Khalidy's person did make a considerable difference – elegance of manner always does – but his belonging to the club of establishment Arabs who are acceptable to the West was the most important thing. In Mas'ari's case, it was his *not* belonging. Both presented their positions in London, and London is ahead of all other cities in the world in being the centre where Middle East and West meet, agree and disagree, and arrive at positions which shape their attitude towards each other. What happens in London between the new establishment Arabs and their Western counterparts is a mirror of what happens between Western and Arab governments. This is also true of the relatively small group of influential Arabs who deal with Western groups and governments in Paris, Washington and Houston and all over the world. It is a continuation of the exclusive dialogue at the top which has taken place for almost a century; it is what nourishes the historical misunderstanding which plagues Arab-West relations. London is the main place where the illusion that both sides understand each other is perpetuated, still without taking into consideration the fact that the pro-West Arab governments and others involved in this dialogue are not the real Middle East. The compact between Arab London and its Western friends, what was confirmed at the Natural History Museum and denied at the House of Commons, is no more than an extension of the compact between Arab leaders and the Western governments.

There is no shortage of examples of other recent activities which express themselves through this contact. On 28 April 1996 two newspapers carried stories which reveal other aspects of Arab-British contact in London. The front-page story in the *Sunday Times* told how former Cabinet minister David Mellor threatened to plunge John Major's government into a fresh crisis because he refused to disclose income realized from consultancy work of between £100,000 and £350,000 in one year. It was suggested that his consultancies were with the Middle East, in all likelihood with London Arabs with solid governmental connections in the area.

That same day, the financial pages of the *Independent on Sunday* reported that a group led by George Galloway MP planned to protest against the alleged sale by British Aerospace to Saudi Arabia of electric shock batons and land-mines and its involvement in the efforts to deport Dr Al Mas'ari. The same story detailed the worsening relations between Saudi Arabia and Britain over Mas'ari's continued presence in London and how this was threatening the business interests in Saudi Arabia of the engineering company Babcock Wilcox. Nothing much came out of the revelations about Mellor, and Galloway's protest fell on deaf ears.

The situations recorded by the two London newspapers, the Khalidy lecture and Mas'ari's press conference represent the norm of happenings in London which have direct connections with the Middle East. Between the beginning of 1996 and April of the same year, there have been stories about attempts to silence Arab dissidents residing in the city, the moderate Tunisian Islamist Rashed Ghanoushi and two Bahraini human rights activists. There were other stories about how a British-Saudi partnership to transmit Arabic-language programmes to the Middle East, the one between the BBC World Television and the Saudi company Orbit, tried to censor what was broadcast by intercepting specific items about Saudi Arabia. Accusations that British journalists are in the pay of Middle East governments surfaced during the same period. The misery caused to the Iraqi people by UN trade sanctions which the United Kingdom supports briefly became a story. However, it died after it was ignored by the creators of the special atmosphere which exists in London and the press; nobody showed any interest in promoting it. London's position as a base from which things Middle Eastern are decided is solid and the decisions reached are either official and friendly to established dictatorial regimes or the product of the special relationship between the Arab establishment and its friends, a product which does not contradict what happens between governments.

Over twenty years ago, in 1975, Beirut began its process of self-destruction, since when hundreds of thousands of Arabs moved to London and made it the capital of the Middle East. A new Beirut to act as bridge between East and West was needed, a home for regional journalism, political manipulation, commerce, the arms trade, banking and all other activities which have influence on the area. The result has been an Arab London in London, a Beirut-on-Thames which responds to the political, social and economic developments of the Middle East and transmits its responses to the people and governments of the Middle East as well as anybody concerned with the Middle East in the West.

Because the politicians, journalists, merchants, arms dealers, spies and bankers who moved from old Beirut to Beirut-on-Thames are a relatively new Arab élite elevated to position and wealth through their connections with, and acceptability to, the established governments of the Middle East, what they say agrees with the perception of what is happening there promoted by these governments. In fact, one of the reasons why these groups were welcomed to London with open arms is because they were correctly identified as natural supporters of what already existed between Western and Arab governments. They may not run governments in the manner of the sheriffian officers elevated to leadership status in Iraq after the First World War, or deputize for a people for most of a century in the manner of the leading families of Palestine, but they agree with the existing official positions and represent a voice of reason. What they do resembles what former Iraqi premier Nuri Saïd did, and he was the man who always told the West how perfect things were in his country until his people silenced him for ever. What they do agrees with the positions of King Hussein and President Mubarak, the Arab chiefs who believe that Western public opinion comes before that of their people.

But what resulted from the permissive British government attitude in allowing Arab political activists, opinion makers and successful businesses to operate from London, its acceptance of London's strange role as the primary centre for Middle East activities, should not be confused with the innocent presence of regular Arab tourists and immigrants or imply a social or cultural acceptance of the pro-West Arab élite group. In a manner which recalls the post-First World War attitude of the Orientalists towards ordinary Arabs, the tourists and immigrants are not part of this London and the nature of the relationship with the so-called accepted ones is similar to what existed between imperialists and native chiefs earlier this century. In the words of Article 19's Saïd Essoulami, 'There is no cultural interaction with the host country.'[1] In this regard, events such as the Khalidy lecture should be seen strictly for what they are, no more than occasions of mutuality of interest directed exclusively at creating a specific view of the Middle East and not an inclusive social or intellectual convergence.

The presence in London of pro-West Arab politicians, journalists and businessmen is separate beyond the groups' attachment to hummus, pitta bread and Arab pharmacies which cater to their ailments and display neon signs in Arabic. Even the best-known and wealthiest participants in London's Arab politics, journalism, business and the arms trade operate under ethnic constraints. Their contacts with their British associates and friends, be they people in these trades, officials of Her Majesty's Government or British politicians, is aimed exclusively at achieving things of mutual interest in the Middle East. This is definitely an extension of the relationship of today's Arab governments with the West, the relationship of mutuality of interest which finds the West supporting 'friendly' governments regardless of their nature and even their chances of long-term survival. These governments are not accepted, except as the most convenient tools to further immediate Western interests. In private, and I have heard this myself, most British officials are less than enamoured with the corruption of the House of Saud or the public beheadings, floggings and restrictions on non-Muslim religious practices which exist in Saudi Arabia, but publicly they defend the Saudi government as a friend worthy of solid support and protection. The same holds for the Bahraini government's denial of the most basic rights for its majority Shias, and so on down the line.

In London, the separateness of the expatriate Arab élite is best seen through their own behaviour, in how they themselves subscribe to the negative aspects of the contact between the two sides. Establishment Arabs have been known to marry embarrassingly uneducated English girls of humble background, not because lack of education and social background don't matter to them but because the mere act of marrying an English girl is supposed to be elevating and render them pleasing. (They wouldn't think of marrying an Arab girl from a humble background, regardless of her talents.) Arabs feel uncomfortable living in truly English areas of London and, even though they have to pay huge sums of money for their homes, they prefer to live near their compatriots. Chichi Arabs frequent discos such as Annabel's and Tramp and gambling casinos such as Crockfords, Aspinall's and the Ritz, but they are uneasy in the surroundings of a real English club. When both sides are together, the Arabs behave in a subservient way towards their British counterparts which shows in things like telling fellow Arabs how important they are and mentioning their titles and exaggerating their positions. And even after years of London life most Arabs frequent shops which specialize in their type of clothes and dress in an identifiable way. In return, most of the time the British see their Arab guests as a novelty and often speak of them as such, in a manner resembling the way Orientalist-agents spoke of and wrote about Ibn Saud and other Bedouin chiefs decades ago. Very much like Gertrude Bell in the presence of the Bedouin monarch, they feel no need to resort to titles of respect even when the situation requires it.

Moreover, any Arab-British contact on this level, even the friendliest, is usually formal and subordinated to the subject matter which brings it about. Businessmen from both sides develop joint and often mysterious terms of reference which are different from the ones which they use when alone. The influential prince or sheikh able to help them with a deal is never mentioned by name and is uncomfortably referred to as 'His Highness', 'the big man' or 'the chief'. Arab journalists subordinate their appreciation of happenings in the Middle East to the attitude of Western listeners, diluting whatever they have to say. They identify with their surroundings and use an inclusive editorial 'we'; they present what they say in a manner which implies that they and their listeners share a common superior approach towards all Middle East problems. 'We know the consequences' is the type of suggestive phrase they employ to describe Islamic movements on the ground and to reduce these movements' elaborate programmes to an undesirable prospect.

Arab politicians in exile dilute their political positions in the same manner, and this is why so many of them insist on operating as human rights groups and are afraid to admit to a desire to change the political structure of their countries. Even Middle East arms dealers have found ways to present what they do without using language alien or offensive to their Western cohorts and the word 'commission' is so neglected one would think it didn't exist. The overall Arab accommodation amounts to something the British cherish, being played up to in ways which please their inherited colonial make-up. The Arab speakers become sensible, moderate and understandable. The master-slave relationship, however amended from what existed in the past, is essentially intact. The Arabs' acceptance of the British as their superiors and deciders of their fate distances them from their Arabism; yet their linguistic and social subservience is what their compatriots back home oppose. Suffering from economic exploitation, the scourge of corruption and in desperate need of making a political statement, the Arabs of the Middle East find the expatriate Arabs who act as their unofficial representatives in the West as unacceptable as the local governments they reject.

London's Arabic-language press, because it influences all aspects of the Arab presence in London and links and subordinates it to the thinking of pro-West governments in the Middle East, deserves a close look. In view of the fact that publications appear and disappear with greater frequency than is usual in industrialized countries, it is difficult to give the accurate number of London's Arabic dailies and weeklies. Including fifteen political scandal sheets, it is over fifty, greater than the number published in Cairo, Beirut or the whole of Saudi Arabia. In some areas of London Arabic-language newspapers and magazines occupy more news-stand space than their English counterparts.

The freedom enjoyed by the Arab press in London is greater than that which it enjoys in the Middle East, which should mean that the political views of all factions are disseminated and discussed. But this is not what has happened, and London's Arab press serves another purpose. For while Arab publications collect news about and from the Middle East and wouldn't exist had the press there been free, the local Arab press has failed in its ostensible function of handling and perhaps sending back uncensored material. With minor exceptions, Arab journalism in London is nothing but an arena of pamphleteers and purveyors of shallow, sponsored opinion, directed at perpetuating a specific image of Western-Arab relations, the one advanced by the occupiers of Beirut-on-Thames on behalf of the Arab governments of the Middle East, or to please them. The Arab press caters to the people who attended the Khalidy lecture.

Stated simply, Arab publications cannot survive on circulation or advertising. Almost all of them rely on sponsors and reflect their view. Because poor countries cannot afford it and the sponsors are mainly the oil-rich countries, Arab journalism in London is a way to get rich by reflecting the opinion of the oil-producing pro-West governments. Determined that only doctored news reaches their people and the Western governments, institutions and people that matter in terms of overlooking their illegitimacy and providing them with support, these governments exercise direct and indirect censorship on stories and in the process cancel the main reason for the existence of London's Arab press. What remains is a press which provides backing for the unwritten concordat between the Arab governments and Arab establishment in exile on the one hand and, on the other, the West. According to the editor of the leading independent daily *Al Quds Al Arabi*, Abdel Barri Attwan, 'Most [Arab journalists and editors] would like to own their own publications, not to solve the problems of the Middle East, but because that allows them to make more money, drive Rolls-Royces, own houses in the south of France or villas in Marbella.'[2] Indeed the lavish lifestyle Attwan attractively exaggerates is a reflection of what interests them and this allows the pro-West Arab governments to buy them and turn them into propagandists who ignore the plight of their people, promoters of the so-called amity between the Arabs and the West, the unhealthy brutal friendships between Arab rulers and their Western masters. That journalists are paid considerable sums of money by oil-rich countries to safeguard these friendships is obvious. This is why nobody in the West has ever objected to this and the lifestyle of Arab journalists, which reflects that of their paymasters, is unquestioningly accepted. Simultaneously, members of this manifestly compromised group are used as a source of information about the Middle East and the interpreters of what happens there.

Some forty of the fifty daily and weekly publications, the television station MBC and the BBC's World Television Arabic Service have Saudi connections. Kuwaiti newspapers are transmitted to London by facsimile, and because they are beholden to their government at home carry its opinion. Qatar and the United Arab Emirates maintain large press offices which are disproportionate to these countries' size and problems, and so does the small island of Bahrain. This arrangement is augmented by the efforts of the PLO, Egypt, Iraqi exiles and occasionally British companies working in the Middle East, which have on occasion sponsored Arabic publications. Small, poor ones which carry contrary opinion exist, but the opinions which prevail are those of the Saudi and Kuwaiti press and what is disseminated by lavishly financed press offices. Sometimes, because there is no conflict of interest between two countries, for example Saudi Arabia and Kuwait or Oman and Qatar, publications have dual sponsors. Regardless of the sponsor, the aim is the same: to have a mouthpiece in London that would advance a specific point of view similar to that of the privileged Arabs and the British who deal with the Middle East and to present the combined viewpoint to the rest of the non-Arab world.

Because the Saudis have tried to buy every journalist who writes on the Middle East, Arab and outsider alike, and have used their financial leverage to put the press which opposes them out of business, they represent a special large group within this establishment. In addition, what Saudi Arabia has to say is important because the country is important both to itself and as the West's leading regional Arab ally. The distortion of reality this exposes goes to the heart of the matter in terms of showing how the Arab establishment and the West interact in London to mislead and conceal corruption, abuse of power, the retardation of democracy and the overall disaster which will result from overlooking corruption, deterring democracy and pretending that all is well in the Middle East.

Al Sharq Al Awsat (The Middle East), distinctive in being printed on green paper, is a daily newspaper which is edited in London and is transmitted by facsimile to three cities in Saudi Arabia, and Cairo, Casablanca, Frankfurt, Paris and New York. The paper is rich, reportedly backed by Prince Salman bin Abdel Aziz, Governor of the Province of Riyadh and a full brother of King Fahd.

The paper makes no attempt to disguise its connection with the House of Saud, a laudable act of honesty which contrasts favourably with secret supporters of the Saudi royals who feign total independence. The question then is not whether it reflects the opinion of the House of Saud, or a faction of it, but why the House of Saud needs a London-edited Arabic newspaper when there are so many of them under its direct control in their country. The answer is simple: the readership of *Al Sharq Al Awsat* is made up of a different group of people, a new Arab élite which operates out of London and has a subsidiary presence in other parts of Europe and America. Newspapers published in Saudi Arabia are relied upon to stop some news from reaching the Saudi people, but those published in London are used to advance the Saudi point of view to the new Arab élite, which represents it to the world.

There is no definite opinion in *Al Sharq Al Awsat* regarding the Arab-Israeli peace process, even three years after the Oslo accord. The PLO's submissiveness and the Syrian hard line are treated in practically the same tone. There has been little reporting of the disastrous economic conditions brought about by the embargo on Iraq. And coverage of the anti-government riots in Bahrain is kept to a minimum. In all these cases any full treatment of the subject matter follows official Saudi policy towards the issues in question. In a way, Saudi Arab policy determines what constitutes news and what doesn't.

The situation is somewhat clearer when it comes to stories about the Kingdom. In 1995 there were official Saudi government announcements of the execution of over 66 drug traffickers. The paper carried the announcements in small news items. The issue of executing drug traffickers in the Kingdom in accordance with the Saudi interpretation of Islamic Sharia laws and the possibility that the people beheaded publicly were denied due process of law is one which has occupied international human rights organizations such as Amnesty International, Middle East Watch and Liberty.

Most human rights organizations object to the punishment in principle:

they find it disproportionate and inhumane. Saudi opposition groups in exile, mainly Islamic and supportive of the principle of Islamic punishment, claim that the Saudi government is not enforcing the true Sharia law, which requires several witnesses to any crime and provides the accused with ample right to defend his or her self. The paper accepts the official Saudi position and the lack of editorial content in reporting the story implies that there are no questions regarding the two issues raised by human rights organizations and Saudi opposition groups.

Meanwhile King Fahd's 1995 decision to sponsor the hajj of 5000 Muslims from former USSR republics was carried by the London-based Saudi press with relish, as if his pocket and the treasury were not one and the same. Fahd's attempt to be more Islamic than the fundamentalists, to the point of creating what might be called royal fundamentalism to appeal to Muslim feelings everywhere, was followed by reports in many Saudi-sponsored publications of the charitable contributions of Prince Abdel Aziz, Fahd's twenty-three-year-old favourite son and adviser, who holds ministerial rank. Naturally other good deeds of members of the 20,000-member family (male and female) are highlighted, as are their weddings, travels, official attendances and Islamic behaviour. According to Saudi-owned publications, the House of Saud is one big, normal and happy Islamic family.

Overlooking or de-emphasizing stories and highlighting others, a legitimate activity, is followed by attempts in Saudi-owned and sponsored publications to elevate their contents through using foreign journalists and diplomats as contributors and presenting them as the accepted Western experts on the Middle East. This is not a lie: the contributors, judged by how the West and the pro-West Arab governments see things, are indeed the accepted experts on the Middle East. But in this case too, natural unwritten restrictions are in effect. For example, to revert to *Al Sharq Al Awsat*, the newspaper's Western contributors are either partisans, insipid innocents or others with no moral position regarding the House of Saud and their governance. Most, if not all, are willing to avoid controversial subjects such as public beheadings and floggings and unemployment among recent college graduates. Nevertheless, using them is beneficial, and it endows the newspaper with an aura of relying on non-Arab voices, by implication highly educated and competent professional writers, to present the same points of view as the Saudi press espouses. Western writers who hold critical or questionable views are avoided.

In addition to addressing its readership in Beirut-on-Thames and similar groups in Europe and the US, the people who run and work for *Al Sharq Al Awsat* speak to them through other media. Journalists on the paper are invited to appear on BBC radio and television, CNN, ABC and French state radio as experts on the Middle East and they are consulted for the same reason by British journalists and London-based ones who cover the region for American and other media. Over the past year they have opined on Saudi Arabia's Islamic and Arab roles, its oil policy, the bombing of the buildings housing American military personnel in Riyadh and Al Khobar, the nature of the opposition to the House of Saud and the overall role of the country as a loyal friend of the West. They do a good partisan job. The one-sidedness of their views, understandable as it is, eliminates the need to listen to voices which reflect the feelings of many of the people of Saudi Arabia and the Middle East. The real story is pre-empted.

The advocacy position of the Saudi-owned press, its regular staff and most of the people who contribute to it is legitimate propaganda aimed at the same group of people who made up the audience at the Khalidy lecture. The message which they advance, that all is well in Saudi Arabia, is accepted by the select group of Arabs whom the West trusts, Western supporters of the Arab establishment (as, in this case, represented by the House of Saud) and the Western press. The latter either refuses or doesn't know enough but to follow the line of friendly voices and this picture is passed on by them to the wider audience, the public in general, who are utterly incapable of judging any Middle East situation by themselves. Furthermore, even in non-interview situations, professionals who don't know much about conditions in Saudi Arabia – and very few are acquainted with the true picture – rely on Saudi publications and their employees for behind-the-scenes guidance and information. The efforts of news-papers like *Al Sharq Al Awsat*, pre-emptive as they are, are open, legitimate and understandable.

But legitimate and understandable as all this activity is, it must be judged in terms of whether the true story of Saudi Arabia and its policies is being covered by anybody else whose opinions reflect an unofficial appreciation of what is really happening in that country and the importance of these events. *Al Quds Al Arabi*, the already mentioned independent daily, is one of the few Arab publications in London which carries Saudi stories from a totally independent point of view.

The newspaper's editor, Abdel Barri Attwan, openly admits, 'We can't afford to pay the salaries paid by newspapers beholden to Saudi Arabia – we simply don't have the money.' In fact, his financial problems don't stop there. *Al Quds* is Palestinian in origin and its coverage of Saudi news deemed unfriendly to the monarchist regime is unacceptable to wealthy Palestinians who are members of the Beirut-on-Thames establishment.

Attwan has been telephoned by some of them and asked to desist from 'his attacks' (in fact, straight reporting) and some members of this group have taken their objections further and issued what amount to warnings against persisting. This strange situation is rendered stranger still by the fact that most of Attwan's reports about the Kingdom are translations of stories in foreign publications, something the people who object to Attwan's activity dismiss because foreigners aren't expected to be as subservient as Arabs or because the Arab people are the issue. And in strictly business terms, Attwan's situation is equally perilous and his newspaper receives no advertising because most of the media companies who place advertising are specialists in the Middle East who have to deal with Saudi-sponsored publications who in turn make it plain that advertising in *Al Quds* would endanger their relationship with them. Also, advertisers in Middle East publications are invariably companies which want to protect their business in Saudi Arabia, Kuwait and the rest of the pro-West countries. Unable to pay good salaries and devoid of sponsorship or support from the Arab establishment of London, and without advertising, Attwan has to rely on circulation to exist, a constantly threatening situation. 'We're all right for the coming two months or so, but I can't predict four or five months from now – we live on the edge,' is the way he describes his financial predicament. This is why other newspapers and magazines committed to an impartial reporting of the news find it difficult to survive. The voice which tells the whole Saudi story is muffled in an open, objectionable way, at the very least diminished.

In fact, the Saudi attempt to influence the content of London's Arab press extends to people who are not accused of any crimes except wishing to remain independent. Dr Saïd Muhammad Al Shehabi, editor of the Islamic magazine *Al 'Aalam*, puts his case succinctly: 'We're not anti anybody; we want to advance Islam in a modern way.'[3] But he is his own man and therefore opposed. Because the Saudis want to use Beirut-on-Thames to monopolize Islamic teachings and advance their version of Islam, they have banned *Al 'Aalam* and this publication also receives no advertising.

But, however deplorable, this too is legitimate. Unless we are taking a moral position or lamenting the undoubted results – the misconceptions this type of reporting produces and its potential disastrous effects on the future of the Middle East – there is nothing new in putting pressure on the opposition, commercial or otherwise. It certainly doesn't compare with the strident, menacing tone of the Saudi-sponsored newspaper *Al Hayyat*. Owned by Prince Khalid bin Sultan, commander of the Arab forces during the Gulf War, it published four years ago a column in which its editor accused some of the people opposed to Saudi hegemony over the Arab press of 'being more Zionist than Larry Smith' (a Zionist member of the US Congress) and proceeded to describe them as 'sick souls' and 'non-Arabs' 'whose ambition is to be spies for Israel'.

These seriously defamatory accusations, perhaps a potential source of physical danger to the accused, went unopposed. As an objector to Saudi control of the Arab press I refrained from suing the editor because I do not have the financial means to fight a legal case against a Saudi publication and in this case its very rich owners. The author of the article is a celebrated journalist, the only Arab journalist to be granted an exclusive interview with former British Prime Minister Margaret Thatcher. The then Prime Minister would never have granted an exclusive interview to an Arab journalist without solid establishment, in this case Saudi, connections, even if the publication he or she represented reflected the opinion of the majority of the people. When she spoke to *Al Hayyat*, Margaret Thatcher was addressing a loyalist readership. Putting pressure on individuals and being favoured with exclusive interviews is another way to support the press which backs the official pro-West Saudi point of view. Abdel Barri Attwan and his reporters have a difficult time even reaching official spokespeople.

Late in 1991 seven Palestinian multi-millionaires met in the Kensington home of a construction tycoon to plan the removal of the PLO's Yasser Arafat. The PLO's pro-Saddam Gulf War stand had endangered their business and affected their standing in Saudi Arabia, Kuwait and other Gulf states. Of particular concern to them was their position with these and other pro-West Arab governments as spokesmen to governments, institutions and important people in the West. In short, the PLO's Gulf War position had threatened their dual connections, and without these connections their functions and the status they engendered would disappear.

It was an empty threat. The powerless Palestinian cabal, charter members of Beirut-on-Thames with little stomach for political combat, were out-of-touch Arabs with no following. Like the rest of them in London, it is the local atmosphere which accords them importance and which misled them into thinking that they have power and represent their people and gave them their consequent desire to manipulate the fate of the Palestinian problem from the luxury of Kensington. Both the lack of political muscle and the utter lack of appreciation of the dynamics of the political process on their home ground is typical of most Arabs who speak the voice of reason to the West. In this case, Western friends, official and otherwise, were told of the move to replace the then unacceptable Arafat and welcomed and encouraged it. Nobody thought of asking the concerned rich men whom they represented. It didn't matter: they were a self-appointed group capable of speaking a voice of reason pleasing to the West, the type of people who have deputized for it for most of this century.

Most Iraqi exiles in London, because the original, anti-monarchist revolution in their country took place in 1958 and they came to Britain before the other Arabs who arrived in the 1970s, have been infected by London's atmosphere and belong to this category of out-of-touch people with political pretensions accepted in the West. 'I don't understand how the country which produced all those civilized people produced Saddam Hussein, and why the Iraqi people don't opt for them instead,' lamented my book publisher friend Peter Hopkins.

Hopkins was right: the Iraqi members of the *ancien régime* or rather the *ancien ancien régime*, are educated, well-spoken, worldly and devoid of the crudeness which is the trademark of many Gulf Arabs. In London they hold lavish parties where even their women drink 'whaiske' and they discuss Saddam, the Arabs and the good old days as well as books, theatre, architecture and other things that civilized people discuss. Indeed the word 'civilized' applies here without being a patronizing exaggeration.

Above all, the Iraqi exiles recite long lists of Saddam's crimes with disgust and relish. In addition to the hundreds of mainly true stories which have been reported and accepted, there is Saddam's son Udai relegating women who refuse him a night of pleasure to a den full of lions and some of them, out of despair, committing suicide. Of course, Saddam taught his sons how to use the gun to eliminate opponents the way any normal father teaches his kids how to play Scrabble. And they don't stop at Saddam: many of them are die-hard monarchists who go back to General Abdel Karim Kassem, the general who overthrew their country's monarchy in 1958, and offer proof of his unworthiness by telling how his mother used to wash clothes to make a living. Even people who didn't attain the top spot in their country don't escape their scrutiny and disparagement – for example, General Hardan Tikriti, the one-time Minister of Defence, who had the unfortunate habit of scratching his balls in public all the time.

Most people who listen to these unattractive characteristics of the non-establishment Iraqi leadership react in the manner of my friend Peter Hopkins. Most aren't as educated or knowledgeable in the ways of the Middle East as Hopkins, but practically all of them are either involved Western people or old or new Arab élite who believe that the son of a washerwoman is unsuitable leadership material. To members of the Arab establishment and their Western friends, including the Americans, Arab leaders should come from a certain class and the maxim that all people are created equal has no relevance to the Middle East.

This is a fundamental and inclusive attitude which covers and renders unfit non-establishment Arabs in positions of leadership or in the public eye and often even individuals with an independent voice. Abdel Barri Attwan has suffered from being patronized by London's Palestinian establishment because he grew up in a refugee camp. He tells of an incident when a chichi Palestinian lady from a leading family congratulated him on being the editor of a major Arabic newspaper and added, 'After all, it is really an achievement for a refugee.' I myself am not acceptable to members of the Arab establishment who liaise with Western people in London because I come from the village of Bethany and cannot be counted on to subscribe to the traditional unwritten rules which govern the behaviour of establishment Arabs and their Western counterparts. The exclusiveness of the Arab club is augmented by the attitude of Western writers and experts who don't want people to pre-empt their role. A refugee or a villager, however educated or capable, is not seen as an achiever but someone who is a threat to their position as explainers of things Middle Eastern. This works both ways.

When the Palestinian community in London recently selected people to make a presentation about the reporting of their problem in the Western media, Attwan and I, though recognized experts in this field, were considered unfit. Some speakers had clearly been chosen for who they were rather than for their knowledge, a fact which manifested itself during these presentations.

But how can a Western or civilized Arab listener not sympathize with anyone objecting to the crimes of Saddam? The killing of the Harrow-educated descendant of the Prophet, King Faisal II of Iraq, in 1958 is bad enough without being reminded of Kassem's obvious lack of social background and his inability to speak English in a proper manner or to carry out a civilized discourse about books and the arts. And we all know what it means to scratch your balls in public. But when the Iraqi establishment speaks to the West, Saddam's eradication of illiteracy, his health care programmes and his championing of women's rights, Kassem's commitment to building houses for the poor and Tikriti's military talents are subordinated to their social status and rendered irrelevant – though others who are pro-West but from equally humble backgrounds are absolved. Of course, Western people relate to Palestinians who tell them that there is no opposition to the new pro-West Yasser Arafat and that Hamas and other opponents of the peace process are all evil people and shouldn't be taken into consideration, even with their obvious popularity.

But, taking further the important example of Iraq, is there anything beyond social acceptability, anything substantial, which binds the Iraqi members of the *ancien régime* to their listeners? Are these Iraqis able to offer solutions to the substantial problems of their country? The answer is no. Having consorted with them for years – and they are indeed good, civilized company – I have never heard them espouse a sensible political programme or do anything but complain or hanker for a reimposition of a minority pro-West regime which would elevate them to leaders of their people. The descendants of sheriffian officers, old *sayyed* families, rich merchants under the monarchy or privileged tribal sheikhs, they live in a world apart from the average Iraqi, and the great majority of them are too comfortable to involve themselves in concrete political action. The reality of conditions in their country escapes them to the extent that they dismiss totally the simple fact that Saddam presides over a fairly well-organized political party with a substantial following, although undoubtedly a cruel minority one. The atmosphere created by the mutual admiration between the Iraqi exiles and their hosts precludes substantive discussion of the pressing issues of hunger and malnutrition in present-day Iraq and what should be done about the Shia–Sunni division to guarantee the survival of the country as a whole. This is why some of them, against all evidence and sound political judgement which demonstrates its unworkability, support the restoration of the monarchy under a certain Prince Ali, a Hashemite whom the Iraqi people don't even know.

The least of what the Palestinians who conspired against Arafat wanted was to redefine their connections with him to protect their pro-West positions and status. What most Iraqis in exile basically want – though few would admit it – is for the West to change the Iraqi government in their favour. After all, the West, whether colonial or committed to exercising indirect control, ran Iraq in the past, so why not now? Why not turn the clock back, occupy Iraq and hand it to members of the *ancien régime*, the friends of the West with nothing to offer except their ability to speak a language the West understands? Indeed why not an unknown Hashemite by the name of Ali? To the Iraqi advocates of this policy Iraq is the same as it was in 1921, when the West imported King Faisal I and created a special class of people to back him and run his government. This is why members of this group rush to accuse Saddam of crimes which would justify Western military action against him, as when some of them alleged that he was behind the June 1996 bombing of the American compound in Al Khobar.

The voice of reason that these groups use may very well be an unrealistic voice which ignores the majority of the people – after all, practically all speakers in Western forums either have no following or pursue political programmes which, like the idea of confederacy, are unworkable – but it is the only voice heard because it accepts Western supremacy in the Middle East. Even the Lebanese ladies who gather daily at the Express Café in Knightsbridge speak the voice of reason and appeal to their listeners with moans about the Lebanese 'mountains, sea and cedars' in an attractive French accent. Not a word about how they, mainly members of the minority Maronite establishment, abused Lebanon's Shias for decades. These usually bejewelled ladies would like someone, in this case preferably France, to act on their laments, occupy their beautiful country and put them back in power, not to speak of the possibility of killing members of Hizbollah and others to guarantee their maintenance of power. In fact, helping a pro-West Lebanese group eliminate Hizbollah isn't as far-fetched as it sounds, because there is little or no understanding of what led to the emergence of this political group and no one is willing to admit that it represents an important part of Lebanon's population. The Lebanon the Western listener wants restored to Maronite control is a beautiful country inhabited by civilized people and not one which affords all its citizens equal rights.

But occasionally there are more important, more difficult aspects to Arab politics which also demonstrate both the special relationship between the West and the Arab establishment which lives in London and other Western cities and how it works as an extension of the governing classes in the Middle East. Years ago, when Saddam Hussein was acceptable to the West, he used the Iraqi Cultural Centre in Tottenham Court Road to conduct intelligence operations against dissident Iraqis, mainly advocates of democracy, and on occasion to eliminate some of them (in 1975 Saddam's gunmen assassinated former Iraqi Premier Nayyef Abdel Razzak in front of Park Lane's Intercontinental Hotel and the whole incident was hushed up). London hosted secret meetings in the 1970s and 80s between King Hussein and Israeli politicians Shimon Peres and Yitzhak Rabin, non-violent accommodations of a policy opposed by Jordan's people. It was from here that Kuwait helped precipitate the Gulf War by trying to sell Iraqi debt notes at 20 per cent of their value, a move equivalent to declaring economic war against Iraq because it would have destroyed Iraq's ability to borrow money on the international market.[4] Even the dozens of Saudi princes competing for the throne and splitting their royal family into feuding factions promote themselves from London through appeals to both sides who make up Beirut-on-Thames and tell the world the story of the Middle East. Years ago, London was the city from which Libyan exiles organized an ill-fated landing against Qaddafi.

Although the tensions and occasional violence which result from the hard Middle East politics and journalism are things which the British government would rather do without, in the past it has been a direct or indirect contributor to them. Would the British government tolerate dangerous accusations of being Mossad agents by non-Saudis or would they have considered them an unacceptable prelude, perhaps an incitement, to violence? Was the kidnapping of Mordechai Vanunu (the man who disclosed Israel's nuclear secrets) by Mossad agents investigated as thoroughly as it should have been or did the British government's friendly attitude towards Israel play a role in what appears to have been a cover-up? What were the results of the investigations into the murders of PLO representative Saïd Hammami and Palestinian cartoonist Naji Al Ali? Who really kidnapped the brother of United Arab Emirates ambassador Mahdi Al Tajir and why haven't we heard much about the involvement of arms merchants and the CIA in the case? Has the British government investigated London press reports of Saudi hit squads sent to eliminate members of the opposition to the House of Saud? Is the British government's treatment of political exiles the same or does it practise selective morality and differentiate between them according to whether their activities are directed against friendly or unfriendly countries?

In fact, discriminating in favour of friendly regimes and against groups opposed to them, is an open and pervasive policy which covers the people who act on behalf of both sides. It doesn't differ from how the West behaves towards the geographic Middle East. Even Saddam was allowed to murder in the middle of London when his government was following policies friendly to the West. The Middle East countries which follow a pro-West line are always accommodated and those who oppose are opposed, even when this covers groups hardly involved or connected to the ever-present prospect of violence. Groups championing human rights and freedom of speech, such as Liberty, Middle East Watch, Article 19 and the Arab Organization for Human Rights, though staffed by gentle, well-meaning people are critical of countries like Saudi Arabia and hence afforded no comfort. According to Liberty's Sultan Azzam, 'We feel no pressure here, but there is an atmosphere, perhaps indirect pressure.'[5] Says Carmel Bedford of Article 19, 'When we issued *The Silent Kingdom*, our report on press and other freedoms in Saudi Arabia, we received calls from former British-officer types objecting to it, strenuously.' But there is more to it and members of the British Cabinet, including Foreign Secretary Malcolm Rifkind, have been dismissive of and objected to the contents of reports by these groups because their members are opposed to 'friends'. As we have seen from the treatment accorded such groups as the moderate Bahraini Islamic opposition, the London press overlooks the reports' contents and think-tanks pretend they don't exist. The Arab and Western components of Beirut-on-Thames condemn the reports of human rights organizations and dismiss the appeals of other political groups without reading what they have to say because, to them, the people who issue the reports and appeals are tiresome outsiders.

It is even more serious than that. The PKK, the Kurdish rebel group fighting for Kurdish ethnic rights in Turkey, is watched closely because Turkey is a friendly country, though the West is on record as supporting Kurdish rights. But Kurds opposed to Saddam are given a free rein even when they are more violent and in some cases no more than the representatives of feudal landlords with reprehensible records who want to enslave their own people. The Sudanese Liberation Front, violent and with a programme that would lead to the dismemberment of the Sudan and destabilization of a good part of Africa, is tolerated, but Malcolm Rifkind repeats his criticism of the Bahraini Shia opposition who try to use London as a base to advocate a peaceful change in their country that would grant them nothing more than equal rights. It is a case of sordid cynicism, an extension of the colonial policy of supporting criminal friends and opposing the most peace-loving of enemies, a frustration of legitimacy and democracy which Britain has practised in the Middle East for most of this century.

It is worthwhile detailing some of the activities and the official and unofficial reaction to them of a friendly group and an unfriendly one. Even today, and despite its apparent ineffectiveness, the Iraqi National Congress (INC), reportedly sponsored by the CIA, uses London to try to overthrow Saddam. Its political programme, a call to create an Iraqi federation which presupposes considerable political maturity on the part of the Iraqi people and their leadership, is utterly unrealistic and the various groups which make up the INC are already quarrelling. But it still functions and not only issues press releases to maintain the anti-Saddam mood of Western governments and the Western press, but also shuttles brave people who are willing to combat his forces inside and outside Iraq. However laudable their activities, they should be seen for what they are, a self-serving group capable of resorting to violence to overthrow Saddam. Furthermore, among the Council's members are former associates of Saddam and the criminal Ba'ath regime in Iraq who are themselves guilty of acts of violence against the Iraqi people. Because they are members of a pro-West organization their crimes are overlooked. INC members operate freely and whatever they do is applauded and encouraged by official Britain, other Western governments, so-called Middle East experts and members of the chichi Arab establishment. Not a word is said about their lies.

Compare this with the already mentioned Committee for the Legitimate Rights (of the Saudi people) and the new, moderate and apparently popular Reformation Committee, which both do nothing more than use modern technology to spread a moderate anti-House of Saud message. Their fax machines and regular telephones are monitored, and though their exhortations are there for everyone to hear, the British government and the residents of Beirut-on-Thames insist on accusing them of terrorism, and the label is widely accepted. I have given up questioning this.

The Saudi groups are opposed because they don't follow a totally subservient pro-West policy but one which advocates open discourse and cooperation between equals. On the other hand, INC is supported because it accepts everything advanced by its Western friends and nothing else matters. The Islamic Front for the Liberation of Bahrain is also opposed. The Bahrainis too have been labelled incorrectly, as when members of the British government – Douglas Hurd did this several times – associated them with terrorism without providing a shred of proof. This is a familiar use of an old propaganda trick, dredging up hated buzzwords to frighten audiences and undermine totally innocent groups. *The Times* stopped short of accusing them of being terrorists but wanted them deported for threatening Britain's relations with friendly regimes. The *Sunday Telegraph* accused them, without naming its source, of carrying out terrorist activity which originates in Iran. The brutal status quo in Bahrain is defended.

The arms trade is another activity which demonstrates the unwritten concordat between the West and Middle East groups beholden to it, in a way which exposes how the West destabilizes the region and condones corruption. How regimes are destabilized has been covered elsewhere in this book, but the arms trade, manifestly corrupt and corrupting by nature, is identified differently when it is practised by friends. This is why participation in it by London's Arab establishment is a legitimate activity.

Sellers and buyers of military hardware, Britain, Saudi Arabia, Kuwait, the United Arab Emirates, China, Russia, Chile, Argentina, Brazil and at least twenty other countries, use London as a centre for their operations. So do the Khashoggis, Gerhard Mertin, Sam Cummins, Robert Jarman and other arms dealers. Certainly less important Palestinian, Lebanese, Jordanian, Kurdish, Armenian, Russian, South African, Argentinian and Pakistani arms dealers operate here.

The rules governing the sale of arms to the Middle East from London are elastic and this once again means that the attitude of the British government matters as much as the rules themselves. For example, in the 1980s Chile used London to sell Saddam cluster bombs and Portugal did the same with heavy 155mm artillery shells. Because the West, despite proclamations of neutrality during the Iran-Iraq War, wanted Saddam to prevail, the British government looked the other way and did nothing to stop the transactions. The deals were organized by 'acceptable' Iraqis. Trying to do the same today would lead to disclosures in the press, calls for stopping them in parliament and attempts by the British government to act against the seller and the buyer. The rules haven't changed – only the attitude.

In the mid-1970s, and even now, sales of British-made military hardware were subject to this superseding attitude. The sale of 'lethal weapons' had to be approved by the government in a way which suggested special care was paid to where they went. But what this meant was subject to selective interpretation. When Iraq, then the largest Arab purchaser of arms, tried to buy Jaguar fighter-bombers from British Aerospace and Lynx helicopters from Westland, all these elements came into play.

The intermediaries on the deals, Arab Resources Management of Beirut, proved the genuineness of their request for the aircraft, the validity of their claim to represent the Iraqi government, and talked British Aerospace and Westland into signing commission agreements covering their products. The agreements were legal, indeed subject to the laws of England and Wales, and all that was needed to conclude the deals was the approval of the British government.

The briefs prepared by BAe to obtain British governmental approval for its proposed sale argued in favour of accepting the credentials of the intermediaries on the basis of Iraq being 'a friendly country'. The approval was granted, with full government knowledge of the commissions and the corrupt nature of the deal. Later, after the approval of the proposed sale of Jaguar aircraft set the precedent, the same company, BAe, made an offer to build several Iraq Military Aircraft Installations, airfields. And Westland, following suit, offered and sold Iraq the sophisticated Lynx helicopter.[6]

The act of accepting the corruption of 'a friendly country' was followed by the outright dishonesty of bribing British corporate officers. John Speechily, at the time the managing director of the helicopter division of Westland, was privately offered and accepted a bribe to facilitate the transaction. With this, the corrupt nature of the deal covered the intermediaries, the Iraqi generals behind them and the British businessman involved. There is good reason to believe that British government officials weren't far behind; to this day, the huge sums of money resulting from these deals which go to British corporate officers imply that there are others in tow, in all likelihood the officials who approved the deals. There is no need to analyse the consequences of what would happen now or had this degree of corruption been the result of a deal with an 'unfriendly country'.

The corruption surrounding this kind of deal nullifies all British government talk – Margaret Thatcher in particular was good at this – of government-to-government transactions being clean. Like the Iraqi deals, the multi-billion Yamama 2 deal with Saudi Arabia and all military sales since have been to 'friendly countries' with 'legitimate needs'. These combinations of words evoke the 'voice of reason' discussed earlier: in the case of arms deals they are made, in London, to describe a certain attitude which justifies corruption and the presence of arms merchants. Consistent press reports, in practically every London newspaper, that huge commissions have been attached to Yamama 2 have led nowhere.

But despite the inherent corruption and cynicism involved, these deals are nothing more than a natural expression of how Beirut-on-Thames functions, how unsound political positions and corrupt business deals by friends become acceptable. The people from the Middle East are indeed the special group I have identified and the reasons behind their comfort is greater than convenience and language: it is the Beirut-on-Thames atmosphere of facilitating the corruption of establishment friends. I know no fewer than ten Arab arms dealers who are not only prominent citizens of Beirut-on-Thames but major contributors to what makes it. Where else in the industrialized world would an arms dealer representing a friendly country dine with the Prime Minister at her official residence? And London is not alone in accepting corrupt friends and elevating them. It was Adnan Khashoggi who set the precedent by establishing close relations with American decision-makers during the Nixon administration and by making contributions to the presidential campaign of Ronald Reagan.

I am in possession of documents which show how Hong Kong, Panamanian, German, Swiss and Irish companies have used London during the past ten years to conclude arms sales agreements with Middle East governments. Undoubtedly there have been many more. Contrary to accepted wisdom, the negotiations for these deals were no more secret than a regular business transaction which involves hiding facts from competitors. The British acceptance of this activity is similar and as selective as their acceptance of London-based Middle East politics and journalism. With these activities in London, there is a chance of influencing and, when necessary, intercepting them, and certainly this is one way of closely monitoring the sales of Western military equipment to the Middle East. The ones which serve the purposes of the British and their friends are allowed, while other deals are stopped in a legal manner or through the exertion of influence, and there is the added benefit of knowing what is happening in this important area. The corrupt nature of the deals is never a factor unless the deal doesn't fit the political designs of Britain.

The existence of a Beirut-on-Thames has more to it than the way it manifests itself in the politics, journalism and arms trade between the West and the Middle East. Says Jotta Simon, an attractive female arms dealer who knows and uses London openly, 'It's a convenience problem and in a way a language problem. People from the Middle East are comfortable here.' One could argue that Beirut-on-Thames was created to accommodate an overall old colonial attitude separating good pro-West Arabs from unacceptable anti-West ones. The separation, in fact discrimination, is the culmination, the modern expression of this attitude.

The well-known Egyptian writer Muhammad Heikal, one of the most celebrated analysts of Middle East affairs, speaks of the Middle East being divided between rich Arabs who, on a full- or part-time basis, live overseas and the poor ones who stay behind.[7] Heikal is correct, for most rich Arabs have made their money out of connections with pro-West governments, including through acting for them in the West, and their loyalties are to the policies which made them. They are at the centre of the Beirut-on-Thames syndrome.

The Home Office, the department which decides who is allowed to reside in Britain and who is denied this right, refused to grant this writer an on-the-record interview about the rules and regulations governing the Arab presence in London. However, speaking on a non-attribution basis, a spokesman told me, 'People with independent means are allowed to stay, but we don't want people with an undesirable background. Character, conduct or association is a factor.'[8]

In essence, Britain is interested in the privileged few who came into existence through the regimes that the West created in the Middle East and who resemble the constituencies of sheikhs, merchants and minorities that it created earlier this century to support its appointed rulers. They are akin to the intellectuals who, caught in a time-warp, still proffer effete appeals to their friends to solve Jerusalem's and Palestine's problems attractively from a distance. This is why, dismissing all warnings of impending danger as expressed in the rising tide of Islamic fundamentalism, the West insists that a Middle East in the hands of these people is what is needed.

With a major part of the Middle East which matters to Western eyes in London acting in a manner which resembles the behaviour of the leadership of the Arab governments, dealing with average Arabs on the ground is seen as unnecessary, and Heikal's statement deserves its intended importance. This is very similar to the British use of leading Palestinian families in the 1920s and 30s, resembles Western reliance on Egyptian pashas under an alien monarchy and is the same as the creation of a new Iraqi establishment of former Turkish officers in the period following the First World War. This continuing process of adopting people with similar interests or creating people in their own image and dealing exclusively with these groups means that there is no need to convert or defer to the opinion of the poor masses of the Middle East, and that is one of the reasons why they, in utter frustration, become rabid nationalists or Islamic extremists, potential bombers.

In accordance with the cynical, corrupt and unsound British policy of looking with favour on people with money and connections, a known arms dealer who spent five years in the prisons of Jordan and the United Arab Emirates has been granted residence in London, while an Egyptian electronics engineer who objects to his country's human rights policies has been denied it. Despite his prison terms the arms dealer still has high connections in a third country, and this qualifies him. A man accused in the Middle East of embezzling the huge sum of £40 million, but a member of the establishment, is allowed to remain in London and afforded protection and legal aid, but a simple worker is deported for defaulting on paying his electricity bills. A former aide to Yasser Arafat turned intermediary is granted asylum, received by members of the Cabinet and the police are asked to drop a case against his hoodlum son for attacking an elderly passenger in a bus, but a Palestinian Islamist, a good family man who obeys impeccably the laws of the land, is refused asylum on the mere suspicion that he is connected with the Islamic movement Hamas.

According to Detective Inspector Thomasz Dorantt of the National Criminal Investigation Service (NCIS), people with 'antecedent history', a record of having been imprisoned or detained in their country without being sentenced, are subject to special police attention.[9] Dorantt spoke attractively of how this works, in reality, because it is never applied, of how this is supposed to work. The information on which NCIS and other government departments' assessment of 'antecedent history' is made comes from Middle East governments. This is why the rich arms dealer's file wasn't transmitted to London. Thus Middle East governments have as much say in how the British view anyone who has antecedent history as do the British. Political antecedent history is doctored by Middle East governments to fit their politics, and officials' pockets. This not only explains friendly Arab governments' protests when the British don't follow this line to the end, as in the case of Mas'ari and Saudi insistence that he be deported. It also explains the situation of the Egyptian electronics engineer and Palestinian Islamist who had no official backing. The British know this and accept it because the information which reaches them is provided by friends and not enemies like Libya, Iraq, Iran, another unfriendly country or Hamas and Hizbollah.

The interviews with the Home Office and Dorantt were followed by a refusal by Scotland Yard officers to grant me interviews on or off the record. This was expected. Scotland Yard officers could not answer for Her Majesty's Government's attitude and any statements made by them regarding applicable laws as they understood them were likely to be refuted by evidence that these laws were applied in a discriminatory fashion. The way laws are applied is beyond Scotland Yard's control. In fact, one cannot but sympathize with Scotland Yard's refusal to discuss these matters. Once again the laws don't really matter as long as the British government's policy and ensuing attitude subordinate the vague laws to accommodating friends, affording them assistance in the dissemination of their opinion and accepting their ways – even when these are violent.

The state of moral decay which exists in London is similar to condoning and justifying arms deals with countries which cannot use the military hardware they purchase and similar also to overlooking the human rights, freedom of speech and other crimes against the average Arab by pro-West Arab countries. The corrupt nature of the intercourse between the British government and the pro-West Arab regimes is the godfather of what happens daily in London.

In fact, the widespread corruption of the Arabs of Beirut-on-Thames appears to have infected their British hosts. There have been press allegations of phoney consultancies amounting to influence-peddling, of outright bribes to officials to facilitate arms deals, and another claiming that MPs received bribes to raise specific questions in Parliament. Moreover, the British government itself has reneged on its promises, made during the Gulf War, to control the flow of arms to the Middle East. The laxity concerning the Arab presence in London has produced questionable ethics on the British side which are likely to continue.

The game played out in London repeats itself in both Paris and Washington, albeit on a smaller scale because neither claims the same primacy in Middle East affairs or hosts as many Arab expatriates. Dealing mainly with Lebanon, which it has always claimed as its sphere of influence,

France hosts former Lebanese Presidents Amin Gemayal and Michel Aoun and provides them with a platform to advocate the reimposition of the old system which guarantees the supremacy of the minority Maronites. The two men, and many of their followers, meet with French officialdom, obtain unqualified statements of support and proceed to act in a way which threatens the stability of their country. For example, on 19 June 1996, in a statement more flagrant than most, the two former presidents and Dory Chamoun, the son of another former president, issued a proclamation against the new election law which does not guarantee Maronite supremacy and, instead of being dismissed, this statement was carried by official French radio.[10] The unwritten concordat between the people who issued the statement and the French, an agreement which suggests acceptance of the return of a Maronite-controlled Lebanon to France's fold, precludes listening to anybody else. In fact, the efforts of the Lebanese Shias to present their point of view in France are cancelled by the refusal of the French to grant their representatives hearings, if they are granted visas.

What happens in Paris in the areas of Middle East politics, business, journalism and the arms trade resembles what occurs in London. The rules and regulations are different, but once again it is the attitude of officials and other people involved in things Middle Eastern which matters.

In Washington, the situation is broader than in France and considerably worse. The pervasive anti-Arab and anti-Muslim atmosphere in the United States is used to justify attempts at a process aimed at eliminating all voices except pro-American ones. The environment is so biased in this direction that even ostensibly all-Arab organizations dealing with the Middle East are constantly fighting to separate themselves from the mainstream of Middle East politics in order to survive. In the end, organizations such as the Arab Institute and the Arab Anti-Defamation League spend most of their time trying to gain acceptance and, in the process of endearing themselves to anti-Arab official and unofficial Washington, remove themselves from the reality of conditions in the Middle East. Other organizations are Middle Eastern in name only from the start, made up of people with no constituency on the ground; others depend on creating a phoney activity of being Middle East experts to make a living (as advisers to American news organizations etc); and a third group has the sole function of pretending to solve Middle East problems in the manner of the people at the Khalidy lecture.

Naturally there are groups and organizations which do not fall within these definitions, but overall what is allowed in Washington adheres to the unwritten rules of discrimination against anything which might represent the thinking of the Arab people.

On 9 September 1994 a Washington gathering held to celebrate the first anniversary of the Arafat–Rabin meeting in the same city was attended by no fewer than 300 American, Palestinian, Israeli and Arab luminaries. The speakers were Nabil Sha'ath (via satellite television), Yasser Arafat's latest chief political adviser; Yossi Beilin, the Israeli Deputy Foreign Minister, and Sari Nusseibeh, a West Bank politician and academic. Everybody toasted a year of peace and spoke of the prospects for implementing the various peace agreements between the Palestinians and Israel, but there was no mention of the acceptability of the agreements to the Palestinian people or appropriate mention of the simple fact that some Palestinian groups and individuals oppose them, the way they were being implemented or both. The atmosphere of the meeting resembled the atmosphere at the Khalidy lecture: it reflected the opinion of politicians and intellectuals connected to each other and a common pro-West policy but without a strong, acceptable link with the people on whose behalf they spoke. In fact, inadvertently, the meeting produced one of the most disturbing examples of 'the club' trying to impose its will on a people, in this case the Palestinians, known to this writer.

When discussing the various peace accords, Yossi Beilin, trying to put a positive face on things, stated that the Oslo, Washington and other agreements were not the first reached by the Palestinians and Israel. He referred to a previous agreement which had been secretly negotiated between the Israelis and Sari Nusseibeh, but which, for unmentioned reasons, was never implemented. Amazingly, there were no questions regarding this in the question-and-answer period which followed the presentations.

Analysing this statement and its significance has to take into consideration the person of Sari Nusseibeh and his position among the Palestinian people. Very much like Walid Khalidy, Nusseibeh is a scholar and a gentleman of the old school, a soft-spoken professor of philosophy, a man of character who also belongs to one of Palestine's leading families. And once again the condemnation of the event, Nusseibeh's negotiations of some sort of agreement with Israel, should be separated from his person as a man of considerable honour.

But who authorized Nusseibeh to negotiate for the Palestinians, and why weren't they told about it? Is it a case of someone capable of representing the Palestinian point of view, and Nusseibeh is, or is it a case of the Israelis negotiating with the old families in the same way that the British confused what the old families wanted with the desires of the people? Why did all those attending the event accept this without question? Indeed all one has to do is to think of the reaction which would have followed a Beilin statement about negotiations and agreements between

Israel and a popular leader such as George Habbash or any representatives of the various Muslim groups with considerable street following. The issue is not Nusseibeh's suitability; the issue is his unquestioned acceptance when there was colossal doubt regarding the support of the people in whose name he was ostensibly speaking.

As the above demonstrates, Washington is part and parcel, perhaps an extreme example, of the Beirut-on-Thames syndrome. However, unlike London and Paris, Washington pays less attention to the social background of the Arabs who deputize for their people and deals more crudely with the nature of their connections with pro-West governments and groups within the Middle East. This is why Khashoggi was openly accepted, and why people who are a clear extension of the old ruling Arab classes, committed as they are to airs and graces, tend to reside in London instead.

But, to repeat, there is nothing new in the Beirut-on-Thames mentality. It is difficult to distinguish the British attempt to silence the Saudi dissident Muhammad Al Mas'ari and stop him criticizing the Saudis from British efforts to stifle criticism of King Faisal I of Iraq by deporting Sayyed Taleb Naqib to Ceylon. And the same holds true of the efforts to undermine the Bahraini opposition and Omani, Egyptian and other groups opposed to corrupt pro-West governments.

Selective Western support for the Kurds, in London, Paris and Washington, resembles British support for the same people from the 1920s to the late 50s and American support from the 1960s until now. There is no ideological content to it and the Kurds have been dropped by the West whenever there was a pro-West central government in Iraq. The support for Iraqi Kurds is always dependent on their acting as an instrument of Western policy aimed at destabilizing unfriendly Iraqi regimes, and the support for the Kurds in Western cities is an extension of it. This formula excludes supporting the Kurds' just demands in friendly Turkey.

Overall, blind opposition to Islamic groups in London and everywhere else is similar to Western opposition to all popular movements in the Middle East throughout this century. In the 1950s and 60s Arabs living in the West who supported Nasser were frowned upon, dismissed out of hand and given little chance to present their point of view. In the 1960s the FBI ordered the deportation from America of my brother Munif for doing nothing more than voicing support for the then populist PLO, and there are many examples of this in Britain and France.

Even the condescending social attitude of people in the West is the same as it was earlier this century. The treatment of the Arabs of Beirut-on-Thames is almost identical to how colonial officers treated pro-West leaders like Nuri Saïd of Iraq and King Abdallah of Jordan. Social interaction with them was limited to having them perform a specific function and had little to do with accepting them as equal social or political partners.

The lopsided relationship which exists today is accepted by descendants of the same people who supported the West earlier this century, plus new moneyed groups promoted to establishment status by governments beholden to the West. The new groups are similar in behaviour to the pro-West Syrian officers of the 1950s, then a new ruling élite which was used to replace and expand the role of traditional leaders.

Beirut-on-Thames and its equivalents in other places are perpetuating a myth. However civilized, subservient and committed to Western supremacy the Arabs who are part of this scene are, they will never replace the need to deal with the Arab people. The Islamic militancy about which we hear daily is the direct result of the behaviour of Western and Arab governments and the activities of participants in the world of Beirut-on-Thames. The march towards disaster cannot be halted by total acceptance of Khalidy and total rejection of Mas'ari.

The 'complex of complexes' from which Nuri Saïd suffered is still very much with us, and so is Western commitment to the chosen few. What happened in Iraq in 1958 will repeat itself throughout the Arab Middle East. There is no light at the end of the tunnel.

Notes

Chapter 1: A Cruel Harmony, a Brutal Friendship

1. Cited in Noam Chomsky, *World Orders, New And Old*, p.155
2. H.V.F. Winstone, *Gertrude Bell*, p.200
3. David Fromkin, *A Peace to End All Peace*, p.106
4. Lawrence James, *The Life and Legend of Lawrence of Arabia*, p.61
5. Sarah Searight, *The British in the Middle East*, p.80
6. Hisham Sharabi, *Neopatriarchy, A Theory of Distorted Change in Arab Society*, p.VII
7. Uriel Dann, ed., *The Great Powers in the Middle East*, p.192
8. James Morris, *The Hashemite Kings*, p.27
9. Saïd K. Aburish, *The Rise, Corruption and Coming Fall of the House of Saud*, pp.18–19
10. Zaine N. Zaine, *Arab-Turkish Relations and Arab Nationalism*, p.60
11. Fromkin, ibid., p.106, quotes Sir Arthur Hirtzel as saying, 'What we need is a weak and disunited Arabia.'
12. Desmond Stewart, *The Temple of Janus*, p.166
13. Morris, ibid., p.65
14. James, ibid., p.313
15. Dann, ibid., p.94
16. Cited in Edward Said, *Culture and Imperialism*, p.239
17. Morris, ibid., p.32; Charles Glass, *Tribes with Flags*, p.180; *Punch* magazine, December 1917, described Allenby's entry into Jerusalem as 'The Last Crusade'
18. Edward Said, *Peace and Its Discontents*, pp.88–9

Chapter 2: Images and Reality

1. David Gilmour, letter, November 1995
2. Christopher Harper, interview, New York, June 1995
3. Cited in J.C. Bartlet, *Global Conflict*, p.313
4. A classmate of the writer, Saud Ibrahim Al Muammar, was tortured to death in a Saudi prison
5. Interview with Saïd Es Soulami of Article 19, September 1995, London

6. Steve Emerson, *The American House of Saud*, pp.298–302
7. Ramsey Clark, *Report on US War Crimes Against Iraq*, p.13
8. John Marlowe, *Imperialism and Arab Nationalism*, p.212
9. Thomas Friedman, *From Beirut to Jerusalem*, p.324
10. Jimmy Carter, *Blood of Abraham*, p.185
11. Gerald de Gaury, *Faisal*, p.97
12. John Bulloch and Harvey Morris, *No Friend But the Mountains*, p.3
13. Alan Hart, *Arafat*, p.53
14. Paul Johnson, *Modern Times*, p.774
15. Muhammad Heikal, *Autumn of Fury*, pp.179, 182
16. H.V.F. Winstone, *The Illicit Adventure*, p.177
17. Conversation with Senator Claybourn Pell, Newport, Rhode Island, September 1993
18. Christine Moss Helms, *Iraq, Eastern Flank of The Arab World*, p.18
19. The writer is in possession of a copy of the Pfaulder Corporation's design
20. James Morris, *The Hashemite Kings*, p.39, describes General Allenby as 'the last Christian conqueror of Jerusalem'. Charles Glass, *Tribes With Flags*, p.180, recounts General Gouraud's statement on occupying Damascus, '*Nous revoilà, Saladin.*'
21. Elie Kedourie, *Politics in the Middle East*, p.100, alleges that Lord Kitchener, as Secretary of War, wanted to make Hussein I caliphate
22. Roger Owen, *State Power and Politics in the Middle East*, p.95
23. Miles Copeland, *The Game Player*, pp.142–57
24. Elie Kedourie, *Political Memoirs and Other Studies*, p.37
25. Jochen Hippler and Andrea Lueg, *The Next Threat*, p.97
26. Interview with Zakki Badawi, Muslim scholar and head of London's Islamic College, September 1995
27. Muhammad Heikal, *Autumn of Fury*, p.124
28. Heikal, ibid., pp.124–5
29. Patrick Seale, *The Struggle for the Middle East*, p.335
30. Hippler and Lueg, ibid., p.128

Chapter 3: The Gift of God, a Gift from Satan

1. *World Bank Statistical Abstract*, 1993
2. Marion Kent, *Oil and Empire*, pp.126–7
3. Daniel Yeargin, *The Prize*, p.262
4. Yeargin, ibid., p.288, cites Ibn Saud telling his aide, 'Oh Philby, if anybody would give me a million pounds, I would give him all the concessions he wants.'
5. Ibid., p.451
6. Muhammad Rumaihi, *Beyond Oil*, p.34
7. Saïd K. Aburish, *The Rise, Corruption and Coming Fall of the House of Saud*, p.38
8. Miles Copeland, *The Game of Nations*, p.208. The suggestion in the book was confirmed to me by the writer in 1988.
9. Anwar Abdallah, *Petroleum and Manners*, p.50

10. The author attended this school at the time
11. Yeargin, ibid., p.451
12. Interview with Abdallah Tariki, 1962
13. Anthony Sampson, *The Seven Sisters*, pp.175–6
14. *Al Naft Al Arabi*, April 1969
15. Sampson, ibid., p.24
16. Dr Ramzi Zakki, *The Arab Economy Under Siege*, p.33
17. Tewfic Al Sheikh, *Petroleum and Politics*, p.225
18. Pierre Terrezian, *OPEC*, p.264
19. Sampson, ibid., p.276
20. Sa'ad Bazzaz, *The Gulf War and the One After*, pp.212 and 216
21. Dr Fadhel Chalabi, Director, Centre for Global Energy Studies, November 1995 speech
22. Ibid.
23. Yahya Sadowski, *Guns or Butter*, p.3. The Peace Institute of Stockholm puts the figure at a staggering 11.6 per cent of GDP.
24. Khalid Kishtainy, *Social And Political Affairs in Iraq*, p.72
25. H.V.F. Winstone, *The Illicit Adventure*, p.172
26. James Morris, *The Hashemite Kings*, pp.24–5
27. David Fromkin, *A Peace to End All Peace*, pp.224, 260, 512, 560
28. Muhammad Heikal, *Secret Channels*, p.40
29. Robert Lacey, *The Kingdom*, p.219
30. Conversation with Yunan Badawi, descendant of Assyrian leaders
31. Heikal, ibid., p.75
32. Cited in Jean Lacouture, *Nasser*, p.61
33. Morris, ibid., p.113
34. Ibid, p.161
35. Conversation with former Syrian Minister of Defence Ahmad Sharabatti
36. Interview with former Ba'ath Party leader Hani Fkaiki, London, October 1995
37. Christine Moss Helms, *Iraq, Eastern Flank of The Arab World*, pp.76–8
38. The writer is in possession of a copy of the Pfaulder Corporation design
39. Alan Friedman, *Spider's Web*, p.27
40. Patrick Cockburn, *Independent*, August 1993
41. Ismael Aref, *The Secrets of the 14 July Revolution and Establishment of the Iraqi Republic* (Arabic), p.310
42. Milton Viorst, *Sandcastles*, p.251. Viorst claims that both Kuwait and Saudi overproduced to undermine Iraq
43. Saïd K. Aburish, *The Rise, Corruption and Coming Fall of the House of Saud*, p.245
44. Conversation with Anthony Cordesman, Washington DC, September 1995
45. Barbara Newman, *The Covenant*, p.100
46. Interview with filmmaker Gwynne Roberts, who produced conclusive evidence that the chemical attack was an Iraqi one

Chapter 4: Coups For Sale

1. Eliezer Be'er, *Army Officers in Arab Politics and Society*, p.243
2. Liona Lukitz, *Iraq, The Search for National Identity*, p.25
3. Lutfi Farraj, *King Ghazi*, p.113
4. Farraj, ibid., p.99
5. Ibid., p.93
6. Ja'afar Al Askari, *Memoirs* (Arabic), p.189
7. Dr Muhammad Zubeidi, *King Ghazi And His Aides*, p.142
8. Dr Abdel Rahman Al Jalibi, *King Ghazi And His Murderers* (Arabic), p.191
9. FO memo 20/7/1936 PRO 374/20017
   A.G. Kerr to Eden 19/6/1936 no. 297
   PRO F.O. 371/20017
10. Farraj, ibid., p.235
11. Hanna Batatu, *The Old Social Classes and Revolutionary Movements of Iraq*, p.343
12. Zubeidi, ibid., p.143
13. Ibid., p.104
14. Farraj, ibid., p.270
15. Ibid.
16. Jalibi, ibid., 137
17. Farraj, ibid., p.275
18. Ibid., p.270
19. Zubeidi, ibid., p.181
20. Ibid., p.196
21. Tewfic Sweidi, *Iraqi Faces*, p.158
22. Zubeidi, ibid., p.275
23. Charles Issawi, cited in S.E. Finer, *The Man on Horseback*, p.228
24. Miles Copeland, *The Game of Nations*, p.42
25. Richard Pipes, *Greater Syria*, p.59
26. Interview with Miles Copeland, London, 1986
27. Abu Saïd is the writer's father and he recalled his involvement in this during interviews in London and Seattle, in 1987 and 1995
28. Be'er, ibid., p.229
29. Noam Chomsky, in *World Orders, Old And New*, quotes secretary of State John Foster Dulles as describing Nasser as an 'extremely dangerous fanatic'
30. Interviews with Radi Abdallah, New York, 1969, and London, 1982
31. The writer asked the king about this in a press conference and received 'We will see' as an answer
32. Conversations with Suheil Abu Hammad, London, 1986, 1987
33. Conversations with James Russell Barracks, New York, 1963
34. Interview with James Critchfield, Washington DC, September 1994
35. Cited in Ismael Aref, *The Revolution of 14 July and Establishment of the Iraqi Republic* (Arabic), p.285
36. Muhammad Heikal, *The Cairo Documents*, p.140
37. Critchfield, ibid.
38. Aref, ibid., p.251

39. Interview with Hani Fkaiki, member of the Command of the Ba'ath Party at the time, London, October 1995
40. Malik Mufti, *Renewed Unionism, 1963–1964* (unpublished)
41. Fkaiki, ibid.
42. The source for this is another American correspondent for *Time*, who declines to be named
43. The Iraqi sources for this information, including Iraqis who were involved in the coup, do not wish to be named
44. Dr Ahmad Al Bayati, *The Coup of February 8, 1963 in Iraq* (Arabic), p.167
45. Cited in Robert Kaplan, *The Arabists*, p.173
46. Dr Ghassan Attiyah, *Al Quds Al Arabi*, London, 14 February 1996
47. Dr Ghassan Attiyah cites Heikal in *Al Quds Al Arabi*, 12 November 1994
48. Radi Abdallah, ibid.
49. Sa'ad Bazzaz, *The Gulf War and the One After*, thesis of book (Arabic)
50. Ismael Aref, ibid., p.310
51. Fkaiki, ibid.
52. Ibid.
53. Attiyah, *Al Quds Al Arabi*, ibid.
54. Fkaiki, ibid.

Chapter 5: The Palestinians Against Themselves

1. Bernard Kimmerling and Joel S. Migdal, *Palestinians, The Making of a People*, p.5
2. A.W. Kayyali, *Palestine, A Modern History*, p.12
3. The writer's grandfather, a classmate of the Mufti at Al Azhar, spoke of people admiring the blueness of the Mufti's eyes
4. Kayyali, ibid., p.54
5. Bayan Nuehid Al Hout, *Leadership and Political Organizations in Palestine, 1917–1948* (Arabic), p.56
6. Ibid., pp.203–4
7. Philip Mattar, *Mufti of Jerusalem*, p.26
8. Izzat Darawazah, *About the Modern Arab Movement*, vol. 3 (Arabic), p.47
9. Kayyali, ibid., p.12
10. Ibid., p.36
11. The writer's grandmother often recited the song: 'They've made mules out of us, Mustapha Kamal come back and help us' (*Hamalouna hmal wa ja'louna Bghal, Mustapha Kamal, Ishfa'i fina ho*)
12. Kimmerling and Migdal, ibid., p.29
13. Kayyali, ibid., p.110
14. Derek Hopwood, *Tales of Empire*, p.144
15. Hout, ibid., p.230
16. Mattar, ibid., p.70
17. Mattar hints at this on p.46. My grandfather claimed that the Mufti saw the Muslim world as the only source of a solution to the problem.
18. Kayyali, ibid., p.119
19. Ibid., p.120

20. Mattar, ibid., p.62
21. Hout, ibid., p.326
22. Mattar, ibid., p.69; Hout, ibid., p.331
23. Kayyali, ibid., pp.200–1
24. Ibid., p.206; Mattar, ibid., p.122
25. Hopwood, ibid., p.149; Kayyali, ibid., p.195; Kimmerling and Migdal, ibid., p.118
26. Mattar, ibid., p.82
27. Ibid., p.83
28. Majid Khadduri, *Arab Personalities* (Arabic), p.143
29. Colonel R. Meinertzhagen, *Middle East Diary*, pp.179–80
30. Khadduri, ibid., p.145
31. Larry Collins and Dominique Lapierre, *O Jerusalem*, p.55
32. Interview with M.B., former treasurer, Arab Higher Committee
33. Saïd K. Aburish, *The St George Hotel Bar*, pp.150–4
34. Janet and John Wallach, *Arafat, The Eyes of the Beholder*, p.11
35. Andrew Gowers and Tony Walker, *Yasser Arafat and the Palestinian Revolution*, p.41
36. Ibid., p.42
37. John Bulloch, *Final Conflict*, p.162
38. Gowers and Walker, ibid., p.85
39. Kimmerling and Migdal, ibid., p.265
40. Gowers and Walker, ibid., p.103
41. Bulloch, ibid., p.162
42. Gowers and Walker, ibid., p.140
43. Ibid., p.86
44. Samuel Katz, *Soldier Spies*, p.276
45. Seymour Hersh, *The Price of Power*, p.407
46. Ibid., pp.405–7
47. Interview with former member of PLFP command, Munif Aburish, the writer's brother
48. Alan Hart, *Arafat*, p.401
49. Muhammad Heikal, *Secret Channels*, p.390
50. Hart, ibid., p.405
51. Ian Black and Benny Morris, *Israel's Secret War*, p.373
52. Hart, ibid., p.415
53. Conversation with writer and journalist John Bulloch, 1991
54. Muhammad Rabi', *US-PLO Dialogue*, p.85

Chapter 6: A Case of Religious Abuse

1. Conversation in 1989 with Raymond Eddé, the son of Emile Eddé and a leading Lebanese politician in his own right
2. Wade R. Goria, *Sovereignty and Leadership in Lebanon*, p.19
3. Kamal Salibi, *A House of Many Mansions*, p.35
4. Nadim Shehadek et al., *Lebanon, A History of Conflict and Consensus*, p.104
5. Meir Zamir, *The Formation of Modern Lebanon*, p.102

6. M.E. Yapp, *The Near East Since World War I*, p.265
7. William Crane Eveland, *Ropes of Sand*, p.248
8. Goria, ibid., p.29
9. Interview with Jordanian Minister of Interior Radi Abdallah, 1961
10. Interview with *Time* correspondent Abu Saïd, Seattle, 1995
11. David Gilmour, *Lebanon, a Fractured Country*, p.31
12. Goria, ibid., p.31
13. Gilmour, ibid., p.32, cites Admiral Holloway as saying, 'Chamoun called us to protect himself.'
14. Samir Khalaf, *Lebanon's Predicament*, p.132
15. Khalaf, ibid., p.136
16. Gilmour, ibid., p.32
17. Goria, ibid., p.215
18. Jonathan Randall, *The Tragedy of Lebanon*, pp.84–5
19. Robert Fisk, *Pity the Nation*, p.78
20. Gilmour, ibid., p.137
21. Ibid., p.146
22. Ithmar Rabonovich, *The War in Lebanon*, p.96
23. Milton Viorst, *Sandcastles*, p.137; Jimmy Carter, *The Blood of Abraham*, p.96
24. Carter, ibid., p.97
25. Ibid., p.96
26. Fisk, ibid., p.268

Chapter 7: The Obedient Offspring

1. Uriel Dann, *The Great Powers in the Middle East*, p.94
2. Gerald de Gaury, *Faisal*, p.30
3. Avi Shlaim, *The Politics of Partition: King Abdallah, the Zionists and Palestine*, p.45
4. King Hussein, *Uneasy Lies the Head*, p.45
5. Conversations with Wilton Wynn and Harry Ellis
6. Interview with Abul Hafez Bazzian, 1979
7. Dan Raviv and Yossi Melman, *Every Spy a Prince*, p.213
8. Ian Black and Benny Morris, *Israel's Secret War*, p.238
9. Raviv and Melman, ibid., p.214
10. Muhammad Heikal, *Secret Channels*, p.310
11. Morris and Black, ibid., p.321
12. Raviv and Melman, ibid., p.265
13. Robert Lacey, *The Kingdom*, p.137
14. Saïd K. Aburish, *The Rise, Corruption and Coming Fall of the House of Saud*, p.13
15. Harry St John Philby, *Arabian Jubilee*, pp.208–11
16. Philby, ibid., p.218
17. Dann, ibid., pp.184–6
18. Lacey, ibid., p.279
19. Ibid., pp.303–5
20. *Sourakia* magazine, 8 March 1988

21. Sandra Mackey, *The Saudis*, pp.227–8; Lacey, ibid., p.447
22. Simon Henderson, *After Fahd*, p.215
23. Mackey, ibid., pp.74–9
24. Anthony Sampson, *The Money Lenders*, pp.125–6
25. Dr Ramzi Zakki, *The Arab Economy Under Siege*, p.47
26. Washington Institute, *The Economy of Saudi Arabia*, number 38, Appendix X
27. Yahya M. Sadowski, *Guns or Butter*, p.68
28. Interview with Anthony Cordesman, Washington DC, September 1994
29. Sadowski, ibid., p.21

Chapter 8: Friends, Renegades and Revolvers

1. Ismael Aref, *Secrets of the 14 July Revolution and Establishment of the Iraqi Republic* (Arabic), p.83
2. Liona Lukitz, *Iraq, The Search for National Identity*, p.82
3. Lutfi Ja'afar, *King Ghazi* (Arabic), p.178
4. Interview with Rifa'at Chederchi, London, August 1995. Chederchi, a scholar, is the son of Iraqi politician Kamel Chederchi.
5. Ja'afar, ibid., p.113
6. Hanna Batatu, *The Old Social Classes and Revolutionary Movements of Iraq*, p.334
7. Desmond Stewart, *Temple of Janus*, p.354
8. James Morris, *The Hashemite Kings*, p.163
9. Lukitz, ibid., p.84
10. Tewfic Sweidi, *Arab Faces in History* (Arabic), pp.84, 85, 86
11. Gertrude Bell, *Letters*, p.303
12. Eliezer Be'er, *Army Officers in Arab Politics*, p.446
13. Miles Copeland, *The Game of Nations*, p.208
14. Majid Khadouri, *Arab Personalities* (Arabic), p.84
15. Jean Lacouture, *Nasser*, p.28
16. Muhammad Heikal, *The Cairo Documents*, p.29
17. Lacouture, ibid., p.59
18. Derek Hopwood, *Egypt, Politics and Society, 1945–1990*, p.86
19. P. J. Vatikiotis, *The History of Modern Egypt*, p.335
20. Copeland, ibid., pp.51–2
21. Audeh, Farouk, *Beginning and End* (Arabic), p.396
22. Lacouture, ibid., p.67
23. Heikal, ibid. p.84
24. Ibid, p.134
25. Interview in 1960 with Wasfi Tel, Jordanian Ambassador to Iran in 1958 and later Prime Minister. Tel had documents proving this.
26. Interview with Hani Fkaiki and Abdel Sattar Douri, London, September 1995
27. Conversations with CIA agent James Russell Barracks and NBC correspondent John Chancellor. The former was involved in the American landing and the latter confirmed and broadcast this.
28. Interview with the Mufti of Palestine, Beirut, 1960
29. Heikal, ibid., pp.187–225

30. *Le Monde*, 17 February 1970
31. Robert Lacey, *The Kingdom*, p.124
32. Gerald de Gaury, *Faisal*, p.74
33. Interview with Jordanian Foreign Minister Jamal Toukan, 1961
34. Interview in 1992 with Walter Pincas, *Washington Post* journalist and maker of *The Secret File*, a documentary about US–Saudi relations
35. Saïd K. Aburish, *The Rise, Corruption and Coming Fall of the House of Saud*, p.161
36. Jochen Hippler and Andrea Lueg, *The Next Threat*, pp.106–7
37. *Al Musawar* magazine, April 1959. Conversations between the writer and CIA agent James Russell Barracks, 1961.

Chapter 9: The Players

1. Cited in Anthony Cave Brown, *Treason in the Blood*, p.68
2. Interview with James Critchfield, Washington DC, September 1994
3. Robert Kaplan, in *The Arabists*, p.39, claims that in 1900 there were ninety-five American schools in Syria
4. Riyyad Al Rayyes, *Spies Among the Arabs*, p.55
5. Harry St John Philby, *Arabian Jubilee*, p.47
6. H.V.F. Winstone, *Gertrude Bell*, p.95
7. Ibid., p.241
8. Ibid., p.240
9. Brown, ibid., p.52
10. Gerald de Gaurey, *Faisal*, p.21
11. Brown, ibid., p.54
12. Mary C. Wilson, *King Abdallah, Britain and the Making of Jordan*, p.68
13. Brown, ibid., p.83
14. Nasser Al Saïd, *History of the House of Saud*, p.170
15. Al Saïd, ibid., p.644
16. Kaplan, ibid., p.58
17. Karl Twitchell, *Saudi Arabia*, p.79
18. Brown, ibid., pp.301–4
19. Kaplan, ibid., p.56
20. Trevor Royle, *The Life and Times of Sir John Bagot Glubb*, p.67
21. Royle, ibid., p.169
22. Avi Shlaim, *The Politics of Partition*, p.203
23. James Morris, *The Hashemite Kings*, p.105
24. Shlaim, ibid., p.78
25. Morris, ibid., p.111
26. Royle, ibid., p.243
27. Shlaim, ibid., p.180
28. Muhammad Heikal, *Secret Channels*, p.79
29. Heikal, ibid., p.82
30. Shlaim, ibid., pp.181–4
31. Royle, ibid., p.365
32. Miles Copeland, *The Game of Nations*, p.41

33. Miles Copeland, *The Game Player*, p.83
34. Ibid., p.44
35. Copeland, *The Game of Nations*, p.77
36. Ibid., p.162
37. Copeland, *The Game Player*, p.134
38. Brown, ibid., p.476
39. Conversation with Bill Eveland, London, 1981
40. Wilbur Crane Eveland, *Ropes of Sand*, p.250
41. Conversation with Abul Hafez Bazzian, 1969
42. Ian Black and Benny Morris, *Israel's Secret War*, p.321; Samuel M. Katz, *Soldier Spies*, p.107; Dan Raviv and Yossi Melman, *Every Spy a Prince*, pp.213, 261

Chapter 10: The Beirut-on-Thames Syndrome

1. Interview with Saïd Essoulami, London, March 1994
2. Interview with Abdel Barri Attwan, London, March 1996
3. Interview with Dr Saïd Muhammad Shehabi, London, April 1995
4. Saïd K. Aburish, *The Rise, Corruption and Coming Fall of the House of Saud*, p.173
5. Interview with Sultan Azzam, London, April 1994
6. Copies of these offers are with the writer
7. Muhammad Heikal, *Al Quds Al Arabi*, 13 March 1996
8. Interview with two officials of the Home Office, March 1995
9. Ibid.
10. *Al Quds Al Arabi*, 20 June 1996

Sources

SELECT BIBLIOGRAPHY

Memoirs of King Abdallah of Transjordan, London, 1950
Abdel Hai, Tewfik, *Death of a Princess*, London, 1988 (Arabic)
Abdel Rahman, Faiz, *Scandals of the Oil Kings*, Beirut, 1990 (Arabic)
Aburish, Saïd K., *Pay-off, Wheeling and Dealing in the Arab World*, London, 1984
—— *The St George Hotel Bar*, London, 1989
—— *The Rise, Corruption and Coming Fall of the House of Saud*, London, 1994
Ajami, Fuad, *The Arab Predicament*, Oxford, 1992
Alawi, Hassan, *Walls of Mud*, London, 1993 (Arabic)
Al Askari, Ja'afar, *The Memoirs of Ja'afar Al Askari*, London, 1988 (Arabic)
Al Bayati, Dr Hamid, *The Coup of February 8 1963 in Iraq*, London, 1996 (Arabic)
Al Ja'fari, Muhammad Hamdi, *The End of Kasr Al Rihab*, Beirut, 1991 (Arabic)
Al Sheikh, Tewfic, *Petroleum and Politics in Saudi Arabia*, London, 1989 (Arabic)
Antonius, George, *The Arab Awakening*, London, 1938
Anwar, Abdallah, *Petroleum and Manners*, London, 1980 (Arabic)
Aref, Ismael, *Secrets of the 14 July Revolution and Establishment of the Iraqi
    Republic*, London, 1986 (Arabic)
Armstrong, H.C., *Lord of Arabia*, Princeton, 1966
Attiyah, Ghassan, *The Emergence of the Iraqi State 1908–1921*, London, 1988
Audeh, Farouk, *Beginning and End*, Cairo, 1995 (Arabic)
Ayoub, Nazih N., *Overstating the Arab State*, London, 1995
Bartlet, J.C., *The Global Conflict: The International Rivalry of the Great Powers*,
    London, 1994
Batatu, Hanna, *The Old Social Classes and Revolutionary Movements of Iraq*,
    Princeton, 1978
Bazzaz, Sa'ad, *The Gulf War and the One After*, Beirut, 1995 (Arabic)
Be'er, Eliezer, *Arab Army Officers in Arab Politics and Society*, London, 1970
Bell, Gertrude, *Letters*, London, 1953
Birdwood, Lord, *Nuri Said: A Study in Arab Leadership*, London, 1959
Black, Ian, and Benny Morris, *Israel's Secret War: A History of Israel's Intelligence
    Service*, London, 1991
Blandford, Linda, *The Oil Sheikhs*, London, 1976
Braudel, Fernand, *A History of Civilization*, London, 1993
Brown, Anthony Cave, *Treason in the Blood*, London, 1994
Bulloch, John, *Final Conflict*, London, 1983

Bullock, Alan, *Ernest Bevin, Foreign Secretary*, London, 1983

Carter, Jimmy, *The Blood of Abraham*, London, 1985

Chomsky, Noam, *Human Rights and American Foreign Policy*, London, 1978

––––– *World Orders, Old and New*, London, 1994

Cleveland, William L., *The Making of an Arab Nationalist*, London, 1971

Cobban, Helena, *The Making of Modern Lebanon*, London, 1985

Cockburn, Andrew, and Leslie Cockburn, *Dangerous Liaison: The Secret Story of American–Israeli Intelligence*, London, 1992

Cooley, John, *Payback: America's Long War in the Middle East*, London, 1992

Copeland, Miles, *The Game of Nations*, New York, 1962

––––– *The Real Spy World*, New York, 1972

––––– *The Game Player*, New York, 1989

Dann, Uriel (ed.), *The Great Powers in the Middle East*, London, 1988

Daniel, Robert, *American Philanthropy in the Middle East*, Boston, 1970

Deegan, Heather, *The Middle East and Problems of Democracy*, London, 1983

de Gaury, Gerald, *Faisal*, London, 1966

Demir, Suleiman, *Arab Development Funds in the Middle East*, London, 1979

Eban, Abba, *Personal Witness*, London, 1993

Eden, Sir Anthony, *Full Circle*, London, 1960

Emerson, Steven, *The American House of Saud*, New York, 1985

Findley, Paul, *They Dared Speak Out*, Chicago, 1989

––––– *Deliberate Deceptions: Facing the Facts about the US–Israeli Relationship*, Chicago, 1993

Finer, S.E., *The Man on Horseback*, London, 1962

Fisk, Robert, *Pity the Nation*, London, 1990

Fkaiki, Hani, *Dens of Defeat*, London, 1993 (Arabic)

Foster, Henry A., *The Making of Modern Iraq*, London, 1936

Friedman, Alan, *Spider's Web: Bush, Saddam, Thatcher and the Decade of Deceit*, London, 1993

Friedman, Thomas, *From Beirut to Jerusalem*, London, 1989

Gellner, Ernest, *Postmodernism, Reason and Religion*, London, 1992

Gerber, Haim, *The Social Origins of the Modern Middle East*, London, 1987

Gerges, Fawaz, *The Superpowers and the Middle East, 1955–1967*, New York, 1994

Ghahtani, Fahd, *Struggle of the Branches*, Beirut, 1981

––––– *The Jumeyhan Earthquake in Mecca*, Beirut, 1992

––––– *Yamani and the House of Saud*, Beirut, 1994 (Arabic)

Gilmour, David, *Lebanon: A Fractured Country*, London, 1983

––––– *Curzon*, London, 1995

Glubb, Sir John Bagot, *Soldier with the Arabs*, London, 1959

––––– *Britain and the Arabs*, London, 1982

Goldberg, Jacob, *The Foreign Policy of Saudi Arabia, 1902–1918*, Harvard, 1988

Goria, Wade R., *Sovereignty and Leadership in Lebanon, 1943–1976*, London, 1985

Gowers, Andrew, and Tony Walker, *Yasser Arafat and the Palestinian Revolution*, London, 1990

Hamdi, Walid M.S., Dr, *The Nationalist Movement in Iraq 1939–41*, Baghdad, 1987

Hamilton, Adrian, *Oil, the Price of Power*, London, 1986

Heikal, Muhammad, *The Cairo Documents*, London, 1971

—— *Autumn of Fury*, London, 1983
—— *Illusions of Triumph*, London, 1993
—— *Secret Channels*, London, 1996
Helms, Christine Moss, *Iraq, the Eastern Flank of the Arab World*, London, 1984
Henderson, Simon, *After Fahd*, London, 1995
Hirst, David, *The Gun and the Olive Branch*, London, 1977
Hitti, Philip, *History of the Arabs*, New York, 1952
Holden, David, *Farewell to Arabia*, London, 1966
Holden, David, and Richard Johns, *The House of Saud*, London, 1981
Hopwood, Derek, *Tales of Empire*, London, 1985
—— *Syria 1945–1986*, London, 1988
—— *Egypt, Politics and Society 1945–1990*, London, 1993
Hourani, Albert, *A History of the Arab People*, London, 1991
Hout, Bayan Nueihid, *Leadership and Political Organizations in Palestine, 1917–1948*, Beirut, 1981 (Arabic)
Howarth, David, *The Desert King*, London, 1964
Horowitz, H.C., *The Struggle for Palestine*, London, 1950
Hudson, Michael C., *Arab Politics and the Search for Legitimacy*, London, 1981
Ionides, Michael, *Divide and Lose: The Arab Revolt, 1955–1958*, London, 1960
James, Lawrence, *Imperial Warrior: Field Marshal Viscount Allenby*, London, 1993
Kabbani, Rana, *Imperial Fictions: Europe's Myths of Orient*, London, 1986
Kaplan, Robert, *The Arabists*, New York, 1993
Kayyali, A.W., *Palestine, A Modern History*, London, 1990
Kedourie, Elie, *Political Memoirs and Other Studies*, London, 1974
—— *England and the Middle East: The Destruction of the Ottoman Empire*, London, 1987
Kerr, Malcolm, *The Arab Cold War: Gamal Abdel Nasser and his Rivals, 1958–1970*, London, 1971
Kent, Marion, *Oil and Empire*, London, 1976
Kessler, Ronald, *The Rise and Fall of the World's Richest Man*, London, 1986
Khadduri, Majid, *Republican Iraq*, London, 1969
—— *Contemporary Arabs: The Role of Leaders in Politics*, London, 1982 (Arabic)
Khalaf, Samir, *Lebanon's Predicament*, London, 1987
Khaysoun, Ali, *The Tanks of Ramadan*, London, 1988 (Arabic)
Kiernan, Victor, *The Lords of Humankind*, London, 1995
Kimmerling, Bernard, and Joel S. Migdal, *Palestinians: The Making of a People*, London, 1993
Kissinger, Henry, *Diplomacy*, London, 1994
Kurm, George, *Arab–European Economic and Financial Relations*, London, 1994
Lacey, Robert, *The Kingdom*, London, 1981
Lacouture, Jean, *Nasser*, London, 1973
Lacqueur, Walter, *The Struggle for the Middle East*, London, 1969
Lawrence, T.E., *Seven Pillars of Wisdom*, London, 1926
Lenczowski, George, *Political Elites in the Middle East*, London, 1974
Lukitz, Liona, *Iraq: The Search for National Identity*, London, 1995
Mackey, Sandra, *The Saudis*, New York, 1987
Makki, Alia, *A Woman's Diary in a Saudi Prison*, London, 1991 (Arabic)
Ma'alouf, Amin, *The Crusades through Arab Eyes*, London, 1983

Ma'oz, Moshe, *Asad, the Sphinx of Damascus*, London, 1988

Marlowe, John, *The Seat of Pilate*, London, 1959

Mattar, Philip, *The Mufti of Jerusalem*, London, 1988

Matthews, Roderick D., *Education in the Arab Countries of the Near East*, New York, 1949

Miller, Aaron, *Search for Security: Saudi Arabian Oil and US Foreign Policy*, New York, 1980

Morris, James, *The Hashemite Kings*, London, 1959

―――― *Farewell the Trumpets*, London, 1978

Munif, Abdel Rahman, *Cities of Salt*, London, 1992

Naqeeb, Khaldoun, *Society and State in the Gulf and Arabian Peninsula*, Beirut, 1982 (Arabic)

Ostrovsky, Victor, *By Way of Deception*, London, 1990

Ozrie, Abdel Karim, *The Problem of Governance in Iraq*, London, 1991 (Arabic)

Parenti, Michael, *The Sword and the Dollar*, New York, 1989

―――― *Against Empire*, New York, 1995

Payne, Ronald, *Mossad, Israel's Most Secret Service*, London, 1990

Perlman, Maurice, *Mufti of Jerusalem: Study of Haj Amin Al Husseini*, London, 1947

Philby, Kim, *My Silent War*, London, 1968

Philby, Harry St John, *Arabian Jubilee*, London, 1952

Pipes, Daniel, *Greater Syria: The History of an Ambition*, London, 1990

Qhahtani, Fahd, *Yamani and the House of Saud*, Beirut, 1988 (Arabic)

Quandt, William, *Saudi Arabia in the 1980s*, Washington, 1981

―――― *The Middle East*, Washington, 1988

Rabi', Mohammad, *US–PLO Dialogue*, New York, 1992

Rabin, Yitzhak, *The Rabin Memoirs*, London, 1979

Randall, Jonathan, *The Tragedy of Lebanon*, London, 1990

Rashid, Dr Abdel Wahab Hamid, *External Trade and Arab Dependence*, Beirut, 1983 (Arabic)

Raviv, Dan, and Yossi Melman, *Every Spy a Prince*, London, 1990

Richards, Alan, and John Waterbury, *A Political Economy of the Middle East: State, Class and Economic Development*, Boulder, Col., 1990

Robinson, Jeffrey, *Yamani*, London, 1988

Rumeihi, Mohammad, *Beyond Oil*, London, 1983

Ruthven, Malise, *Islam in the World*, London, 1991

Sadowski, Yahya, *Guns or Butter*, Washington, 1993

Salameh, Dr Ghassan, *Democracy without Democrats*, London, 1995

Said, Edward, *Orientalism*, London, 1978

―――― *Culture and Imperialism*, London, 1993

―――― *Peace and Its Discontents*, London, 1995

Saïd, Nasser, *History of the House of Saud*, Beirut, 1981 (Arabic)

Saleh, Zaki, *Britain and Iraq*, London, 1995

Salibi, Kamal, *A House of Many Mansions: The History of Lebanon Reconsidered*, London, 1988

Salinger, Pierre, *The Gulf War Documents*, London, 1992

Sampson, Anthony, *The Seven Sisters*, London, 1975

―――― *The Arms Bazaar*, London, 1977

―――― *The Money Lenders*, London, 1981

Seale, Patrick, *The Struggle for Syria*, London, 1978
—— *Asad: The Struggle for the Middle East*, London, 1988
—— *Abu Nidal, the World's Most Notorious Terrorist*, London, 1992
Searight, Sarah, *The British in the Middle East*, London, 1979
Seekt, Ian, *OPEC . . . 25 Years of Price and Politics*, London, 1984
Seymour, Ian, *OPEC . . . Instrument of Change*, London, 1980
Sharabi, Hisham, *Neopatriarchy, A Theory of Distorted Change in Arab Society*, London, 1988
Shoukri, Ghali, *Egypt: Portrait of a President*, London, 1981
Shukeiri, Ahmad, *40 Years in Arab and World Affairs*, Beirut, 1972 (Arabic)
Solh, Raghid, *Britain's Two Wars with Iraq, 1941–1991*, London, 1994 (Arabic)
Sweidi, Tewfic, *Iraqi Faces through History*, London, 1987 (Arabic)
Taylor, Philip M., *War and the Media: Propaganda and Persuasion in the Gulf War*, London, 1992
Terrezian, Pierre, *OPEC: The Inside Story*, London, 1983
Twitchell, Karl, *Saudi Arabia*, Princeton, 1948
van Nortseda, D., *Governments and Politics in the Middle East in the 20th Century*, London, 1962
Vatikiotis, P.J., *The History of Modern Egypt*, London, 1991
Viorst, Milton, *Sandcastles*, London, 1994
Wardi, Dr Ali, *A Study of the Society of Iraq*, Beirut, 1989 (Arabic)
Weizmann, Chaim, *Trial and Error*, London, 1949
Williams, Henry, *The Making of Modern Iraq*, London, 1936
Wilson, Keith M., *Imperialism and Nationalism in the Middle East*, London, 1983
Wilson, Mary C. (ed.), *Britain and the Making of Jordan*, London, 1987
Winstone, H.V.F., *The Illicit Adventure*, London, 1982
—— *Gertrude Bell*, London, 1993
Yapp, M.E., *The Near East since the First World War*, London, 1991
Yeargin, Daniel, *The Prize*, London, 1991
Zakki, Dr Ramzi, *The Arab Economy under Siege*, Beirut, 1989 (Arabic)
Zamir, Meir, *The Formation of Modern Lebanon*, London, 1985
Zakkaria, Ghassan, *The Red Sultan*, London, 1991 (Arabic)

UNPUBLISHED MANUSCRIPTS

Singleton, Jenny, *The National Democratic Party of Pre-Revolutionary Iraq*, 1996
Asst. Professor Malik Mufti, *Renewed Unionism, 1963–1964*

INTERVIEWS (INCLUDING THOSE CONDUCTED BY THE WRITER AS A NEWS CORRESPONDENT)

Abdallah, Colonel Muhammad Radi
Abdallah, General Radi
Abu Hammad, Suheil
Aburish, Abu Saïd
Abu Sherrif, Bassam
Akins, James
Al Ma'asari, Dr Muhammad
Alummedine, Najib
Al Ullum, His Eminence Sheik Ibrahim
    Bahr
Alawi, Abdel Ameer
Anderson, Bobby
Attwan, Abdel Barri
Azzam, Sultan
Badawi, Zakki
Bustani, Myrna
Canistrero, Vincent
Chalabi, Ahmad
Chederchi, Rifa'at
Copeland, Miles
Cordesman, Anthony
Critchfield, James
Dhagastani, Tamara
Douri, Abdel Sattar
Dorantt, Chief Inspector Thomasz
Eddé, Raymond
Essoulami, Saïd
Eveland, Wilbur Crane
Faqih, Dr Sa'ad
Firzli, Suleiman

Fistere, John
Fkaiki, Hani
Freij, Elias
Galloway, George
Gilmour, David (correspondence)
Gubser, Peter (correspondence)
Harper, Christopher
Heikal, Muhammad (correspondence)
Hussein, King of Jordan
Husseini, Heidar
Jawad, Ghanim
Khilewi, Muhammad
Llewellyn, Tim
Murad, Dr Amneh
Odone, Toby
Ozrie, Abdel Karim
Parker, Paul
Roush, Patricia (correspondence)
Shehabi, Saïd Muhammad
Shukri, Dr Subhi
Simon, Jotta
Sindi, Dr Muhammad (correspondence)
Solh, Dr Raghid
Tariki, Abdallah
Tel, Wasfi
Toledano, Shmuel
Tveit, Karsten
Zakkaria, Ghassan
Zakki, Dr Saniha
Zogbi, James (correspondence)

OFF-THE-RECORD INTERVIEWS

Representative of British Home Office
Three CIA agents (one by correspondence)
Two former members of Jordanian Cabinet
Three members of Palestine National Council
Two oil experts
Six former US and UK diplomats
Eight academics and think-tank members
Two members of Saudi opposition in exile
Two members of Hamas

PUBLICATIONS, RADIO AND TELEVISION

Arabic-language
    Al Hayyat
    Al Sharq Al Awsar
    Al Quds Al Arabi
    Al Quds
    Al Musawar
    Al Hawadess
    Al Thawra
    Middle East Broadcasting
    Radio Baghdad

English-language
    Independent
    Independent on Sunday
    Sunday Times
    Spectator
    Washington Post
    Sunday Telegraph
    Jerusalem Post
    Guardian
    Christian Science Monitor
    International Herald Tribune
    Petroleum Intelligence Weekly
    Time
    The Times (London)
    New York Times

THINK-TANKS AND GOVERNMENT OFFICES

Royal United Services Institute
The Washington Institute
Centre for Strategic And International Studies
International Institute for Strategic Studies
Rand Foundation
Public Record Office, London

Index